Judaism and Other Religions

Previous Publications

Alan Brill, *Thinking God: The Mysticism of Rabbi Zadok of Lublin* (2002)

Judaism and Other Religions

Models of Understanding

Alan Brill

First published in 2010 by
PALGRAVE MACMILLAN®
in the United States—a division of St. Martin's Press LLC,
175 Fifth Avenue, New York, NY 10010.

Where this book is distributed in the UK, Europe and the rest of the world,
this is by Palgrave Macmillan, a division of Macmillan Publishers Limited,
registered in England, company number 785998, of Houndmills,
Basingstoke, Hampshire RG21 6XS.

Palgrave Macmillan is the global academic imprint of the above companies
and has companies and representatives throughout the world.

Palgrave® and Macmillan® are registered trademarks in the United States,
the United Kingdom, Europe and other countries.

ISBN: 978–0–230–62226–5

Library of Congress Cataloging-in-Publication Data

Brill, Alan.
    Judaism and other religions : models of understanding / Alan Brill.
        p. cm.
    ISBN 978–0–230–62226–5 (hardback)
    1. Judaism—Relations. 2. Christianity and other religions. 3. Gentiles
in the Bible. 4. Gentiles in rabbinical literature. 5. Judaism—Doctrines.
    I. Title.

BM534.B75 2010
296.3'9—dc22   2009039951

A catalogue record of the book is available from the British Library.

Design by Newgen Imaging Systems (P) Ltd., Chennai, India.

First edition: March 2010

D 10 9 8 7 6 5 4 3 2

Printed in the United States of America.

CONTENTS

Preface vii

1 Beginning the Conversation 1

2 Theological Categories 15

3 Biblical and Talmudic Texts 31

4 The Inclusivist Tradition 63

5 The Universalist Tradition 99

6 Pluralism 129

7 The Exclusivist Tradition 151

8 Gentiles 175

9 The Phenomena of Religion 207

10 At the Dawn of a New Century 225

Notes 241

Selected Bibliography 259

Index 269

PREFACE

In 2001, the Israeli journalist Yossi Klein Halevi published his award-winning book *At the Entrance to the Garden of Eden: A Jew's Search for God with Christians and Muslims in the Holy Land.* The book describes his important spiritual journey as a religious Jew into the worlds of Christianity and Islam in Israel and the Palestinian territories. Halevi joined in prayers and meditations in mosques and monasteries, in an attempt to experience their devotional lives and thereby create a religious language of reconciliation among the three monotheistic faiths. His quest for reconciliation was an attempt to move beyond the fear and hatred of gentiles inherited from having been raised in a Holocaust survivor household in Brooklyn. This fear had originally led him to the right-wing politics of a Jewish defense against the non-Jewish world as "Never Again." Many of his contemporaries continued their journey by supporting right-wing rhetoric upon moving to Israel. Halevi left his comfort zone to determine whether religion can be a source of peace and reconciliation.

My journey was not as dramatic as Halevi's. I, too, was raised in the survivor community, and as I tell people, the people in *Maus* were my neighbors and family friends. While I imbibed many of the same attitudes toward gentiles as Yossi Klein Halevi, my greater exposure to the broader world of the era, and my awareness of being part of the vast tapestry of different urban-ethnic groups in New York tempered this fear. A county away in Queens, I played with neighbors who made up the multiethnic and multireligious kaleidoscope of New York, and I imbibed the diversity of American religion. I accepted the xenophobia of the older generation as a passing phenomenon of an immigrant community similar to speaking Yiddish, eating *petcha,* or warding off the evil eye. As in the case of Yossi Klein Halevi, the state of Israel served as a comfort zone for these encounters, in that Christianity in Israel is a small, somewhat quaint minority religion, neither to be feared nor overwhelmed by its presence.

My interest in theology and Hasidic thought led me to choose mysticism as a field of study, bringing me to doctoral studies at Fordham University, a Jesuit institution. During my theological studies, I was accepted socially and made to feel comfortable as a student in the theology program due to the immense accomplishments of the Jewish-Christian encounter. Unlike Yossi Klein Halevi, I did not have to leave my comfort zone. Nor did I even need a special visa to enter a foreign territory where one remains conscious of one's temporary status. I was accepted as an ordinary student along with the other non-Catholics, including Evangelicals, Mennonites, Greek Orthodox, and other Jewish students. The courses included discussion on the possibilities of empirical comparisons between religions and the similarities of spiritual paths. My doctoral advisor, Ewert Cousins, garnered a cadre of students who listened eagerly to his intellectual and spiritual autobiography, which took leaps over the chasms between different spiritual worlds. Under his editorial guidance, the *Classics of Western Spirituality* made the category of spirituality, then fresh and exciting but now overused, a source of religious encounter. For me, mysticism and knowledge of the higher realms drowned out, at the time, almost any social concerns or encounter implications.

I entered the field of interfaith encounters long after the great strides made in *Nostrae Aetate,* and during the time of trajectories set into motion as John Paul II acknowledged Judaism as a living faith, recognized the Holocaust, and finally made his historic official visit to the state of Israel. The main topic of discussion of the era was the difference in terminology between reconciliation and *teshuvah* (return or repentance). In this context, I met several of my current departmental colleagues who were involved in elucidating these differences. Encounter at this point was no longer based on the liberating sense of dialogue and brotherhood of the 1960s. Now, it was complex activity, more academic and more informal, more concerned with protecting the interests of world Jewry and the need for specific local ethnic encounters, a more cautious and calculated encounter. The original participants of the early 1960s were passing away, including my own teacher Rabbi Walter Wurzburger, who originally brought me into the interfaith discussions. At this point, there was a greater divergence between the perspective of the academy and those who represented specific religious traditions than in the original heady days of Jewish-Christian dialogue.

As heir of the latter half of the twentieth century, I am the one explaining contemporary Christian theology to Christians, rather than the one who it needs to be explained.. Instead of tentatively learning to understand Christianity, I am the one helping Christians catch allusions to Christian classics and compare Church documents. The Christians I encounter are comfortable and knowledgeable about Jews; most have attended a synagogue service, and many go out of their way to wish me greetings before Jewish holidays. The original obstacles to a Jewish-Christian encounter seem remote when one teaches in a department that situates early Christianity in a Jewish context, teaches Christian students to read rabbinic Hebrew, and grants certificates in Holocaust studies to Christian students.

When I read accounts of Jews involved in interfaith work, even those only two decades my senior, I come across their straining personal justifications as to why they read Christian theologians. In contrast, while in a Jewish college, I read the Lutheran classics that were so dear, at the time, to modern Orthodox thinkers. Then, as part of a seemingly, at the time, natural progression, I expanded the canon to include Rahner, Moltmann, Ratzinger, Lindbeck, and many other theologians. The wisdom contained in these works did not need justification. Other religions and their theologies do not appear to be an incomprehensible realm. I have taught Orthodox Jewish students who had expressed a natural "sacred envy" for Christian or Buddhist practice and who are comfortable comparing, as a mental experiment, their practice to those of other faiths. Some of my students have even entered the field professionally, knowing in advance the academic training they will need. Yet when I read the writings of my senior colleagues, I am amazed as they point out how the liturgical and ritual world of Christianity remains entirely impenetrable to them, even after years of study and encounter.

The sources in this book were collected over decades, but my writing started at the June 2001 International Catholic-Jewish Liaison Committee (ILC) meeting in New York. At the meeting, one of the Jewish presenters warned against the dangers of Cardinal Ratzinger's *Dominus Iesus*. The presenter pointed out how the Christian God differs from the Jewish God, and he voiced his rejection of the recent publication of *Dabru Emet* (a statement made in 2000 by a group of Jewish scholars that stresses the common ground of Judaism and Christianity), which stated that Jews and Christians worship the same God. In contrast, Cardinal Kasper, who attended the meeting, immediately explained the language of *Dominus Iesus* based on traditional inclusivism theology. After the talk, I had a conversation with two colleagues, Rabbi Michael Signer, of blessed memory, one of the drafters of *Dabru Emet*, and Prof. Lawrence Schifman, who opposed the document. I suggested that *Dabru Emet* could have been formulated not in terms of an either/or dichotomy of a same or different God, but as a qualified statement reflecting some of the traditional Jewish texts. At this point, I started to point out subtleties and distinctions that could have been added to the first paragraph of *Dabru Emet* to make the statement closer to the inclusivist or universal statements of other texts. I also noted that the Catholic encounter partners use a language of inclusivism and not pluralism, so an emended document would have more weight in a traditional context. Both of my colleagues were intrigued by the idea, yet were unconvinced, and I proceeded to write up my first thoughts.

Then, and with great urgency after the tragic events of 9/11, there was an awakening to the issues concerning encounter with other religions, and to the special problems in an era of globalization. Many of those involved in interfaith encounter, myself included, were asked to give presentations on the seeming clash of civilizations and the new role that religion played in our lives. The *New York Times* began a series of articles on the role of religion in Islamic countries; it also began to openly view the role of Evangelicals in the United States and discuss the religious backdrop to current events and political agendas. Those of us in interfaith encounter were required to explain the importance of moderate positions and also to serve as moderate voices. The challenge is to discuss the difficulties practically, historically, and textually in implementing moderate positions, even those positions with long pedigrees and cherished stature. Rather than falling into a sharp dichotomy between contemporary pluralism and absolute fundamentalism, moderate positions tend to use texts from former ages to create a more inclusive position without diminishing allegiance to religion. Those years left many people confused about the rise of religion during the previous twenty years. From 2001 through 2005 there was a need for a positive message to counterbalance the anxiety that many felt, and the need for data or cultural buoys that would help make sense of current events.

After 9/11 one thing was certain, the expectation that members of diverse religions would meet each other as liberal secular thinkers and place their religion aside was no longer a possibility. To identify the public sphere with liberalism devoid of religion was both an insult to religion and an obstacle to fruitful discussions. I do not necessarily reject liberalism or a public sphere devoid of religion, but there was a change. Centers of religion and culture, religion and media, religion and the public sphere began to open in order to discuss this cultural shift.

With others who take a moderate position based on classic texts, this collection has served me in many contemporary discussions. This work started as a florilegium—a collection of sources—but with the encouragement of my colleagues, the bouquet of erudition became a book. The starting categories were exclusivist, pluralist, and inclusivist, and these subdivided over time. Finally, the bouquet of sources needed to be set in a vase. Public talks needed contemporary points as well as texts, hence the surrounding chapters.

In 2003, a first draft was presented at the "Fifth Academic Meeting between Judaism and Orthodox Christianity" held in Thessaloniki, Greece. In 2004, the World Jewish Congress invited a select group of Catholic Cardinals to New York, and at that gathering the core of chapters two through five were given as a paper. Shortly afterward, a prematurely edited transcript of the speech "Judaism and Other Religions: An Orthodox Perspective" was available on the website of the Boston College Center for Christian-Jewish Learning. In 2005, the World Jewish Congress invited a different group of Cardinals, to whom I presented a draft of the last chapter of this book. The same year, Alon Goshen-Gottstein and the Elijah Institute held a conference gracefully hosted by Marc Shapiro at the University of Scranton, which offered me the extraordinary opportunity to deliver the thesis before many of the best Jewish authors in the field without the usual press coverage. In September 2005, I attended a conference in Rome on the ramifications of *Nostrae Aetate* forty years later. At that conference, I presented a version of the material geared for that occasion. Finally, I presented on Judaism and Eastern religions at Florida International University. Through my current circuit of community lectures, I have gained further clarification of my own work.

Because this book grew out of encounters between Catholics and Jews and between Jews and Jews, it became clear that it needed to be adjusted to apply to other groups, such as Muslims, Evangelicals, and Hindus. I was quite gratified to learn that a group of Muslims I met in Seville at the World Congress of Rabbis and Imams for Peace had read my online article about Judaism and other religions. They felt at home translating their own terms into my schema of Jewish positions. The sources were similarly useful when I received in my home a contingent of Israeli Arab educators from Al-Kasami College in Baqa El Gharbia. Nevertheless, I know some of the framing issues would change if geared specifically for a Jewish–Muslim encounter, but this can be easily done since many of the Jewish texts were originally written in Arabic about Islam of which they were intimately aware. Finally, as I finish this volume, I have just met with Imams from Iraq brought by the U.S. State Department, an opening created by the new administration. For them, the question of how to seek their own moderate positions, especially neglected medieval positions, is the only route to appreciating religious difference that they are comfortable following.

Most Jews are not remotely aware of the texts in this volume. When interfaith positions began to be classified as inclusivist, exclusivist, and pluralist in the 1980s, categories that became the professional terminology in the 1990s, there should have been a Jewish compilation of theological opinions about other religions to complement the Christian versions. But alas, most Jewish works concentrated on personal theories, or debated the virtues of dialogue, thereby neglecting their own internal theological self-formulation. Many proceeded from a projected medieval exclusivism to an affirmation of pluralism, even when they really meant inclusivism or universalism. And many, as a reaction, ran headlong from this pluralism into new forms of exclusivism.

I consider this volume a necessary tool for a serious discussion of the attitude of Judaism toward other religions. This book is not about dialogue, it is about Jews knowing their own sources. It is not enough to cite only the inclusivist position of Maimonides or the halakhic leniency of Rabbenu Tam, and then use them as a justification for pluralism, or conversely use them as a justification for exclusivism. The gamut of Jewish texts cannot be aligned in a single direction or single valence. We are far from any concluding point and all apparent conclusions in this work remain open to discussion. I would be pleased if this work produced follow-up volumes weighing the material. The various opinions need to be formulated and evaluated. Even when accepted, the positions need translation into modern religious categories.

I cast my net wide in my collection in order to show the diversity of the materials. For some, eager to settle on a contemporary position, my net might be much too wide. To those who want to have a fixed conclusion, consider the book a resource tool for teaching historical opinions and formulating current opinions. Others will object to my inclusion of statements from Jewish texts that demonize other religions, and they will argue that these statements should not be aired in public. It should be noted that almost every negative statement is already easily accessible on the web, readily available for all to see. In today's world of readily available information, little religious doctrine can remain secret. These texts are already out there and there is nothing to be gained by hiding from them. It is important to respond to these questionable texts. Still other readers will object to my specific selection of texts, arguing for texts they consider normative or that they accept. Others may find most of these texts illiberal or superseded in the modern age. To these latter readers, I say that these texts still frame many of the traditional discussions, and their points of view are still held by more people than those who accept some of the liberal positions. My book reflects an Orthodox training and erudition, but it is not limited to Orthodox thinkers. All thinkers who contribute to the discussion are included.

A pluralist author who writes a theology of other religions needs to give a fair presentation of the exclusivist position, and an exclusivist author needs to give a fair presentation of the pluralist position. They should not merely shout names at each other across a fence: fundamentalist, relativist, obscurantist, heretic, immoral, nihilist. Those disturbed about the inclusion of the negative portrayals of gentiles will probably argue that I want to destroy the tradition. On the other hand, those readers upset by my inclusion of a vast array of medieval texts rather than starting with the contemporary pluralists will probably think that I am a fundamentalist rallying against liberalism. My goal was to collect the original texts because I am convinced that any attempt to create contemporary theologies before the groundwork is done will not answer the basic questions.

Why do I still use the outdated term of theologies of other religions, implying that Judaism is judging the world? I can speak from personal experience, as someone who formerly taught at a Jewish college that would not and could not entertain creating a religion department, and who currently teaches in a college that does have a religion department, carved within recent memory from the theology department, but still refers within the required courses to "the other religions." I can assert that the basic questions still need to be addressed from a traditional position. Many believers are still trying to formulate their positions in a nonrestrictive way. If interfaith encounter is to change people then it has to start with acknowledging and working to change the contemporary lack of clarity.

I am more than surprised at frequent interfaith encounters where the Catholic speaks from the official Church teachings, the Muslim speaks from traditional teachings, and the Jewish representative addresses the assembled from the general perspective of comparative religion, politics, or anthropology. There need to be Jewish theologies of other religions.

Many authors who work in interfaith relations divide their books into two different books. The first book presents the general interfaith categories of inclusive, exclusive, and pluralistic thought. The second volume gives the specifics of how faith relates to the specifics of other religions. In keeping with that approach, there will be a follow-up volume to this book called *Judaism and World Religions*, which will deal with specifics of how Judaism relates to Islam, Christianity, Buddhism, and Hinduism. It will deal with the important topics of covenant theology, comparative religion, and the ability to compare religions. It will discuss the important thinkers that are conspicuous by their absence in this work: Rosenzweig, Baeck, Herberg, Heschel, Soloveitchik, Wyschogrod, Novak, Levinson, Neusner, and Levinas.

Currently, I occupy a position that was named in honor of Sister Rose Thering, a feisty nun who was instrumental in an account of Jewish-Christian relations in many ways—examining how Judaism is taught in American Catholic schools, instrumental in instituting the first state-mandated Holocaust curriculum requirement, and educating Catholics about the need to learn about and respect Judaism. What we say on interfaith topics does matter; it does lead to greater understanding, and it leads to practical change.

Since this work came to be both in public events and in email, I wish to thank everyone who offered useful comments at the various stages: Marc Angel, Gavriel Bellino, Philip Cunningham, Ari Gordon, Alon Goshen-Gottstein, Ann Heekin, Nathaniel Helfgott, Ruth Langer, Nathan Katz, Menachem Kellner, Eugene Korn, Menachem Kallus, Deborah Lerner, Len Moskovitz, Anthony Sciglitano, Marc Shapiro, Michael Shmidman, Marvin Simkovich, Aviad Stollman, Larry Yudelson, and Peter Zaas For the formal invitations and original request for the talks that produced this volume, I wish to thank Avi Beker, Israel Singer, Pinchas Shapiro, and David Rosen. I thank my editors Patty Lee and Tara Gellene, my graduate assistants Meghan Chapuran and Sasha Makuka, and the immense help of Jay Wofferman, who runs our department. For making the book a reality, I thank my agent Neil Salkind and my editor at Palgrave Macmillan Chris Chappell. Finally, I dedicate this work to my loving wife Debi, for her continuous love, support, and devotion; she entered a foreign terrain of both new lands and a new life.

CHAPTER 1

Beginning the Conversation

Does Judaism have a theology of other religions? Emphatically, yes. Judaism has a wide range of texts that offer thoughts on other religions. In this book, my goal is to present this broad range of traditional sources bearing on this question of the theological relationship between Judaism and other religions in order to start discussion about a Jewish theology of other religions. We will begin to explore the important questions about other religions.

- If God is one, then what is the value of the other religions?
- Does God only care about one small people or does His plan include the wider world?
- How does one theologically account for the differences between religions?
- How do Jews think about other religions?
- How do we balance our multifaith world with the Jewish texts?

Before turning to these important questions, I must first present the importance of the return of religion in our age. I will then present a brief insight into the role that a theology of other religions plays in an era when people seem to affirm both particularist and pluralist positions at the same time, followed by a brief history of Jewish–Christian dialogue explaining why this book was not written until now. Finally, I will turn to the nature of the texts collected and the acceptance of texts in an age of hermeneutics.

From Tolerance to Theological Politics

Many Jews view modernity as a major change separating the premodern and the modern. This has led many to approach other religions solely from the perspective of modern tolerance. Many base the entire possibility of dialogue on the modern condition, where Jews and Christians coexist within a larger, secular world.

Jacob Katz, the eminent historian of Jewish entrance into modernity, narrated that modern tolerance was due to the eighteenth-century Enlightenment thought of Moses Mendelssohn and the concurrent creation of a neutral society. In Katz's view, Jews at the end of the eighteenth century moved from the Ghetto restrictions that limited their relationship with the surrounding culture to the post-Enlightenment integration into civil society through enfranchisement and emancipation. Thus, as Gentile attitudes toward Jews changed, the Jewish response toward Christians moved from exclusivism and polemics to Mendelssohn's universal tolerance.[1]

In modernity, the encounter between religions presupposes a civil society built on Enlightenment tolerance and common sense over the certainty and authority of revelation. In the modernist approach, John Locke serves as the enduring hero who championed the right of private conscience in religious matters and separated it from the public sphere. Thomas Hobbs and Gotthold Ephraim Lessing showed that one cannot adjudicate between opposing religious truth claims, so one cannot refer to them. And the achievement of the Great Awakening of the 1730s was the belief that religious experience is inherently subjective. Tolerance, religious freedom, and religious liberties are taken for granted in a secularized Western world.

However, as a prelude to encountering other religions, Jews need to learn to kick the secularization habit, viewing the outside world as secular. The same forces that allowed the upswing of traditional Judaism during the last decades also led to the rise of Christian, Islamic, and Hindu traditionalism. In the 1990s people still thought that traditional religion and religious conflicts were simply a throwback to a premodern era. Religion now plays a major role in the entire public sphere of politics, media, and culture.

Currently, "everywhere we look, we have religious problems." "Globalization has propelled traditionalism as a barrier against change and "for the prosperous suburbanite it has become a lifestyle coach."[2] Mark Lila, professor at Columbia University, wrote that "wherever we now cast our gaze we are met with the spectacle of individuals and whole cultures set spiritually ablaze and eager to spread the flame to others" Many who still think that Western society is about secularization "find it hard to believe that people can still take God seriously and want to shape society according to its dictates."[3]

In a post–9/11 world, religion in its traditional forms has returned as a force in politics and civil society. In order to come to terms with the current clash of civilizations and the increasing tensions between forces of globalization and those of tradition, we need to view the conflict as a moral challenge for faith.[4] Religion offers an essential means of providing dignity, sanctity, and spirituality to meet these new challenges. I reject, therefore, the notion that the solution to conflict must come in the form of a secularized meeting and dialogue, where one's religious identity is bracketed. Naturally, we do not want to return to theocratic religion. Yet, a straightforward acceptance of Enlightenment values is discordant with twenty-first-century reality.

In recent decades, religion has returned to the public sphere, and many, but not all, elements of traditional religion have reemerged. Traditional sources are now playing a greater role in discussions; hence I approach the encounter with other religions from the full range of textual sources.

Rather than seeing a drastic contrast between the religious exclusivity of medieval relations and the magnanimity of modern times, I contend that many medieval thinkers constructed theories of other religions and, in contrast, many contemporary moderns spew forth invective against other religions and exhibit xenophobia. At this point, the urgent agenda is to construct usable moderate theologies from traditional religious positions.[5]

In this new globalized world, encountering other religions is a constantly occurring and a growing phenomenon on many levels and is no longer an academic or ecclesiastical rarity. Religion can, and does, serve as meeting place of encounter within our globalized world. Facing others in a post-secular age, therefore, means that we must choose the moderate positions from within our own tradition as a basis for discussion. This book is a collection of resources for understanding Jewish positions. As I will demonstrate for Jewish thought, traditional texts offer ample resources to make this possible. In choosing to meet as moderates in an extreme world, we need to know that conflict resolution can only occur by bringing the most recalcitrant positions, even our own, to the table. The entire spectrum of positions must be represented and honestly presented.

My starting point is, therefore, not a tolerance based solely on eighteenth-century Enlightenment ideas, which would place interreligious encounter in secular terms. Nor is my goal simply, for pragmatic reasons, to hammer the idea of tolerance into the traditional texts. I find that presupposing liberalism in a traditional text is not useful for several reasons. First, liberal tolerance is not empirically sensitive to the complex nature of religion because it does not discuss the public dimensions of religion; and it imposes alien categories not always commensurate with religion. Second, it does not respect religious positions because it claims that they are really secular or all that counts is the secular. Third, it does not respond to the role of religion in an age of religious resurgence because it downplays religious ideals.

Finally, mere tolerance without communication or understanding is not enough and it is in fact patronizing. Tolerance remains solely a refusal to interfere with others with whom I disagree. For many, the public acceptance of tolerance is placed alongside the unchanged preexisting exclusivist views of religion. Some Jews with a seemingly tolerant position are in fact quite reluctant to have actual encounters; for them, conceptual tolerance is sufficient. They typify contradictory extremes of a public tolerance and a private exclusivism. Conceptual tolerance without encounter means that one does not actually confront anyone else, either to articulate one's position or to broaden one's perspective.

Locally

This quest for a meaningful approach for mediating traditional texts about other religions and contemporary life is just as important locally as globally. Americans operate without a clear theology or self-understanding of the relationship of their own faith to the existence of other religions.

Robert Wuthnow, a leading sociologist of religion, notes that Americans give respect to all religions but at the same time harbor exclusivist views denying this very respect to other religions. The result, he says, is "a kind of tension that cannot be easily resolved; a tattered view of the world held together only by the loosest of logic." Wuthnow notes that other scholars more pessimistic think that American "beliefs are so shallow that inconsistencies make no difference." They can accept "incommensurate beliefs in their personal life."

Wuthnow points out how Americans grapple with political tolerance and religious liberty to give coherence to their opinions, but it does not reflect their actual positions. He stresses that Americans create pluralism, or even relativism, of exclusivist opinions.[6]

> You could call it tolerance and, of course, people use the language of tolerance, because when you press them, then they'll say, "Well, of course, a Hindu, or a Muslim, or a Buddhist has every right to practice, just as we do." They flip into the language of rights—civil rights, civil liberties, and so forth. Push people, though, and say, "Well, but theologically, what do you think? They really believe something different from you." And it's, "Well, that's okay. That may be true for them. What I believe is true for me."

Americans alternate between various forms of pluralism and particularism. They accept a plurality of exclusivist positions, not worrying about the principle of noncontradiction. Therefore, an honest rendering of the texts that build their religious consciousness will help close the gaps and bring unified, and hopefully moderate, views grounded in their traditions.

Wuthnow concludes that we need to articulate middle positions between the extremes of public pluralism and private exclusivism. Wuthnow advocates a process of examination and investigation and learning in order to articulate middle positions. This requires an ongoing, ever-adjusting process since "finding a middle ground is not something they can determine once and for all." Respect and listening are slow gradual processes. Wuthnow calls for people to learn as much as possible about other religions. He stresses that we need to be interested in the substantive elements "issues, teachings, or practices, rather than somehow attempting to rise above such matters."[7]

Dialogue

Much of the serious contemporary discussion on interfaith started as a result of the initiative of the Catholic Church in convening the Second Vatican Council that culminated in *Nostra Aetate* (the 1965 Declaration on the Relation of the Church to Non-Christian Religions of the Second Vatican Council), an official statement on other religions. The document discussed the many religions of the world, and affirmed that notwithstanding the Christian doctrine of universal salvation, God's presence can be available in other religions as rays of truth. With regard to Jews, it absolved them of deicide, decried anti-Semitism, and acknowledged that God still has a covenant with the Jewish descendents of Abraham. It then goes on to affirm the unique spiritual patrimony common to Christians and Jews.

Yet, there were nascent beginnings already in the late nineteenth century where many Americans were coming to the realization that other religions are not idolatrous. In 1893, Chicago hosted the World's Parliament of Religions, the first attempt to create a global dialogue of faiths. In the twentieth century, there was a start of a broad ecumenicism, when Nathan Söderblom won the 1930 Nobel peace prize for his ecumenical work that focused on the personal religion behind organized religions.

The term "dialogue of religions" attained its modern meaning in the years after World War II and was closely connected with Existentialism, especially the *I –Thou* philosophy of Martin Buber. Dialogue meant approaching the other side as one encounters another person in dialogue—outside of doctrine, institution, or any objective standards. According to Eric Sharpe (d. 2000), a historian of religions and one of the leading academic experts on the history of modern interfaith encounter, only liberal Christians used the term "dialogue" whereas conservative Christians avoided it. The official term used at Vatican II for *Nostra Aetate* was "relation with other religions," implying that Catholic theology and doctrine confronts others religions, not that it is a humanistic dialogue of equals outside of doctrinal restraint. Most of this book remains at that level since its aforementioned purpose is presenting the classical texts in order to show how they confront other religions.

Eric Sharpe notes that the use of the term dialogue broadened, so that in the past fifty years there have been at least four uses of it: doctrinal dialogue (an intellectual activity), humanistic dialogue (which bypasses community and doctrine), secular dialogue (calling for joint action), and spiritual dialogue ("advocated chiefly by those who have been trained in the contemplative and monastic traditions").[8] In addition, the term dialogue has been used as a generic one for all forms of encounter, prayer, meeting, discussion, joint statement, and working together.[9]

This broadening of usages of the term dialogue occurred after *Nostra Aetate*, when there was a flurry of diverse interfaith activity. In the case of Judaism's encounter with Catholicism, there was a mixture of Jewish-Christian encounter events, prayer breakfasts, pulpit exchanges, discussions of the Jewishness of early Christianity, and joint commemoration of the Holocaust. The term dialogue absorbed a confusion of historical encounters, theological responses, and personal meetings, it merges the intellectual, with the political, and the pastoral.

An example of this mixing of issues is the following preface from a 1967 introduction to dialogue typifying that era. The goal of the book was to provide an introduction to Jewish-Christian relations, to state the theological differences between the two religions, and to explain Vatican II:

> "Yesterday: Auschwitz. And today a new day in Jewish-Christian rapprochement." In a massive outburst of Christian conscience, the impact of which cannot be fully measured or predicted, opportunity for dialogue between Jews and Christians are proliferating at a rate which even a year ago would have seemed impossible...Religious texts are being revised, courses on Judaism introduced in Christian seminaries, joint Judeo-Christian scholarly ventures in Bible study initiated...Jews and Catholics are led in common prayer and psalm by priest and cantor.[10]

The theological statements took the exclusivist position as the outdated default position of the tradition to be replaced, in a supersessional way, by dialogue. On the popular level, dialogue implied a before and after narrative of Jewish-Christian disputation to dialogue, and from Holocaust to responding to brotherhood.

A still valuable perspective on this era was provided by Ben Zion Bokser (d. 1984), in his *Judaism and the Christian Predicament* (1967). Bokser, following the usage described earlier, defines dialogue as all forms of encounter, and therefore he argues that it is not a modern invention as encounters occurred in all ages—but most in his opinion were polemical and make for "melancholy reading." [11] Bokser's goal was to help set the post–Vatican II agenda for the dialogue by pointing out the Christian insensitivity to Jewish needs and that the very language of Christianity, the New Testament and the theology of the Church, is anti-Jewish. As a theology of other religions, he only offers Rabbi Abraham Isaac Kook's vision that the other religions all contribute to history and will share in the glory of God. Nevertheless, he warns, "Judaism...sees every religion as potentially capable of rising to the dimension of universality and thus meet the spiritual needs of its adherents...But where Judaism finds itself in divergence from Christianity, Judaism will be itself, expressing the divergence respectfully but unequivocally."[12] Dialogue was the agenda not theology, not that the erudite Bokser could not have written a theological response, but it was not the issue of the day.

Robert Gordis (d. 1992), pulpit rabbi and one of the creators of the post–World War II Conservative movement, wrote the widely circulated "Ground Rules for a Christian-Jewish Dialogue." His guidelines show that at the time both religions did not know the other side. He stated clearly that (1) Judaism is not inferior or primitive compared to Christianity; (2) Judaism should not be painted as judgment compared to Christian mercy; (3) the New Testament should not be taken as the correct interpretation for the Hebrew Bible; (4) Christians need to understand that Jews do not share in their beliefs; (5) Jews need to move beyond seeing Christians solely through historic memories of persecutions and contempt.[13]

Gordis emphasizes that Jews need to learn to appreciate the fact that Christians come to God though belief in the Incarnation, Passion, and Resurrection. "The Trinitarian concept of Christianity, which Judaism emphatically repudiated as impugning the unity of God, was not generally regarded as sufficient to deny to Christianity the character of a monotheistic faith." He cites as support the statements of Yehudah Halevi, Meiri, and Tosafot (these will be explained in later chapters). Gordis did not think that that we should look to turn the obvious differences into theological abysses. Overcoming differences was a means of overcoming contempt, not one of historic or theological research. Gordis still feels Christian theology is strange and Jews do not understand dogmatics. "Yet the Jew should see in Christian doctrine an effort to apprehend the nature of the divine that is worthy of respect and understanding." [14]

But a Jewish theology of other religions is not just a Jewish understanding of Jesus or of Christianity, based on either historical study or interfaith dialogue.

Theology did come more than twenty years later, when two volumes appeared that brought to light most of the still current thinking on dialogue.

A 1991 volume had articles by David Hartman and Irving "Yitz" Greenberg, and a 1994 one had articles by Elliott Dorff, David Novak, and Michael Wyschogrod. (Some of their ideas will be dealt with later in the course of this book.) Many of these essays created important Jewish theologies of pluralism and covenant thinking. However, the 1991 volume's introduction still focused on the goal of dialogue as part of a need to heal centuries of hate. We need an acceptance of the faith of other human beings, as persons not as objects, and to learn to talk to one another with respect and dignity.[15] The analogy of interfaith activity was to the process of overcoming racism though blacks and whites learning to see the other side as people.

Furthermore, dialogue, the original post–World War II word for any religious encounter, has begun to define itself into separate activities. Theological discussion between religions is not the same as working for Holocaust recognition among Christians, working for recognition of the needs of the state of Israel, or dealing with the interfaith representation on the local community board. They are all separate activities, with different people engaged in each. These activities are all beyond the scope of this book; we are limited to the self-understanding of a theology of other religions.

The agenda for theology in the late 1980s focused on the acknowledgment of the Holocaust, the meaning of the State of Israel, and creating a common moral language. Jews tended to see *Nostra Aetate* only as a political declaration against anti-Semitism and as a compromise to Jews rather than the Church's own theological understanding of Christianity. Jews need to move beyond the social and political understanding of these encounters. They still tend to think that Christian belief is what they read about in the study of medieval history. They do not reflect on the changes during the course of the centuries within Christian theology. In fact, many Jews still have not acknowledged *Nostra Aetate* as a permanent change in Catholic understanding. And when Jews do acknowledge Vatican II, many mistakenly assume it affirmed a religious tolerance toward Judaism based on pluralism, rather the stated covenantal inclusivism.

The current Jewish encounter with other religions on the personal level has the potential to influence future Jewish thinking. Such influence will come not from any process of the trading of principles, but rather from the self-understanding gained in our own awareness of the ways in which people experience the Divine and articulate their faith. Our self-understanding needs to be broadened to see Judaism itself as part of the greater human religious quests. Jews did not parallel their Christian counterparts in developing full theologies of other religions; this book is an effort to help Jewish theology catch up in a process it has sorely neglected.

Theology

I believe that the conception of dialogue held by many contemporary Jewish thinkers is much too limited. I think the role of theology has not been developed sufficiently. As a believing Jew by commitment and a theologian by temperament and profession, I feel that the potential encounter in the realm of ideas—an encounter of theology and doctrine—is much more interesting and probably of much more profound importance.

When the dialogue first started, theology was not the Jewish agenda, and so there were no Jewish equivalents of Rahner, Panikkar, or Kung, not to mention Knitter and Hick. At that time, when the terminologies inclusivist, exclusivist, and pluralist were becoming well known, there should have been a Jewish response, such as this book, to serve as a basis for future work on Jewish thinking about other religions. But there was not.

This work will lay the foundation for the necessary self-understanding among Jews. I am laying out the possibilities with which Jewish theology can understand other religions and construct a theology of other religions based on traditional sources. Although not my primary objective, I also intend to provide non-Jews with an insight into Jewish thought through the variety of Jewish perspectives toward other religions.

The first step is to understand some of the basic terms used for categorizing these texts: exclusivist, pluralist, inclusivist, and universalist.

Exclusivism states that one's own community, tradition, and encounter with God comprise the one and only exclusive truth; all other claims on encountering God are a priori false.

Pluralism takes the opposite position, accepting that no one tradition can claim to possess the singular truth. The beliefs and practices of all groups are equally valid. It is widely taught among Western academics.

Inclusivism situates itself between these two extremes, where one acknowledges that many communities possess their own traditions and truths, but maintains the importance of one's comprehension as culminating, or subsuming, other truths. One's own group possesses the truth; other religious groups contain parts of the truth.

Universalism proposes a universal monotheism; it was widely taught by medieval Jewish philosophers who postulated a common Neo-platonic or Aristotelian truth to all religions.

Can we compare other religions to Judaism? Both medieval texts and modern scholars have offered insights into whether we share monotheism, Biblical narrative, or human religious expressions. In addition, many are unaware that there are numerous references in Jewish texts to Eastern religions, especially to Brahmins and Indian religions.

The important point of all these texts and discussions is to avoid the false dichotomy of a medieval exclusivism or a modern pluralist individualism. One should learn not to seek a position where everything is equal or a common ground syncretism. Equal legitimacy of everything practiced in another faith is not a prerequisite for an encounter. Encountering others is not a zero-sum game of exclusivism or relativism.

I met a young rabbi who in his false humility and modern emphasis on the self told a group of clergy from another faith that he cannot speak about God in Judaism since one can never be certain about God. He emphasized that since he could not speak about his own tradition, he certainly could not affirm any commonality. For him, all commonality would be existentially false. Rather, for him, we can only speak as humans; God is not part of reality. Each community just lives as its ethnic community. This is not a useful approach for a theology of other religions. Many of those who say that a person cannot know anything certain about his or her own religion, thinking they are thereby creating pluralism, are in effect creating an exclusivism. A religion that cannot be articulated remains particularist. If all we each have is our own subjective practices without any grounding, then it is a pluralism of human stories, not religion.

Knowing the Jewish texts about other religions demonstrates that Judaism does indeed have different rules than other religions. We need to come to the table with the breadth and depth of our conviction. There are many positions and many sources. Different situations require different texts. All of them do play a role and all of them continue to be used in the community. We need to appreciate what the wide palette of traditional texts says about other religions and stop thinking that we already know the range of opinions. Our religious community has a robust tradition of varying interpretations of the texts, often yielding competing understandings. We have to be open to the multiple voices that can speak to the various sides of this discussion.

We must be humble and honest in the acceptance of who others are and who we are. I reject a simplistic view that treats all religions in some collective approach where differences are minimized. Only when each member of a community comes to the discussion with firm beliefs and a desire to grow can he or she expect to cash in on the encounter with other religions. As Avery Cardinal Dulles (d. 2008) wrote "it takes considerable self-confidence to listen patiently while others tell you why they think you are wrong. Groups that have not reflected on their theology quite understandably shy away."[16] We need to listen to the other with honesty, humility, and openness and let each other be surprised by our differences. The goal is not to find parallels that minimize differences between religions or that leave out essential texts or defining aspects. Many of the challenges facing contemporary theologians are shared between Jews and other religions today and should thus serve as a meeting place in the midst of our globalization. It is here that this work acts as the beginning of such a meeting place in an age of post-secularization.

This book

This book will begin to answer the questions presented at the start of this chapter. To begin the discussion, I have selected sources which highlight the widest array of opinions. The goal is not the definitive word on the meaning of these texts or a fixed theological conclusion on other religions. Rather, these selections will, I believe, testify to the broad spectrum of texts available from previous centuries.

This book will go back to the Jewish tradition for texts that can serve as new resources in our contemporary discussions and present a range of traditional sources bearing on Judaism's conceptualization of other religions. The volume also collects some of the best adaptations of these ideas by contemporary thinkers for the current era. My goal is a rich collection and juxtaposition of texts that will allow the defining range of voices to be heard.

The breadth of the texts collected in this volume might take one aback. One may find the canon too large, too historically divergent, and not in line with the current normative canon. Many of the figures discussed would not tolerate being placed in any grouping with many of the others. Those looking for a halakhic-Jewish legal analysis will be sorely disappointed. A reader might also object to the temporary suspension of almost any evaluation of the importance of given texts, or the lack of deference to the texts that are cited the most frequently today. Finally, one might also consider it inappropriate and embarrassing to the Jewish community to present extreme exclusivist positions in public.

As stated earlier, however, this work aims to stimulate engagement with these texts and the only way to accomplish this is by laying them out for discussion. It would be welcome if work continuing this project would begin the important task of evaluation, but all evaluation must start with the data. One also needs to admit that the tradition has positions that one does not accept, and openly reject or move beyond the rejected positions. The range of texts presented here serves a very valuable service in giving those who engage in encounter the ability to respond adequately in new situations. When one encounters more committed traditions, or more metaphysical faiths, one requires a larger palette of texts in which to frame one's own response.

To me, an authentic Jewish theological position must meet the criterion of textuality, of being true to the sources. I spend most of my time, therefore, on Rabbinic based thought, medieval thinkers such as Yehudah Halevi, and the early modern positions such as Yaakov Emden together with their interpretations. As did the medieval thinkers before me, I insist that a theology fit the rubrics of the Tanakh and the Talmud, as interpreted by later generations.

I have selected these texts for their utility in articulating previous Jewish theologies, as well as in guiding future ones. Accordingly, I have omitted polemics and statements in *passim*. Each of these texts represents an entire theological position, a worldview within which the question of other religions is only one aspect. These are real positions that to this day remain live options for Jews seeking theological direction. I have included some positions that are no longer live options, because these either framed the original discussions or continue to shape the debate. I also include many texts that I would not follow or recommend but that are important for understanding the issues.

At their core, most of these texts reflect the classical philosophical tradition that, in Islamic translation, inspired the first formal Jewish theologies of the early medieval period. Classical philosophy seeks universals and distinguishes between the essence of an object and its attributes. This philosophic recognition of the essential creates the possibility of philosophic tolerance and respect, since through the acknowledgment we share a common, universal focus, wherein the differences between us are only secondary attributes. There is a common core of monotheism, where the differences relate to the very core of their commonality and there is a primacy of God's responsibility for humanity. In this philosophic tradition, the witness of monotheistic religions is that there is one God, and differences occur due to a lack of understanding that destroys unity.[17]

The vision of this book is not just historical documentation, to record positions from previous ages. Rather, it is a prolegomena that opens up the questions in order to carry this work further. Our question will be of what we can learn from earlier Jewish theological approaches, however much we might not agree with their metaphysics or representation of other religions. In our hermeneutical age, theologians are returning to textual traditions seeking resources long unnoticed, depreciated, and in many cases hidden by modern habits of thought. Returning to texts helps us move beyond modernist apologetics. Yet, some traditional passages are easier to live with whereas others are harder to live with and brush up against modern sensibilities. However, in the hermeneutical age, no single text constitutes an entire theology and every text has potential theological significance. I am showing the multiple registers, diverse situations, and untapped potentials. The goal is to create a full narrative that is not just choosing one opinion and rejecting others but incorporating them all. The objective is not to be partisan for a specific interpretation of Judaism or to write from the myopia of triumphalism.

The concern for the textual tradition, a hallmark of post-liberal thought, may be unpalatable to both the traditionalist and the liberal. A textual understanding of truth may be too provisional for conservatives, but my recognition of differences between religions and starting with texts contradicts the liberal assumption that all religions are essentially the same and start in human experience.

Jews travel heavy and do not throw texts away. They may think that they do not have a use for a given text anymore, so they lay it aside for a while. Then when the need arrives they reach into their satchel to retrieve one of these texts. But in the process of retrieving one text, they can be surprised by the unleashing of many other minimized voices or the sounds of the many new voices speaking in conversation.

Taken together, all the positions can help create a fuller theological narrative for self-understanding. Some Jews will seek to oscillate between the positions contained in this book depending on the contexts; others will treat the different positions as alternate models; still others will attempt a grand synthesis. I would be most gratified if this anthology generates varied theological schemes. In the new realm of encountering other religions in an age of post-secular globalization, Jews have a need to learn when, and in what context, to apply a given text and how to put the texts together into a broader theory.

CHAPTER 2

Theological Categories

When a Jew sees a member of another faith, how does he/she explain it to himself/herself?

- Does God only relate to Jews?
- Do other religions share in the Jewish God?
- Is God greater than any one religion?
- Do different peoples create their own religions?

A theology of other religions asks these questions. It seeks to interpret the meaning of the encounter of other religions based on what we know of other religions in conjunction with the tenets of our own starting religion. Some of this theological activity requires one to stretch one's own conceptual framework to encounter the strangeness of the other religion, and still to find that it resonates with his or her own views. The goal is to honor both sides of the equation.

How I Categorize the Sources

The aspiration of a theology of other religions is not the chronology or the sociohistoric setting of each text. Rather, the categories, both major and minor, used to analyze Judaism's attitude toward other religions are most important. The sources need to be categorized in multiple dimensions; to divide them simply between "pro-dialogue" and "anti-dialogue" mutes their richness. The most obvious of these dimensions is the division that categorizes positions as exclusivist, inclusivist, or universalist/pluralistic.

Alan Race created these categories in 1982 and their popularization in the writings of John Hick (b. 1922), a British philosopher of religion, made them widely used in the field of theology for the past twenty-five years.[1] This book is the first extended application of these categories to a wide variety of Jewish opinions.

Nevertheless, even as they are first being applied to Judaism, these categories are beginning to reach their limits of usefulness and have already had their critics. Many have noted that in practice, most theologians do not fit tightly into one of the three categories. Only philosophers who construct their theories a priori can fit totally into a single category; theologians who work with the complexity of textual traditions and social circumstance cannot be thus restricted; and lived communities of faith can never operate in a single mode. Some figures will be included in one, two, or all three categories.

Furthermore, these three categories have so many subdivisions that a proponent of one of the positions will inevitably need to define his or her position against alternate similar positions. (See later, where I further subdivide these positions.)

- **Exclusivism**, *"There is only one true religion."* Exclusivism states that one's own community, tradition, and encounter with God comprise the one and only exclusive truth; all other claims on encountering God are, a priori, false. There is *only* one way to God and salvation. Thus one religion is uniquely and supremely true and all other religions are false. Those who accept exclusivism usually affirm that other religions possess some elements of wisdom, but these religions do not teach "the truth" of salvation and revelation.
- **Pluralism**, *"All major world religions have some truth."* Religious pluralism takes the opposite position, accepting that no one tradition can claim to possess the singular truth. All groups' beliefs and practices are equally valid, when interpreted within their own culture. Thus, no one religion is inherently better or superior to any other major world religion. For pluralists, there may be differences in rituals and beliefs among these groups, but on the most important issues, there is great similarity. Most religions, they claim, stress love for God, and have a form of the Golden Rule.
- **Inclusivism**, *"One religion is best but weaker forms of religion are possible in other religions."* Inclusivism situates itself between these two extremes, where one acknowledges that many communities possess their own traditions and truths, but maintains the importance of one's comprehension as culminating, subsuming, or perfecting all other truths. One's own group possesses the truth; other religious groups contain parts of the truth. They do believe, though, that truth, wisdom, and even revelation can be found in other religions.

- **Universalism**, *"The truth is One."* Universalism is midpoint between inclusivism and pluralism, where one acknowledges that the universal truths of God, soul, intellect, and ethics have been made available by God to all people. This is usually a God-centered approach, in which the theism transcends the other elements of religion.

From an inclusivist perspective, other religions are explained by one's own religion: one may acknowledge a world beyond one's own, but must rely on one's own worldview to make it comprehensible and to give it meaning. An inclusivist speaks the language of his or her own theology and uses its vocabulary to describe outsiders. Sometimes the inclusivist finds language in the other religion to help explain itself and make itself understood by a wider audience. An inclusivist allows any real adherent of one of the great religions to be already informed by the Word of God by finding a common denominator such as monotheism or a moral code.

Many post–Vatican II Catholic theologians have tended to follow this approach, accepting that God is God overall for all people, and that other religions can give witness or fulfill aspects of one's own religion. There is one basis for religious fulfillment but several means of access. For the inclusivist, God is concerned with not just one faith but with members of other religions. The other religions have a real encounter with the Divine and have some connection to monotheism, revelation, and redemption.

Inclusivism affirms a uniqueness of Judaism, like the exclusivist, but rejects the idea that there is no value in other religion. One can, however, still acknowledge that there are differences in these essential theological points from Judaism and even consider their views mistaken. Yet one can say these mistakes are due to social, cultural, and historical circumstances or that they have distorted the truth but nevertheless they have some of the truth.

Inclusivism is able to appreciate general aspects of ethics, mission, searching for God, and revelation in other faiths, but it brackets out the other religion's views of ritual, feasts, and theology. For some, inclusivism is seen as colonial and liberal in that it forces one religion into the cultural and linguistic norms of one's own religion. One is only seeing the good from his/her own understanding and not from the self-understanding of the other religion. A philosophic problem of the inclusivist position is its creation of a wedge between the ontological and the epistemological, between seeing the world as a multiplicity of religions and explaining them according to one's particular perspective.

Jewish inclusivists tend to discuss an ethic that is derived from a Torah ethic, or they claim that there is a historic mission for the other religions, as in both Halevi and Maimonides. One calls the member of the other faith an anonymous member of your own faith. The Jewish inclusivist would claim that Christianity and Islam are daughter religions, even though it means that the other religions brought more people to God than Judaism. Finally, inclusivists relegate the Biblical command to destroy idolatry to a distant past. To accept this position, one has to separate the Biblical paganism, at whom the Biblical commandment is directed, from contemporary forms of religion.

The universalist assumes that God and ethics are greater than the specifics of organized religion. Medieval Jewish universalists accepted the universalism of the Neo-Platonists and Aristotelians. Universalists have a firm belief in God, revelation, and the soul but consider relationship with God as available to all humanity. God as creator made all humans in the image of God. They postulate a universality of faith that says all actually share God, revelation, or providence. The universal position focuses on a God-centered religion while the philosophic pluralist, in contrast, makes them human constructs.

This category does not exist in the standard Christian typology since historically they required salvation through Christ. Currently, the universal positions created by contemporary Catholic theologians are still viewed with suspicion by those responsible for Catholic doctrine. Medieval Jewish philosophers, however, could freely accept a God greater than any one religion, especially since the Islamic philosophers had a similar position. Similarly in the eighteenth-century Enlightenment, despite the social exclusion, Jewish thinkers attempted to hold together enlightenment and universal religious truths. (When Christian theologians do accept universalism, it is either seen as a more liberal inclusivism or as a form of the mystical pluralist.)

The pluralist recognizes that the great world religions have equally valid religious claims and addresses others in their own language. There is no universal court or absolute philosophy in which the rival truth claims can be adjudicated. There are several types of pluralism: *philosophic pluralism* is based on the limits of human understanding; *mystical pluralism* envisions a God beyond human categories; and *ethical pluralism* only sees the common good works of religion. The *philosophic pluralist* requires a major shift in thinking toward the fundamental fact of the pluralism of our religious world. The *mystical pluralist* sees the limitations of reason and feels that the ineffable mystery of God transcends human perspectives, dissolving categories before the blinding light of the Divine. The *ethical pluralist* has a universal commitment to goodness, justice, and human welfare.

John Hick, who originally popularized the categories of exclusivist, inclusivist, and pluralist, accepts a philosophic pluralism that functions as a kind of a priori commitment to the *philosophia perennialis*, which claims that all religions are fundamentally the same, or similar to the neo-Hindu model that there is a single absolute behind the many religions. Hick rejects or radically revises

divine revelation, creation or miracles, and considers most religious statements as myths or as poetic expression. For example, Sinai is to be understood
metaphorically. For his critics, Hick's insistence that all religions eventually
abandon their claims to uniqueness and universality results not in interfaith
dialogue at all but in a roundtable of liberals at which none of the actual religious cards is ever laid on the table. For some, this kind of tolerance is thus
both patronizing and unfaithful.

Pluralism as a category to replace universalism took off as the popular position in 1987 when Hick and Paul Knitter consolidated the pluralist position
by gathering in a single volume essays by many scholars who agreed with the
pluralist position. For them, any claim of uniqueness is only historical and
personal in meaning. Pluralism goes beyond acknowledging the plurality of
religions. Rather, they maintain a rough parity among religions concerning
truth. "No one revelation can be used as universal criteria for all the others."[2]
The parity was already advocated by the Enlightenment and defended by
Hobbes, Lessing, and a host of others but the Eighteenth-century thinkers
condescendingly looked down on organized religion. Now, the pluralism is
occurring within theology itself. Deism was the original home for tolerance
and equality; in the 1980s theological pluralism replaced deism as the home
for equalitarian thinking.

Those influenced by pluralism designated anyone who is the opposite of
an exclusivist as a pluralist. Many inclusivist and universalists are incorrectly
labeled together with philosophic pluralists since they find God's truth in
many forms, they engage in interfaith encounter, and can be portrayed as
the opposite of exclusivism. But those who share the same opponent are not
necessarily in theological agreement. On the other hand, any inclusivists and
universalists who reject pluralism and certain forms of dialogue are not to be
labeled as exclusivist; one can be a universalist or inclusivist and place limits
on irenic trends.

The philosophic pluralist model has merits for understanding the human
condition but Hick and most other pluralists ask the theologian to make a
"Copernican shift" to accepting pluralism as a starting point and then to ask
when one's own religion fits into the pluralism. Then one is no one longer
speaking from within a given faith, but as a theology of pluralism.

For the exclusivist, other religions are simply false. There is no broader,
outside world whose claims need to be harmonized and addressed; instead,
there is only the realm of the "other side." For those who accept this position,
there is a questioning or denial of the salvation of the believers in other faiths
or the value to other religions. The exclusivist position has a broad spectrum
of formulations from the need to actually belong ethnically and tribally to a
given religion, to those giving special status to one's belief.

The exclusivist position generally retains a very high degree of urgency about the imperative for outreach to others. It is ontically dependent on the unique elements of that religion, for example, Christ in Christianity, or halakhah in contemporary Orthodox Judaism. Truth and salvation are available solely through these unique elements. Exclusivism also has a strong sense of the reality of evil in the world and a need to overcome it through the discipline of a specific religion.

The more extreme form of exclusivism is restrictivism, where salvation can only come from the explicit teaching and acceptance of the details of one religion. The restrictive perspective views religion as a small lifeboat, in which only a few can enter, rendering God as only concerned with a small number of people. Even among exclusivists there is a tendency to recoil from the extremes of the position. What of God's concern for humanity? Do we think that God limits His concern to a small percentage of earth's people? Less restrictive versions of this approach, popular in engaged evangelical circles, leave open the possibility that God has more possibilities than He tells humans about: God has the option to save others after death, or that God works in mysterious ways, or that unique individuals in other faith might earn an individual redemption.

While this position may sometimes be at odds with ethical and universal sensitivities, it plays a powerful sociological role for groups who feel embattled and threatened by the majority culture. As Mary Douglas has observed, exclusivist thinking creates strong group identities. Unfortunately, many exclusivists seek to make it a zero sum question that if one's own faith is true then the other is completely false. The danger is not the exclusivism itself, it is the dualism and lack of other opinions. The danger is the single voice of the exclusivist arbiter, precluding a polyphonic symphony, where exclusivism is but one of several possible instruments.

For the Jewish exclusivist the universe is Judeo-centric and the other religions are not relevant; at best the exclusivist can speak of individual gentiles as righteous and admit the possibility that there is knowledge among the nations. Jews can judge doctrines based on Jewish criteria and even see an overlap on some ideas like monotheism or ethics, but the overlap remains in the realm of their coincidental adaptation of acceptable Jewish ideas. We find the restrictive position among some of the halakhic approaches that require the gentile to formally and publicly submit to Judaism and enter into a semi-conversion of a separate religion of the seven Noahite laws as defined by the rabbis.

Current forms of Jewish exclusivism, products of the postmodern culture wars, accept a radical perspectivism in which every person is entitled to have a different perspective, incommensurate with any commonalities. For these exclusivists, Judaism is absolutely true and other religions are false, but they assume and accept that other faiths should feel the same way toward their own faith.

For Judaism, the exclusivist position creates a chiasmic splitting of the world around us in two groups, Jews and all others. Most of the time such a viewpoint remains a form of myopia, assuming that Jews are the only protagonists in the march of history. At its most particular, Judaism has a tribal view of itself as the only possessor of morality and portrays contemporary gentiles as bereft of morals, sometimes considering all gentile morality as analogous to the immoral Roman tenth legion that was stationed, during the Rabbinic era, in the Golan.

Application of the Terms

The terms exclusivist, inclusivist, and pluralist were originally focused on the Christian theological question of salvation: Who can be saved? For many Christians, one could only be saved by faith in Jesus: "I am the way and the truth and the life. No one comes to the Father except through me" (John 14:6). In the discussion of Judaism, the terms are used to focus on the significance and meaning given to other religions. Since almost all Jewish positions grant the possibility of salvation to individual gentiles, they would all be a form of inclusivists, despite the wide gap from the universalism of the Maimonideans to the demonization of gentiles in Lurianic Kabbalah. In modern usage, contemporary scholars such as Robert Wuthnow and Diana Eck still use the three models, not as categories of salvation, but because they work to describe three basic sociological positions. Exclusivists start with essentials and their own faith commitment. The inclusivist (and universalist) sees some truth or the fulfilling of mission outside of one's faith. Pluralists start with the human perspective.

For a Jewish example of how each of these positions can play out theologically, let me look at how the *shema* can be imagined differently for each of the positions. For the exclusivist, the *shema*'s significance lies in its particularistic call for martyrdom, a reminder of the position of a besieged minority comprised of the sole bearers and oppressed proclaimers of the truth of God's unity. An inclusivist may hear the *shema* as a vision of all faiths acknowledging God's kingship, either now or at the eschaton. And for the universalist, it speaks of a unity of God so profound that all are included. For the pluralist, this proclaims a Jewish version of a common religious truth.

I do not think that one needs to choose between the models, we accept different approaches in different situations. As dutiful Jews, we need not always choose one position over the others; each can play a role in our religious lives. There will be days when our recitation of *shema* will carry universal intentions, and days where we will close our eyes and think exclusively. Among the components from which we build our religious lives and identities are the exclusive martyrdoms of the Maccabees and Crusader victims; the inclusivism of the Psalms, and medieval thinkers like Halevi and Maimonides; and the universalism from Isaiah, Ibn Gabirol, and Rabbi Abraham Isaac Kook.

We live by narratives that allow or even encourage us to shift our stories between inclusivist, exclusivist, and pluralist positions in accordance with our own inner dialogues, external contexts, and practical situations. As noted earlier, "Very few people seem to fit in any one of the three categories."[3] On a practical level, people employ all three positions, shifting stances depending on their circumstances. We should learn to pay attention to how we use different texts to guide us in different aspects of our lives. Different contexts call for appropriate responses in the situations they present. For example, sociologists note that in civic situations such as health care as well as in most pragmatic scenarios the majority of Americans are pluralists in religion, while they may have a different default position of exclusivist faith at their own place of worship. Many Orthodox Jews, as full participants in American civil society, are outraged when it is insinuated that they would withhold health care from a gentile in the name of religion, but are comfortable with an exclusivist theology in the synagogue.

Between these two extremes of health care and the house of worship there is a vast expanse of scenarios that could be understood in different ways. What is the best of the three positions for discussing civil religion, religion in the public sphere, or the role of religion after 9/11? Which should be used to discuss the importance of global responsibility, social activism, or meaning in history? I am not looking for a midpoint because I think that we do indeed use different rubrics in different situations. Rather, I seek to help articulate the implications of each position for encountering other religions, to illuminate how we do have different theologies in different situations, and to help formulate middle positions when people seem to accept contradictory positions in the same situation.

Currently, authors tend to write in more autobiographical narratives about how they came to their positions, delineating the slow changes in achieving openness to other religions and encountering other faiths. Today, encounters with other religions tend to be less intellectual, theoretical, and abstract and instead more practical, communal, and commonplace. And, in the broader American context, encountering other religions overlaps with the broader American pluralism in which the current climate moves beyond the meeting of discrete religions into a discourse highlighting the multifaith, the multicultural, and the multiethnic. When one sees a member of another faith engaged in worship, then what does it mean? For universalists, inclusivists, and even many contemporary exclusivists, I can still recognize their piety even as I fit it into my own system.

Subdivisions

Each of the three categories can be further subdivided into historical-mission, metaphysical, and humanist. I offer the following chart to give the reader an indication of where the book is going for the next five chapters. In the course of this book, I will explain these subdivisions as they arise from the texts. In the interim, a working definition for each of the subdivisions is as follows:

Inclusivism

- Historical mission—where knowledge of God and His will play themselves out in the wider world of other religions.
- Metaphysical, theocentric—where all references to God must point to the one true God.
- Revelation, Sinai-centered—where the teachings and ethics of Sinai are known throughout the world.
- Natural Law—where the teachings of Sinai are known to all people through natural means of understanding the natural order.
- Humanistic, theocentric—where there is a divine concern for humanity as made in the image of God.

Universal

- Theocentric—where God is a universal available to all humans in the minds or souls.
- Humanistic—where there is a common core of all humanity under God.
- Historic—where the divine has been fragmented among many nations.

Pluralistic

- Pluralism, ethical—all ethical people are on the right path.
- Pluralism, mystical—the encounter with God transcends any human categories.
- Pluralism, epistemological—there are limits to human knowledge or we have to accept the reality of the truth of all religions.

Exclusivism

- Historic—Chosen People where there is an oppositional mission of Judaism to other historic religions.
- Historic—other religions are one of the evil and transitory kingdoms of the book of Ezekiel or Daniel.

- Metaphysical—the other religions involve idolatry.
- Anti-humanism—where the humanism of others is downplayed or denied.
- Revelation—where the other nations are blamed for lacking Torah.
- Demonizing—where others are treated as essentially lacking souls, meaning, or value.

Ecclesiology or religious law

- Halakhah-centric, institution-centered ecclesiocentrism—in the case of Judaism it is all based on the halakhah and the truth of the halakhah or the rabbinic tradition containing all truths.

The historical-mission approach sees history as an unfolding of God's plan for bringing knowledge to the world culminating in the messianic age. Those who accept a historical position place other religions, usually Christianity and Islam, in a scheme that brings knowledge of God to the world (while by contrast these religions, from an exclusivist position, prevent the messianic age). An historical approach can ask about the relationships between these religions using biblical typology and can even subject their texts to a Jewish interpretation since the march of history is greater than any one faith. Exclusivists who use the historical-mission approach will stress the chosenness and uniqueness of the Jewish people as overriding any commonality.

The metaphysical approach distinguishes between levels of knowledge of God in that there is a hierarchy, usually based on Kabbalah, in the conception of God, from lower to higher understanding of God. The difference between the positions hinges on whether the other faith will eventually share the Jewish vision, have a limited perspective, or be severed from connection to the Divine.

Another metaphysical position acknowledges one common source for revelation and then asks how the revelations of the other religions relate to the Jewish concept of revelation. In this revelation-centric approach one can classify the other religions as derived from Sinai, as opposed to Sinai, or argue that revelation is available to all nations irrespective of Sinai. Morality can be considered a natural revelation available to all; then as long as gentiles are moral, they are fulfilling God's revelatory will.

The humanist approach starts with an axiological premise that all humans share a common Adamic origin and are made in the image of God. There are also antihumanist texts presenting a demonizing hatred of gentiles and the dehumanizing of their very humanity, let alone their religion. These texts are dangerous. This is the only explicit editorial point in the book: I condemn these texts in no uncertain terms. However, I see all other positions as undeveloped and needing discussion of the strengths and weaknesses of the position before any judgment can be made.

Acceptance model

Besides the three categories described earlier, there are new perspectives that move the empiricism of the academy to a theological position that has elements of the other three models. This approach is generally called the acceptance model, since it accepts all differences. It is also called the particularity model, since it respects all particularities and calls for mutual acceptance. There are three major forms.

- Post-liberal
- Comparative theology
- Different goals

In the post-liberal model I can only speak about and from within my own tradition. George Lindbeck is the major proponent of this position that accepts a theology of other religions but not dialogue. Religion is not doctrinal or expressive; rather it is cultural-linguistic, a textual or linguistic framework that shapes one's life. A cultural-linguistic perspective views religions as self-enclosed language based on grammatical rules. A particular faith must understand the world its own language primarily through its own texts and narrative. Theological faithfulness is within the texts of a given community. Theological reflection is based on the texts and even experience is related to the text.

In the case of Judaism it means that the texts of Judaism and the actions, thought patterns, and images that come from the texts are a cultural world that precedes any articulation as doctrine or experience. Religions are therefore incommensurate since they provide different cultural worlds. There is no neutral point to adopt. Encounter of religions is more of a good neighbor's policy in which there may be a fence but no mutually owned commons. Yet, Lindbeck concedes that "although we cannot get outside of our systems, what is outside our systems can nevertheless hit us hard enough to make dents in our systems." One could, if one wanted, treat this entire volume on *Judaism and Other Religions* not as fixed doctrine but as offering the conceptual system and grammatical rules of the Jewish texts on other religions.[4]

In the comparative theology model one compares texts from one's own faith to those of another faith and lets texts play off of each other without offering a broad or overarching theory. Francis X. Clooney, the proponent of this method, teaches that one understands the other religion within the categories of one's own faith. Starting with the perspective of belief in one's own faith seeking to understand others, one can compare and contrast Christian and Hindu love as a believer in a single tradition, deepening the understanding of love in religion.[5]

This volume is not comparative; rather it is entirely about and from within Jewish texts. The comparative approach would open a totally different set of questions based on commenting on the texts of other religions from a Jewish perspective.

In the different ends model, one can acknowledge that other religions may have nothing in common with one's own since the goal of the other religion may be different. S. Mark Heim, the proponent of this view, states that different religions are not just different paths but different goals. Differences are not skin deep or language deep but categorically different goals. Different religions answer different questions and have disparate and unique things to teach. For example, some forms of Buddhism may offer meditative liberation but not salvation. Religions cannot be compared because each religion is unique in its offerings.[6]

This approach shows the limits of the universal and pluralistic Jewish positions in that they seek commonality or diversity, rather than accepting that many practices in other religions may have no correspondence, for good or for bad, in Judaism.

These three new positions consider that the models of exclusivism, inclusivism, universalism, and pluralism inoculate one against actually knowing anything new or confronting the novelty of the other faith. These new models necessitate that one actually studies the other religion. Part of the importance of the new post-liberal models is that they show there are limits to all the positions and that moderns impose their own categories on the study of religion.

Even more contemporary is the non-foundational position of Kathryn Tanner, who considers religious identity as entirely negotiated and constructed, emerging through ground-level interactions between religious traditions and the cultures in which they are embedded. She highlights how religious identity develops through conflict and choice, and foregrounds practices (rather than beliefs or metanarratives) as the principal arena in which identity is constructed. Since she limits all religions to the cultural, one cannot compose a theology of other religions. Tanner argues that those who think all religions are completely different, or conversely the same, transcendental impulses are unacceptable and imposing their own values. For her, one should not minimize the differences for the sake of theological neatness; one must recognize the depth of the differences.[7]

Empirical Truth

If everything is a collection of texts, then what becomes of truth claims?

Henry Siegman, an Orthodox rabbi by original training and former executive director of the, currently defunct, Synagogue Council of America, argued the need for more practical encounters than theological ones but nevertheless noted that Jews have been less than daring in a process of self-reflection. For Jews to acknowledge that Christians who live a decent life do so despite, not because of, their Christianity is not daring.

> As a believing Jew, I affirm that Judaism is the "truest" religion. That affirmation is part of what makes me a believing Jew, and I do not expect Christians to be offended by it. I cannot be offended by parallel affirmations of faith made by Christians—or by Muslims, Hindus, or Buddhists, for that matter. To insist that Christians may not entertain such beliefs about their own faith is to cut the ground from under the Jewish position. It is to say that Jews can talk only to those who are less secure in their own faith than we are.[8]

For Siegman, we can deny the mystery and saving ability of their faith and yet we do not ask them to change and they should not ask us to change. We are not looking for validation and do not need pluralism—we need respect and to accept difference. Encounter is important for self-understanding and self-definition. If one, however, did not think one's faith was the best then why practice it?

The question of what is truth and how to evaluate different truth claims is part of the huge academic field of the epistemology of belief. Theology of other religions involves the question of how to formulate a coherent, cogent, and faithful religious response. Theology is not about what is defendable epistemologically. There are many fine discussions written by philosophers about whether religious belief is a correspondence or cohesive theory of truth, and many recent works on what makes a justified belief. There is also substantial literature on whether religious truth claims work the same way philosophic truth claims do. All of this is beyond the scope of this book. Nevertheless, a few points are worth noting.

Many appeal to religious experience in interfaith discussions. But there remains the epistemological question of whether we are all experiencing the same thing when we experience God. But there is actually a variety of opinions on the topic: many think that all religious experience is of the same object of ultimate reality; some think we experience aspects of the same divine reality but like a snowflake we do not have the same experience; and some others think all the experiences are different since we cannot escape our cultural construct.[9]

Many others involved in interfaith encounter take refuge in the ambiguous and multivalent marriage metaphor. The analogy is to the language that a husband would use of his wife saying: "you are the most beautiful woman in the world." Yet, this does not solve anything, since for the pluralist the husband's affirmation is only in the context of marriage, not an objective statement. The husband certainly knows that every husband says the same thing to his wife, and that there is little novel in these romantic proclamations. The exclusivist sees the marriage love as private and nontransferable and feels that one cannot even discuss the emotions of marriage in public. One has to have an absolute faith in one's private decisions of love. The inclusivist knows that one has affirmed a specific spouse and that the beauty and charms of one's wife are absolute in the moment but also knows that he is attracted to a certain type of beauty and is not attracted to others. His declaration of beauty is starting from a given perspective. The metaphor can be used by all positions. The pluralist assumes that if one is firm in one's marriage then one appreciates the beauty of others, as opposed to the exclusivist who assumes that one's emotional decisions need to be taken as absolutes. The inclusivist knows that every husband says to his wife that she is the most beautiful, but knows that we still live in a world of commitments and the need for continuous compliments. He finds the pluralist too close to taking the wife for granted while he finds the exclusivist not playing the game of love and attraction, just a defense of home and hearth.

All three monotheistic religions trace their origins back to a definitive revelation in history: Jews claim that revelation culminated in Moses; Christians accept Jesus Christ as the definitive revelation of God; and Muslims confess Muhammad as the last and final prophet of salvation history. And this is precisely the rub: as Thomas Hobbes pointed out, no revelation can trump another, for to do so would be to step outside the circle of the elect recipients of that revelation. The modern position of the eighteenth through twentieth century was that no religion could prove their unique revelation.

In contrast to Hobbes, who understands the revelations in complete contrast with one another, Jewish thinkers, from the Middle Ages until today, understand that other opinions can express truth even if in error or inexact. Inclusivists accept there is a single revelation, viewing the others as natural or a lesser form. Universalists view truth as not dependent on a historical event, hence available in all religions. Many exclusivists move the entire discussion out of questions of truth and into ethnic-national terms of the chosen people.

Paul Griffiths, a contemporary philosopher of religion, observes that an exclusivist approach, or one that does not see commonalities, "commits anyone who holds it to the claim that no alien religious teaching is identical with any teaching of the home community." According to Griffiths "if there were any such instance of identity, it would immediately follow that if the relevant teaching of the home community is true, that of the alien religion must also be true" I have had many students who have taken that attitude and they instinctively reject any commonality between religions. They prefer to think of everything in Judaism as unique and unprecedented. Their exclusivism might be doctrinally and existentially validated, nevertheless according to Griffiths, one can assume no overlap with others only if one has isolation from knowledge of other religions.[10]

These approaches to truth are based on following one's preexisting a priori assumptions. Schubert Ogden offers an option beyond the a-priori claims of the other approaches[11] Ogden holds that religions other than one's own can also be formally true even if, in point of fact, none of them actually are true or has yet been shown to be true in a reasoned way. In other words, for Ogden, the question of validity is fully empirical and a posteriori, derived from experience, and should not be decided in advance. Western acceptance of many aspects of other religions, such as yoga or meditation, is based on experience. This approach exhibits the following characteristics. First, all the conclusions different religions form about each other must be empirically based and not derived from a priori doctrines. We have to go, see, and experience the other. Each religious community, moreover, will make its judgments the basis of its own standards and values. Second, no doctrines, including those with a claim to particularism, are excluded a priori. As a result, he claims that the exclusivist need not fear an abandonment or reconstruction of fundamental doctrine. One can start from the particularism of one's tradition but still allow for other options.

Ogden's empirical approach allows one to see wisdom in all nations. As Paul Griffiths points out, there are many overlaps between religions; between one's own religion and other religions; for example, one can see love, joy, prayer, and kindness. Therefore, one can say those in the other religion are acting correctly, ethically, and with wisdom. Much of the actual lived practice and public teachings of most religions fall into this category of accepting of wisdom in other cultures. One could also find elements that seem similar to one's own religion's revelation and can either accept that the other faith has its own revelation or at least that the other faith has lesser forms of revelation through visions, intuitions, and true dreams.

Finally, we need to acknowledge that those inclined to spirituality and mysticism do not have trouble comparing notes on the human elements in their experiences. For many of the spiritual adepts, there is a certainty of the same empirical mystical reality greater than any theological scheme. This universalism is not a pluralism in which religions are all partly right, but of learning to respect the other on his or her own terms. To be a person that can give witness to other acts of faith, one must recognize the common phenomenology of spiritual techniques. A theology of mystical pluralist assumes that mysticism transcends any religion; in contrast, the empirical mystic knows that he or she can compare techniques with other mystics but does not make it a principle of a formal theology. An example of this ability to compare the human elements of religion will suffice.

On one of my visits to a kabbalistic Yeshiva in Israel, I met an ultra-orthodox kabbalistic follower of Lurianic Kabbalah meditation techniques; his theology was entirely sectarian and exclusive. Yet, he told me that we could learn techniques from all faiths, especially Hinduism and Buddhism. According to this ultra-orthodox Jewish mystic, everyone has partial knowledge of the technology of meditation. He himself had met with Indian meditators to aid in his own kabbalistic technique. Yet, he still accepted the exclusivist Lurianic theology as his core belief.

Many find a lack of substance within interreligious discussions because they either think "we're all really just the same" or that we're really all different." The categories of the theology of other religions offer intellectual categories to move beyond this simple dichotomy. Most people on both extremes expect little of others and therefore engage in serious misrepresentation of others. In addition, a generic social tolerance, without a theology of other religions, requires respect out of social principle but has no curiosity or respect for the difference of others. A theology of other religions requires one to encounter the other, appreciate the other, and actually fit the complexities of other faiths into terms understood by one's own religion.

CHAPTER 3

Biblical and Talmudic Texts

This chapter provides an overview of the views toward other religions expressed in the Hebrew Bible and the rabbinic corpus. Since this book concerns the writers of later centuries who interpreted and elaborated on the views of these foundational texts, I will focus on the passages that are discussed by these subsequent writers. I will not undertake independent historical and philological research on the biblical and rabbinic texts, but will offer a theological summary of the existing scholarship written by experts in these fields.

Before proceeding with the presentation of the sources, it is important to note that Judaism generally does not seek guidance from a direct and unmediated reading of the Bible. Rather, it generally understands the Bible through the complex matrix of rabbinic Judaism, later Jewish thought, and Jewish historical experience.

Furthermore, as a Jew, one does not ask when approaching these discussions whether gentiles have access to God or whether or not Christians should become Jews. Jews do not fret over who has access to God.

However, Jews do ask about the implications of being called a chosen people and a unique nation. In the Bible and Talmud, according to the Jewish reading, only Jews are seen as a special chosen nation; these texts blur the line between religion and nation. In modern terms, Jews ask: what is the relationship between Judaism as an ethnicity or nationality and Judaism as a religion?

The Hebrew Bible: Tanakh

The Bible contains many statements on the religions of the other nations. Most obvious are the repeated demands that Jews have no foreign gods and the characterization of heathen practices as foolish abominations. In Deuteronomy, the Israelites are both required to destroy all idols in the land and are severely chastised when they do not. They are seen as having a different mandate and destiny than the other nations who worship images. Therefore, in many biblical stories, gentiles are generally allowed to worship their gods. For example, in Ruth, Orpah is not chastised for returning to her father's god.

This tolerance is supported by the prophetic vision that predicts an eventual universal monotheism for all the nations. Isaiah offers us a universalistic vision of God's dominion over the world, in which the Jewish people and Jerusalem are central. Zephaniah and Zechariah offer an eschatological vision of all people serving one God, speaking one language, and living according to like-minded values. Most strikingly, Amos insists that God has interceded for other peoples as well. For the prophets, the standard by which God measures peoples is morality; access to God is not essentially exclusive. However, in Joshua and Ezekiel, God is seemingly a national God for the Israelites alone. (In these contexts, the correct phrase to use is "Biblical God" to avoid the implicit universal implications of the word God.)

In this chapter, I present the biblical texts in detail. They are arranged according to six broad theological categories. (i) Idolatry; (ii) natural religion; (iii) greatest of gods; (iv) universalism; (v) mission and proclamation; and (vi) national God.

Idolatry

Idolatry in the Hebrew Bible has two functional meanings: the worship of a being other than the Biblical God, and the use of imagery in worship.

> You should have no other gods before me. You shall not make a graven image or any likeness that is on the earth below, or that is in the water under the earth; you shall nor bow down to them or serve them; for I am the Lord your God am a jealous God." (Exod. 19:3–5)
>
> Thus shall you say to them: the gods who did not make the heaven and the earth shall perish from the earth and from under the heavens...every man is stupid and without knowledge; every goldsmith is put to shame by his idols, for his images are false and there is no breath in them. They are worthless, a work of delusion." (Jer. 10:11)

In these passages, idolatry is defined in three ways. It can be either the worship of idols as gods, the worship of polytheistic gods by use of idols (or images), or the use of idols in the worship of the true God. The first two types of idolatry involve rejecting the Biblical God, thereby violating the Covenant, while the third involves the use of representations to worship the true God.

According to the noted Israeli scholar Yehezkel Kaufman (d. 1963), the Bible represents monotheism as entirely separate from its polytheistic predecessors, rather than as an evolution of polytheistic practices. Within the Bible, local gods are consistently represented as false. They typically appear as purely material objects of gold, silver, wood, or stone. They are described as the work of men's hands, unable to speak, see, hear, smell, eat, grasp, or feel, and powerless either to injure or to benefit mankind (Ps. 135:15–18). Kaufman reads the biblical commandments regarding idolatry, most of the time, according to their most literal sense of treating inanimate objects as gods. For Kaufman, "The Biblical author's whole condemnation revolves around the taunt of fetishism."[1]

However, Kaufman acknowledges that in some cases idols appear to have been mere representations of gods. For instance, in 1 Kings 18:27, Elijah challenges the priests of Baal atop Mount Carmel to persuade their god to perform a miracle. The pagan priests beseech their god without the use of an idol, which, in Kaufman's view, indicates that Baal was not an idol, but instead a god that could be worshipped through the use of an idol.

Finally, the Bible contains instances of idolatrous worship of the Biblical God, as when Jeroboam sets up idols at Beth El and Dan (1 Kings 12:28–29). Since the Biblical God is aniconic, one cannot use images to worship God. It is important to note, therefore, that though it may seem counterintuitive to worship God and still call it idolatry because of our contemporary sense of the term "idolatry," the use of representations of God in worship constitutes monotheistic idolatry according to biblical terminology.[2]

In addition, there is textual and archeological evidence that Israelite religion incorporated this third form of idolatry into traditional practice, and there are various accounts to explain why Israelites preserved these elements of primitive paganism. According to Mark Smith, a contemporary scholar of biblical history, the religion of the Bible shared many elements with Canaanite religion in practice, but simultaneously sought to define itself by outlawing these customs. The evidence of the Bible, for Smith, points to the lingering fossils of older misunderstood ideas of religion. In contrast, the scholar Morton Smith (d. 1991) argued years ago that the extra-biblical evidence demonstrates that the worship of additional gods had strong popular support and were often promoted by kings and members of the royal court. Ziony Zevit, an expert in ancient Israelite religion, argues that the ancient Israelites still had an iconic love of the visual, and more significantly, incorporated into their worship polydoxies and polypraxes. In Zevit's reading, the tolerance toward representation we find in certain passages of the Book of Kings is consistent with the editorial approach of the book, since the book focused on denouncing royal idolatry rather than on popular syncretic practices.[3]

However, the arguments of these scholars, based on archeology and knowledge of the ancient near east, are not particularly significant for understanding the interpretations of idolatry produced by later Jewish writers of the rabbinic and medieval periods. The tradition of Jewish reflection on idolatry was not based in archeology, but rather in inherited textual tradition, rabbinic interpretations, and theological categories. Kaufman's approach may not be the most historically accurate one but his own inclusivist position offers a better guide for how later millennium read the Bible.

Natural religion

Many biblical passages assume that gentiles know the one true God. According to contemporary scholars, the biblical view is one of *monolatry*—the belief that all deities are simply different names for a single God.

Rabbinic thought explains that the existence of these different names is the result of a devolution from a primordial monotheism. Originally, all people of the world could, and did, know God. Adam worshiped one God, and those who now do not do so have forgotten the original truth. In the rabbinic view of biblical religion, God is available to all through the natural human tendency to monotheism, a universal knowledge.

Several important passages support the principle of monolatry. For instance, Melchizedek recognized God Most High as Abraham's God. "Melchizedek king of Salem brought out bread and wine; now he was a priest of God Most High. He blessed him and said, 'Blessed be Abram of God Most High, Possessor of heaven and earth'" (Gen. 14:18–9).

On the other hand, Naaman came to recognize the Lord of the Bible but still linked the biblical God with possession of earth from the biblical land. Yet, Elisha did not seek to correct Naaman's theology. And Elisha, according to most interpretations, accepted Naaman's request to be forgiven for still needing to worship, for political reasons, in a Temple dedicated to a foreign god.

> Then Naaman and all his attendants went back to the man of God. He stood before him and said, "Now I know that there is no God in all the world except in Israel. Please accept now a gift from your servant."...The prophet answered, "As surely as the Lord lives, whom I serve, I will not accept a thing." And even though Naaman urged him, he refused. "If you will not," said Naaman, "please let me, your servant, be given as much earth as a pair of mules can carry, for your servant will never again make sacrifices to any other god but the Lord.
>
> But may the Lord forgive your servant for this one thing: When my master enters the temple of Rimmon to bow down and he is leaning

on my arm and I bow there also—when I bow down in the temple of Rimmon, may the Lord forgive your servant for this." "Go in peace," Elisha said. (2 Kings 5:15; 18–19)

Malachi supports the notion that worship to any deity in any nation is in fact worship of the Biblical God. "'For from the rising of the sun even to its setting, My name will be great among the nations, and in every place incense is going to be offered to My name, and a grain offering that is pure; for My name will be great among the nations,' says the LORD of hosts" (Mal. 1:11–12). (Maimonides, Kimhi, Menashe ben Israel, and others make this verse a linchpin of their approach to other religions, see later chapters.)

While all of these passages reflect the principle of monolatry, there are clear differences in their individual logic. In the nineteenth century, the preferred term for the concept of monolatry was *henotheism*, where God is considered the singular deity behind all the lower manifestations. This term enables us to differentiate better between Melchizedek who eschewed the lower deities and only worshiped the "God most high," Naaman who understood that his deity was not to be worshiped anymore, and Malachi who understands that behind every lower form of worship is the true worship.

In other passages, the Bible speaks of one God over all who rewards righteousness. In these passages, there is no clear line between ethics and religion. For example, "Righteousness exalts a nation, but sin is a disgrace to any people" (Prov. 14:34). Passages of this sort reflect the universality of the true morality and religion, despite differences of national or religious custom.

What is the theology behind monolatry? Does accepting one God allow actual acceptance of idolatry for others, as long as they are ethical? Or does it merely enable a begrudging tolerance for the deviance of others? There are three broad readings of these texts.

One reading of the biblical position takes the view that as long as the members of other traditions leave us Jews alone, we should leave them alone in return. Jews have no responsibility to get involved in the beliefs of other nations. The Bible reveals that God expects non-Jews to be righteous and ethical, but regards them only with this minimal concern. This reading supports an attitude of neighborly pluralism, tolerant of others and indifferent to the details of other religions.[4]

A second reading focuses on biblical visions in which other nations come to acknowledge the one true God, understanding these moments as figures for the universal acknowledgment of God in the end of days. The actual method of worship is incidental. This reading supports a competitive pluralism, a universalism in which the worship of others is acknowledged, but God undoubtedly wins the contest.

The third reading of these texts privileges the Deuteronomistic mandate to destroy the worship of the seven nations in the land of Canaan during the conquest of the land and to wage war against them and their religions. An alternate form is that the land of Israel is special and that God has a zealousness to keep the land free of other deities (2 Kings 17). This is vehement exclusivist intolerance, in stark contrast with the first two opinions. However, the many other passages that mention the ordinary gentile who serves a local deity implies that many biblical texts take one of the first two approaches, rather than the third approach of vehemence.

To reiterate a major theme of this book, the choice is not between an acceptance of idolatry and a vehement intolerance toward others. The first two models of neighborly and competitive tolerance are both important and justifiable interpretations of the text in which either a universal ethic or a monotheism is available to all religions as part of the legacy of creation.

As a modern application, regardless of their representations, which may be considered idolatrous, the other contemporary religions—Christianity, Buddhism, Hinduism—can be productively considered from these intermediate positions.

Incompatible and greatest of the gods

The Bible, for theologians, affirms the idea that God is incompatible with any other god or power.[5] He is unique, singular, and omnipotent. The emphasis is on His wondrous, separate, and holy nature, deserving to be loved and feared. "Hear, O Israel! The LORD is our God, the LORD is one!" (Deut. 6:4). God is the great king and ruler who does not compromise or share his power with lesser beings. "For what nation is there so great, who has God so near to them, as the LORD our God is in all things that we call on him for?" (Deut. 4:7). In the later Jewish philosophic tradition, these biblical premises are abstracted to a philosophic monotheism characterized by Divine unity, indivisibility, noncorporeality, necessity, and uniqueness.

According to many scholars, this firm monotheism was preceded by monolatry and henotheism.. These henotheistic passages depict a divine council staffed by lesser supernatural figures. Mark Smith called the biblical monolarity a streamlined bureaucracy headed by an absolute monarch. The important distinction between the Biblical God and the pagan gods of the ancient near east, according to scholars Nachum Sarna and Mark Smith, was that the Biblical God did not have relatives, sex, children, or any need to fight lesser deities. This categorical distinction, despite the persistent belief in lesser or local deities, produced a sense of His superior greatness to other gods and a sense of His status as the only one true God.[6]

On the other hand, Yehezkel Kaufman, as stated earlier, maintains a radical separation between monotheism and preceding polytheisms. He reads passages that suggest a henotheistic cosmology as mere poetic fragments integrated into the biblical books.

Traditional Jewish commentators, who lived within the closed cosmology of medieval monotheism and who did not consider the possibility of a monolatry, treat these "gods" as the mighty warriors of Egypt, as powerful men, as angels, and as celestial forces (see Rashi, Ibn Ezra, and Radak on the verses cited below).

> Who is like unto thee, O LORD, among the gods? who is like thee, glorious in holiness, fearful in praises, doing wonders? (Exod. 15:11)
>
> God stands up in the Assembly of El (KJV the mighty); In the midst of the gods he judges. (Ps. 82)
>
> The heavens will praise Your wonders, O LORD; Your faithfulness also in the assembly of the saints. For who in the heavens can be compared to the LORD? [Who] among the sons of the mighty can be likened to the LORD? God is greatly to be feared in the assembly of the saints, And to be held in reverence by all [those] around Him. O LORD God of hosts, Who [is] mighty like You, O LORD? Your faithfulness also surrounds You. (Ps. 89:6–8)

Universalism

The prophets proclaim that one God is over all nations and envision a messianic ideal of peace and knowledge of God for all nations. The restoration of the people Israel, the rebuilding of the city of Zion, and the acceptance of one God are combined in a single eschatological image, and the attitude toward other religions remains vague.

> For then will I turn to the people a pure language, that they may all call upon the name of the LORD, to serve him with one consent. (Zeph. 3:9)
>
> And the LORD shall be king over all the earth: in that day shall there be one LORD, and his name one. (Zech. 14:9)
>
> And the glory of the LORD shall be revealed, and all flesh shall see it together: for the mouth of the LORD hath spoken it. (Isa. 40:5)
>
> For I know their works and their thoughts; the time is coming to gather all nations and tongues. And they shall come and see My glory. (Isa. 66:18)

These verses are interpreted by Maimonides, and many others, to promote an association between the monotheistic religions, specifically Islam and Christianity, as bringing knowledge of the Biblical God to the world. According to this perspective, their shared belief in one God is part of the unfolding of a messianic path.

Mission and proclamation

The Biblical God wants His power to be recognized by all people. He wants the world to know that He is not like the false gods revered by other nations. In Exodus, the Biblical God shows his power to the Egyptians by his own hand. "I will harden Pharaoh's heart that he shall follow after them; and I will be honored on Pharaoh, and on all his host; that the Egyptians may know that I am the LORD. And they did so" (Exod. 14:4). Isaiah instructs the nation of Israel to be light unto the nations and to make God's name known in the world.

> Now therefore, O LORD our God, save us from his hand, that all the kingdoms of the earth may know that you are the LORD, even you only. (Isa. 37:20).
> Give thanks to the LORD, acclaim his name; among the nations make known his deeds, proclaim how exalted is His name. (Isa. 12:4)
> He says, "It is too small a thing that you should be my servant to raise up the tribes of Jacob and to restore the preserved ones of Israel; I will also make You a light of the nations. So that My salvation may reach to the end of the earth." (Isa. 49:6)

What does it mean for God to be known by the nations in post-biblical times? Texts from the medieval and early modern eras state that God is known among the nations when they acknowledge His existence, miracles, and providence. Therefore, the influence of the Bible upon its daughter religions ensures that the monotheism of the Biblical God reigns. In the modern era, especially the religious thinkers of the nineteenth and early twentieth centuries, the knowledge of God was reflected in worldwide justice, morality, and pure monotheism.

National God

Some biblical verses suggest a sharp division between the nation of Israel who is chosen by her one true God and the other nations with their false gods. When the psalmist states, "He has not dealt thus with any other nation; they do not know his rules" (Ps. 147:20), he asserts a relationship to the Biblical God unique to the Jewish people. In a real sense, the verse proclaims that a non-Jew reading the Bible is reading someone else's mail.

These verses collapse ethnicity, national identity, and religion into a single category. This collapse of national and religious categories especially occurs in representations of a nationalistic God who displays His glory when Israel defeats other nations in war.

The Lord delivered them into the hand of Israel, so that they defeated. (Josh. 11:8)

There was no day like that before it or after it, when the LORD listened to the voice of a man; for the Lord fought for Israel. (Josh. 10:14)

And the LORD gave them rest round about, according to all that he swore unto their fathers: and there stood not a man of all their enemies before them; the Lord delivered all their enemies into their hand. (Josh. 21:44)

Your sudden roar, God of Jacob, knocked the wind out of horse and rider. Fierce you are, and fearsome! Who can stand up to your rising anger? (Ps. 76:6–7)

To be sovereign as a nation means that the Biblical God is sovereign as the deity who guarantees their success in war.[7]

Other texts present Israel as an agent of divine vengeance against these nations. The idea of a national God does not allow for talk of a universal religion or other religions in general. "I will lay my vengeance upon Edom by the hand of my people Israel: and they shall do in Edom according to mine anger and according to my fury; and they shall know my vengeance, said the Lord GOD"(Ezek. 25:14).

Biblical texts that emphasize the covenant between God and the single people of Israel evade discussions of who can know God, focusing instead on a typological reading in which the nation Israel alone has God, while the other nations are inherently idolatrous. These idolatrous peoples and nations—the Moabite, Ammonite, Egyptian, Amalek, Jebusite, Assyrian—are not considered religious in any relevant sense. Rather, they are divided into those that dwell in the Land of Canaan, which must be destroyed, those that attacked Israel and deserve punishment, and those that are simply devoid of God's covenant.

Israel was chosen among the peoples, but as a result of this, God is doubly strict in His demands upon this nation, and doubly severe in His punishment of its transgressions.[8] In contrast, God is less concerned with other nations. And even more importantly, other lands are portrayed as devoid of the Biblical God and as ruled by other gods. "Then the Lord will scatter you among all peoples, from one end of the earth to the other, and there you shall serve other gods, which neither you nor your fathers have known-wood and stone" (Deut. 28:64).

I will not devote time here to the Second Temple texts because they did not generally serve as independent sources for later Jewish writers. In the Second Temple era, there were many ideologies of strict separation from the gentiles, no possibility of conversion, and strict rejection of foreign gods. There are also cosmological texts portraying the other nations as arrayed as seventy nations around Israel, with their own access to God. These latter texts will be discussed briefly in later chapters.

Rabbinic Judaism

The Talmud includes a tractate entitled *avodah zarah*, literally "foreign worship," but it focuses more on the "other"—gentiles, pagans, and foreigners—than on the cults of antiquity and their religious content or significance. Rabbinic texts have a distrust of gentiles as an ethnic other—so much so that, according to rabbinic teaching, one should even avoid receiving a haircut from a gentile.

However, the rabbinic literature offers a wide variety of positions on the relationship of gentiles to true religion, from universalism—gentiles are able to study the Torah and part of the Sinai revelation—to an exclusivism shaped on the anvil of the Hadrianic persecutions in 135 CE.

Greco-Roman religion, when mentioned, is the subject of disrespect and disdain from the Talmudic Sages, who suggest obscene variations on the names of the ancient deities and recommend that idols be referred to with snide nicknames.[9]

Yet the Talmud maintains a category for virtuous gentiles who merit the world to come. Despite the general anti-gentile opprobrium, some of the rabbis seem willing to adopt the view that "some of my best friends are gentile" and are willing to adopt a friendly attitude toward gentiles. They offer tolerance without adopting a universal theory of religious salvation. Gentiles who live the virtuous life get into heaven, apparently without the help of religion.

However, the rabbinic texts also clearly differentiate Jews from idolaters and heretics. The latter category is amorphous enough to include various sectarians, Gnostics, early Christians, and those who don't accept rabbinic authority.

Why are there so many conflicting statements in rabbinical literature Scholars respond to this question in various ways. Some scholars account for the difference by distinguishing between schools of thought, for example, between Rabbi Yohanan b. Zakkai and Rabban Gamaliel, Rabbi Akiva and Rabbi Ishmael, and between R. Shimon Bar Yochai and Rabbi Yehudah. Others scholars separate texts into the following historical periods: Second

Temple sectarianism, the tumultuous struggles of the second-century Mishnaic period, the peaceful third century, the difficult fifth century in Israel, and the acculturated Persian sixth century in Babylonia.

I have sorted texts thematically, selecting primarily those that are quoted in later centuries. A complete arrangement and analysis of the variety of statements in the huge sea of rabbinic literature is far beyond the scope of this chapter. I am neither attempting a literary analysis of the texts nor a historical one. Nor is my goal to enter into the scholarly debates about the range of meanings of a passage. The current literature interpreting rabbinic narrative and history is enormous. My presentation, based on the following points, accepts the rabbinic literature as the core texts of the Jewish tradition, which serve as background for the latter chapters: (i) The righteous of all nations; (ii) Greco-Roman religion; (iii) Jews as separate; (iv) universal and inclusivist trends; (v) Noahite laws; (vi) separation and exclusivism; (vii) heretics; (viii) Christianity; (ix) Jesus; and (x) Alenu.

The righteous of all nations

Rabbinic texts have the potential to encourage tolerance and respect for difference because the question at the core of Christian theological discussion of the other, that is, the question of salvation, plays a relatively minor role in them. Behind the silence on the topic of salvation is the universally accepted Talmudic dictum: "the righteous of all nations has a share in the World to Come" (*Tosefta Sanhedrin* chapter13; TB *Sanhedrin* 102). This dictum became an axiom and has shaped the basic Jewish attitude for more than a millennium.

The *Tosefta* records two positions. The first—that of Rabbi Eliezer— promotes a restrictive doctrine and denies salvation to members of other religions.

> Rabbi Eliezer said: all gentiles do not have a share in the world to come as it is written: The wicked will return to Sheol, [even all the nations who forget God.] (Psalms 9:17); All the nations forget God, "the wicked will return to Sheol" these refer to the wicked of Israel.

In this case, the only way for gentiles to achieve the world to come is through conversion. The second position—that of Rabbi Joshua—holds that only the wicked are excluded from salvation.

> Rabbi Joshua said to him: if the text had said "the wicked will return, to sheol all nations, and was quiet, then I would say like you said. But now

that the verse said those who forget God. Behold there are saints among the nations they have a share in the world to come."

In this case, the righteous of all the nations can attain the world to come. While these two positions coexist in the *Tosefta*, one restrictive and one inclusive, the latter one was accepted and codified from the early middle ages onward.

From a broad perspective that casts its net over the breadth of rabbinic literature, the text of the *Tosefta* is not representative of the theological variety contained within rabbinic literature; there are many counter-voices. However, from the perspective of received theology and halakhah, this text is decisive and formative of the Jewish ethos. While we still find restrictive statements in early Ashkenaz, the emphasis was placed mainly on ensuring the world to come for all Jews, rather than denying eternity to gentiles. Soteriology was removed from the theological table and replaced by a tendency to evaluate gentiles according to their acceptance of the God of the creation (and Exodus and Sinai) and their moral behavior.

In his influential twelfth-century *Mishneh* commentary, Maimonides codified this rabbinic dictum as "All Israel have a share in the world to come and the pious of the nations have a share in the world to come."[10] The formulation by Maimonides shifts the terminology of the rabbinic texts from the religious ("saints of the nations") to the moral ("pious of the nations").

In theological hands, the admission of the "righteous of the nations" into heaven assumes a basic morality for all humanity. Secondary debates in later centuries exist about where this morality comes from. Some suggest that gentiles acquire their morals from an inborn potential to intuit the right and the good or that morality is rationally universal. Others propose that the morality of gentiles is originally derived from Sinai. For most, however, the acknowledgment by the *Tosefta* of righteous gentiles, who come to God by virtue of their morals rather than through religion, became a sufficient reason to ignore the question of gentile religion altogether.

Greco-Roman religion: statues

During the rise of Hellenism at the end of the Second Temple period, Jewish texts represented the other religions of the Greco-Roman world as mute statues unworthy of any adoration or belief.

The characterization of Abraham as the destroyer of the idols of his father is first recorded in the *Pseudepigrapha* work *Apocalypse of Abraham* (*ca.* 70–150 CE), but the narrative was more widely known among Jews as taught by

Rabbi Hiyya (~ 200 CE) through a version from the *Genesis Rabbah* five centuries later.

> Rabbi Hiyya said: Terah was a manufacturer of idols. He once went away somewhere and left Abraham to sell them in his place. A man came and wished to buy one. "How old are you?" Abraham asked him. "Fifty years" was the reply. "Woe to such a man," he exclaimed, "you are fifty years old and would worship a day-old object!" At this he became ashamed and departed.
>
> On another occasion a woman came with a plateful of flour and requested him, "Take this and offer it to them." So he took a stick, broke them, and put the stick in the hand of the largest. When his father returned he demanded, "What have you done to them?" "I cannot conceal it from you," he rejoined. "A woman came with a plateful of fine meal and requested me to offer it to them. One claimed 'I must eat first,' while another claimed 'I must eat first.' Thereupon the largest arose, took the stick and broke them." "Why do you make sport of me," [Terah] cried out, "have they then any knowledge?" "Should not your ears listen to what your mouth is saying," [Abraham] retorted.[11]

The rabbis reiterate the psalmist who declared that idols cannot hear, speak, or touch; only God is real. The midrashic story treats the idolatrous faith of Abraham's father, and by extension all belief in idols, as false. Only Abraham's God is real.[12] Treating other beliefs as false and irrational is widespread in rabbinic literature. It does not appear as an attack on any specific religion, but instead the falsehood of idols was displayed in stories as ordinary common sense available to all.

Another story ridicules the method of idolatrous worship by reducing all service of idols to an absurdity of an excrement joke.

> Sabta, a townsman of Avlas, once hired out a donkey to a gentile woman. When she came to Peor, she said to him, "Wait till I enter and come out again." When she came out, he told her, "Now you wait for me until I go in and come out." "But are you not a Jew?" she asked. "What does it concern you?" he replied. He then entered, uncovered himself before it, and wiped himself on the idol's nose. The acolytes praised him, saying, "No one has ever served this idol so consummately!" He that uncovers himself before Baal Peor thereby serves it, even if his intention was to degrade it. He who casts a stone at Merculis thereby serves it, even if his intention was to bruise it. (*Sanhedrin* 64a)

In the story, Peor (see Num. 25), which the rabbis imaginatively portray in scatological terms, is the prototype to ridicule idolatry, including everything from ancient Baal worship to the contemporary homage to the god Mercury. For most scholars, the rabbis do not seem interested in contemporary religions and are just continuing biblical anti–idolatry. The few references are solely basic knowledge of one's environment. Yet, some scholars do argue for the vitality of pagan cults among Jews and that they are knowledgeable about their contemporary local practices.[13]

The stories, nevertheless, reflect a lack of speculation on the role of icon and external representation in religion. This tale, as an exemplar of other midrashim, treats the statues as if they themselves are gods. The stylized approach in rabbinic texts demonstrates limited ethnographic interest in other religions and deters inquiry regarding the accuracy of their characterization. Rabbinic texts are not interested in the logic of iconic representation for other worshipers. In this they were similar to the ancient Greek thinkers (500–200 BCE), such as Heraclitus, Xenophanes, and Antisthenes, who also rejected the use of images in religious worship and were nostalgic for an earlier religious age free of statues and images.

Before I continue, I must point out that there is confusion in English terminology between idolatry and *avodah zarah* (foreign worship). "Idol" is literally "image" from the original Greek *eidōlon*. "Idolatry" is the worship of images, which by the time of the *Septuagint* was used for images of gods. In the *Mishneh, avodah zara* is defined technically as the worship of idols, the worship of statue.[14] However, over time both words drifted in meaning to include the worship, even without a statute, of other gods or other religions. The meaning was further expanded in rabbinic literature to include any unfaithfulness to God or negative character trait.[15]

In the *Mishneh*, the worship of a statue is *avodah zarah*, even when done by Jews as in the case of the golden calf in the wilderness or under Jeroboam. In contrast, one who accepted a false belief was called, depending on the belief, *apikorus, min*, or *kofer*, not an *avodah zarah*. The definitions of these boundaries creating terms are complex, varied, and beyond our scope. However, it is important to note that one can be monotheistic *avodah zarah* if images are used, and be a polytheist and not violate the mishnaic concept of *avodah zarah*.

For the background of the rabbinic view of other religions, it is also important to note that in the world of late antiquity, Jews and philosophic pagans were both against icons. A philosophic pagan monotheist who eschews idols, as many of the philosophers did, is not guilty of *avodah zarah* despite the recognition of the pagan gods. Sage and Hellenistic philosopher were on the same side against popular paganism.[16] (Later, medieval Jewish philosophers clearly treated Plato and Aristotle as monotheists.) Philosophers saw statues as bereft of intrinsic value, and Plotinus called them "blank darkness" far removed from any force or intelligence.[17] Yet, cultic paganism accepted icons, while some Christians accepted anthropomorphism and saw icons as pointing to the biblical monotheistic God.

The ever presence of statues, icons, and images in popular Greco-Roman culture was overwhelming to rabbinic Jews. "If one wished to write all the names of idols, all the parchment scrolls in the world would be insufficient" (*Sifre Deuteronomy* 43). More importantly, they assumed that idolatry used to be worse in ancient Mesopotamia. Abraham needed four hundred chapters on the laws of *avodah zarah* (Avodah Zarah 14b). Hence, both rabbinic Judaism and the medieval Jewish thinkers refer to the Chaldeans of the Bible as the idolaters, not the Greco-Roman world. There was already a logic, despite the ever presence of images, that the use of image in the rabbinic era was unlike the biblical era idolatry. The Talmud states "the temptation of idolatry was subdued in the time of Ezra" (*Sanhedrin* 64a).[18]

Idols were functionally defined as for the sake of worship. Those statues that were ornamental, functional, or not worshiped were permitted.

If one finds utensils upon which is the figure of the sun or moon or a dragon, he casts them into the Dead Sea. Rabban Shimon ben Gamaliel says: if [one of these figures] is upon precious utensils they are prohibited, but if upon common utensils they are permitted. (*Avodah Zarah* 3:3)

Proclos, son of a Pilosphos, asked Rabban Gamaliel in Acco when the latter was bathing in the bathhouse of aphrodite. He said to him, "It is written in your Torah, 'let nothing that has been proscribed stick to your hand (Deuteronomy 13:18)'; why are you bathing in the bathhouse of Aphrodite?" He replied to him, "We do not answer in a bathhouse." When he came out, he said to him, "I did not come into her domain, she has come into mine. People do not say, 'the bath was made as an adornment for Aphrodite'; rather they say, 'Aphrodite was made as an adornment for the bath.' Another reason is, even if you were given a large sum of money, you would not enter the presence of your idol while you were nude or had experienced seminal emission, nor would you urinate before it. But this [statue of Aphrodite] stands by a gutter and all people urinate before it. It is only stated, 'their gods' (Deuteronomy 12:3): what is treated as a god is prohibited, what is not treated as a deity is permitted." (*Avodah Zarah* 3:4)

By the third century statues were everywhere. If the Jews were to adopt an overly strict attitude toward these statues, and consider them idols, they would effectively be prohibited from taking part in most of Greco-Roman society, including such communal institutions as the bathhouse, roads, bridges, and marketplaces. Moshe Halbertal notes that the distinction between the cultic and the aesthetic created neutral space between pagans and Jews.[19] The statues are entirely functional and not considered a deity; The passage reflects the Roman concept that a statue is only an idol if one shows it respect or gratitude. Aphrodite was merely placed there as adornment. Rabban Gamaliel further points out that if this sculpture of Aphrodite were truly considered to be a goddess, people would not walk naked in front of her, or perform bodily functions.[20]

According to the noted scholar Ephraim Urbach, by the third century the rabbis no longer considered the Greco-Roman world as truly pagan. To put it in contemporary terms, gentile contemporaries no longer believed in their ancestral religion, but only using the ancient forms as a cultural practice. Rabbi Yohanan, a sage from the Land of Israel, said "their idolatry is only an ancestral custom." According to his thinking, there is a practical indifference toward the idols themselves. "One can bathe in a bathhouse before a statue of Aphrodite," he rules, "because it is only for decoration."[21] Having declared his neighbors to be cultural pagans rather than religious pagans, Rabbi Yohanan defines true religion in a way that is neither cultural nor concerned with theological specifics: "Anyone who rejects idolatry is a Jew."[22]

A similar betokening of tolerance toward Greco-Roman paganism is shown by the Babylonian Rav, who considers Roman religion a civil or natural religion, rather than a theological religion. "The Saturnalia and the Calends originated with Adam and were based on purely human sentiments" ('Ab. Zarah 8a; Yer. 'Ab. Zarah 39c). According to Rav, one should not participate in these rituals, but one can at least understand that the festival is a manifestation of universal sentiment and is not idolatry.

In another acknowledgment of pagan religion, the rabbinic texts record and respond to the practice of placing stones at crossroads as a cairn to Mercury, the god of journeys and transport. The *Mishneh* states "Three stones next to each other," placed near a Markulis (Mercury) pillar, "are forbidden." However, since the Talmud does not offer a discussion of the guiding theology behind Mercury worship, this practice was probably singled out because of its prevalence on roads of the land of Israel and its use of stones making it seem similar to those stone piles mentioned in Deuteronomistic prohibitions (*massabah*).

Some rabbinic texts offer a version of the biblical view of neighborly tolerance, by not concerning itself that much with the religion of the gentiles. These texts limit the ban on idolatry to Judaism and not to gentiles, or they limit it to the land of Israel and are not concerned with other lands.

It is written: Let them be only thine own, and not strangers' with thee (Prov. 5:17). The Holy One blessed by He said, "I do not warn idolators concerning idolatry, but you," as it is said: Ye shall make you no idols (Lev. 26:1). Only to you have I given judgment, for it says: Hear this, O ye priests, and attend, ye house of Israel, and give ear, O house of the King, for unto you pertaineth the judgment (Hos. 5:1). (*Exodos Rabbah* 15:23)

These texts prescribe forbearance toward the use of images by non-Jews, the religions of the other nations. This later position dovetails with those who use tosafot (see chapter on gentiles later in this volume) to allow a lower standard of either iconography or monotheism to gentiles. It also supports those medieval thinkers who accept positions that state that gentiles do not believe in the statues as gods, only as representation.

Universalism and inclusivism

The rabbinic texts contain universal statements about the Torah as accessible to all gentiles. Some texts seem to create a Torah outside of the Jewish ethnos and its laws. "Whosoever recognizes idols has denied the entire Torah; and whosoever denies idols has recognized the entire Torah" (*Sifre*, Deut. 54), whereas others seem to imply that Torah was not to be limited to Jews, but was to apply to all of humanity.[23]

"They encamped in the wilderness" (Exodus 19:2). The Torah was given in a free place. For had the Torah been given in the land of Israel, the Israelites could have said to the nations of the world, "You have no share in it." But now that it was given in the wilderness publicly and openly, in a place that is free for all, everyone wishing to accept it, could come and accept it." (*Mekhilta de R. Yishmael bahodesh*, 198)

"When the Holy One, blessed be He, revealed himself to give the Torah to Israel, he revealed Himself not only to Israel but to all the other nations." (*Sifrei Devarim* 343)

According to these passages, all people, not just Jews, can freely partake of Sinai. In other texts, gentiles can acquire access to Torah through study and through following its teachings.

R. Meir said: What is the proof that even a gentile who occupies himself with Torah is like a high priest? Scripture says, "With which if a man occupy himself, he shall live by them" (Lev. 18:5). It does not say, "A priest, a Levite, an Israelite," but, "A man."

Hence you may infer that even a non-Jew who occupies himself with Torah is like a high priest. (*Baba Kamma* 38a)

R. Jeremiah used to say: What is the proof that even a gentile who keeps the Torah is like a high priest? The verse "Which if a man do, he shall live by them.". . . Thus even a gentile who keeps the Torah is like a high priest. (*Sifra Leviticus* 86b)

[The prophet] Elijah said: I call heaven and earth to witness that whether it be Jew or gentile, man or woman, manservant or maidservant, the holy spirit will rest on each in proportion to the deeds he or she performs. (*Tanna devei Eliyahu*, ed. Freidmann, 48)

This group of texts creates an opening for many of the medieval positions accepting the availability of revelation to gentiles. The latter passage, reminiscent of *Galatians (3:28)*, serves as one of the strongest universal rabbinic statements about the availability of prophecy, but *Tanna devei Eliyahu* is a late work that already has many characteristics of early medieval works.

One of these universal strains presents an inclusive interpretation of Jewish ancestry. The following passage states that even converts who are not ethnically Jewish can be regarded as descendents of Abraham, and thereby incorporated into Judaism.

R. Yehudah taught: a convert brings [first fruits] and recites. What is the reason? "For I make you the father of a multitude of nations" (Genesis 17:5) in the past you were the father of Aram and from now on you are the father to all the nations [*av-hamon*]. (JT *Bikkurim* 5)

The first fruit offering *(bikkurim)* was to be accompanied by a recitation from Deuteronomy that stated that originally Abraham, *our forefather*, worshiped idols and then came to God. The passage explains that the convert can rightly recite this claim to Abraham's line because the concept of conversion breaks the identification of the Jewish religion with a specific ethnic group. Converts can identify with a historical mission that stretches from Abraham to the Messiah.

These texts suggest that gentiles can be as worthy as Jews if they follow the Torah. What was the ultimate vision of early rabbinic Jewry for the nations? There are two available interpretations of this—either gentiles who follow Torah are incorporated into Judaism, or Torah offers a form of a general revelation available to all humanity. Was it an eschatological conversion of all to Judaism or a moral conversion to serve God, and thereby fulfill Torah? Most scholars accept the former, but some scholars, such as Paula Fredrickson, argue for the latter:

The roots of the first-century Law-free mission are not Christian, nor even Jewish-Christian. They are specifically Jewish. They grew in the soil of apocalyptic eschatology. The belief that, at the End of Days when

God revealed himself in glory, Gentiles would repudiate their idols and as Gentiles (that is, without converting to Judaism) acknowledge and worship the true God together with Israel is native to ancient Judaism itself.[24]

There are also universal strains in the rabbinic texts that follow an idea of the universal mercy of God, which cannot be limited.

The Holy One declares no creature unfit, but receives all. The gates of mercy are open at all times, and he who wishes to enter may enter. (*Shemot Rabbah* 19:4. *Baba Kamma* 38a)

"In justice and plenteous righteousness, he will not afflict" (Job 37:23): God does not withhold reward from gentiles who perform His commandments. (*JT Peah* 1:1)

Most of these universal statements found in the rabbinic writings are overshadowed by statements that limit the Torah to Israel. The collection of sources in this book opens up many important questions on the meaning of the chosenness of Israel. However, it is important to note that there is a view that presents Torah as a gift from God, which acknowledges Jewish chosenness and particularism without producing a negative view of other religions. The Oral law cannot be given to gentiles or universalized because it is a mystery given only to God's children.[25] "The Holy One Blessed be He says to the nations of the world: You claim that you are my children, but I know that only those who know My secrets (*mysterion*) are my children. Where are His secrets? In the *Mishneh*, which was given orally" (*Tanhuma ki-tissa* 34:27; cf. *Gittin* 60b). What is the status of chosen people after creating a theology of other religions? Why is the difference between Judaism and other religions if they also have truth? What if other religions have Torah or prophecy? These questions deserve their own volume, but this passage is a useful beginning. Only Israel as children of God has access to certain mysteries, but presumably gentiles may possess the Written Torah and maintain a relationship with God.

Separated and exclusivism

Many rabbinic texts argue the intrinsic righteousness of Israel as separate and holy, and distinguish Israel from the nations who lack its special status.[26] A well-known Talmudic passage that has become part of the liturgy declares "[God] distinguishes between sacred and secular, between light and dark, between Israel and the nations, between the seventh day and the six days of creation."

This separation is carried further in other passages that present gentiles as the very opposite of the Torah. "When Israel eat and drink they engage in words of Torah...but the nations...engage in obscenities" (*Megillah* 12b, *Esther Rabbah* 3:13). Eliezer b. Hyrcanus offers another example: "the mind of every non-Jew is always intent upon idolatry" (Git. 45b). Levi b. Hama offers a more general essentialist view that the religion of the gentiles and that of the Jews creates different types of people.

> R. Levi b. Hama said, "If an idolater resembles his idol, as is written (Ps. 115), 'Those who worship them are like them,' how much more so will one who worships the Holy One Blessed Be He resemble Him. And how do we know this to be so? It is written (Jer. 17:7), 'Blessed is the man who trusts in the Lord.' " (*Deut. Rabbah* 1:12)

These influential texts move the discussion from a ban on idolatry to a rejection of gentiles in general. This approach reaches an extreme in Simon ben Yohai's dictum "The best among the Gentiles deserves to be killed" (*Mek, beshallah*, 27a). There is a large body of apologetic literature that attempts to soften the intent of this statement, and these readings are important for contemporary self-understandings, but do not relate to our concerns with other religions.

Sacha Stern, a scholar of rabbinic thought, explains that the strong differentiation between Jews and gentiles in rabbinic texts stems from an equation of gentiles with idolatry, and of both with immorality. The Talmudic tractate on idolatry primarily emphasizes social separation from gentiles, but Stern posits this equation as a corollary: all gentiles are idolatrous since only Jews have God.

Gary Porton, a scholar of rabbinic texts, represents the standard academic approach to these texts. He states that idolatry was a potential attraction to Jews and prohibitions were designed to discourage the practice among Jews. Stern, however, argues that there was no attraction to idolatry, and that the Talmud takes an incredulous view of non-Jewish worship. Stern concludes that idolatry (*avodah zarah*) functioned as a halakhic Jewish law metaphor for non-Jewishness and the threat to Jewish identity. The rabbis actively "created boundaries" and, in Stern's bold words, retreated into solipsism and introversion. "The praxis of Jewish identity is thus to our sources a fundamentally solitary experience," in which "exclusory solipsism can be itself a strategy for the protection of self-identity."[27] Stern notes that these texts do not discuss differences between Jewish and gentile practices in the typical Talmudic manner for presenting legal test cases or ethical principles. Rather, he sees in them an anxious assertion that "without the Torah, indeed, there would be no difference between Israel and the nations."

Besides identifying gentiles with idolatry, many rabbinic texts also identify gentiles with immorality. These moral arguments about gentiles generated a Jewish concept of original sin, in which those who were not at Sinai are forever tainted by Eve's sin. "Why are idolaters contaminated (*mezuhamin*)? Because they did not stand at Mount Sinai. For the serpent came upon Eve he injected her with filth: the Israelites who stood at Sinai, their pollution departed" (*TB Yevamot* 103b). If Sinai removes the original sin, or acts as a break in theological history between the polluted generation and the purified, then revelation becomes spiritualized as the means of moral perfection. The Jewish view of original sin is a negligible minority position today, but the doctrine influenced many later kabbalists.[28]

Noahite laws

The Talmud, in a single discussion, introduces the concept that all of humanity is bound by the Noahie laws.[29] "The descendants of Noah were commanded with seven precepts: to establish laws, (and the prohibitions of) blasphemy, idolatry, adultery, bloodshed, theft, and eating the blood of a living animal" (*Sanhedrin* 56a; Tosefta Avodah Zarah 8.4; and compare *Sifre Deut.* 343:4).[30] When unpacked, this short statement yields a list of seven prohibitions:

1. Prohibition of idolatry: You shall not have any idols before God.
2. Prohibition of murder: You shall not murder (Gen. 9:6).
3. Prohibition of theft: You shall not steal.
4. Prohibition of sexual promiscuity: You shall not commit adultery.
5. Prohibition of blasphemy: You shall not blaspheme God's name.
6. Dietary law: Do not eat flesh taken from an animal while it is still alive (Gen. 9:4).
7. Requirement to have just laws: You shall set up an effective judiciary to enforce the preceding six laws fairly.

These seven are each, in turn, seen as broad cluster concepts that each incorporate or generate many detailed prohibitions yielding well over a hundred separate rules of conduct.

The Talmud debates how and when humanity became aware of the Noahite commandments, and whether these obligations are exclusively moral or also entail specific commitments. Normative Talmudic opinion (*Sanhedrin* 56a–57a) regards the commandments as intended for all people, using the original commandment of Genesis 2:16 (not to eat the fruit of the tree) as evidence that all humanity is required to listen to God's mandates. The Talmud gives further biblical verses to show that each of the commandments are found in the Bible and constitute its implicit moral code. It is important to note in the context of other religions that these seven Noahite laws are considered the Jewish basis for universal morality, not the Ten Commandments or the prophets This list has similarities to the list in Acts 15 of prohibitions given to gentile Christians. (This comparison was already noted by Rabbi Yaakov Emden in Eighteenth century, see chapter 4.)

There is significant rabbinic and scholarly debate over whether Noahite laws were ever meant to serve as a foundation for gentile morality, or whether they were a theoretical category necessary only for Jewish rule over non-Jews. Furthermore, medieval and modern rabbinic opinion is divided on whether Jews have an obligation to compel gentiles to observe Noahite standards. Maimonides (*Mishneh Torah, Laws of Kings* 8:10) maintains that Jews are obligated to enforce these standards on gentiles, and Nahmanides (commentary on Gen. 26:5) disagrees. Some Jewish thinkers maintained that these laws were derived from reason or natural law, and that all civilized cultures create a legal-religious system.[31] However, exclusivists require an explicit rejection of other religions to follow the Talmudic Noahite laws. Some even embrace the restrictivist requirement for the gentile to appear before a Jewish court (*beth din*) in order to convert to Noahite religion.

Sasha Stern, however, demurs, and goes so far as to state that the Noahite laws functioned explicitly to exclude gentiles from Jewish law and never intended any implicit inclusivism. He bases his own position on rabbinic statements such as "God gave the nations shapeless commandments, to keep them busy; he did not distinguish, in them, between impure and pure" (ExR 30:9).[32] Rather than providing a universal standard, they are yet another way for rabbinic thought to evade the question of gentiles.

However Rabbi Isadore Epstein (1894–1962), the translator of the Soncino Talmud into English, offers an explanation of the Noahite laws, as a moral standard for all mankind and a sign of God's universal love, shared by many moderns.

> These commandments may be regarded as the foundations of all human and moral progress. *Judaism has both a national and a universal* outlook in life. In the former sense it is particularistic, setting up a people distinct and separate from others by its peculiar religious law. But in the latter, it recognizes that moral progress and its concomitant Divine love and approval are the privilege and obligation of all mankind. And hence the *Talmud lays down the seven Noachian precepts, by the observance of which all mankind may attain spiritual perfection.* (*Sanhedrin* 56a)

The understanding of this idea promoted by later thinkers is incorporated elsewhere throughout this book.

Heresy and sectarians

Rabbinic texts have a fear of unnamed heretics, calling all of them sectarians (*min, minim*). The nineteenth-century Jewish historian Heinrich Graetz considered all these polemics a necessary precaution against the widespread Gnostic influence. In contrast, many twentieth-century historians considered them veiled polemics against the presence of Christians or Judeo-Christians. However, probably neither is the case.

The polemics against sectarians most likely refer to a rabbinic category that blurs Judeo-Gnostics, Judeo-Christians, Christians, Zoroastrians, Jewish sects, and all those outside of rabbinic authority into a single linguistic and conceptual category. Analogous to the early Christian usage of "gnostic," which covered all heretics and schismatics, sectarian (*minim*) covers all manner of heretics. According to Naomi Janowitz, a scholar of late antiquity,

> Picking a specific identity for a min is a bit like taking a Rorschach, revealing the favorite heretic of each scholar. Was he a non-rabbinic Jew, heretical rabbi, Christian, Jewish-Christian, Gnostic, imperial official, or some other flavor of heretic? Collecting all the references which denounce "minim" does not settle the issue since the specific issues they are denounced for vary so widely from anecdote to anecdote; according to the rabbinic texts themselves there were twenty-four kinds of "minim" at the time of the destruction of the Temple. Marcel Simon concludes "Minim designated simply any dissident body, whatever its particular characteristics, which rejected in any respect the thought or practice of Jewish orthodoxy."[33]

"Sectarian," Janowitz argues, is just a value-laden term to represent a heterodox believer.

My concerns are not with the academic historian who attempts to figure out who was the sectarian in any given passage. Scholars themselves ask if the group identified by *minim* changed or if only their rabbinic portrayals did. I accept the broad historical distinction that in Tannaic sources the sectarian are an acute internal threat, while in Babylonian Talmudic sources they are stylized. In these later texts, heretic is a general term for the proximal other, the deviant position from within one's own ethnic national group.[34]

My concern is to elucidate that sectarians accept beliefs that are unacceptable for Jews, and may, or may not, be unacceptable to gentiles. This is important to note because some of these texts about sectarians might have applied to early doctrines of the followers of Jesus. Christians, however, if they were of Jewish birth were probably seen as sectarians and not as a part of a separate religion. The discussion of sectarians is also important because many of the discussions of monotheism occur in these passages. Finally, the term sectarian had social implication since Second Temple Judaism was highly sectarian and many groups practiced social separatism. They avoided contact with both gentiles and those outside of their sect.

There are affinities between the pseudoepigraphic work *Jubilees* and the Rules of the Dead Sea Sect with the rabbinic thinking about gentiles and heretics. *Jubilees* encourages separation from Gentiles, while the Qumran sect goes further and applies the concept of separation to other Jews. Rabbinic legal texts reflect both interpretations of separation; they differentiate Jews from both gentiles and Jewish sectarians. The rabbis prohibit common eating and intermarriage between Jews and non-Jews. Jewish sectarians are seen as magicians who argue over the meaning of biblical passages, their children are considered illegitimate, and their meat is prohibited.

> Meat which is found in the possession of a gentile is permitted for gain; in the possession of a *min* it is prohibited for gain ... Their bread [is deemed] the bread of a Samaritan, and their wine is deemed wine used for idolatrous purposes. And their produce is deemed wholly untithed, and their books are deemed magical books, and their children are mamzerim All are permitted to perform an act of slaughtering [of an animal], even a Samaritan, even an uncircumcised, and even an Israelite apostate. But the slaughter [performed by] a min is deemed as idolatry, and that of a Gentile is invalid. (*Tosefta Hullin* 20)

According to Aharon Shemesh, a scholar of rabbinics, the Tannaitic laws are rooted in the ancient "Laws of Separation" of the Second Temple era, and as we see here, they were clearly invoked by the rabbis against other Jews.[35]

Sectarians appear to have different conceptions of divinity than the rabbis, hence the original hypothesis that they were Gnostics. Here we have a sectarian portrayed as treating the mountains and winds as emanations of separate deities.

> A certain *min* once said to Rabbi, "He who formed the mountains did not create the wind, and he who created the wind did not form the mountains, for it is written, 'For lo, He who forms the mountains and creates the wind (Amos 4.13).'" He [Rabbi] replied, "You fool, turn to the end of the verse, 'the Lord of Hosts is His name.'"

This passage does not attack any specific pagan or Christian belief. Instead it shows, through a hypothetical case, that anyone who is not worshiping the true God is worshipping foolish and false idols.

In another series of passages, a heterodox theological opinion, that there is a plurality of deities, is corrected by examining discrepancies between putative misinterpretations and actual biblical verses.

> R. Johanan said: In all the passages which the Minim have taken [as grounds] for their heresy, their refutation is found near at hand. Thus:
>
> Let us make man in our image,—And God created [sing.] man in His own image;
>
> Come, let us go down and there confound their language,—And the Lord came down [sing.] to see the city and the tower.
>
> Because there were revealed [plur.] to him God,—Unto God who answereth [sing.] me in the day of my distress;
>
> For what great nation is there that hath God so nigh [plur.] unto it, as the Lord our God is [unto us] whensoever we call upon Him [sing.]; And what one nation in the earth is like thy people, [like] Israel, whom God went [plur.] to redeem for a people unto himself [sing.], Till thrones were placed and one that was ancient did sit. Said R. Eleazar b. Azariah But one was a throne, the other a footstool:

In all the passages, plurality is rejected and God is unique. The last passage from Eleazar ben Azariah presents as the rabbinic position a proto-kabbalistic image, in which God sits on a throne and has both a seat and a footstool in support of His feet. All the dismissed sectarian statements represent an obvious rejection of rabbinic monotheism of one God. However, Christians, and later early Muslims, thought Jews violated monotheism in their veneration of angels, the divine glory, and the divine throne.[36] Janowitz concludes, "The charge of being insufficiently monotheistic was widely made in the late antique period."

Talmudic texts on Christianity

Robert Travers Herford (d. 1950), a Christian scholar of the Talmud, characterizes the discussions of Christianity in the Talmud as entirely marginal, separate from the self-definition of the rabbis. "Judaism released itself from what it considered to be the danger of Christianity. It preserved only a careless and contemptuous tradition about Jesus."[37] Herford espouses the regnant opinion that the doctrine of incarnation, with its implied doctrines of hypostases, trinity, faith, and ascension, was of little theological concern to the Talmudic rabbis. They considered the entire discussion of these themes contradictory to Judaism. Sasha Stern notes that all discussions of Christianity seem to still use sources from the Second Temple era and are indifferent to historical realities.[38]

Recently, Daniel Boyarin has argued that a strong definition of Christian doctrines was important in creating a rabbinic self-identification through rejection, but the rabbinic texts seem to express aversion rather than encourage debate.[39] For instance, one Talmudic passage explicit in its rejection of Christian belief argues *ad hominem* instead of theologically. "R. Abahu said: If a man says to you, 'I am God,' he is a liar; if [he says, 'I am] the son of man,' in the end people will laugh at him; if [he says], 'I will go up to heaven,' he says, but he shall not perform it" (*Jerusalem Talmud, Taanit* 65b). While the cited Talmudic text does encourage laughing derision of the false doctrine, it does not explicitly place Christians as outside monotheism.

There are also many rabbinic parables that invert the Christian parable of vineyard owner and the tenants, which appears in Matthew 21:33–44 and Luke 19:9–19. In the New Testament version, the vineyard is taken from Israel and given to nations. In the rabbinic version, the vineyard begins in the hands of the nations and is given to Jacob. Abraham and Isaac had impure offspring, identified with the other nations, but this impure age is over and the divine inheritance is now entirely in Jewish hands.

> For the portion of the Lord is his people [Deut 32:9] A parable. A king had a field which he leased to tenants. When the tenants began to steal from it, he took it away from them and leased it to their children When the children began to act worse than the fathers, he took it away from them and gave it the original tenants grandchildren. When these too became worse than their predecessors, a son was born to him. He then said to the grandchildren "leave my property. You may not remain therein. Give me back my portion, so that I may repossess it." thus also, when our father Abraham came into the world, unworthy [descendants] issued from him. Ishmael and all of Keturah's children. When Isaac came into the world, unworthy [descendants] issued from him, Esau and all the princes of Edom, and they became worse than their predecessors. When Jacob came into the world, he did not produce unworthy [descendants] rather all his children were worthy. (*Sifrei Deut.* 312)

Parables that emphasize Jews as the chosen of God, over and against similar parables from Christianity, continue in later midrashic collections and are further developed in the kabbalistic corpus.

Jesus

The Talmud does, however, contain several negative stories involving a protagonist called Jesus or Joshua who may refer in some of the cases to the Jesus of the New Testament. Yet these stories are not central within the Talmud, which only wanted to distance Jews from the new religion. The stories are anachronistic and are of interest only in that they reflect what the Persian-period rabbis of the Talmud thought about the Jesus legends that they were hearing. The rabbis do not have historical evidence and many of the stories are similar to, if not borrowed from, the anti-Christian stories presented by the pagan Celsus.[40]

The rabbis have no knowledge of or interest in Jesus' incarnation, divinity, or saving power; they only address stories in which Jesus appears to have magical abilities. The stories are explicit in their condemnation of Jesus for sorcery and apostasy, yet they lose their force by blurring the lines between Jesus and a certain Ben Stada, a Jewish sorcerer (*ca.* 100 CE) who used Egyptian spells.

The following story, told centuries after the gospels, is noteworthy because it takes responsibility for putting Jesus to death on the charges of sorcery and misleading Israel.

It was taught: On the eve of the Passover Yeshua, the Nazarene was hanged. For forty days before the execution took place a herald went forth and cried, "He is going forth to be stoned because he has practiced sorcery and enticed Israel to apostasy. Anyone who can say anything in his favor, let him come and plead on his behalf." And since nothing was brought forward in his favor, he was hanged on the eve of Passover.

Ulla said: Why should we look for exonerating evidence for him? He was an enticer, as the verse said (Deuteronomy 13:9) "Show him no pity or compassion, and do not shield him." Yeshua was different because he was close to the government. (TB *Sanhedrin* 43a)

This passage revises the Gospel account of Jesus' execution in several respects. First, it shows that fairness was always the rabbinic practice, even in the case of Jesus. Second, according to this polemical Jewish text, Jesus' Jewish contemporaries are proud to have killed Jesus and take full responsibility, though an argument on Christ's behalf had to be mounted by the *Sanhedrin* because Jesus had "close connections with the non-Jewish authorities who were interested in his acquittal." Third, since the Talmud was not seeking a historical account, the Jesus of the Talmud is placed in the era of Shimon ben Shetach (*ca.* 120–140 BCE), a Jewish monarch known for killing witches by imperial demand, who lived a full century before the common era. In the story, the Romans play a protective role and the Jewish king and the rabbinic court are imagined as having full power to execute.

There are many historically inaccurate features of this account, but it nevertheless functioned to shape a rabbinic position on Jesus. Steven Bayme of the American Jewish Committee astutely notes about the earlier given passage:

> Pointedly, Jews did not argue that crucifixion was a Roman punishment and therefore no Jewish court could have advocated it.
>
> [T]he passage suggests rabbinic willingness to take responsibility for the execution of Jesus. No effort is made to pin his death upon the Romans. In all likelihood, the passage in question emanates from fourth-century Babylon, then the center of Talmudic scholarship, and beyond the reach of both Rome and Christianity. Although several hundred years had elapsed since the lifetime of Jesus, and therefore this is not at all a contemporary source, the Talmudic passage indicates rabbinic willingness to acknowledge, at least in principle, that in a Jewish court and in a Jewish land, a real-life Jesus would indeed have been executed.

Another text portrays Jesus suffering in the afterlife for mocking the words of the Sages. In this text, Jesus is conjoined with Balaam, who also did not seek the benefit of Israel. Together they represent the fate of those who act against Israel, those who do not listen to the rabbis, and who practice sorcery.

> Onkelos bar Kalonikus called up Balaam from the dead. [Onkelos] asked: Who is honored in that world? [Balaam] replied: Israel. [Onkelos asked:] What about joining them? [Balaam] replied: (Deut. 23:7) "You shall not seek their peace or welfare all your days." [Onkelos] asked: What is your punishment? [Balaam answered]: In boiling semen.
>
> [Onkelos bar Kalonikus] called up Jesus from the dead. He asked: Who is honored in that world? He said to him: Israel. What about joining them? He replied: Seek their good. Do not seek their harm. Every one who injures them is as if he injured the apple of his eye. [Onkelos] asked: What is your punishment? [He replied]: In boiling excrement. As a teacher said: Whoever mocks the words of the sages in punished in boiling excrement.[41]

In a well known statement made in a polemic context in 1240, Yehiel of Paris denied that this text referred to Jesus, rather the story refers than to another man named Jesus since it does not mention the Nazerene: However, the image of Jesus the magician prevailed in Jewish texts and folklore regardless of the actual identity of the Jesus of the Talmud stories. The following is a story advising readers not to enlist the healing powers of a wonder-working Jesus:

> It once happened that Rabbi Elazar ben Dama was bitten by a snake, and Jacob of Kefar Sama came to heal him in the name of Jesus son of

Pantera, but Rabbi Ishmael did not allow him. He said to him: "You are not permitted, Ben Dama!" He said to him: "I shall bring you proof that he may heal me," but he did not have time to bring the proof before he dropped dead. Said Rabbi Ishmael: "Happy are you, Ben Dama, for you have expired in peace, and you did not break down the hedge erected by sages. For whoever breaks down the hedge erected by sages eventually suffers punishment, as it is said: 'He who breaks down a hedge is bitten by a snake.'" (Eccles. 10:8)

In these texts, Jesus and Christianity are not seen as another religion, but as either an internal Jewish heresy, a Second Temple era antagonist, or a phenomenon vaguely forbidden despite its healing properties.

Jewish texts call Christians "Nazarenes" (*Notzrim*) following the Gospels, which often refer to Jesus as the Nazarene. Originally, the term seems to have embraced all those Christians who had been born Jews and still lived as Jews. The Church Father Jerome provides an account in which Nazerenes are also called Ebionites and *minim* (sectarians). However, starting in late antiquity and continuing into the medieval literature, the term was extended and became the generic Hebrew word for Christians.

Alenu

The Alenu hymn is currently recited at the end of all traditional liturgies and exerts significant influence on the Jewish understanding of other religions. Attributed to Rav, a third-century Babylonian rabbi, a version of the hymn is mentioned in the Jerusalem Talmud (*Rosh Hashanah* 1:3 57a, *Avodah Zarah* 1:2 39c), which refers to the Rosh Hashanah service. By the twelfth century, according to the *Mahzor Vitry*, a French prayer book edited between the twelfth and fourteenth centuries, Alenu was already used to conclude daily services.

The hymn begins with a rejection of the gods of the nations as vanity and folly, and asserts the need for Jews to acknowledge their chosen status. The second paragraph contains an inclusive messianic vision of all people accepting the one true God in the end of days. In its entirety, the prayer offers a complex combination of diverse biblical statements, including a call for exclusivity, an acknowledgment of Jewish chosenness, a recognition of the uniqueness of monotheism, a foreshadowing of the eventual eradication of idolatry, and an inclusivist acknowledgment that all nations will eventually recognize the one true God. Many interpreters read the prayer as an affirmation that all people are invited and encouraged to praise the true God and king. Others, however, who concentrate on the opening section, find the hymn rejectionist.

The prayer is representative of an early textual style, and the language is sufficiently archaic to not reflect contemporary rabbinic concerns. In general, liturgy based on collected citations is never univocal. The hymn was also integrated into the heikhalot literature, the descriptions of heavenly ascents to the divine throne. In these texts, the hymn serves as adoration for God's everlasting dominion.

Any discussion of this hymn should start with the fact that it differentiates the nations arrayed around the Jewish nation from the chosen people. As stated elsewhere in this chapter, this persistent notion deserves its own academic study. The nations invoked in this early hymn are connected to the genealogies of nations delineated in Genesis; it embodies an ancient idea of nationalism, in which each nation has a celestial advocate, as well as the biblical antagonism toward nations who do not know God. Hence, the hymn's biblical imagery does not refer to post-biblical religions, or to Christianity.

Nevertheless, the hymn has been read by many Jews and Christians as an attack on Christianity. While the contentious third sentence of the first paragraph—"For they bow down to emptiness and vanity and to a God that cannot save"—was taken from Isaiah (30:7 and 45:20) and originally referred to idolworshipers, for many Jews, Alenu constituted a refutation of the Church and its savior. In 1399, Pesach Peter, a baptized Jew, popularized the assertion that the hymn alludes to Jesus through the words "and folly" because the Hebrew letters of both words are equal in numerical value, amounting to 316. The phrase was deleted under repeated pressure from Christian censors between the fourteenth and seventeenth centuries. The aforementioned association of the word "and folly" by numerical value (*gematria*) to Christianity is in fact explicitly mentioned in the commentary *Arugat Ha-Bosem* by R. Abraham b. Azriel from the 1200s. This controversial line of the prayer was eventually eradicated from the Ashkenazi prayer book entirely, but was recently reprinted and reinserted in the new Israeli editions.[42]

Alenu appears here in its entirety. One can readily see that the text can be read to support inclusive, exclusive, and universal visions. The exclusivist emphasizes the line discussed earlier. The universalist emphasizes the reference to the one "Lord of the universe" whose kingship will reign over the whole earth. The inclusivist emphasizes the balance between references to God's kingship over all and the specialness of the chosen people. For the inclusivist, the text refers only to the "nations of the land," which can be limited to only ancient pagans, exempting those religions that accept the biblical God. (See Maimonides, Kimkhi, and Nahmonides in later chapters.)

> It is incumbent upon us to give praise to the Lord of the Universe, to glorify Him who formed creation, for He hath not made us to be like the nations of the lands, nor hath He made us like the families of the earth;

He hath not set our portion with theirs, nor our lot with their multitude;

for they prostrate themselves before vanity and folly, and pray to a god who cannot help. But we bend the knee and prostrate ourselves and bow down before the King of the Kings of Kings, the Holy One, blessed be He! For it is He who stretched forth the heavens and laid the foundations of the earth, and the seat of His glory is in the heavens above, and His mighty dwelling-place (Shekhinah) is in the loftiest heights. "He is our God, and there is none other." In truth, He is our King, there is none besides Him, as it is written in His Torah: "And thou shall know this day and lay it to thine heart that the Lord is God in heaven above and upon the earth beneath: and there is none other."

Therefore do we wait for Thee, O Lord our God, soon to behold Thy mighty glory, when Thou wilt remove the abominations from the earth, and idols shall be exterminated; when the world shall be regenerated by the kingdom of the Almighty, and all the children of flesh invoke Thy name; when all the wicked of the earth shall be turned unto Thee. Then shall all the inhabitants of the world perceive and confess that unto Thee every knee must bend, and every tongue be sworn. Before Thee, O Lord our God, shall they kneel and fall down, and unto Thy glorious name give honor. So will they accept the yoke of Thy kingdom, and Thou shall be King over them speedily forever and aye. For Thine is the kingdom, and to all eternity Thou wilt reign in glory, as it is written in Thy Torah: "The Lord shall reign forever and aye." And it is also said: "And the Lord shall be King over all the earth; on that day the Lord shall be One and His name be One."

Since the text never mentions other religions, but rather speaks of "the nations of the land" and those that pray to "idols" and "abominations," the inclusivist and universalist read exclusive statements as limited to the ancient nations and contemporaries who worship gods alien to the Bible. Contemporary gentiles and certainly Christianity and Islam can be included as daughter religions of the biblical God. A study of the various interpretations of the hymn throughout history would offer insight into how different communities at different times understood their relationships to other religions.

If the original reference is clearly to idolaters who worship statues, then my questions for our age are:

- Can we separate the medieval Ashkenz historical experience where Alenu referred to Christianity from the original meaning of the text, whose origins is Rosh Hashanah liturgy?

- Can we disentangle the biblical-rabbinic concepts of nation from the separate category of other religions?
- Can we read "The One who spread out the heavens, and made the foundations of the Earth" to apply to all religions who teach that one God founded the Earth?
- Finally, in many debates, Alenu has been cast as a prayer for the conversion of the world. Can we show in the exegesis of Alenu and Zechariah that the prayer is for a moral conversion by recognition of one God, and not an actual conversion?

Conclusion

In order to serve contemporary needs for tolerance, many would concur with E.E. Urbach's reading of rabbinic thought: "In their relations with other nations, most of the Sages would have satisfied themselves with the declaration of Micah 4:5." That is, "All people will walk, each in the names of their Gods, and we will walk in the name of the Lord our God for ever and ever."[43] Relying on Urbach, Krister Stendahl, the late Bishop of Stockholm, called the rabbinic approach "a stunning vision" of accepting others. Similarly, Robert Goldenberg summarized his study of ancient Jewish attitudes toward non-Jews, "Neither Jewish monotheism nor Jewish 'universalism' necessarily entailed that the one true God could only be reached through Israel's covenant with Him."[44]

But the rabbinic discussions of heresy, Christianity, and sectarianism temper this stunning vision. Urbach's notion of rabbinic tolerance was certainly important for twentieth century self-definition, but in the twenty-first-century interfaith encounter, we need to take ownership and responsibility for all of our classic texts. A textual commitment to the rabbinic corpus as a whole demands that its contradictions and plural interpretations must be weighed against each other to formulate a contemporary religious discourse.

CHAPTER 4

The Inclusivist Tradition

Inclusivism sees other faiths as included within Jewish concepts, especially the concept of God as a philosophic monotheism. This theological monotheism allowed them to treat the first cause doctrine of the philosophers, the god of Plato and Aristotle, Christian Trinitarians, and all other people of faith as one essential unique God, even though these non-Jewish believers might have an incorrect view of the attributes of God. This inclusivism works because medieval Jewish thinkers understood the Bible as teaching a doctrine of philosophic monotheism (e.g., they understood Isaiah's vision of God's providence as a cosmological argument). In addition, inclusivism can view that the other religion are derivation of the Jewish concepts of revelation, ethics, or messianism. For inclusivists the biblical knowledge of these ideas were spread by the daughter religions of Christianity and Islam.

Halevi, Maimonides, Nahmanides, Emden, Hirsch, and Kook all look to biblical history in which the other nations play a role in the unfolding of God's plan. Kimkhi, Gikitilla, and Zohar take a metaphysical approach focused on the all-encompassing Divine. Aderet and Arama speak of the meaning of revelation, and finally Seforno looks to the image of God possessed by all members of humanity.

Inclusivism

- Historical mission—where knowledge of God and His will play themselves out in the wider world of other religions.
- Metaphysical, theocentric hierarchy—where all references to God must point to the one true God.

- Revelation, Sinai-centered—where the teachings and ethics of Sinai are known throughout the world.
- Humanistic, theocentric—where there is a Divine concern for humanity as made in the image of God.

Historical mission

The historical mission variation on inclusivism maintains that Judaism has a messianic mission to spread the doctrine of monotheism throughout the world. According to this view, the monotheistic religions of other nations both reflect the success of the mission until now and play a role in the mission's continued advance toward the messianic age.

Yehudah Halevi

Yehudah Halevi (*ca.* 1075–1141), the twelfth-century heir to Spanish philosophical and poetic traditions, wrote a defense of Judaism called *Treatise in Defense of a Despised Tradition*, popularly known as the *Kuzari*. The work has been popular over the centuries and is still read today by students seeking a guide to the basics of Jewish theology. The opening of Halevi's book is written in the form of a fictitious dialogue in which a Jew, a Moslem, and a Christian, each attempt to convince a pagan king about the truth of his religion. This dialogue shows how Halevi used a discussion of other religions as a means of formulating his own Jewish theology.

In defending the Jewish tradition, Halevi emphasizes God relates to all people, yet God singled out Judaism's centrality. Halevi likens the centrality to the heart in a body or to the trunk of a tree.

> Israel among the nations is like a heart among the organs of the body. It is the healthiest, as well as the one most prone to disease. As the verse [Amos 3:2] states, "Only you have I known from all of the families of the earth; therefore shall I punish you for your iniquities."[1]
>
> God has a secret and wise design concerning the Jewish people. This may be compared to a seed that falls to the ground, where it undergoes external transformation through its contact with earth, water, and dung, until it is virtually unrecognizable. However, it is the seed itself that transforms earth and water to its own substance, carrying them from one level to another until it refines these elements and transmutes them to its own form. The [plant] casts off its husks and leaves to reveal a heart that has been purified and refined and is fit to bear fruit like itself.
>
> Similarly, all religions that came after the Torah of Moses are part of the process of bringing humanity closer to the essence of Judaism, even

through they appear its opposite. The nations serve to introduce and pave the way for the long-awaited messiah. He is the fruit and they, in turn, will all become his fruit when they acknowledge Him. Then all nations will become one tree, recognizing the common root they had previously scorned.[2]

For Yehudah Halevi, Israel is a chosen people, who transform the world. He follows the biblical text by giving the Jewish people a special historical status, which he explains as part of the cunning of divine history. Employing the natural metaphor, he expounds that other religions share a common root of Judaism; all religions are of the same tree with Judaism as the trunk. These other religions are not needed for a Jew to understand her obligations from Mosaic prophecy, but to fail to recognize the nature of the branch religions is to fail to properly understand the world and, in effect, God's providential plan.

Many misread Yehudah Halevi's position as if he were arguing for the exclusive uniqueness of Judaism and the corollary falseness of other religions, implying that we are true and they are wrong. However, as the passage given earlier shows, Halevi does not deny the importance of the other religions; he merely notes that the other religions are only limbs on the trunk of Judaism. Eventually, all will bear fruit on a single tree. His example demonstrates that openness to discussing other religions does not preclude finding a place for the other religion within one's own system even if it includes rejecting part of their theologies, nor does it prevent understanding them in one's own inclusivist terms.

Yehudah Halevi's finding of a common root and endpoint is reminiscent of the thinking of *Nostra Aetate* (the 1965 Declaration on the Relation of the Church to Non-Christian Religions of the Second Vatican Council) that stated that Christianity, as a branch, is grafted onto the Jewish Abrahamic tree trunk. It is important to note that for Yehudah Halevi the base of the trunk, the fountain of all true revelation, is not Abrahamic faith, but Mosaic faith. The nations of the world are all part of the divine plan, not bereft of historical providence. For Halevi, other religions will be reintegrated back into the biblical vision at the end of days.

Halevi limits prophecy to Judaism, but that does not preclude the availability of some form of natural revelation for all. The book itself opens with a story of a gentile king getting inspiration from God through a true dream and thereby, through his search, coming to learn of the higher Mosaic revelation.[3] For Halevi, true dreams and divine inspiration are available to all faiths as a general revelation, while the special revelation of Sinai prophecy was only available to Jews. Biblical prophecy was, for Halevi, the highest form of connection to God ever attained, and keeping the commandments allows the Jew to attain a lower form of this same prophetic vision. Yet Halevi credits Socrates, Zoroaster, and Hermes with some form of prophetic connection (III: 1–15). This approach of recognizing a natural revelation available to all offers a means of creating a universal approach in our age of globalization that can include the many religions of the world.

Halevi still uses a combination of medieval science and Ismaeli prophetic theory to create a hierarchy of being from animals to prophets. He credits the descendants of Jacob with having angelic qualities not given to the other genealogies of the book of Genesis. He connects this angelic quality to the neo-Platonic metaphor of fruit and shells. Those directly connected to the divine are the fruit and those distant from the divine good are immersed in the shells.

> Would it not have been best for all animals to have been reasonable beings? Thou base, apparently, forgotten what we said previously concerning the genealogy of Adam's progeny, and how the spirit of divine prophecy rested on one person, who was chosen from his brethren, and the essence of his father. It was he in whom this divine light was concentrated. He was the kernel, whilst the others were as shells which had no share in it. The sons of Jacob were, however, distinguished from other people by godly qualities, which made them, so to speak, an angelic caste. Each of them, being permeated by the divine essence, endeavored to attain the degree of prophecy, and most of them succeeded in so doing. Those who were not successful strove to approach it by means of pious acts, sanctity, purity, and intercourse with prophets.[4]

Halevi concludes the aforementioned passage about the descendents of Jacob having prophecy by advocating the need to be separated from matter and entirely spiritualized. A religion is to be judged by its ability to aid in the attainment of immortality and acquiring a vision of the divine light. Select spiritual virtuosos among Jews can see glimpses of the divine in everything and seek to use those glimmers to attain greater divine light.

> Know that he who converses with a prophet experiences spiritualization during the time he listens to his oration. He differs from his own kind in the purity of soul, in a yearning for the [higher] degrees and attachment to the qualities of meekness and purity. This was a manifest proof to them, and a clear and convincing sign of reward hereafter. For the only result to be expected from this is that the human soul becomes divine, being detached from material senses, joining the highest world, and enjoying the vision of the divine light, and hearing

the divine speech. Such a soul is safe from death, even after its physical organs have perished.

If thou, then, findest a religion the knowledge and practice of which assists in the attainment of this degree, at the place pointed out and with the conditions laid down by it, this is beyond doubt the religion which insures the immortality of the soul after the demise of the body.

At this point Halevi has moved from his historical argument to a metaphysical emphasis on which religion gives access to God. This theme was picked up by several kabbalists (see later in this chapter), and is related to the universal versions of this argument in Ibn Gabirol and Ibn Ezra (see the chapter on universalists).

Before proceeding it is important to note with our first inclusivist text that even though Halevi recognizes the quest for God in other religions and their purpose in the divine scheme, he still rejects ideas in other religions that he deems incorrect. For example, Halevi rejects the Christian doctrines of virgin birth, incarnation, and Trinitarianism as not based on logic (*Kuzari* I: 5) without rejecting the common core that Judaism and Christianity share in their belief in the God of the Bible.

This rejection is succinctly stated by Hasdai Crescas (*ca.* 1340–1410), an important fourteenth-century legal scholar and philosopher, in a text entitled *The Refutation of Christian Principles*:

The Christian says God has three separate attributes, calls Persons, and the Jew denies this. The Christian believes that God has an attribute called Son, generated from the Father, and the Jew denies this. The Christian believes that God, may He be blessed, has an attribute which proceeded from the Father and the Son called Spirit, and the Jew denies this. The Christian believes that the Son took on flesh in the womb of the virgin . . The Jew denies this.

How much he knew of the logic of trinity, or if he thought Christians accepted an Arian position of tri-theism, or how much he knew of the other elements of Christian thought is beyond the scope of this book. This understanding of other faiths using the categories of one's own faith to view other religions and to accept and reject parts of the other religion defines the entire inclusivist position.

Maimonides

Maimonides (1138–1204), the great codifier and systematizer of medieval Jewish law and theology, presents several highly influential statements about

Christianity and Islam almost as side notes to his grand vision. Some of the same sentiments expressed in Halevi's work are found in Maimonides' writings, although they are there embedded within a more theologically multifaceted and contradictory halakhic grid. A presentation of the full complexity of Maimonides' position is far beyond the scope of this book and is already the subject of several fine studies.[5] I will simply provide some of the basic texts used in discussions.

The most important text for his inclusivist position is the original version in the uncensored texts of Maimonides' *Code of Jewish Law, Laws of Kings* 11: 3, entirely excised in most printings. In this famous passage Maimonides simultaneously acknowledges that Christianity has been a distortion of Judaism, incorrect theologically, misleading people, and a persecutor of Israel, yet it has still brought knowledge of God, the Bible, and the commandments to the world. God's messianic cunning for bringing knowledge of God to the world is beyond human keen and not subject to political and denominational observations. Even more than a historical cunning of reason, this is a divine plan, a transcendental perspective above the ordinary perception.

> Even Jesus of Nazereth, who imagined that he was the Messiah, but was put to death by the court, Daniel had prophesized, as it is written, "And the children of the violent among your people shall lift themselves up to establish a vision; but they shall stumble" (Daniel 11.14). For has there ever been a greater stumbling block than this? All the prophets affirmed that the Messiah would redeem Israel, save them, gather their dispersed, and confirm the commandments. But he caused Israel to be destroyed by the sword, their remnant to dispersed and humiliated. He was instrumental in changing the Torah and causing the world to err and serve another besides God.
>
> The human mind has no power to reach the thoughts of the Creator, "for His thoughts and ways are unlike ours" (Isaiah 55:8). All these matters of Jesus of Nazareth and of the Ishmaelite who stood up after him are only intended to pave the way for the Anointed King, and to mend the entire world to worship God together, thus: "For then I shall turn a clear tongue to the nations to call all in the Name of the Lord and to worship him with one shoulder" (Zeph. 3:9).Thus the messianic hope, the Torah, and the commandments have become familiar topics of conversation among the inhabitants of the far isles and many peoples, uncircumcised of heart and flesh.

This text shows that Maimonides accepted that Christianity and Islam are believers in the biblical God of Israel. In the *Guide of the Perplexed*, Maimonides casually reiterates this point of the universality of the biblical God and applies it to the entire civilized world. "Most people, as we see at present, agree in praising and glorifying Him, No one opposes or ignores Him, except some ignoble remnants of the nations left in the remote corners of the earth."[6] Maimonidean inclusivism is based on a common core of monotheism as found in the Bible and the commandments firmly situated in a messianic sense of biblical mission found in the books of Isaiah and Zephaniah.

Another text showing Maimonides' inclusivist perspective is a responsum about teaching Torah to gentiles. Maimonides' position is that teaching Christians Torah is permitted since they accept the Bible as it is written and canonized. By teaching them Torah, according to Maimonides, one can show Christians the true Jewish position. But, he argues, one should not teach Muslims because, although they are unquestionably monothesists, they do not accept the Hebrew Bible. Islamic polemics say the Bible was falsified or mistaken and that the Koran records the correct version of the stories (*tahrif*).

> It is permitted to teach the commandments to Christians and draw them to our law. But it is not permitted to teach anything from it to Muslims because it is known to you about their belief that this Torah [of ours] is not from God...and if one can convince the Christians of the correct interpretation [of Scripture], it is possible that they might return to what is good.[7]

The importance of this responsum, and further casuistry based on it, for interfaith encounters and study sessions cannot be emphasized enough. It creates an ability to speak of a shared biblical heritage and to discuss scripture.

While this anthology of texts has refrained from quoting polemical texts, Maimonides' polemical *Epistle to Yemen* has been used by many to undercut, and even to reject, his more inclusivist statements. The *Epistle to Yemen* was a letter of comfort to Yeminite Jews facing forced conversion to Islam that exhorted them not to give up hope. Here is one of his polemical statements against Christianity; he has many similar statements about Islam.

> It resolved to lay claim to prophecy and to found a new faith, contrary to our Divine religion, and to contend that it was equally God-given. The first one to have adopted this plan was Jesus the Nazarene, may his bones be ground to dust. He impelled people to believe that he was a prophet sent by God to clarify perplexities in the Torah, and that he was the Messiah that was predicted by each and every seer. He interpreted the Torah and its precepts in such a fashion as to lead to their total annulment, to the abolition of all its commandments and to the violation of its prohibitions.

The categorical language of annulment, abolition, and violation in a polemical letter should not be seen as rejecting his more philosophic opinions found elsewhere. There is a substantial literature on Maimonides' position that seeks to explain or resolve the tensions in his writings. (For his views on idolatry, see chapter nine and for his view that Christianity is idolatry, see chapter eight in this volume.)

Nahmanides, the great Barecelona Talmudist and kabbalist (1194–1270), presents an important citation and interpretation of inclusivism in the messianic *Mishneh Torah* passage.

> The nations, close to the center of civilization are also inheritors of Torah, since the Christians and Moslems absorbed and study the Torah. When Rome conquered the ends of the earth they had learned from [the Christians] Torah and made statutes and laws on the model of the Torah...
>
> Those later [nations] are completing the path to the King Messiah. How? The world is becoming filled with the messianic idea and words of Torah and they engage in these matters and the commandments of the Torah. Therefore Maimonides wrote... [citation and paraphrase of above passage].
>
> Some say the commandments are no more and have been nullified, do not apply in our age, and are not to be practiced for generations, while others think that the commandments have esoteric non-literal meanings. When the messiah comes as prophesized and successfully sets up the exalted Messianic King, then immediately all will return and know that their forefathers lead them in false paths.[8]

The passage clearly affirms an inclusivist doctrine in which the other two religions are based on Judaism. The innovation of Nahmanides is to actually state that the other religions are inheritors of Torah and they study it. While not respecting the narratives of the other religions in the contemporary sense, this text can be used by rabbinic authors wishing to accept an inclusivist reading of Maimonides' approach. However, the messianic vision in which all would recognize the errant nature of their ways and that they were blinded by their leaders bears a close similarity to traditional Pauline doctrines about Jews.

Rabbi Abraham, the son of Maimonides (thirteenth century), while true to his father's inclusivism also has a concept of being a light unto the nations. Abraham explains revelation as needing to be taught to the entire world through the nation of Israel and the phrase "kingdom of priests" to refer to a teaching function.

> The meaning of a "kingdom of priests" is that the priest of a congregation is its leader, for he is its most honored member, serves as its model,

in as much as the members of the congregation will walk in his footsteps and, through him, will find the straight path. Thus God said: "You, by observing My commandments, will become the leaders of the world. Your relationship to them [the nations of the world] will be like the relationship of the priest to his congregation. All the world will follow in your wake, they will imitate your actions, and walk in your path."[9]

Abarbanel

Don Isaac Abarbanel (1437–1508) was a financier and biblical commentator. In the late fifteenth century, there was a turn from medieval philosophy to a more realistic approach to reading texts. Abarbanel, following this trend, turns toward a humanistic and realistic approach to the Bible and marginalizes the medieval universals based on metaphysics. Abarbanel's biblical commentary offers an early modern perspective of historic realism and realpolitik. Many twentieth-century thinkers who prefer concrete realistic thinking to philosophy also treat religious encounters from the perspective of Jewish peoplehood, not metaphysical truth.

Like Maimonides, Abarbanel sees the spread of Christianity and Islam as part of a divine plan for the world to know God; however, unlike Maimonides, he relates it specifically to the fate of Judaism. Rather than seeing in Christianity and Islam a universal vision of the world coming to acknowledge one God, Abarbanel reduces their value, arguing that they merely provided the means by which the Jews retained a connection with biblical faith in exile. Abarbanel in no way denies metaphysical inclusivism, granting that the other religions have correct notions of God. Yet, unlike the other inclusivists, he does not speak of the righteousness of other religions nor of their contribution to the world, only their role in the drama of the Jewish people. At points, Abarbanel comes close to maintaining an exclusivism position.

There is no doubt that this was the most powerful of providential acts that God brought about so that the Torah should not be lost completely. For when He foresaw the long duration of this great exile, He realized that if the Jews were to live among the idolatrous cultures of antiquity, who had neither heard of the Torah nor witnessed its greatness, then Torah would soon be forgotten...That is why He prepared the cure before the disease by exiling Jewry among nations who supported the Torah, and in this way it sustained by us during this long exile. For as we see with our eyes, these nations acknowledge the truth [of the Torah] and hold it in high regard, and there is no difference [between them and us] except in their understanding of it. Because of this the Torah remains strong and enduring among us.

We should consider Christians and Muslims as instruments that will help bring about the recognition of God by all men on earth. While the nations worshipped their idols and denied the existence of God, and thus recognized neither the power of God nor the principle of reward and punishment, the existence of Christians and Muslims helped disseminate among the nations the awareness of God's existence, and introduced into the most distant lands the realization that there is a God who rules the world, who rewards and punishes, and who has revealed Himself to men. Indeed, thinking Christian scholars have not only taught the nations to accept the written revelation but have also acted as defenders of the oral revelation which is equally of Divine origin. For when vicious people from our own midst, sworn enemies of the Law of God, conspired to abrogate the Talmud and to do away with it, there arose from among the non-Jews defenders who fought against these attempts. (Abarbanel, Commentary to Deut. 4)

Christians and Muslims thus only have an instrumental function in this world; in the hierarchy of religions, they serve their role by letting Israel supersede them. Abarbanel acknowledges that friendly Christians have defended the oral law for Jews against polemicists intent on defaming Judaism, and also that Christians and Muslims recognize a biblical conception of God.

Whereas philosophic thinkers look for commonalities with talk of roots and branches or wholes and parts, a historical realist who seeks to harmonize texts finds biblical verses critical of the ancient gentiles and applies them to contemporary gentiles. The historical humanist perceives references to the four ancient kingdoms as a realistic geopolitical statement, which leads him to equate the last of the kingdoms Edom with the contemporary gentile religions of Christianity and Islam.

For example, in the following commentary on Isaiah 52, Abarbanel uses the thirteenth-century insight of Rabbi David Kimkhi, amplified by his own social observations, to discuss the immorality of both Christianity and Islam.

Every person turns to Islam and Christianity, called Ishmael and Esau (or Edom) because they include all four kingdoms.[10]
   "...because there will no more come to you the uncircumcised and impure" (Isaiah 52:1). This alludes to the Kingdom of Edom because they are uncircumcised and the kingdom of Ishmael because they are impure in their evil actions even though they make themselves appear pure with their bathing.[11]

In addition, many negative observations about other religions are included in his commentaries and many were censored out. His original uncensored statements were more vitriolic concerning gentiles, which leaves us to ponder the positive role that censorship of texts can play in interreligious encounters. When offensive passages are excised, then even though scholars might still concern themselves with those passages, the effect of the texts on society is more sanguine.[12]

Yaakov Emden

Yaakov Emden (1697–1776) of Hamburg is an exemplar of a traditionalist pulpit rabbi and Talmudist responding to the eighteenth-century Enlightenment who stretches the traditional inclusivist position of Maimonides into eighteenth-century directions.

> We should consider Christians and Moslems as instruments for the fulfillment of the prophecy that the knowledge of God will one day spread throughout the earth. Whereas the nations before them worshipped idols, denied God's existence, and thus did not recognize God's power or retribution, the rise of Christianity and Islam served to spread among the nations, to the furthest ends of the earth, the knowledge that there is One God who rules the world, who rewards and punishes and reveals Himself to man. Indeed, Christian scholars have not only won acceptance among the nations for the revelation of the Written Torah but have also defended God's Oral Law. For when, in their hostility to the Torah, ruthless persons in their own midst sought to abrogate and uproot the Talmud, others from among them arose to defend it and to repulse the attempts. (Commentary to Pirkey Avot 4:13)
>
> All those who believe in the Torah of Moses, be they from whatever nation, are not in the category of idol-worshipers and the like, even though they do not fully observe the Torah, for they are not commanded to do so. (Commentary on the siddur II)

Emden's position is less overtly messianic than Halevi's and, consequently, apparently more positive about Christians and Muslims in the present world. Emden believes that other religions share our God (who commands on Sinai and rewards and punishes) and acknowledge our Scripture; accordingly, they have become our religious allies in this world. Emden's abstraction of the concept of Mosaic Torah as the acceptance of Scripture allows him to view Christians and Muslims as sharing our devotion to Torah even if they do not formally accept the Jewish formulations of the laws. And this broad definition of the fulfillment of prophecy tacitly accepts Christian scriptures as the fulfillment of prophecy.

Emden presents a model of interreligious cooperation premised on a shared world of dogma and belief in God. In contrast, his younger contemporary

Mendelssohn contended that respect could only exist in a realm of tolerance based on universal truths. For Emden, respect is grounded on our shared commitment to God, His commands, and His providence. From Emden's perspective, Zephaniah's vision of tolerance and harmony does not require a messianic change, but a current moral aspiration. God dispersed Israel among the nations in order that they become an ethical light among the nations.

Emden shows a unique Enlightenment spirit by analyzing the gospels from a rabbinic perspective as part of his own historical investigations in *Seder Olam Rabbah veZutta*. The tract was a polemic against the heretical sect of the Frankists and has references to the writings of Jewish converts to Christianity such as Johann Christoph Wagenseil (1633–1705); however, its views agree with his positions elsewhere. Emden credits Jesus and Paul with maintaining the law for Jews and only offering their new faith to gentiles. The Gospels, according to Emden, show that Pauline doctrine did not apply to contemporary Jews. Christianity, in Emden's opinion, was instrumental in weaning the world from idolatry and offering it a moral standard even higher than Judaism.

> Therefore you must realize—and accept the truth from him who speaks it[13]—that we see clearly here that the Nazarene and his Apostles did not wish to destroy the Torah from Israel, God forbid; for it is written so in Matthew (Mt. 5:17), the Nazarene having said, "Do not suppose that I have come to abolish the Torah. I did not come to abolish, but to fulfill. I tell you this: So long as heaven and earth endure, not a letter, not a stroke, will disappear from the Torah until it is achieved. If any man therefore sets aside even the least of the Torahs demands, and teaches others to do the same, he will have the lowest place in the Kingdom of Heaven, whereas anyone who keeps the Torah, and teaches others so, will stand high in the Kingdom of Heaven." This is also recorded in Luke (Lk. 16:17). It is therefore exceedingly clear that the Nazarene never dreamed of destroying the Torah.
>
> The writers of the Gospels never meant to say that the Nazarene came to abolish Judaism, but only that he came to establish a religion for the Gentiles from that time onward. Nor was it new, but actually ancient; they being the Seven Commandments of the Sons of Noah, which were forgotten. The Apostles of the Nazarene then established them anew. However, those born as Jews, or circumcised as converts to Judaism (Ex. 12:49; one law shall be to him that is home-born, and unto the stranger) are obligated to observe all commandments of the Torah without exception. But for the gentiles he reserved the seven Commandments which they have always been obliged to fulfill. It is for that reason that they

were forbidden pollutions of idols, fornication, blood, and things stran-
gled. (Acts 15)

It is therefore a habitual saying of mine...that the Nazarene brought
about a double kindness in the world. On the one hand, he strengthened
the Torah of Moses majestically, as mentioned earlier, and not one of our
Sages spoke out more emphatically concerning the immutability of the
Torah. And on the other hand, he [the Nazarene] did much good for the
Gentiles...by doing away with idolatry and removing the images from
their midst. He obligated them with the Seven Commandments so that
they should not be as the beasts of the field. He also bestowed upon them
ethical ways, and in this respect he was much more stringent with them
than the Torah of Moses.

The Christians keep distant even from certain practices that are permitted to Jews...They have many admirable and saintly traits, such the
piousness of not only avoiding vengeance but also refraining causing evil
to an enemy.[14]

He, understandably, rejects the notion that Jesus is the Son of God—and
then proceeds apologetically to interpret the *New Testament* as a Jewish
work, rejecting Christian doctrine and situating Jesus in a Jewish context.
Nevertheless, he offers a unique model of a rabbinic Jew reading the New
Testament as part of the Jewish mission. Many of the modern positions that
seek the historical Jesus as Jew are similar to Emden's in treating Jesus as a
moral teacher. They are also similar in praising Jesus' teachings as proper
Jewish teachings while distancing him from Paul, the founder of Christianity,
a competing religion.

In our time, Lawrence Boadt has asked, "Can Jews recognize a place for
Christianity as a legitimate extension of the first covenant?"[15] Emden would
answer affirmatively, seeing Christianity not as a new path, but rather as
an interplay of Jewish monotheism and messianism sufficient for non-Jews.
Emden can thus serve as a model of a rabbinic scholar willing to listen and
show a deep respect for another faith community and its scripture. Those traditionalists who seek a theological starting point for a theology of other religions usually start with Emden. S.R. Hirsch builds on Emden, as does Isaac
Bar Levensohn in his nineteenth-century defense of Judaism's *Efes Damim*,
and Eliyahu Soloweyczyk uses Emden as a model for a Jewish commentary
on Matthew (see later). Abraham Joshua Heschel, in his essay "No Religion is
an Island," used the thought of both Yehudah Halevi and Yaakov Emden to
find a common divine plan for Jews and other religions.[16] And contemporary
twenty-first-century rabbi Jonathan Sacks relies on Emden's positive appreciation of Christianity (see chapter six in this volume).

Samson Raphael Hirsch

Samson Raphael Hirsch (1808–1888) was the Frankfurt pulpit rabbi and ideo-
logue behind the neo-Orthodox philosophy of remaining true to the Torah while
accepting the cultural, aesthetic, and intellectual mores of the wider culture. His
biblical commentary and the school he founded were major cultural influences.

Hirsch's ideology is best exemplified by his acceptance of Western civil
society, with the understanding that the Jewish religion serves as a light unto
the nations (Isa. 42:6). In this context Abraham represents the Jews as the light
unto the nations while in other places, especially his earlier writings, he offers
a universalistic biblical religion. Commenting on Genesis 12:2—"And I will
make you into a great nation, and I will bless you, and I will make your name
great; become a blessing"—he writes:

> The people of Abraham, in private and in public, follow one calling: to
> become a blessing. They dedicate themselves to the Divine purpose of
> bringing happiness to the world by serving as model for all nations and
> to restore mankind to the pure spiritual status that Adam had possessed.
> God will grant His blessing of the renewal of life and the awakening and
> enlightenment of the nations, and the name of the People of Abraham
> shall shine forth.
>
> Balaam believed in the unique God, as do many in our country
> [nineteenth-century Germany]. But the uniqueness of Judaism is that Judaism
> supports this faith with an absolute demand to integrate it into all of life. But
> Balaam supported his faith for earthly purposes, e.g. for greed. (Num. 22:7).
>
> The distinction between Israel and the nations continuously lessens
> through the influence of the mission of Israel and quiet exemplar activ-
> ities amidst the nations.[17]

The prophetic call of Jews, as the children of Abraham, to be a "light unto the
nation" plays a central role throughout Hirsch's theology. It is not only a tool by
which to interpret non-Jewish religions, but serves as a consistent trope in his moral
interpretations of the *mitzvot*. Jews are to be role models, spreading the enlightenment of experienced, nonintellectual knowledge of God to all. Hirsch bases this
theology on his direct readings of the words of the Scripture, mediated by the thirteenth-century commentary of Rabbi David Kimkhi, who had already explained
the verses as teaching that the goal of Judaism is to be a Light unto the Nations.[18]

Hirsch embraces a universal loving God who accepts the upright of all
peoples. According to Hirsch, the era of the idolatrous nations is over and the
nations that we now live among fulfill the will of God.

> Judaism does not say, "There is no salvation outside of me." Although
> disparaged because of its alleged particularism, the Jewish religion

actually teaches that the upright of all peoples are headed toward the highest goal.[19]

In particular, they have been at pains to stress that, while in other respects their views and ways of life may differ from those of Judaism, the peoples in whose midst the Jews are now living have accepted the Jewish Bible of the Old Testament as a book of Divine revelation. They profess their belief in the God of heaven and earth as proclaimed in the Bible and they acknowledge the sovereignty of Divine Providence in both this life and the next. Their acceptance of the practical duties incumbent upon all men by the Will of God distinguishes these nations from the heathen and idolatrous nations of the Talmudic era.[20]

For Hirsch, there is one true and loving God over all humanity creating one brotherhood. Hirsch does not seek to define Noahite laws or the upright life in terms of narrow rabbinic parameters, but instead appeals to the universal common edifice of mankind. Christians share with Jews, at least on the abstract level of universals, the same God, scripture, and acceptance of providence.

Significantly, Hirsch speaks of returning to the spiritual status of prelapsarian Adam; God's covenant with the children of Abraham aims to restore the children of Adam. However, he reflects his nineteenth-century European, colonialist setting, implicitly assuming that while the Jews themselves may not directly spread light throughout the globe, those whom they have encountered, influenced, and inspired—the Christians—will complete the universal task.

It is also worth noting that Hirsch's approach is practically devoid of metaphysics or messianic postponement. He speaks not of roots and branches, but rather of exemplar biblical heroes and moral influences.

Rabbi Yehudah Leib Alter

Rabbi Yehudah Leib Alter of Gur (1847–1905) was a major leader of Polish Jewry at the end of the nineteenth century. He offers a Hasidic approach of interiority, where the adept find God in the heart and reconnect to their true Divine natures. Selections from his thought are having an increased role in the current turn to spirituality. "You might think that [chosenness] is to cause distance from the nations, but on the contrary this is a deep ruse of God to bring the nations to Him by means of Israel. The children of Israel understand this and they desire to bring all to Him."[21] The goal of Jewish chosenness is for God to ultimately connect with all nations, thereby bringing them to God. Rabbi Yehudah Leib Alter here transforms a blatantly particular text into a description of Israel's universal mission, in which chosenness is only a means to a universal end. Maimonides' idea a divine ruse becomes part of Hasidic thought of bringing God to the world.

Particularly noteworthy here is the speaker. Unlike his contemporary Hirsch, who lived in the modern world of Enlightenment Germany and addressed a community that had long since embraced emancipation, R. Yehudah Leib Alter was speaking to his non-emancipated, Polish Hasidic community, the exact locale where we usually find the stereotypical views of exclusion to be articulated. However, this passage and those similar to it in his writings do not offer much practical guidance. He and his listeners remained in their parochial all-Jewish world.

Rabbi Abraham Isaac Kook

Rabbi Abraham Isaac Kook (1865–1935) was the first Ashkenazi chief rabbi of the Zionist return to the land of Israel. His writings embrace modernism by offering a vision of the restored land of Israel, a vision at once evolutionary and Hegelian while at the same time mystical and messianic. Offering a Zionist dream of renewal of religious Judaism, his influence is widespread and significant. Rav Kook's idea of renewal is evident in his writing:

> As for other religions, in my opinion, it is not the goal of Israel's light to uproot or destroy them, just as we do not aim for the general destruction of the world and all its nations, but rather their correction and elevation, the removal of dross. Then, of themselves, they shall join the Source of Israel, from whence a dew of light will flow over them. "And I will take away the blood from his mouth and his detestable things from between his teeth, and he, too, shall remain for our God" (Zechariah 9:7). This applies even to idolatry—all the more so to those religions that are partially based upon the light of Israel's Torah.[22]
>
> It is necessary to study all the wisdoms in the world, all ways of life, all different cultures, along with the ethical systems and religions of all nations and languages, so that, with greatness of soul, one will know how to purify them all.[23]

Rav Kook acknowledges that other nations have other religions, and that many of them are based on the Torah. He obviously does not mean Torah in the narrow sense; rather, he recognizes that religions bring God's presence into the world. Their existence is not an obstacle to messianic times, but rather a challenge. It is part of the Jewish messianic task to "elevate" and "purify" the religions, along with the entire world. He leaves unanswered the precise meaning and method of purifying other religions, shrouding it behind his vision of renewal.

Rav Kook seems to echo strains of the messianic theology of the seventeenth- century kabbalist Abraham Azulai, who wrote, "The gentiles will completely lose their bad, to be included in those...righteous of the nations who already have a share in the world to come."[24] Azulai treats the relationship of light and dross as relative terms, in which all can aspire to light (compare the dualism advocated by the kabbalists in chapter seven). But whereas Azulai and many other kabbalists make the purification of the gentiles posthistorical, Rav Kook makes the transformation historical, since he envisions the changes of the contemporary historical age as messianic.

Rav Kook does not seem to assign special historical significance to Christianity and Islam for their status as "branches." In a move that accepts the already-globalizing situation of the early twentieth century, he grants that even the Eastern religions contain gold and holiness, which await elevation and unity with the Source of Israel. One can encounter and empirically study them, yet more importantly it is a Jewish task to purify these other religions. The actual process of study, purification and unification, however, is left frustratingly vague. Nevertheless, what is clear is that personally Rav Kook was able to look at other religions—and even at atheism—and see the truth of the Torah within them.

Much more so than Halevi, Emden, or Hirsch, Kook believes that the main work to be done ("purification") is to be done by the Jews. Other religions are taken as a condition of the world, whose elevation is a Jewish task; the other religions themselves are not necessarily the main protagonists in the drama of history. While this position may seem to grant less dignity to other faith communities through a self-centered approach to history, it also appears to mandate a much more positive attitude toward encounter with other religions. Where other inclusivists see religions working on their own to advance the cause of God, for Kook, Jews must advance the divine plan by studying and understanding the other religions.

The historical inclusivist approach enables Judaism to respect and appreciate Islam and Christianity in Jewish terms, even if not on their terms. It transforms the millennia of Diaspora into part of the redemptive progress of history, with all that entails for remembering and feeling the pains accumulated along the way. Hirsch and Kook in particular provide a model of integrating other religions into the Jewish framework without nullifying these religions. Rather than preaching conversion, they would call on Judaism to connect the other religions to the divine blessing (Kook) or teach the essence of religion (Hirsch). For many, this approach of limiting oneself to one's own terms of superiority and mission does not function in a dialogical context.

Yet, is this approach still valid in a world of globalization? Does being a light to the gentiles work today? Is it our task to connect Buddhism, Hinduism, and Shintoism to the biblical God? Are we to support the monotheistic global religions in their missionary challenge? What is the Jewish role in the global age?

Are we supposed to go out and encounter others and learn from them or stay home and fantasize about a supposed religious role in the world?

Metaphysical: theocentric hierarchy

In this second variation of the inclusive approach, non-Jewish religion finds its place not as part of a historical progression, but rather in the metaphysical realm. Other religions are seen not as means of bringing individuals or nations to God, as in the historical approach, but are instead seen as binding themselves to metaphysical realms, just as Israel is bound to God. The metaphysical position places the understanding of God found in other faiths on a lower level than that found in Judaism. According to this view, the drama of separate religions that we see here on Earth is just a manifestation or epiphenomenon of the metaphysical situation.

Rabbi David Kimhi

Rabbi David Kimhi (1160–1235, Provençe), a Maimonidean rationalist, wrote an extensive commentary on the Bible focusing on the literal sense of the Bible, which was used by Jews and Christians alike.

Kimhi's writings are filled with polemics against the Christian interpretation of Scripture, especially Isaiah, as well as polemics against Christian theological doctrines. Nevertheless, he offers a clear and precise version of the philosophic tradition's metaphysical inclusivism. The verse in *Malakhi* 1:11 reads "Great is Thy name among the nations, and in every place incense is offered to my name, and a pure offering, for great is my name among the nations, said the Lord." The Talmud comments on this verse, "They call him the god of gods, even if they are known to be idolatrous" (*Menachot* 110). For Kimhi, this is an opening to present a lucid statement that the other nations share the belief in one God with Judaism, since everyone accepts a first cause. However, they are lower than Judaism because they add intermediaries. "For even though they worship the constellations of the heavens, they acknowledge Me as the first cause; however, they worship them based on their opinion that they are intermediaries between Myself and them, and thus the Rabbis said, 'They call him the God of gods.'" Many variants of this statement are found whenever the worship of other gods is mentioned, in the traditional rabbinic biblical commentaries of Nahmanides, Gersonides, and elsewhere in Kimhi. The many biblical mentions of other gods become a natural opening in their commentaries to explain ancient gods based on theistic inclusivism. Isaac Arama (discussed below) has a variant of this understanding of Malachi based on Deuteronomy 4:19 that "the nations are not obligated in the prohibition against idolatry" and are seen as worshiping the one God.

Kimhi's position creates an important distinction between belief in theism and polytheistic practice; that is to say, other religions may still be classified as idolatrous or having a polytheistic practice, yet they may still be considered monotheism since from our perspective they are still serving the ultimate being, the first cause. This constitutes a kind of philosophic theism. It is no longer just that Christianity may have, from a Jewish perspective, an incorrect formulation of God, and may simultaneously be both monotheistic (since Christians are theists) and idolatrous (since Christian representations are problematic). But, even Hinduism and other religions that are polytheistic in practice may still be seen as worshiping the monotheistic first cause.

Rabbi Adin Steinsaltz, contemporary author and translator of the Talmud into Modern Hebrew, wrote that Indian religions are sufficiently monotheistic for gentiles and the multitude of gods are all names for the one true God. Leniencies in conceptions of God are allowed to gentiles in order to make monotheism easier to practice.

> In the ancient religions grouped under the name of Hinduism, there are many gods and local shrines, but the theological principles that guide belief and provide a uniformity of moral standards assume that all the deities revered in India or elsewhere are forms of, expressions of, or names for, one ultimate reality or God.
>
> It is possible to assume that Hinduism and Buddhism are sufficiently monotheistic in principle for moral Hindus and Buddhists to enter the gentiles' gate into heaven. Jewish law regards the compromises made or tolerated by the world's major religions as ways of rendering essentially monotheistic theologies easier in practice for large populations of adherents.[25]

Rabbi Yosef Gikitilla

Rabbi Yosef Gikitilla (*ca.* 1248–after 1305, Castile), one of the foremost kabbalists of the thirteenth century, is the author of the classic introduction to Jewish theosophy, *Gates of Light*. The book offers a glossary of the major kabbalistic symbols, arranged as a vertical hierarchy of inter-divine structures, combined with reflections on their theological meaning. It explains how divine energies or powers descend to bestow blessings on the world based on human performance of commandments, provided that the actions follow the prescribed kabbalistic patterns.

As a kabbalist, Gikitilla affirms that all religions are based on the divine powers. The ability to differentiate attributes of God into a vertical hierarchy, however, allows him to differentiate religions.

> Do not believe the words of emptiness of some ignorant people who say that there is no power in the god of the nations and that they are not

called gods (*e-lohim*). But you should know that God gives strength and dominion and the scepter to each minister of the ministers of the nations to judge and adjudicate his people and nation. The ministers are called *e-lohim* because it judges his nation. Know and believe there these other gods have no power, the gods of the nations, but their power is given to them to judge and sustain their nations.[26]

In an unambiguous statement, Gikitilla affirms that all religions partake of the true divinity, albeit in a particular form for their nation. Only Israel, however, can draw the powers of the Tetragrammaton, while all other religions refer to singular and limited aspects of God's powers. Israel has direct access to the highest realms of the inter-divine sefirotic system, and the other gods are only lower points of the system.

The heavenly constellation is arrayed around the seventy princes, some of whom are included as knowers of the secrets through the essence of the formation called Adam (man)...All their eyes look toward the Name YHVH to give them strength and sustenance for them to live and each one can sustain its nation. They do not, however, each have their own power or light, for it comes from YHVH, who is the source, the wellspring, from whom all draw and are sustained.

When God unites with Israel and one merges with the other, then all the heavenly princes will be made into one group to worship God, may He be Blessed. They will all serve the community of Israel, because it is from her that they will be sustained.

When you understand this, comprehend what the prophets have said: "And YHVH will be King over the land..." (Zechariah 14:9). When will this be? "On that day when YHVH will be one and his name one" (Zechariah 14:9). On the day when YHVH unites with the community of Israel, then the faith of all nations will look toward YHVH, may He be Blessed, and because they so intensely desire to cleave to the name YHVH, may he be Blessed, they will worship Israel.

As it is said [in the Rosh Hashanah liturgy], "Therefore make all Your creation aware of Your awe, YHVH our God, and Your creatures will fear You and all of Creation will bow before You as one unity to do Your will with a pure heart." God may He be Blessed, will remove all His appellations in the future in order to receive the community of Israel so that He can unite with Her, then all the nations will serve God; the nations will be outside and the Name YHVH will stand inside with the community of Israel joyful and tranquil.[27]

The notion that each of the nations has a corresponding heavenly power—an angel—goes back to the phrase "prince of princes" (Dan. 8:25) and resonates with many Second Temple and rabbinic sources. For example, in the second century BCE, the Apocrypha work *Ben Sira* (17:7) mentions how "every nation has a governor" and we find similar views in diverse works from the third to the tenth century CE, such as the Heikhalot tract *3 Enoch* and mystical midrash *Tanna debei Eliyahu*. The theme of heavenly powers for each nation continues in Ashkenaz esotericism and early Kabbalah, in twelfth-century *Sodai Razaya*, *Bahir*, and the thirteenth-century kabbalist Ezra of Gerona. There are so many references and variants of this idea that an entire book can be written to explain the differences between these texts. In these classical contexts, the hierarchy of divine agents creates a distinction between direct divine providence granted to Jews and the indirect guidance granted through the ministering angels or lower forms to the other nations. Not a particularism, but a vision of a hierarchy of religions into higher and lower forms.

Here, Gikitilla adds the notion of different divine names. All God's names are not equally holy. The apparent implication is that the religions of the gentiles provide access to some of the names of God, even if not as directly as does Judaism, which connects Israel to the greatest and most powerful of names, YHVH. The entire world and everything in it is sustained by the single divine name, the Tetragrammaton, only known in the other religions through a glass darkly. There is one single God of creation, of whom only limited aspects are known in our non-messianic age. Currently, the unified perspective of a single God is veiled, but eventually God will reveal Himself fully to all.

There are many variants on this approach, all of them accepting metaphysical structures. Their virtue is the ability to avoid the political and historical elements of the encounter of religions and to instead talk of God's presence as light available to humans, direct and indirect, clear and refracted.[28]

These metaphysical constructs indicate a basis for encounter not predicated on the principles of modernity. Their metaphysical foundationalism leads to a firm recognition of other religions. Such an approach might be a particularly useful basis for discussions with metaphysically inclined churches; I can envision a mutual encounter with the Greek Orthodox Church concerning theories of divine glory, blessings, and energies. However, metaphysical models are limited in their utility in an era where few embrace, or even understand, metaphysical language. Premising our encounter on a theology of angels and the power of divine names would not be prudent for a Jewish community that puts little stock in either.

Zohar

The *Zohar* (*ca.* late thirteenth century) is the major text of the Kabbalah, incorporating prior midrashic, theosophic, and mystical passages and ideas. For many, the work is one of the classic primary texts of Judaism. The corpus includes both inclusivist and exclusivist statements, the latter will be dealt with later in this book.

The *Zohar* combines the basic rabbinic concept of national diversity with midrashic ideas of the division of the world into seventy nations after the tower of Babel. It also projects Yehudah Halevi's idea of Israel as the center of the historic nations into the spatial realm of the inter-divine sefirotic hierarchy. The resulting image is of Israel as the center of a metaphysical process and Jerusalem as a metaphysical *axis mundi*. The terrestrial map functions as a metaphor for the metaphysical map delineating center and periphery from the Divine.

> Jerusalem is the center of the seventy nations [because] the settlement of all seventy nations surround Jerusalem. Jerusalem dwells in the center of all settlement as it is written, "This is Jerusalem! I have set her in the midst of the nations and countries are around about her." (Ezek. 5:5).[29]

The *Zohar* uses Empedoclean, Neoplatonic, and alchemical schemes of right, left, and mediating middle, symbolized by colors, planets, and patriarchs, to portray a spatial triad. In the following text, this schema is applied typologically, with Ishmael and Esau to refer respectively to Islam and Christianity.

> There are two other nations that are close in their unity to Israel.[30]
> The rainbow is never enclothed except in the colors of the primordial patriarchs, green, red, and white. Green colors the enclothment of Abraham when Yishmael went forth, Red colors Isaac when Esau came forth, White is the good enclothment of Jacob who did not ever change his continence.[31]

In this passage of the *Zohar*, the discussion of religion becomes a question of who has the best connection to divinity: the right, left, or middle? Other religions are certainly not demonic; rather, as in the theology of Gikitilla, other religions simply focus on a partial revelation. They remain colored and do not reflect the full spectrum of white light. The *Zohar*, echoing the historic approach, treats metaphysics as a process in which all three colors are needed in the world. But Judaism is the culmination of a metaphysical process. Gradually, dross becomes purified and yields white. Judaism proceeds from the dross of the other two faiths, just as Ishmael and Esau preceded Jacob.

This theme of including two other religions to the right and left of Judaism became the first part of the seventh stanza of Rabbi Shlomo Alkebetz's famous sixteenth-century Shabbat hymn "Lecha Dodi": "For you shall spread out right and left, and you shall extol the might of God."[32] Shlomo Alkebetz, the author of the hymn, explains his own *Zohar*-influenced theology of religions as a slow process of the gradual purification of the colors of other religions into the pure white light of Judaism. In the messianic age, they will be drawn back into the Abrahamic stock. "Yishmael is derivative from Abraham, the beginning of the drawing of the consequence of the light, of the right side. Another byproduct draws from darkness on the left side. The secret is 'Esau went to Yishmael' (Genesis 28:9). Then both derivatives will be joined together to be one principle."[33] Alkebetz's inclusive position accentuates the impurity and differences and leaves the commonality for a future messianic purity. Similar to the Halevi model given earlier, the other nations are, in some way, part of the unfolding of the divine. Here, history serves as a metaphysical process of purifying the world from the differences, but from our penultimate perspective the world that we see consists of right, left, and middle, Islam, Christianity, and Judaism.

Hasidic unity

Early Hasidic homilies, those of late-eighteenth-century Ukraine, utilize a variety of variations of the aforementioned metaphysical approaches. These homilies include viewing the world as seventy nations, the completion of all the parts and branches of the holy tree, and that Judaism offers direct access to the divine. These preachers offer an expansive spirituality that seeks to incorporate the entire natural order into a pan-psychism of imaging the metaphysical source of everything in God. This leads them to think that Israel has a paternalistic responsibility for the metaphysical destiny of the nations since we share the same underlying divine unity. In the historical-mission model discussed earlier, the nations of the world are active players in God's drama spreading knowledge of God; here there is a spirituality of taking theurgic responsibility for everything that one sees, in this case gentiles.

Rabbi Yaacov Yosef of Polnoye (d. 1781 Volhynia, Russia), the foremost disciple of the Baal Shem Tov, wrote in several places in his sermons about a metaphysical unity that incorporates all people. Freely mixing metaphors of trees and image of Divine man he writes, "the seventy nations grasp the branches of the holy tree and Israel grasps the roots. Therefore . . . Israel and the nations are included in one face of the complete [divine] man."[34] Another early disciple of the Baal Shem Tov writes, "I heard in the name of the Baal Shem Tov that through the seven Noahite commandments, Israel has responsibility for the nations."[35] These statements are important to compensate for much of the exclusive, dehumanizing, and demonic approaches found in

Hasidic texts (see the later chapters). For those raised in the Hasidic world, or who develop their spirituality from Hasidic texts, who now serve as rabbis around the globe and attend the requisite interfaith encounters, these homilies create an necessary opening for a more expansive approach.

Revelation: Sinai

This approach makes the dividing line between faiths their acceptance of Mosaic revelation and the importance of understanding revelation through the rabbinic tradition. It assumes that knowledge, morals, and law come solely from Sinai, broadly defined, and the other religions are derivatives from Sinai. Following midrashic tropes, the revelation at Sinai was not just for Jews but for the entire world.

Rabbi Solomon Aderet

Rabbi Solomon Aderet (known as Rashba, ca. 1235–1310) was a major rabbinical figure and Talmudic commentator, and the author of thousands of legal responses that form the backbone of Jewish law until today. In particular, he wrote two long epistles dealing respectively with Islam and Christianity. Rabbi Aderet was conversant with the medieval critiques of Judaism, and his writings offer responses to various other thinkers, including Ibn Hazm, Thomas Aquinas, and Ramon Lull. His letters contain an important repository of medieval Jewish thinking about religion; their translation is a desideratum.

Rabbi Aderet acknowledges a natural religion of the philosophers, which is available to all. Yet he clarifies that superior religion listens to revelation, while natural religion does not. Specifically, revelation offers a law available to all nations that have a prophet. In an expansive move, Rabbi Aderet acknowledges that other religions may possess revelation, and he uses revelation as the starting point for his inclusivist discussions. The strength of Rabbi Aderet's position is his recognition within the other nations of both natural religion and general revelation.

Aderet's acceptance of the natural religion of philosophers as a category, reminiscent of Aquinas, opens up a conceptual range to treat ritual and prophecy as natural. In addition, his category of defining revelation as prophecy is pluralistic in that it accepts that other religions have prophecy and offers the possibility that this option should not be limited to the three major Western religions.

The great philosophers, Plato and Aristotle, recognize religion and acknowledge that the prophetic soul is above the philosophic soul. The second group believes that religion was given from God through His prophet, this religious group includes the three nations known to us, the Hebrews [Jews], Ishmaelites, and Christians—and maybe more. These three acknowledge that the religion of Moses, our teacher, is true and his Torah is true.

They do not deny this except that one of these nations divides *mizvot* into three groups. The first group of mizvot are optional because they are parables and typologies, such as not plowing a bull and a donkey together or not eating animals that do not chew their cud. They undress these from their meanings and garb them in false typologies. The second group they accept their meaning but limit their temporal applicability like sacrifices because they prefigure a future allusion that will nullify the original form... The third group they accept the original meaning was without a time limit of the Sabbath, circumcision, and the priestly garments. But they state that according to God's will there was a time to change the religion through a prophet. We the congregation of the community of Israel accept all the mizvot in their meaning without allegory, parables, or limited time frame but the whole Torah is eternal, as is the heavens and the earth.[36]

Though he is expansive in the range of revealed religions he acknowledges, he nevertheless critiques other religions, especially concerning the quality of Mohammed's revelation and the metaphysical problematic of the Trinity. In the full text of these letters, Rabbi Aderet has many unkind things of polemical intent to say about Christianity and Islam.

Rabbi Aderet makes Moses the pivot of his theology. All three faiths are Mosaic faiths that accepted his prophecy on Mt. Sinai; their differences lie in their understanding of law. Similar to twentieth-century author Trude Weiss-Rosmarin, who divided Christianity from Judaism based on creed versus deed, Rabbi Aderet rejects the Pauline and Koranic allegorical interpretations as desiccating the law.[37] The truth of Judaism compared to others religion stems from the Jewish rejection of the false allegories and typologies that spiritualize the law. The theological concern for Rabbi Aderet becomes a matter of needing to accept the rabbinic tradition as method and meaning of Mosaic prophecy.

Rabbi Aderet also offers a Jewish rejection of the Trinity by answering seemingly Augustinian and Thomistic arguments, and, most interestingly, those of Raymond Lull (1232–1316). Lull, credited by many as a medieval Christian inclusivist, spoke of the three monotheistic faiths, but saw Christianity as the most exalted form of monotheism. To all of these theologians, Aderet says, "We unify the unified one, and the other nations differ with us in this belief."[38] Aderet criticizes Christianity with having a lesser form of monotheism, without a unified deity, compared to Judaism. Aderet even explains the doxology of the *shema* as a proclamation of this simple unity to refute the Christian trinity. Many contemporary Jews lack the theological comfort by which medieval Jews compared their theology to other faiths, a skill essential for many of these topics.[39]

Rabbi Isaac Arama

Rabbi Isaac Arama (1420–1494), community leader, preacher, and Talmudist, exerted a wide influence on Jewish theology for centuries, especially since he combined the three prime medieval fields of Talmud, Kabbalah, and Maimonidean philosophy. Arama's biblical commentary, *Akedat Yitzhak,* combines reasoned theology with respectful polemics offering a rejoinder to Catholic theology. He argues in favor of Judaism by rejecting both universal philosophy and Christianity's redemption through grace without physical mizvot. Arama's theology necessitates both revelation and commandment.

There are also strong humanistic statements in his nearly unexplored book *Hazut Kashah,* a unique Jewish work on the history of religion, idolatry, and heresy. Arama builds a theory of religion around the creation of Adam as the progenitor of all humanity, which shows that all people are equal before God. Everyone originally knew the true God, but many were distracted by the falseness of material representation and materialism. (On henotheism, see chapter nine in this volume.) According to Arama, the virtue of the Jewish religion is quantitative—that it fell less into the abyss of the material world and false representations.

In a fashion similar to Rabbi Abraham Aderet, Rabbi Isaac Arama assumes that only Judaism keeps the law given at revelation. He acknowledges, however, that there are those who do have a natural religion or who accept revealed religion without the commands. Arama considers mizvot and the ensuing communion with God as the definition of true religion. He knows, however, that many acknowledge God, yet they have a defective divine religion because of their incorrect moral doctrine.

> The people of the world are divided into those that do not have any divine religion [natural religion] and those that do have divine religion. Those who have religion are divided into two, those religions that have illusory Divine, and those religions that have a true God. The latter group has a tradition about the world to come and immortality based on Divine command but say that the mizvot of the Torah are not required for this...

The third group are the people of the Divine Torah who say that the mizvot of the Torah [are required] given by the faithful God to lead his beloved.[40]

How could the critics fail to perceive the intensity of the Divine communion and the spiritual wealth attained by members of our nation while still dwelling in this ephemeral world wherein our souls remain anchored in the crudeness of the earth. How much more so will this come to pass upon man's separation from the material [world]? This wondrous message underlines Moses' declaration: "But you that did cleave to the Lord your God are alive every one of you this day . . . " This day, in your this-worldly existence, you are [nevertheless] able to experience the proximity of and communion with God.[41]

The sects of the nations are divided into three groups. "The first believe that all things that come to a person good or bad is decreed from above . . . there is no way to change the decree right or left . . . this is most Islamic sects.

The second is the opposite that everything is based on human effort based on knowledge to request through the worship of the powers of heaven. They worship the sun, moon, and stars and the other foreign gods of the land; these are the sects of idolatry . . . Today these are completely wiped out from our lands but they exist in distant lands.

The third acknowledges that the blessed God has providence over the world and good and evil come from Him according to God's daily will corresponding to [human] actions . . . but they call God by a false name.[42]

Arama makes the decision of the true religion hinge on the acceptance of free will and the concurrent rejection of occasionalism (where all events are caused by God) and grace (where salvation is unearned). The role of human initiative in the workings of religions becomes the debate between the faiths. It also acknowledges that one can have a correct theology of God's existence, revelation, providence, and required human actions but still attribute a false name to God. The crux of naming God is not that one cannot call Him by another name; the problem is the false conception of the Deity, obviously referring to the Trinity. Judaism does not have the problem of "in no other name" because, unlike Christianity, which requires knowledge of a specific historic person and event, Judaism in Arama's approach to inclusivism only requires a pristine conception of the Deity, regardless of the name. There is an opening here for Judaism to accept as the name of God not just Allah, but also the Confucian naming of God as Heaven, or the Hindu name of Atman-Brahmin.

Arama has no difficulties accepting Balaam as a real prophet, but he condemns the latter for not teaching the eternal moral way of life, but only materialism. Morality becomes the criteria of the true religion. Arama also points out that Balaam thought humans are playing out a predetermined scenario over which our actions can exert no meaningful control or influence. A real prophet, on the other hand, knows that his teachings have to guide our choices.

Arama has recently served as a lynchpin of a modern theology of other religions. Emmanuel Levinas, Charles Touati, and George Vajda, in a 1968 report to a commission established by Chief Rabbi Jacob Kaplan of France, presented a striking reading of Arama, showing that he cited and developed the Talmudic statement of Rabbi Yohanan that "Gentiles that accept God are to be called Israel." The authors interpreted, based on Zunz's reading of the passage in Arama, that the latter actually meant that all righteous men, even gentiles, are called Israel.[43] The report, however, had a significant minority that differed with its bold formulations, and it was withdrawn before public presentation.

Rabbi Eliyahu Soloweyczyk

Rabbi Eliyahu (Elie) Soloweyczyk was a scion of the illustrious Soloveitchik family of Talmudic scholars. Rabbi Soloweyczyk defended Christianity to Jews by writing a commentary of the New Testament book of Matthew called *Kol kore o' Hatalmud ve haberit Hahadashah* (1867, French edition 1875).[44] Rabbi Soloweyczyk drew his inspiration from the pioneering work of Rabbi Yaakov Emden on Christianity.

On the title page of *Kol Kore*, Rabbi Soloweyczyk sets out to interpret "The Book of Matthew with a commentary sufficient to show to all that the *New Testament* came to sow the unity of the Creator, blessed be His name, in the whole entire world and to strengthen the Torah of Moshe." He claims that Christianity was originally part of Judaism and then digressed into a less true doctrine.

> Jesus the Nazarene brought double good to the world. On one hand he strengthened Moses' Torah with all his strength (according to what was written in *Matthew*). There is not one of the sages that spoke more on the obligation of the eternal fulfillment of the Torah and on the other hand he brought much good to the nations of the world except they falsified his desired intentions. (2)
>
> May God grant us all, Jews and Christians, that we may follow the teachings of Jesus and his shining example, for our well being in this world and our salvation in the next. Amen. (9)

The book contains a detailed review of Maimonides' thirteen principles and shows that the Christianity of the *New Testament* accords completely with accepted Jewish beliefs. Despite this expansive theological expansion of Maimonides' thirteen principles, he writes, seemingly based on his reading of Emden, that in the end, our salvation is based on good deeds and not on theology.

> My dear reader, now you have seen with your own eyes that all thirteen principles of our faith are supported by both the *Talmud* and the *New Testament*. Now my Christian brethren, place your heart on our ways to ask why do you quarrel with your Jewish brethren whether Jesus sits to the right or left of God? We do not know. How can we know even if God has a right or a left? Rather, one who is busy with Torah, mitzvot, and good deeds in this world will grasp God's essence according to his merit in the world to come. How can we know who has Grace before God? (51)

For Soloweyczyk, Jesus, his divine status, and his resurrection are left as best forgotten minor points of Second Temple theology, and the Trinity and his Incarnation are taken simply as false folk beliefs. At best, he reduces the Trinity to the philosophic triad of Him, His knowledge, and Life. But as his starting point, Soloweyczyk notes that many Jews also mistakenly deify or treat the messiah as supernatural, so the Christian mistake is natural.

> I have seen that many of our Jewish brethren and almost all of our Christian brethren are believers in the coming of the Messiah...But almost all follow in simplicity and mistakenly think that the messiah will have to be above humanity. They both bring simplistic proofs from scripture that teach their false doctrine that He is above humanity, that is eating, drinking, taking a wife, having children...in their opinion he is an angel and without volition...This leads to idolatry. (42)
>
> When you investigate to know whence idolatry came from and why they sought to abandon God in order to worship the sun and the moon you will find that in the beginning their intentions were for the sake of heaven. (54) They made [Jesus as a] form for a remembrance and to bow down to it. Over the course of many years they forgot His awesome and glorious name.
>
> We find that all the ignorant women and children do not know anything but the form of wood or stone even the wise among them imagine that He is one but that He is three. Which are Him, His knowledge, and His life. (58) We should scrutinize and investigate our ways. Behold, [consider] the brass serpent which God himself commanded to Moses...which Israel went astray and made the serpent a god...therefore it is easy make a

mistake and to say that God is one in three. And even more so to worship the soul of a person when you think their soul is part of God. (60)

Soloweyczyk seeks to exonerate Christian belief in the divinity of Jesus by showing that images of God, considered idolatrous in Jewish law, were originally intended only to serve as representations of the Divine and not as separate gods. He also shows that even the ancient Hebrews fell into the same mistake when they worshiped the golden calf and the brass serpent. Soloweyczyk's approach does not give respect to Christian understanding of its own religious doctrines and assumes that Christianity can be understood outside of its two thousand years of tradition.

Soloweyczyk recounts a rabbinic story of the Caesar and the Rabbi focusing on the Roman Caesar's desire to see a tangible God and the Jewish belief in a non-iconic God. Rabbi Soloweyczyk transforms this dialogue into a tension between the Caesar's desire to know whether God's essence is a single unity or a Trinity and the rabbinic Jewish concentration on the complete unknowability of God. He adopted a Maimonidean unknowability of God to show that the Jewish approach rejects all the metaphysical debates between Trinitarian and Unitarian approaches as unknowable metaphysics.

> The Caesar said to Yehoshua ben Chanania, "I want to see God with my own eyes." He answered him that it's not possible...He pressured him until he said to him "I will show Him to you. We will go out in the middle of the summer day and I will show Him to you. He said to him "I cannot bear to look at the sun." He said to Him "just as the sun is one of his servants that stand before the Holy one Blessed be He and you cannot look at it, all the more so the Shekhinah. (Hullin 60) It is a wonder that the Caesar believed in God.
>
> Certainly he knew that he couldn't see Him. But the explanation of the matter is as follows: the Caesar wanted to know if the Holy one Blessed be He was a simple unity or a Trinitarian unity. He said to him, "just as the sun that you can see and you cannot know its essence, so too the Blessed Creator, that no eye can see, all the more so you can't grasp its essence. (11) From this story my dear reader you will understand that its impossible for a person when he is still connected of body and soul to grasp His blessed essence. Furthermore, it is a great danger. (12)

Humanism

This approach assumes that God cares for all humanity as descendents of Adam, all created in the image of God. He would not leave them without access to God. One does not need a special covenant or revelation to know and worship God. All people can naturally know God.

Rabbi Ovadiah Seforno

Rabbi Ovadiah Seforno (1470–1550) was a rabbinic scholar, exegete, and philosopher in Renaissance Italy. He is noted for teaching Torah to gentiles and dedicating his theological work *Light of the Nations* to King Henry of France. His theological works are based on technical scholastic presentations of the universal ability of the human soul to attain the good. This position looks neither ahead to the future conclusion of history nor up to the supernal realm. Rather, it understands other religions as knowledge of God given to all children of Adam, created in the image of God and in relation with God. Lacking metaphysics, this position proved particularly popular in the latter part of the twentieth century.

Seforno suggests that non-Jews share with Jews this universal relationship with God and thus all humanity is the chosen people. However, after the Fall of Adam, when humanity turned toward materiality, Jews and the pious of the other nations became more special. He uniquely proffers only a quantitative difference between Judaism and the other faiths. The distinction between Israel and other nations is the presence—or absence—of the Sinai revelation. All have the image of God, but the Sinai experience is only for Jews. There are two aspects to our lives: the universal and the particular; The image of God as God's concern for all humanity. The Jewish commitment to Sinai—as understood by rabbinic literature—known through Torah study, ritual law, and peoplehood.

"And now if you will diligently listen to my voice and observe My covenant, you shall be consecrated (segulah) *to Me from all the nations, for all the earth is Mine. And you shall be a kingdom of priests and a holy nation unto Me."* (Exod. 19:5–6)

"You shall be consecrated to Me:" Humanity as a whole is more precious to Me than the lower forms of existence, since man is the central figure in creation. As our Sages taught: "Beloved is man who was created in the Divine image" (*Avot* 3:14). However, the difference between [Jews and non-Jews] in the hierarchy of the universe is that, although "the entire earth belongs to Me," and the righteous of the nations are precious to Me without a doubt, [nevertheless] "you shall be a kingdom of priests unto Me." This is your distinction: You shall be a kingdom of priests to teach all of humanity that they all shall call upon the name of God to serve Him with a common accord (Zephaniah 3:9). It also states, "And you shall be called the priests of God" (Isaiah 61:6), and "For out of Zion shall the Torah come forth" (Isaiah 2:3).

Although You love the nations, all of the holy ones are in your hand; they are
subdued beneath Your feet, for he brought Your word. (Deut. 33:3)

"Although you love the nations": With this You make known that all
of humanity is precious to You. As the Rabbis taught, "Beloved is man,
who was created in the Divine image." Nevertheless, "all holy ones are
in your hand." You declare that all holy ones—the holy myriads who
received the fiery religion are in your hand as silver in [the hand] of the
refiner. "They are subdued:" They are broken, like one who has been
reproved and prays with a broken spirit. "Beneath Your feet:" That is,
at your footstool, Mount Sinai. "He brought Your word:" That is Torah
which Moses commanded. They said to God, "Moses brought us your
word, the Torah which You commanded us to heed."[45]

For Seforno, all humanity is beloved by God and chosen from amongst all
creation. As Zephaniah has prophesied, the nations will, in messianic times,
all call upon God.

With his emphasis on Zephaniah, Seforno prefigures and makes possible the
thinking of Hirsch and Kook. Seforno, though, lacks the strong teleological
thrust that underlies much of Hirschian and Kookian theology. It is important to
note that Rabbi Reines (d. 1904), the founder of religious Zionism, who sought
a broader vision of Judaism, advocated following Seforno's inclusivism.[46]

In many ways, Seforno is structurally similar to Rabbi Joseph B. Soloveitchik's
Confrontation, a universal religious quest through Adam and a particular one
through Sinai. However, Soloveitchik considers the image of God our secular
side, only a universal human religious quest, untranslatable into our covenantal
revelation side. In contrast, Seforno has the Sinai covenant as predicated on our
humanity and a fulfillment of it. Our covenant is translatable to other faiths, and
the non-Jews share our covenant, but Jews claim a quantitative superiority.

Avigdor Kara

Avigdor Kara, a fifteenth-century rabbi and biblical commentator, was witness to the Hussite rebellion (1420–1434) inspired by Jan Huss (ca. 1369–1415)
with its rejection of Catholic theology. Kara offers us an inclusivist model
of a Jew evaluating the monotheism of his Christian contemporaries. His
approach belies those who associate medieval Ashkenazi culture only with
exclusivism. Kara does reject Christian iconography and representation and
seems to accept specific Hussite formulations of Christianity. He couches this
approach in the form of a hymn:

> One, alone unique is God,
> Responsive to the seeking heart that's pure.

God is surely good to Israel. Hallelujah!
Jew, Christian, Arab! Understand!
God has no form that can be seen.
His ways are just and Him we trust. Hallelujah!
The mystery of faith is nowhere found
Except among the Hebrews.
Forbidden altars shall lie on the ground. Hallelujah!
The Kenite, Na'aman-Obadiah too—
Rahab, Na'amah and Ruth of Moab
Entered the saving faith and true. Hallelujah![47]

The hymn, which addresses non-Jews, mentions various biblical proselytes to the God of Israel. It shows an inclusive monotheism in which Christianity and Islam are included. According to Kara, monotheism, not commandments or community, is the essence of Judaism. By accepting monotheism, and praising the one God, Muslims and Hussites have joined the Jewish people as surely as the biblical heroes Ruth, Rahab, and Yael. Everyone needs to accept that "the mystery of faith can only be found among the Hebrews;" only the Jewish revelation has taught faith in God to the world.

Kara's acceptance of Christianity is premised on his sympathies for the Hussite Unitarians and a misreading of the Hussite reform movement as a Judaising, anti-Trinitarian movement that accept a Jewish definition of monotheism. The following "Hussite Saga," a Jewish document, describes Kara's opinions.

a development of the highest consequence was brought about by R. Avigdor Kara of blessed memory, who lived in Prague, the capital of the land of Bohemia. The king of the land took a liking to him, and this grew to a feeling of intense love, until the king learnt from him to acknowledge the true monotheism of the Jewish faith . . . Shortly afterwards the king passed away. There arose after him a priest named Hus. To this day his followers are known as Hussites. And this priest would gather all the inhabitants of the aforementioned capital and preach to them and teach them until they all believed in God's unity. They then arose and destroyed all their houses of idolatry and their idols they committed to flames, and the priests who persisted in cleaving to the faith of "that certain man" they put to death . . . And the Hussites were joined by the majority of the land.

Now the above-mentioned rabbi would compose liturgical songs in Hebrew and Yiddish with the exaltation of monotheism as the theme. These hymns would be sung in public, to the glory of the Jewish faith.

"One, alone, unique is God" ran the caption of one among many similar songs.

This position is noteworthy mostly for its implementation of the inclusivist vision in premodern times in Ashkenazi lands, and also for its concurrent rejection of anti-gentile particularism. There are also elements of a millenarian end of days vision consisting of the recognition of the Jewish truth.

Kara's approach is similar to some of the contemporary twenty-first-century Evangelical approaches that recognize the faith of Malkizedek, Jethro, Rahab, Job, and Naamah. These biblical believers do not have the true mystery of faith, yet they do have a monotheism and recognition of the biblical God. This approach does create an opening for a natural belief in monotheism.

Scholarly inclusivism: Yehezkel Kaufman

Yehezkel Kaufman (1889–1963), professor of Bible at the Hebrew University of Jerusalem, was influential in creating a Jewish-Israeli school of biblical criticism that views the prophets as heirs to the legalistic and priestly Temple cult. Kaufman presents a biblical theology where the moral monotheism of the Bible fought against the immoral paganism. Kaufman portrayed the ideas of Jesus as entirely within Judaism, in which Jesus brought the biblical message to the world.

According to Kaufman, God originally made a covenant to the entire people of Israel, as a nation at Mt.. Sinai. Israel is responsible to this covenant as a nation. The basic difference between Judaism and Christianity is defined by Kaufman as two forms of covenant, both bringing the Hebraic gift of ethical monotheism to the world. Judaism requires the keeping of the law, while the Christian covenant is the moral monotheism without the requirement to keep the law.

Kaufman quotes the passage from Maimonides, presented at the start of this chapter, to state that Christianity and Islam are continuities of the biblical message able to bring a moral monotheism forward to the world without the nationalism. For Kaufman, what counts is that there is a continuity of the moral monotheism of the Bible in both rabbinic Judaism and the New Testament.

The significance of the annulment of the Law was not that it marked the priority of the ethical over the ritual, but that the sacrifice of Jesus thereby became an event of divine salvation overshadowing the revelation of the Law at Sinai. A symbolism of the covenant was created whereby the new Christian would be detached from the congregation of Israel. Moreover, the doctrine of the redemptive sacrifice accorded well with the spiritual attitudes of the gentile judaizers, and facilitated the evolution of a predominantly gentile Christian church. A new protagonist of the faith but not of the nation Israel came into being: the gentile church, heir of the religion of Israel given in a "new testament," and with destiny unencumbered with the fate of exilic Jewry.

The markedly apocalyptic element in the new religion also played its part in the separation of the gentile church from Israel and its development in Jesus' name. Thus, the vehicle was created whereby the religion of Israel would go forth to conquer the world. Pagan nations succumbed little by little by means of this Judaism which was symbolized in the covenant, a fact which neither Jesus nor his disciples nor Paul foresaw or thought possible. Pauline Christianity was not rooted in the ethical teachings of Jesus, and was not the product of Jesus' quarrels with "the Pharisees." It grew out of the legendary, mythological appreciation of the person of Jesus, which prevailed among the earliest followers and was accepted in the end by Jesus himself.[48]

Paul is credited with adding the apocalyptic and mythological elements to Christianity, a view widely shared by liberal Christians in the first half of the twentieth century. Kaufman's approach is no longer accepted in either the scholarly or theological worlds.

Yet, Kaufman's position was highly influential, as required reading, in both the Israeli school system and among Jewish academics. Kaufman was of prime importance for creating a scholarly version of inclusivism that influenced many of the Jewish thinkers of the late twentieth century seeking to create a common covenant with Christianity. According to Kaufman, "the nations are judged for violations of the moral law, but never for idolatry." Therefore, Judaism is not concerned about the theology of the nations and allows a wide range of beliefs among gentile religions.[49]

Conclusions

When considering each of the inclusivist positions, the historical position works best when it allows the other nations to be part of a greater entity of religion and a providential role. It is weakest at its supersessionist moments. Within the metaphysical position, the kabbalistic approaches offer the most to those who are mystically inclined or who still speak of metaphysical entities. The affirmation of Mosaic revelation as a general revelation to humanity has been underdeveloped in twentieth-century Jewish thought.

Inclusivism allows a commitment to one's own texts and theology but still acknowledges other faiths. Inclusivism as a natural theology can point to the commonalities between religions in belief in one God and prophetic knowledge. As historical theology it can fit Christianity and Islam into a Noahite, Abrahamic, or Mosaic context and as an approach to seeking the mystical light of the Divine, it allows an understanding of the common quest while preserving a sense of uniqueness. Many today start their theological work with the inclusivist positions such as that of Yaakov Emden or Seforno, because, for many Jews, the acknowledgment of Christian faith and morality as part of Torah rings true in the contemporary setting. Some may find the inclusivist approach too paternalistic and others may find it too universal but its importance lies in the overcoming of a simple dichotomy between exclusiveness or pluralism, thereby forcing Jewish thinkers to formulate a more nuanced middle position.

CHAPTER 5

The Universalist Tradition

Over the centuries, many Jewish thinkers have embraced a universal approach in which the universalism of the prophets is joined with the philosophic monotheism of the Middle Ages. They accept a universal truth available to all humanity beyond, but not against, revelation. In a universal truth there is no need to refer to Judaism as the single truth; rather all knowledge is grounded in a higher divine knowledge, or a unified sense of rationality, or the natural abilities of the mind and soul. This approach, at times, blurs the line between religion and philosophy or between religion and ethics. However, religiously universalists remain close to the inclusivists in that everything is grounded in the teachings of Judaism.

This universal monotheism is found in Sa'adiah, Ibn Gabirol, and Ibn Ezra, and some of the Maimonideans, and the poets Immanuel of Rome, and Yehudah Abarbanel. Even more universal, Nathaniel ibn Fayumi offers the unique position that allows for a universal potential of revelation. The beginning of the modern era witnessed a shift to a rationalist universalism by Moses Mendelssohn and a moral universalism in the form of thinkers such as Israel Lipschutz, Samuel David Luzzatto, and Mendel Hirsch. Other thinkers in the age of discovery, such as Menashe ben Israel, Elijah Benamozegh, Henry Pereira-Mendes, and Joseph Hertz, presented a historical universalism of a lost truth from Adam that makes itself manifest in cultural diversity.

Universalism

- Universal—a universal availability of God to all humans
  - Monotheism
  - Souls' return

- Perfection of the intellect
- Political need for society
- Love and beauty
- Universal revelation
- Universal rationality without revelation
- Humanistic—a common moral core of all humanity under God
- An original universal truth scattered in history

Medieval Universalism

Sa'adiah

Sa'adiah Gaon (882–942) was a leading rabbi and early medieval Jewish philosopher whose *The Book of Beliefs and Opinions* set the parameters for the tradition of Jewish philosophy by employing the Islamic strategy of freely using Platonic, Aristotelian, and Stoic texts to produce a rational theology. Sa'adiah, as befitting a classical philosopher, presents religion as a universal phenomena and accepts a type of religious truth transcending Judaism, even though his overall approach is inclusivist.

In the introduction to his book, after discussing empirical, rational, and deductive sources of knowledge, which are all clearly universal, he states: "As for ourselves, the community of monotheists, we hold these three sources of knowledge to be genuine. To them, however, we add a fourth source...the validity of authentic tradition...This type of knowledge...corroborates for us the validity of the first three sources of knowledge."[1] In other words, people can rationally attain a universal knowledge of the monotheistic God. Revelation and tradition serve to corroborate this rational knowledge of God.[2] Following the Kalam, the Islamic theological arguments for creation and the unity of God that apply to Islam and Christianity as well as Judaism, Sa'adiah cannot have denied the monotheistic nature of Islam nor that of Christianity, since they accept the God of creation with the attributes of life, power, and knowledge (*Emunot* 2:5). According to Raphael Jospe, professor of medieval Jewish thought, Sa'adiah's argument with the Christian doctrine of the Trinity follows his discussion of essential attributes, not his refutation of dualism and polytheism, and therefore contextually implies that Christianity is not polytheistic, but an incorrect form of monotheism. Moreover Sa'adiah, when discussing believers in the Trinity, refers to "the communities of the monotheists."[3]

Sa'adiah's "community of monotheists" is also found in the usages of later Jewish philosophers. For example, Bahya ibn Paqudah (eleventh century, Spain), in his pietistic work *Duties of the Hearts* 1:1–2, refers to "the people of monotheism," where the distinction is not between Jew and non-Jew, but between varying degrees of comprehension among people who affirm God's unity. Judah Ha-Levi's *Kuzari* 1:4 also refers to "monotheists" in a non-Jewish context, when the Christian spokesman says to the Khazar king: "For we are truly monotheists, although the Trinity appears on our tongues." In Maimonides' *Guide of the Perplexed* 1:53, "we, the community of true monotheists" refers to those who have a correct philosophical understanding of the divine attributes.

Ibn Gabirol and Ibn Ezra

In accordance with the notion of a community of monotheists, the poetry and philosophy of Golden Age Spain produced many works pointing to a universal religious path. Solomon ibn Gabirol (1021–1058, Malaga), a poet and liturgist, presented a universalism that is inspiring to this day. Ibn Gabirol's great philosophical meditation, *The Kingly Crown*, is an elaborate hymn to the transcendent Being and is still included in the Yom Kippur liturgy of many Jewish communities. In the poem, the worshiper speaks in awe of the majesty and intellectual perfection of God; he does not refer to any special relationship between God and Israel or to revealed religion at all. Instead, he stresses that all who sincerely seek God, even if it is through an incorrect form, will be able to know God's majesty.

> Thou art God:
> Every creature is Thy servant and Thy devotee.
> Thy glory never can diminished be
> Because to others some men bend their knee,
> For none intends but to come near to Thee.[4]

It is significant to note that since Ibn Gabirol's writings were universal, his major work *Fountain of Life* (*Makor Hayyim, Fons Vitae*) was not identified as written by a Jewish author until the nineteenth century.

Another important figure from this era was the polymath thinker, exegete, and poet Abraham ibn Ezra (1089–1164) who wandered from Spain to Provence to northern Europe spreading the wisdom of the Judeo-Arabic world. For Ibn Ezra, the human soul comes into being as a separated part of the universal soul, and if worthy, it can become immortal by being reunited and absorbed within that soul.

At the request of Samuel Ibn Jami, a learned and philosophically inclined North African Jew who was himself a poet, Ibn Ezra wrote his *Hayy ben Meqitz*, a Hebraic version of a similar work by the Muslim sage ibn Sina (980–1037, Avicenna), *Hayy ibn Yaqzan* (*Alive son of Awake*). The poem is a universal epistle about the need to cultivate the soul to achieve a cleaving to the Divine, the universal ruler over all and the source of all knowledge, greatness, and compassion.

> There is no God save Him; No Creator except Him.
> There is no limit to His Knowledge; No bound to his wisdom.
> His possessions cannot be enumerated; His contents cannot be known.
> From an abundance of greatness, His Knowledge is hidden from men.
> From the greatness of His appearance, seeing Him is prevented.
> Since the sun is hidden by its light, we cannot know it.
> When it rises at dawn, we barely visualize it.
> In this way souls are unable to know Him.
> Hearts unable to perceive Him; He has neither shape nor likeness.[5]

All humans can undertake training to purify their souls and gaze at the majesty of God. Similar to the modern mystical approaches, the human soul has the potential to attain access to the hidden knowledge of God.

Ibn Ezra makes similar statements in his biblical commentaries written for general Jewish audiences, those who are not philosophically trained. In discussing Ecclesiastes 7:9, he presents the Platonic vision of the exile of the soul, which conditions its need to transcend the body and return to the truth, goodness, and beauty of the Divine.

> Just as the passerby who has been taken prisoner longs to return to his homeland and to be with his family, so does the intellect yearn to grab hold of the higher rungs until she ascends to the formations of the living God, which do not dwell in material houses... This will transpire if the spirit whitens, sanctifying herself above the impurities of disgusting bodily lusts, which sully what is holy... then what is distant will be like what is near, and night like day; then she will be configured to know the real truth, which will be inscribed upon her in such a way so as not to be erased when she departs the body, for the script is the writing of God... (Levin 1985, 288)

Maimonidean universal religion

Many thirteenth- to fifteenth-century followers of, and commentators on, the great thinker Moses Maimonides held universal positions. Each of these thinkers saw revelation as a process of cognition attainable by all who were philosophically and morally worthy. Maimonides himself was an inclusivist who defended Judaism and Jewish revelation as the source for true monotheism, and who considered the other biblical faiths as a means of spreading the knowledge of Judaism. Yet, many of his followers stressed the universal aspects of revelation as a human capacity available to all. They had no problem recognizing other religions as a part of a natural human need to organize one's life around eternal verities and values.

Maimonides explains how using representation to worship God leads to forgetting of God's universal existence. His philosophic abstraction blurs the historic lines between ancient idolatrous worship and the ever-present unreflective religion of the non-philosophic masses who do not understand the true reality of God.

> Whoever performs idolatrous worship does not do it on the assumption that there is no deity except the idol... Rather, it is, worshipped in respect of its being an image of a thing that is an intermediary between ourselves and God... This led to the disappearance of the belief in His existence, may he be exalted, from among the multitude. For the multitude grasp only the actions of worship, not their meanings or the true reality of the Being worshipped through them.[6]

According to these Maimonidean commentators, the idolatrous representation in religions other than Judaism does not invalidate the original universal oneness of God reflected in those religions, just as those Jews with false notions of God do not invalidate Judaism as a monotheism. Their definition of monotheism judges concepts of God based on the essence of God, the monotheism itself, not the attributes of God and historical narratives used to represent truth for the wider community.

Acceptance of universalist positions comes most easily to religious approaches that emphasize inner conviction over social identity in that they need to ask little of the community beyond social stability and being left alone. In this case, the medieval Maimonidean thinkers saw fellow philosophers as having attained the universal truth of philosophy through the study of philosophy, outside of the representational thinking of the religious–political community. For the philosopher, the masses of any religion conceive of religion as a collection of narratives, rituals, and external practices, unaware of the true universal reality of God.

In the educational background of these thinkers are the writings of the Muslim philosopher Al-Farabi (870–950). In his widely read *Political Regime*, Al-Farabi argued that there is but one reality, yet many images or reflections of that reality. There can be many religions therefore, as each nation represents these images of reality in its own ways, although not all possible ways are equally excellent. Al-Farabi also thinks that the creation of a virtuous society, within any religion, requires belief in monotheism. The broad strokes of Al-Farabi's thought were accepted by most of the Islamic philosophers (*falasifa*) and their Jewish translators.

Ibn Kaspi, Jacob Anatoli, and Narboni

Joseph ibn Kaspi (1280–*ca.* 1332, Provençe) sought to explain Maimonides without metaphysics or esotericism. For Ibn Kaspi, religion is a natural part of the human experience, like politics. Every community needs religion for a sense of order and morality. "I swear by the Eternal that Aristotle, his associates and his students all caution us to observe everything in the Torah and in the words of the prophets, and to be especially careful with respect to the commandments calling for action. As Plato said 'Put to death one who has no religion.'"[7] This approach accepts that gentiles all have religion, and, indeed, must have religion. The quote is not by Plato himself, but a truism of the Platonic-Aristotelian tradition as interpreted in Judeo-Islamic sources. To be more exact, the quote was probably from one of the Hebrew translations of al-Ghazzali, a Persian author (1058–1111) whose writings were widely accepted in the Jewish community. According to this interpretation, to create a virtuous society everyone follows the monotheistic religion of his community. This approach seems to have been widespread in Provençe, whether due to contemporary philosophic trends or due to a particularly broad social tolerance in the region. The famous halakhic position of R. Menachem Meiri, which considers contemporary gentiles as people of religion, may have grown out of this approach (see the chapter eight), as did Jacob Anatoli's naturalistic understanding of the Noahite laws.

Jacob Anatoli (*ca.* 1194–1256) was a rabbi in Naples and earned a place in the history of Western civilization as the translator of Arabic philosophical texts in association with the Christian scholar Michael Scot under the patronage of Fredrick II of Italy and the Holy Roman Empire. He played an aggressive role, especially through his sermons, in the Maimonidean controversy of the 1230s defending the honor of Maimonidean rationalism before the onslaught of the anti-Maimonidean, which he considered as theological vulgarity.

Anatoli professed a universal religion, characterized by a knowledge of God's existence, unity, and kingship. Each nation produces its own system of morally upright laws to uphold its religion. Gentiles are understood to be invested with the need to acknowledge God's glory, through philosophy and the moral order, and thereby affirm the universal Noahite laws.

> Noah was a saint (*zaddik*), yet only the seven Noahite laws were given to him and his offspring. It should not be a wonder to you that [Noah] was called a saint for these commandments alone... The righteous of the nations of the world who keep the seven commandments merit the world to come. Just as there is a commandment for Jews to establish courts in their cities, so, too, the children of Noah have to set up courts

in their cities, the righteous of the nations follow in their business deal-
ings according to their courts.

God created for His glory the mighty and the small, and He rules all,
and in His desire the human species was chosen from all lowly things,
and He chose His nation from this species and raised their glory in
Torah...it is fit for every person to praise the God of all existence, of
which all dominion is His.[8]

Anatoli also tries to close the gap between Jewish and Christian theology discussing what appears to be a citation from a version of the Athanasian Creed.
Anatoli attempts to explain the Christian Trinity in a charitable manner as
emanation and not as persons within a triune divine, "God is without doubt
God and king over all. Yet the Christian adds 'eternal God'...He is first, or
he emerges from hiddenness."

Another Provençal R. Yedidyah HaPenini, a poet and philosopher, wrote
to his more conservative correspondent R. Abraham Aderet about the universal ability to enter knowledge of God. In discussing the Talmudic passage
about the four who entered Paradise (Hagigah 13), he interprets the esoteric
knowledge of Judaism to be identical with the Platonic path of Enlightenment
from the darkness of the masses. Yedidyah includes gentiles with those who
know the esoteric secrets of religion that are known to the rabbis.

The Pardes refers to the high vineyard into which the wise of Israel entered
in peace and exited in peace. The word "peace" in the context of entering means to integrate the true theoretical doctrines in agreement with
what one has to believe based on the Torah. That includes throwing away
the shells. The word "peace" in context of exiting means that the now
perfected person leaves his meditative isolation to partake in the practical
world perfected in his virtues and his actions. The elite of the nations are
not withheld from entering [the vineyard] and all those who spend all their
time in study and true knowledge, will arrive at the same place. The Rabbis
already mentioned that pious of the nations have a share in the world to
come, which is only through true knowledge of the Creator of all.[9]

Rabbi Moses ben Joshua Narboni (~1300–1362, Perpignan, Toledo, Valencia),
another thinker of this school, composed detailed commentaries on earlier
philosophical works. In his discussion of other religions, he seems to have
combined elements of Ibn Ezra, Maimonides, and Provençal Maimonideans.
Narboni emphasizes the universal importance of following a correct way of
life in order to attain spiritual perfection culminating with a state of cleaving
to God. In his commentary of Ibn Sina's *Hayy Ibn Yaqzan* Narboni emphasizes

that Islam, just like Judaism, is a purely monotheistic faith. As an example of his recombining older texts into new forms, he explains that the prevalence of circumcision among Muslims is a sign of the purity of their faith. Narboni develops this idea by bringing together two statements of Maimonides. One is Maimonides' assertion in the *Guide of the Perplexed* that circumcision is a sign of one's belief in the unity of God. The other is his statement in the epistle to R. Obadiah the Convert that the Ishmaelites are not idolaters, and that they uphold the oneness of God in the proper manner.[10] Hence, Muslims show the purity of monotheistic faith through circumcision.

False understandings of a true core: Shem Tov ibn Falquera and Isaac Albalag

Some Maimonideans framed their universalism in terms of attaining correct philosophic knowledge instead of emphasizing the prevalence of monotheistic views. Shem Tov Falquera (1225–1290), a Spanish author and poet responsible for the popularizing of Maimonidean ideas, wrote apologies in favor of studying of philosophic works and practicing philosophic religion. Falquera assumes that all religions worship the one true God, and he quotes the prophet Micah to prove his position—all who call, "call to my name." However, he attributes the mistakes of other religions solely to illusory workings of imagination.

> Know that one who worships idolatry does not worship it because he thinks that there is no other God... or that he thinks that the forms of metal, stone and wood created the natural order of heaven and earth or serve as source of providence. This worship [of images] is because of imagination alone as a means of serving God.[11]

Falquera stresses the presence of false beliefs even within Judaism. "Know that when one has anthropomorphism or anthropopathism, it is worse than idolatry." Significantly, Falquera distinguishes not between Judaism and other religions, but between true belief in God and false beliefs.

Isaac Albalag, a Jewish philosopher during the second half of the thirteenth century who probably lived in northern Spain or southern France, translated the Muslim thinker Al Ghazalli's *Aims of the Philosophers*, to which he added his own views and comments. Albalag defended philosophy against the accusation that it undermines religion, stating that religion appeals to the great masses, while philosophy demonstrates with proof. But religion and philosophy agree on the fundamental principles of all positive religion—"the belief in reward and punishment, in immortality, in the existence of a just God, and in Divine Providence." They both follow the same aim, namely to render mankind rightly ordered and happy, but differ in their modes of explanation and presentation. For example, the divine design and providence of the world is taught as ex-nihilo by the biblical account of the Creation, while the philosopher apprehends the same ideas via the Aristotelian theory of the eternity of the world. Albalag stresses the need for biblical language for religion, but accepts philosophic naturalism for the philosophers.

Albalag attributes differences among religions to misunderstandings of the masses, who do not comprehend the philosophic aspects of religion, and who therefore produce wild distortions and misrepresentations. He treats the Christian Trinity as a category mistake about the universal knowledge of God.

> Al Ghazzali explained that God is thought, thinking, and thinker because all is one essence, even though these are three distinct aspects in the understanding [of God]. Perhaps this explains the belief of the gentile masses in the trinity that remains one. When they heard from their wise men [about the trinity] consisting of one understood as three aspects, the masses did not understand [its philosophic meaning]. There is no doubt that this belief [in the trinity] is good and true in itself and not to be considered detrimental, except when understood by the masses who stumbled to be lead to a lesser understanding. Not just to [the Christian masses] did this occur but this occurs in every nation between the wise and the masses.[12]

The sixteen-century thinker Eliezer Ashkenazi developed these medieval universal themes in an exegetical context, which influenced the legal tradition, see chapter eight.

A contemporary version of these medieval universal positions has been presented by Menachem Kellner, a professor at Haifa University specializing in Maimonidean thought. He personally believes that "in the messianic future" the dichotomy between Jews and gentiles "will be overcome, and all human beings will share the same relationship with God. In the messianic world, there will be no Jews and gentiles, only worshippers of the one true God." The distinction between Jews and gentiles will be "overcome," not because all gentiles will convert to Judaism in its particular current form, but because Judaism is really a matter of affirming the truth, rather than merely an ethnic identity. Therefore, by accepting the truth, gentiles, in effect, will become Jewish in a universal sense: "The messianic age will witness not a triumph of Judaism so much as the triumph of truth."[13]

Immanuel of Rome

An Italian Jewish philosopher more concerned with poetry than epistemology, Immanuel of Rome (*ca.* 1261–1328) was a student of the Maimonidean

Zerachiah Hen, a confrere to Dante, and an antagonist of the more traditional Rabbi Hillel of Verona. Immanuel's imitation of Dante's *Divine Comedy*, called *Tofet veEden,* was universalistic in orientation and his poetry was chastised as too risqué in his lifetime. In fact, because Immanuel's description is lacking in its engagement with rabbinical proof texts, it is not an authoritative text for traditional thought. Nevertheless, Immanuel allows us a glimpse of the forces that shaped traditional Jewish thought. His position forced the thirteenth-century critic Rabbi Hillel of Verona to formulate an inclusive humanism that was to influence the position of Rabbi Ovadiah Seforno (discussed in chapter four). He also shows us that universalistic positions are not chronologically limited to the modern era, nor are they necessarily related to post-Enlightenment ideas of tolerance, liberalism, and secularism.

The heaven-rewarded saints observed by the narrator of Immanuel's epic *Tofet veEden* have reached their non-Jewish paradise through intellectual reasoning. Evidently, for Immanuel of Rome, paradise could be reached through a non-Jewish path consisting of self-discovery and intellectual commitment. The various forms of traditional religion, each with its own particular ethnicity, theology, and approach to naming God, pale before the universal truth.

I observed men filled with honor and majesty's spark,
Compared with whose beauty sun and moon were dark...

These are the pious among the gentile state
Who by their intellect and wisdom have become great...
Whist they with their intelligence searched out who formed them, and who was the Creator,
Thro' whose goodness they into being came,
And who brought forth from nothingness to something with a name,
And set them in this world's frame,
And what purpose was of their creation, and what its aim.

And as they passed the Faiths of all other under examination...
But they chose of all beliefs views such as seemed to them right,
Upon which men versed in conscience had no cause to fight...

And when men boastfully would attach a name to God, our hearts trembled; it shook our frame to think that each and every people should give Him some definite name.

We however say, Be His name whatsoever, we believe in the First Existence, the True One, whom we never from our life can ever sever.[14]

According to Immanuel, then, those gentiles who come to God through their own intellect are the pious of the nations. In Immanuel's vision, one can naturally sense that the world is created with purpose and divine goodness. It is the names that men attach to God and to human religious understanding that cause war and strife. In Immanuel's terms, the correct position is to accept a universal God beyond the trappings of organized religion. When his friend Dante wrote that love is known through the Christian Trinity, Immanuel responded with "Love Never Read the Ave Maria," a poem that extols the universal elements of love and ridicules Dante's notion of connecting love solely to the Christian faith.[15]

Judah Abarbanel

The medieval philosophical tradition gave way in the fifteenth century to a Renaissance philosophy of love that retained medieval terminology, but shifted its emphasis to new topics like beauty and myth. Judah Abarbanel (*ca.* 1465–1523, Lisbon, Naples, Genoa) wrote the tremendously influential *The Philosophy of Love Dialoghi d'Amore*,[16] a universal theology that understood religion as love and beauty. This work is important since similar sentiments are found in many Jewish, and non-Jewish, works written in Italy in the Quattrocento and Cinquecento.[17]

Judah Abarbanel accepts the concept of a *sophia perennis*, a perennial wisdom, available to all faiths and considers the ancient Greek myths "rediscovered" in Italian culture as containing this eternal wisdom. Judah, on one level, wanted to show that there exists a fundamental identity between Greek myth and the teachings of the Torah. Yet on a deeper level he argues that the Greeks ultimately derived their teachings from the ancient Israelites and subsequently corrupted them. For instance, Judah argues that Plato studied among the ancient Israelites in Egypt, and that Plato's myth of the Androgyne, found in the *Symposium*, is actually a Greek plagiarism of a Jewish source. Furthermore, he tries to reframe Christian-centric interpretations of biblical passages (e.g., the Garden of Eden and the concept of original sin), claiming that the Jewish version or interpretation of such texts is actually more in keeping with the spirit of the Renaissance than those offered by Christians.

> Sophia: The story is beautiful and ornate, and it is impossible not to believe that it signifies some philosophical beauty, more especially since it was composed by Plato himself in the *Symposium* in the name of Aristophanes. Tell me, therefore, Philo what is the allegory?
>
> Philo: The myth was handed down by earlier writers than the Greeks—in the sacred writings of Moses, concerning the creation of the first human parents, Adam and Eve...it was from [Moses] that Plato took his myth, amplifying and polishing it after Greek oratory, thus giving a confused account of Hebrew matters.[18]

Beauty, that which inspires love and desire, connects all levels of the universe in an interlocking and organic relationship, which Judah refers to as the "universal circle." The result is that everything, both sensual and intelligible, has the potential to reflect God's beauty. The imagination is crucial here because it is the faculty responsible for decoding these reflections by translating the incorporeal into the corporeal and vice versa. Judah distinguishes between three types of beauty that pervade the cosmos. The first is God as the source of beauty, the second is beauty itself, and the third is the physical universe produced by this idea in the intellect of God.[19] In turn, Judah distinguishes among three types of vision. The highest type is God's visual apprehension of himself; next is the vision associated with the angelic world that sees God directly, though not on equal terms; and finally, there is human vision, which is the weakest of the three types and can only visualize the divine indirectly.[20]

Scholarly universalism

Discussions of the Golden Age of Spain, and by extension Provençe and Italy, were common among late-nineteenth-century and early-twentieth-century Jewish historians seeking the universal in Judaism. Among the best examples of this are the writings of Shelomo Dov (Fritz) Goitein (1900–1985). Goitein started his career as a Semitist, and then achieved world renown for his expositions of Jewish life in the Muslim world, which he based on his analysis of thousands of documents from the Cairo Geniza.

Goitein paints a rosy picture of the creativity during "the long and great period of Jewish-Arab symbiosis," in which there is a universalism that transcends any one religion. A symbiosis that concentrates on the *products of mutuality*, in which the "Jew served as a... catalyst in the self-definition of Islam, and the Muslim likewise operated in synergy with a Jewish effort at self-legitimation."[21] Goiten's writings are replete with remarks on the similarity of the two religions.

> A comparison between classical Islam and Judaism is extremely revealing... Apart from many aspects of religious law and literature common to the two religions—a fact which can hardly be due to chance—all main characteristic features of their systems are identical, or almost identical.[22]
>
> Islam, however, is from the very flesh and bone of Judaism.[23]
>
> Muslim philosophy and theology, pietism and mysticism, through their Jewish counterparts, are mirrored in the Hebrew poetry of the Middle Ages.[24]

This universalism had many proponents among twentieth-century European Jewish historians who looked to the Judeo-Islamic synthesis to transcend the exclusivism they saw in their Ashkenazi heritage. Seeking a grand synthesis with the surrounding culture in prior ages is not limited to those who study Spain, but extends to other noble historical portrayals such as Cecil Roth's portrayal of Jews under Christendom in Renaissance Italy.[25]

Universalism—revelation: Nathaniel ibn Fayumi

For some of the rabbis, divine prophecy was self-evidently too powerful to be bound by human categories of Jew or non-Jew. While this idea does not constitute a multi-covenant theology, it is a strand of rabbinic thought that paves the way for such a possibility.

> "The prophet Elijah said: I call heaven and earth to bear witness that anyone—Jew or gentile, man or woman, slave or handmaid—if his deeds are worthy, the Divine Spirit will rest upon him." (*Tanna Debai Eliyahu* 9:1)[26]
>
> "When the Holy One, blessed be He, revealed himself to give the Torah to Israel, he revealed Himself not only to Israel but to all the other nations." (*Sifrei Devarim* 343)

The rabbinic texts contain universal approaches to prophecy that were, at times, emphasized and elaborated by later Jewish thinkers, despite other rabbinic texts that explicitly exclude gentiles from prophecy.

Yemenite Rabbi Nathaniel ibn Fayumi (twelfth century) presented a multi-revelation theory without feeling the need to justify or defend it. In his *Garden of the Intellect, Bustan alAql* (ca. 1165, Yemen) he writes, "God permitted to every people something he forbade to others...God sends a prophet to every people according to their own language."[27] Ibn Fayumi based his position that prophecy is available in all nations on the aforementioned rabbinic statements and on Maimonides' theology of prophecy as a universal perfection. Ibn Fayumi's statement is similar to that of the *Qur'an* (*Sura Ibrahim* 14:4): "He sends a prophet to every people according to their language." He also reflects pluralistic trends in the Isma'ili thought of the "Brethren of Purity" (*Ikhwan al-Safa*) supersession of prophets. In Fayumi's approach, all nations are given a separate but equal revelation.

Ibn Fayumi discusses multiple revelations both before and after the revelation of the Torah. These post-Sinaitic revelations, however, do not abrogate the Torah, which will not be abrogated even in the messianic era:

> Nothing prevents God from sending unto His world whomsoever He wishes, whenever He wishes, since the world of holiness sends forth emanations unceasingly from the light world to the coarse world, to liberate the souls from the sea of matter—in the world of nature—and from

destruction in the fires of Hell. Even before the revelation of the Law, He sent prophets to the nations, as our Sages of blessed memory explain, "Seven prophets prophesied to the nations of the world before the giving of the Torah: Laban, Jethro, Balaam, Job, Eliphaz, Bildad and Zophar." And even after its revelation nothing prevented Him from sending to them whom He wished, that the world might not remain without religion. The prophets declared that the other nations would serve Him from the rising of the sun to the setting thereof: "For from the rising of the sun to the setting thereof great is my name among the nations." (Malachi 1:11)

Religions are like medicines, each adapting themselves to the person for whom they are prescribed. Religions must be different in order to match the different temperaments of men, but in substance they are all the same.[28]

Ibn Fayumi's writings have not had a great influence on Jewish thought outside of Yemen, yet he offers a reading of Maimonides that grants revelation to other nations, even those outside of the biblical purview.

Enlightenment: Moses Mendelssohn

With the advent of Enlightenment and Emancipation, the older universalism based on medieval metaphysics presented in the first half of this chapter gave way to a universalism based on rationality, autonomous ethics, and individual merit.

The Enlightenment religious leader Rabbi Moses Mendelssohn (1729–1786) consistently held universal views and rejected the exclusive claims made by any religion. If the creator is merciful, then truth must be available to all people. Early in 1770, Mendelssohn wrote to Prince Karl-Wilhelm of Brunswick (1735–1806) about liberal Christian reformers.

> They must not base their system...on the hypothesis that Judaism and, even more so, natural religion, are inadequate means to ensure man's salvation. Since all men must have been destined by the Creator to attain eternal bliss, no particular religion can have an exclusive claim to truth. This thesis, I dare to submit, might serve as a criterion of truth in all religious matters. A revelation claiming to show man the only way to salvation cannot be true, for it is not in harmony with the intent of the all-merciful Creator.[29]

In another letter written in 1770, he differentiated between internal, natural religion, which is universal and involves basic demonstrable truths that all people should accept on a rational basis—and a variety of external positive religions. Mendelssohn lacks ethnographic or theological interest in Christianity. His goal is just to point out that the latter is very particular compared to the universalism of Judaism.

> Worship, however, as everyone knows, can be private as well as public, internal as well as external, and one does well to differentiate between the two. The internal worship of the Jew is not based on any principles except those of natural religion. To spread these is, indeed, incumbent upon us... Our external worship, however, is in no way meant to address itself to others, since it consists of rules and prescriptions that are related to specific persons, times and circumstances. I grant that we believe that our religion is the best, because we believe it to be divinely inspired. Nevertheless, it does not follow from this premise that it is absolutely the best. It is the best religion for ourselves and our descendants, the best for certain times, circumstances and conditions.[30]

Mendelssohn considered the moral way of life as taught by Enlightenment rationalism as a fulfillment of the Seven Noahite laws (for a definition of these laws, see chapter three). He portrays Judaism as a universal religion in which "according to the Law of our Torah the Gentiles were obliged to keep only the seven commandments in order to share in the world-to-come." Mendelssohn considers God, reward for righteousness, and immortality as rational beliefs available to all people.

> The nations of the world, even though they recognize the entity of God... they nevertheless worship another entity besides Him. A few worship the angels above believing that God apportioned to each one of them a nation or country... to rule, and they have the power to do good or bad as they please.
>
> These are called "other gods" in the Torah... A few [of the nations of the world] worship the stars in the sky... or people... and bow down to them. The judgment of the intellect does not require forbidding such worship to a Noahite (provided he does not intend to remove himself from the realm of God). Why must he offer service and prayer to God alone?
>
> If he hopes for good and fears for bad from an entity besides Him and acknowledges that also that entity is subject to God, it is not beyond the intellect for him to offer sacrifices, incense, and libation and to pray to this entity be it an angel, demon, or person...[31]

It is worth noting that Mendelssohn is still concerned with relying on the medieval glosses on the Talmud by *tosafot* on association (*shituf*; see chapter eight), and that he interprets them as a general acceptance that non-Jews can use any representation of God or any intermediary.

Humanistic Universalism

Israel Lipschutz: *derech eretz:*
In contrast to Mendelssohn, who minimizes the importance of external worship and rejects the essentiality of revelation to religion, Rabbi Israel Lipschutz (1782–1860), a traditionalist from the port city of Danzig, reflects the sentiments of his era and offers a surprisingly universalistic sentiment in his Mishneh commentary.

> R. Elaezar ben Azaryah said, "If there is no Torah there is no civilization (*derech eretz*: lit. way of the land)." The word "Torah" here cannot be meant literally, since there are many ignorant people who have not learned [Torah], and many pious among the Gentiles who do not keep the Torah and yet are ethical and follow the "way of the land." Rather, the correct interpretation seems to me to be that every people has its own Divine religion, which comprises three foundational principles, (1) belief in a revealed Torah, (2) belief in reward and punishment, and (3) belief in an afterlife. They only disagree on the interpretation of these principles. These three principles are what are called here "Torah."[32]

Lipschutz offers a vision of tolerance based on a generic sense of revelation, reward, and afterlife found in all religions. Rather than approaching religions as other, Lipschutz senses a common core based on morality. Similar to Sa'adiah, he finds the universal gained by gentiles on their own, and Jews have the added direct gift from God.[33]

If one wanted to develop an approach to non-Abrahamic faiths, then his general definitions would offer a useful starting point. According to Lipschutz's claims, enlightenment, karma, and reincarnation can be considered teaching morals and values, forms of Torah for gentiles. Although he did not work out in writing these implications of his ideas, his position was the one cited by the Israeli rabbinate when recently engaged in Hindu-Jewish dialogue.

Rabbi Lipschutz did not respond to the specific ethics or religious beliefs of Christianity like Rabbi Yaakov Emden did a generation before him. However, he did value Christian achievements and morals. Continuing his discussion about praising and appreciating the civilization of the gentiles, he writes,

> Even without these holy words of our rabbis, we would know this from simple logic. "God is right in all His actions and pious in His deeds."

We have come across many good non Jews who in addition to believing in the Creator and accepting the Divine sanctity of the Bible have done great kindnesses not only to Israel but have benefited the whole of mankind. The pious [Edward] Jenner invented inoculation against smallpox, and thus saved the lives of tens of thousands of people and helped them avoid disease and becoming crippled. Drake [Sir Walter Raleigh]...brought potatoes to Europe and thus prevented much famine. Guttenberg invented the printing press.

Some who were not at all rewarded in this world, like the saintly Reuchlin, who put his own life in danger by preventing the Talmud from being burnt on the orders of Emperor Maximilian in 1509, as a result of the pressure from the apostate Pfefferkorn who plotted together with the evil monks. This Reuchlin risked his life, and with his arguments got the Emperor to change his decree. As a result, he was pursued and harassed and his life made bitter by the monks who opposed him, and he died a broken man. Do you think it conceivable that these amazing deeds would not be recognized and rewarded in Heaven? God does not betray any of his creatures.[34]

Samuel David Luzzatto *brotherhood of man*

Rabbi Samuel David Luzzatto (1800–1865), known the his acronym Shadal, was a biblical scholar and humanist at the Padua Rabbinical Seminary. His views on the Bible as a non-metaphysical book of literature and history have become an integral part of modern Jewish education. Luzzatto highlights ethics and compassion as the central focus of religion, and empathy for all human beings as the basic Jewish directive. "The compassion that Judaism commends is universal. It is extended, like God's, to all of his creations. No race is excluded from the Law, because all human beings, according to Judaism's teachings, are brothers as children of the same father, and are created in the image of God."[35] Luzzatto affirms that we all worship one God, which creates a brotherhood among all people.

Luzzatto provides his own theory of other religions wherein he traces religion to Abraham and his descendants who understand the universal implications of creation to be the requirements of mercy, kindness, and righteousness. Judaism in particular is based on the covenant of Abraham, which understands that God, as a single creator, means compassion and providence for all humanity.

According to Luzzatto, Moses added many laws to Abrahamic religion, almost all of them for three reasons: for social organization, to remind the Israelites of God, and to control their passions. Yet the core of the Jewish religion remained Abrahamic. Non-Jews are not expected to follow Moses' law, but only practice the providential faith of Abraham. In contrast, one who rejects religion is outside the Abrahamic covenant.

> The people of Israel did not acquire their religion from Moses, but inherited it from their ancestors, Abraham, Isaac, and Jacob...What was the nature of that religion?...For the sake of future generations, he described its character by portraying the biographies of Abraham, Isaac, Jacob, and his children. Judging from these narratives, we realize that they believed in one God, creator of heaven and earth, judge of the world, Who protects and rewards His faithful, and punishes the wicked in accordance with their deeds.
>
> The numerous precepts and laws in the Torah of Moses are useful for the maintenance of religion.
>
> The ancient Jews and non-Jews believed strongly in Providence of God. The wise man amongst them was one whose acts were done with great care and thoughtfulness. When he was about to undertake something, he considered, not merely the natural consequences that might result, but also that of Providence...
>
> But in our generation, and in that of Maimonides, wisdom no longer includes religion. Even an atheist or non-believer in Providence is called a wise man, and according to some, the only wise man.[36]

Luzzatto's idea of universalism achieved through Adam offers a useful starting point in encountering many contemporary formulations of religion that start with God's plan for creation, while his Abrahamic religion can be fruitfully compared to *Nostra Aetate*. Adam already had the universal ethical demands of religion, while Abraham brought knowledge of God to the world.

Even though the Abrahamic faith of Judaism helped bring knowledge of God to the world, there did and do exist counterforces of atheism, intellectualism, cruelty, and militarism. Luzzatto names these external forces Atticism, the legacy of the skeptical Greeks and militaristic Romans. From Luzzatto's point of view, a movement toward compassion in this world, even the compassionate teachings of Jesus, would be fruitless before the counterforce of Atticism.

> Even though Jesus and his disciples arose and proclaimed God's Torah and the prophets among the nations, all this is of no value. For those nations were unable to strip from themselves the soiled garments, the ways of Greece and Rome. From there have come, and continue to come to this day, the evil ways which dominate in the world and which I call Atticism.[37]

Unlike other Jewish commentators who limit "Love thy neighbor as thyself" (Lev. 19:18) to apply only to fellow Jews, Luzzatto considers it a universal moral principle.[38]

A similar approach to that of Luzzatto was displayed in the midst of a mid-twentieth-century conversation between Ernst Simon and Harold Fisch, both educators in Israel. Whereas Herman Cohen, the liberal theologian, had presented a universal ethic based on philosophy, and then afterward Cohen grounded the ethic in the sources of Judaism, these traditionalist thinkers needed to struggle to find compatible traditional sources that already have the ethic. Ernst Simon argued that whereas earlier authorities were restrictive in their application of "loving one's neighbor" to Jews alone, in the modern era the ethical command should apply to all people. Simon suggested that modern Jews follow R. Yakov Mecklenberg (1785–1865) and Rabbi Meir Loeb Malbim (1809–1879), both of whom treated the divine command to love one's neighbor as a Kantian categorical applicable to all humanity.[39] Fisch responded that rather than seeking modern authorities to give new meaning to the biblical text, noting rabbinic texts about "love of neighbor," we should consider other biblical sources. Fisch states that love (*ahavah*) only applies to Jews, but righteousness (*hesed*, or *caritas* in the Christian tradition) applies to all humanity. Luzzatto himself would have accepted the claims of both Simon and Fisch since he considered both love and charity as universal in applicability.

Luzzatto offers moderns an opportunity to grapple with the moral standards of the Talmudic text even as he accepts the corpus. He is willing to attribute morally repugnant passages to the historical necessity or cultural immorality of their time. Statements in the Talmud that are not ethical should not be regarded as part of the tradition.

> Whatever propositions or story that could be found in the Talmud...which would be in opposition to the sentiments of universal humanity and justice—which are suggested equally by nature and by Sacred Scripture—must be regarded as neither of the dictates of Religion or of Tradition, but as regrettable insinuations of the calamitous circumstances, and of the public and private vexations and cruelties to which the Jews were subjected in the barbaric centuries.[40]

Luzzatto approaches rabbinic texts freely and has no qualms about rejecting immoral passages of the Talmud. In his eyes, even difficult biblical texts need to be interpreted in a charitable way in order to preserve divine universalism. For example, he explains the Deuteronomistic command to destroy the seven nations as a referendum on a disposition to immorality and corrosive influence on the morals of others in those nations, rather than as an intrinsic command.

Mendel Hirsch—universal humanism as message of revelation

Dr. Mendel Hirsch, son of Rabbi Samson Raphael Hirsch, was the principal of Jewish High School (*Bürger- und Realschule*) founded by his father in Frankfurt. His educational principles and curriculum became the model for many Jewish high schools in Europe, Israel, and the United States. Dr. Hirsch wrote the commentary on the prophetic portions of the *Hirsch Biblical Commentary*.

Mendel Hirsch offers to his students a consistent universalist message based on the prophets, similar to the message in his father's early work *The Nineteen Letters*, which relied heavily on the universal biblical prophets. His father, S.R. Hirsch, wrote about universal brotherhood in his early writings.

> The Torah calls Israel a treasured nation. However, this does not imply, as some have mistakenly assumed, that Israel has a monopoly on God's love and favor. On the contrary, it proclaims that God has the sole and exclusive claim to the Jewish people's devotion and service, and that Israel may not worship any other being. Israel's most cherished ideal is that of the universal brotherhood of mankind. Almost every page of our prayers refers to the hastening of this end... All these efforts and accomplishments are the building blocks contributed by the various nations to the common edifice of history; all take part in carrying out the plan of the same One God.[41]

In a similar manner, Mendel Hirsch wrote that all men are created in the image of God and all men are to achieve the highest aims of creation.

> Thus the biblical anthropology, which only knows one ancestor for all races, bestows a two-fold superiority on all men, through their descent from Adam... This also applies to the Divine blessing (Genesis 1:28) pronounced—not upon the Jew but upon man—in the words: "Be fruitful and multiply."
>
> All Jewish proselytism is shown to be inconsistent with the original teaching. The Torah never looks upon men outside the Jewish faith as men doomed to damnation whose only hope of salvation would be their conversion to Judaism. All that is necessary for them is to be pure men, not Jews. By their faithful observance of general human duties they will, as his children, earn their share of the grace of their and our God.[42]

For Dr. Hirsch, there was never any need for conversion to Judaism, since all men can do God's will. Not without a bit of rhetoric, he affirms his commitment to Western culture by proposing the Greeks as stewards of Divine providence. "The ennobling Hellenic art and poetry would appear to serve the higher purpose of Providence."

Mendel Hirsch rejected the perceived tension between secularism and fanaticism, and affirmed instead a religious humanism in which Judaism, when taught correctly, is both the origin of humanist principles and the fullest realization of those principles. Hirsch repeatedly warns his readers of the perils of particularism and exclusivism, opposing them to biblical universalism. He reads verses that seem to imply particularism as simply saying that Israel will lead the way in a prophetic brotherhood of mankind. His biblical commentaries consider the works of Isaiah, Amos, and Micah to contain the heart of the Jewish message.

> The experience of all times has amply shown how easily nations succumb to the danger of looking contemptuously upon everything alien. How great this peril was for a nation deemed worthy of God's direct guidance and raised to a national entity...Thus we can easily understand why it is that the wisdom of the Bible keeps anxiously reminding this people, at each step of its development, that all men are God's children, and that Israel was called upon to lead the way towards the tree of life, or rather to preserve and transmit to men, in the Divine teaching, the fruit of this tree of life.
>
> When, therefore, God speaks of Israel as "my son, my first born," the underlying meaning is that: Through Israel the generating powers of humanity are opened; through Israel the march is started in which all nations shall go forth as "My sons."
>
> But above all, at Sinai, when Israel was to be prepared for the revelation, the conception of all men as subservient to God's purposes was emphasized in particularly clear and precise terms. "Mine is the whole earth" (Ex. 19:5–6)...Yet any misconception with regard to Israel's position is obviated by the emphatic declaration: "All the earth is Mine."
>
> Thus it is Universality, with its broad outlook in the whole of humanity, and the ideal of the loftiness of human destiny which forms the basis as well as the starting point of the Torah in its view of the world.[43]

Even the revelation at Mt. Sinai and the giving of the law was for all mankind, and one should not have the misconception that it was only for Jews.

Universal historical

From the beginning of the age of discovery in the sixteenth century until the 1893 World Parliament of Religions in Chicago, those confronted with the vast differences between the diversity of customs and religions of world peoples needed to make sense of these discoveries. Whereas some explorers saw new peoples as heathen devil worshipers ripe for conversion or annihilation, Judaism conceptualized them with reference to Genesis and its list of many peoples descended from Adam. Judaism envisions a primordial wisdom from Adam scattered through the Fall of Babel and the fanning out of the ancient peoples to the ends of the earth.

Menashe ben Israel, many names

Menashe ben Israel (1604–1657), a rabbi in Holland in the age of discovery, was a member of the "Portuguese" nation in Amsterdam, an acquaintance of Rembrandt, and was widely respected in his time as a Jewish theologian. His works *Nishmat Hayyim* and *The Conciliator* were widely regarded in their day for their amazing erudition and humanism. This same erudition and humanism made Rabbi Menashe ben Israel a model for Western European Jewry from the seventeenth to the nineteenth centuries. His writings present Jews as the chosen people who know God, and he uses this premise to present Judaism in a confident and open way.

Rabbi Menashe sought to reconcile the curse in Jeremiah 10:25—"Pour out thy wrath upon the heathens that know thee not, and upon the families that invoke not thy name"—with the universalism of Malachi 1:11—"Great is thy name among the heathen, and in every place incense is offered to my name, and a pure offering, for great is my name among the heathen, saith the Lord." The verse in Jeremiah suggests that gentiles do not know God, while the verse in Malachi implies the opposite—that all nations know God. Rabbi Menashe gave clear precedence to the verse in Malachi and sees the implication of Jeremiah as limited to immoral heathen practices of antiquity.

Rabbi Menashe proclaims that all nations have knowledge of God. "The knowledge of a First Cause was general to all nations of the earth."[44] To prove his point, he cites Lactantius, Pythagoras, Plato, and Seneca.

Great is my name among the heathen because as shown, they had knowledge of a first cause; "and in every place incense is offered to my name" for they addressed their sacrifices to the Sovereign Lord, the God of gods, with good intentions; yet as will be shown, they were idolaters.[45]

As Marcellius Ficino observes on Plato, that the name of the Lord is written and pronounced by all nations with four letters.[46]

By the Hebrews being dispersed throughout the world, they came to the knowledge of the Divine words, and the prophetical books of the holy Scripture; the people separated themselves from a plurality of Gods, acknowledging the God of Israel, although they could not divest themselves of invoking saints, and the worship of images...the Lord becomes known, for as He sends souls from the celestial to the terrestrial and elemental globe, that they may bring notice of the Divinity and angelic world.[47]

Even their sacrifices are correct once they have a first cause. Jeremiah is when they forget the first cause and become focused on the secondary causes of God. In all the nations of the world there are good and bad, Israel imitated the bad of the heathen, and in zeal did not imitate their good qualities.[48]

According to Rabbi Menashe, all nations worship one God despite differences in language, culture, and name, but not all nations understand the correct attributes of the biblical God, they might not understand His providence, and some nations still hold idolatrous representations and images. Nevertheless, they are all still worshipping the biblical God. Menashe uses the rabbinic statement by Rav—"And all people of the earth shall see that thou art called by the name of the LORD; and they shall be afraid of thee" (Deut. 28:10; Menachot 35b)—to affirm that the ancient peoples of the Mediterranean knew about God. He also acknowledges, without special arguments, that there is moral good and biblical knowledge among the heathens.

Modernity was not the most expansive era for the creation of pluralistic theologies of other religions; the early modern era was remarkably fruitful. Already in the seventeenth century, Judaism could affirm a dignity of all faiths based on the dignity of man, in which a diversity of religions points to a single religion of mankind.

Benamozegh, scattered truth

Rabbi Elijah Benamozegh (1823–1900), a kabbalist and religious leader in nineteenth-century Italy, incorporated the new finding of comparative religion. His work *Israel and Humanity* allows for a universal revelation available to all mankind, and asserts that each religion offers a path to God. The work is an outgrowth of his reply to the conversations he had with Aime Palliere (1875–1949), who wanted to convert to Judaism. Benamozegh argued that there was no need to convert, rather God offered himself to all people and expected them to follow a broadly understood application of the seven Noahite laws as the basis for their practice. Benamozegh not only embraced reading the works of other faiths, but also wanted to bring gentiles, even his Christian contemporaries, back to a true universal monotheism based on the seven Noahite laws.[49]

Benamozegh places Judaism at the heart of the nations, with the nations following the Noahite laws and the Jews following the commandments, yet he continuously refers to God's plan for all humanity and the religions of humanity.

> For Judaism, the world is like a great family, where the father lives in immediate contact with his children, who are the different peoples of the earth. Among these children there is a first-born, who, in conformity with ancient institutions, was the priest of the family, charged with executing the father's orders, and with replacing him in his absence... Such is the Jewish conception of the world. In heaven a single God, father of all humans alike; on earth a family of people, among whom Israel is the "first-born."[50]

In many aspects, Benamozegh continues the inclusive-hierarchy model, which values Jewish monotheism over the Christian Trinity, yet he moves beyond it by seeking to understand Christian thought in Jewish terms. Benamozegh sought to educate Jews to take Christianity with requisite seriousness and respect. All religions are God's children, yet Israel remains the first-born. To explain why he privileges Judaism over Christianity, he rehearses theological reasons why Judaism rejects the Trinity, why the *New Testament* cannot supersede the Sinai revelation, and why Jews accept a progressive revelation in the oral law.

> The idea of the personality of God necessarily implies that of the unity of substance... Christianity, which possesses a trinity of persons while maintaining the unity of God's substance,... might best be called tritheism.[51]
>
> As for those who tell us that Christianity embodies a new revelation, do they not see that if the Christian mysteries were truly a radical innovation, then the entire system of Divine revelation would be overturned?... It could no longer be a question of a unique and perfect Revelation coming, like the material creation, from the sovereign intelligence of God... From the moment that one abandons the notion of a unique revelation—with the intention of combating Judaism—there remains only the hypothesis of multiple religions.
>
> And now we turn to the followers of the two great messianisms, Christian and Moslem. It is to Christians in particular that we wish to address a frank and respectful word, and God knows that it is with fear in our heart lest our advances be taken for hypocrisy. No! No impartial and reasonable man can fail to recognize and appreciate, as is appropriate, the exalted worth of these two great religions, more especially of Christianity. There is no Jew worthy of the name who does not rejoice in the great transformation wrought by them in a world formerly defiled.

We cannot listen to the noblest and most precious names in Judaism, the echoes of its holy books, the recollection of its great events, its hymns and prophecies, in the mouths of so many millions of former pagans of all races, joined together to worship the God of Israel in churches and mosques, without feeling imbued with a legitimate pride of gratitude and love toward the God who effected such great miracles.[52]

Rather than rejecting other faiths, Benamozegh openly compares and contrasts Judaism with Christianity, pagan mysteries, Taoism, and Hinduism. He envisions a single world religion with Judaism at the pinnacle; all religions, he professes, were needed for the progress of mankind.

Benamozegh acknowledges the cultural embeddedness of religion, as well as the idea that there is truth, based on a primitive revelation, in every religion, even if certain conceptions of monotheism and revelation are deficient. He even allows for the influence of these "other children" on the first-born: Israel can learn from the other religions.

A glance at the pagan mysteries will enable us to understand very clearly the influence of paganism upon the educated class in Israel.[53]

Through dispersion among Gentiles, [Judaism] gathers and incorporates the fragments of truth wherever it finds them scattered.

Know that the primitive form of all Revelation, which continues even after the introduction of the Mosaic Law, and which still exists in our day in the heart of the Jewish people, the form which Biblical teachings have long preserved, comes of oral tradition.[54]

Benamozegh, like Yaakov Emden, is able to appreciate the Gospels as part of the Aggadah. Yet he criticized Christianity for failing through "lack of learning" to understand and properly teach "genuine Hebraic" conceptions of God, ethics, and messianism.[55] Benamozegh finds Christianity wanting in monotheism precisely because it has a Trinity, and wanting in revelation because revelation by definition means to be eternal, unique, and not superseded by later revelations.

The reading of certain passages of the Gospels has never left us unresponsive. The simplicity, grandeur, infinite tenderness, which these pages breathe out overwhelms us to the depths of our soul; and we should easily have been won over by the seductiveness of this book if not for a special grace, and if we had not been long familiar with this thrill through the writings of our sages, by the Aggadah above all, of which the Gospel is indeed a chapter.[56]

I hope that Christians will not forget that what speaks in these pages is the Judaism from which Christianity was born; that the interests of the one and of the other are interdependent; and that, finally, it is Christianity, reformed to be sure on its first model [Hebraism], which will always be the religion of the Gentile peoples. And this will come about through Judaism itself. The reconciliation dreamt of by the first Christians as a condition of the Parousia, or final advent of Jesus... will occur, not as it has been expected, but in the only serious, logical, and durable way, and above all in the only way which would be advantageous to the human race. This will be the reconciliation of Hebraism and the religions which were born of it.[57]

Since he was confident in the universal value of religious symbols, Benamozegh was therefore willing to openly discuss the philosophical and religious value of the Trinity, as well as its relationship to the original unity of the Divine. It seems that if he had lived in the twentieth century, Benamozegh could easily have accepted a position treating religious doctrines as symbols for the universal. But living in the nineteenth century, he spoke of fragments of original truth and a perennial religion above its specific manifestations.

Benamozegh notes that Judaism is not nearly so absolute in its monotheism as Jews want to claim. Jewish mystical doctrines depend on belief in divine aspects or emanations. For Benamozegh, the Christian doctrine of the Incarnation is a correctable misapplication, not an idolatrous apostasy. Christianity is based on the Jewish idea of the *shekhinah*, transforming "the divine immanence" into "the conception of a man-god."[58]

The Christian Incarnation is but an imitation of the Hebrew *Shekhinah*, or divine immanence, of the *Malkhut* of the Kabbalah—though with an essential difference. According to Christianity, the descent of God into the finite is accomplished in the bosom of mankind alone, or rather in a single man; but for the Kabbalah, the incarnation exists in and through the very fact of the entire creation, although man occupies the central focus.[59]

The two religions themselves are and will remain sisters... they will know at the proper moment how to join their energies of spirit and intelligence... they will recognized their original kinship, and through an appropriate alliance resume their common work for the accomplishment of their great destinies.[60]

Judaism and Christianity are sisters and need to resolve for common work to accomplish their biblical destinies.

Henry Pereira-Mendes, precious stones

Henry Pereira-Mendes (1862–1937) served as rabbi of New York's traditional Spanish-Portuguese Synagogue. He was the first president of the Union of Orthodox Jewish Congregations of America and a founder of the Jewish Theological Seminary of America in 1887 (it originally met in his Spanish-Portuguese Synagogue). He was also the first professor of Homiletics at Rabbi Isaac Elhanan Theological Seminary in New York.

Mendes attended the 1893 Parliament of Religions in Chicago, an important milestone in the American encounter with other religions, as the representative of traditional Judaism. Rabbi Pereira-Mendes' writings demonstrate his belief in a religious universalism, in which we are all children of the same divine Father, from the creation of Adam and the subsequent division into many religions until the eventual restored unity in the messianic era.

> There is a legend that, when Adam and Eve were turned out of Eden or earthly paradise, an angel smashed the gates, and the fragments flying all over the earth are the precious stones. We can carry the legend further. The precious stones were picked up by the various religions and philosophers of the world. Each claimed and claims that its own fragment alone reflects the light of heaven, forgetting the setting and encrustations which time has added. Patience my brother. In God's own time we shall, all of us, fit our fragments together and reconstruct the gates of paradise. There will be an era of reconciliation of all living faiths and systems, the era of all being in at-one-ment, or atonement, with God. Through the gates shall all people pass to the foot of God's throne.
>
> And Israel, God's first born, who, as his prophets foretold,...shall be but fulfilling his destiny to lead back his brothers to his Father. For that we were chosen; for that we are God's servants or ministers. Yes, the attitude of historical Judaism to the world will be in the future, as in the past—helping mankind with his Bible—until the gates of earthly paradise shall be reconstructed by mankind's joint efforts, and all nations whom Thou, God hast made, shall go through the worship before Thee, O Lord, and shall glorify Thy name![61]

Here we have a traditional thinker who clearly affirms a common core of all religions that over time have became encrusted with historical particulars, thereby leading to the evolution of various faiths. Now, in the modern age, we seek a collective activity of all humanity to return to the original core. In Mendes' terms, the biblical vision of becoming a light unto the nations is part of a joint effort to worship together. The eventual goal is a messianic restoration to Eden. Details are left to a distant eschatological future.

Hertz

Chief Rabbi of England Rabbi Joseph Herman Hertz (1872–1946) was an important rabbinical figure because of his post, his writings, and his political activities, especially his widely used *The Pentateuch and Haftorahs*.

Hertz's approach combines the ethical universalism of the nineteenth century with the rising knowledge of other religions aided by international trade, the study of anthropology, and the history of religions. Hertz echoes the late-nineteenth-century anthropological theories of animism (associated with British anthropologist Sir Edward Burnett Tylor presented in *Primitive Culture*, 1871). For these anthropologists, animism was the most primitive and essential form of religion, yet in hindsight the popular description of animism bore striking similarities to contemporary liberal Protestant thought, which considered religion solely a matter of the heart.

Hertz states that the heathens were not held responsible for a false conception of God and "were judged by God purely by their moral life." This sentiment was shared by many of his contemporaries, including Rabbi Abraham Isaac Kook and Yehezkel Kaufman. Pagan worship serves as a primitive stage of religious belief, which "forms part of God's guidance of humanity." Rabbi Hertz used Malachi 1:11, which states that all nations call to God, as so many did before him.

> Even the heathen nations that worship the heavenly hosts pay tribute to a Supreme Being, and in this way honour My name; and the offerings which they thus present (indirectly) unto Me are animated by a pure spirit, God looking to the heart of the worshipper. This wonderful thought was further developed by the Rabbis, and is characteristic of the universalism of Judaism.[62]

Elsewhere, Hertz used this pure spirit of religion to argue that religion is greater than Christianity, and certainly greater than the internal Christian divisions in England between Angelical Catholic and Methodist. He also offered polemics against Christianity in order to oppose missionaries.

Rabbi Abraham Isaac Kook

It is a sign of Rabbi Kook's breadth and strength as a thinker that despite his strong inclusive position, he at times demonstrates both particularistic and universalistic leanings. Rabbi Kook continues the ethical universalism of the nineteenth century combined with a mystical limitation on attaining truth. In other words, Kook offers ways for a mystical pluralist to transcend finite forms of religion, yet he does not see any need for the encounter with other religions, or any engagement with their particularities. While an inclusivist in discussing the role of Israel amidst the nations, Kook's universalism is about the potentials of the infinite divine known by all. He seeks a universal peace and a harmony of religions, without any need to appreciate the actual diversity of religions.

From Kook's mystical perspective, no one human framework can encompass the Divine. All of our parallel paths are necessary for diversity, and meet in the Infinite. Rabbi Kook does not offer any criteria to aid in distinguishing the good from the bad in the diversity of other paths.

> Since the manner that human thought and feeling connects with the infinite supernal Divine light needs to be in a multiplicity of colors, therefore every nation and society must have a different spiritual way of life.[63]

> The brotherly love of Esau and Jacob, of Isaac and Ishmael will transcend all confusions... The old method of choosing one path to patiently follow can no longer exist or continue. In the beginning of our path, we need to develop and evolve to grasp an integration of the paths to synthesize them into a secure tranquility.[64]

On May 5, 1924, while on a tour of Canada, Rabbi Kook visited Montreal and greeted the dignitaries of the city with a speech that included the following statement: "When all is said and done, the difference of religious belief is only on the surface, the fundamentals being: to do good to all mankind, live up to the teachings of the Bible, and carry out the precepts of the Golden Rule."[65]

Conclusions

The universal positions within Judaism have been considered marginal in most narratives of Jewish identity. As a whole, these religious universalists, with their gaze on the oneness of God, differ sharply from pluralists, who consider all religions as diverse human constructs. Most Jewish universalists affirm that theism, ethics, and revelation can be known naturally. (A discussion of how these positions use rabbinic statements would contribute greatly to developing a theology of other religions.) The important points to note in this chapter are that there are, indeed, medieval universalists; this position did not have to wait until modernity and how much the Enlightenment position of Mendelssohn still has common roots with prior universal thinkers. These positions deserve to enter the discussion as an opening to discuss the role of the universal in Judaism and how the universal differs from the pluralists discussed in the next chapter.

CHAPTER 6

Pluralism

Religious pluralism is a modern philosophic approach that accepts that one's religion is not the sole and exclusive source of truth. On the social level, this approach cherishes difference and diversity. Unlike the universalists who see the possibility for all to come to the same truth, pluralists stress the inadequate nature of any truth. Pluralism sees an impossibility of a universal truth available to all people, suggesting instead that each religion has limited access to truth. They look forward to each religion playing a positive role in the enrichment of the world.

Pluralists are comfortable with viewing religion from a dialogical approach, valuing the mutual enrichment of viewing religious truth in relation to other religions. They stress the need for treating all other faiths with full acceptance of the differences. The Americans among the pluralists, have already imbibed the cultural pluralism inherent in American life, and articulated by Horace Kallen and Mordechai Kaplan. Inbuilt in their pluralism, is a tension between the pluralism of individual choice and need for working within one's particular religious community. In the current era of globalization, they speak of the need for all religions, each in their own manner, to work in their mutuality convergent goals.

Many people, on the popular level, use the term pluralist or the phrase "religious pluralism" as synonyms for any encounter or openness to appreciate other faiths. In this popular definition of pluralism there is a mistaken notion that approaching other religions is an either/or dichotomy of exclusivism or pluralism. If one rejects exclusivism then one must be a pluralist, and universal and inclusivist thinkers are considered precedents for pluralism. Pluralists acknowledge both moral and intellectual truth, but think that the differences between religions are mutually enriching and that one cannot attain an absolute truth outside the human condition. So they refrain from speaking of religious absolutes.

On the hand, some popular supporters of exclusivist thinking fight against anything that could possibly be considered pluralism by regarding all pluralists as relativists. Pluralists actively distinguish themselves from relativists who deny any moral or intellectual truth. Pluralists are firmly committed to theism, ethics, and amelioration of the world. Yet, many of those who reject pluralism take refuge in the opposite extreme of hard perspectivist positions in which one must reject everything except one's own particular perspective.

There are three main types of pluralism, ethical, mystical, and epistemological. There are also two terms that are used often by twenty-first-century pluralists—difference and diversity.

- Pluralism, epistemological—there are limits to human knowledge, therefore, we have to accept reality of the truth of all religions
- Pluralism, ethical—all ethical people are on the right path
- Pluralism, mystical—the encounter with God transcends any human categories
- Difference is the acknowledgment of many different approaches to religion, each to be tolerated and accepted without discrimination
- Diversity is the acknowledgment that the many different approaches to religion are each valuable and desired for the diversity of human life

Many of the Jewish thinkers discussed in this chapter did not start as pluralists, and thus, their presentations include narratives of how they came to adopt this position. Furthermore, most of the thinkers still have inclusivist elements and the authors can still point to these elements to show the traditionalism of their pluralism. This chapter will discuss the thought of David Hartman who started as a universalist and developed different forms of pluralism. Raphael Jospe offers an ethical pluralist viewpoint. Zalman Schachter-Shalomi represents the mystical pluralist example. Irving (Yitz) Greenberg seeking an acceptance of diversity shows how all faiths may each contribute to human dignity. Elliot Dorff embodies a philosophic pluralist who denies the viability of metaphysical truth claims and Michael Kogan offers a Jewish version of the general philosophic pluralist position. Jonathan Sacks seeks to defend differences in a world of absolutes with nods to moral and epistemological pluralism.

David Hartman: From Universalism to Penultimate Things to Pluralism

David Hartman (1931–), a contemporary rabbi and theologian, established the important Shalom Hartman Institute in Israel where he and his disciples continue to work out modern Jewish theological positions on liberalism and pluralism, sometimes beyond the intellectual limits of his initial Orthodox training and community.

In his early work from 1976, entitled "On the Possibility of Religious Pluralism from a Jewish Point of View," written when he was still under the influence of his teacher Rabbi J.B. Soloveitchik, Hartman postulates that the Bible has two covenants—that of creation and that of Sinai. The creation covenant encompasses all of humanity; it is universal and for all generations. The Sinai covenant, on the other hand, deals only with the people Israel. Hartman's early essay echoes the inclusive humanism of Seforno and especially some of the universalistic passages of Soloveitchik's *Lonely Man of Faith*.[1]

In a later work written in 1985, *Conflicting Visions*, Hartman stresses that revelation in history is always fragmentary and incomplete since the divine–human encounter cannot exhaust God's plenitude. Hartman thinks that theology starts with the human, the penultimate, rather than ultimate truth of the divine.

> Revelation expresses God's willingness to meet human beings in their finitude, in their particular historical and social situation, and to speak to them in their own language. All of these constraints prevent one from universalizing the significance of the revelation...Revelation...was not meant to be a source of absolute, eternal, transcendent truth. Rather, it is God's speaking to human beings within the limited framework of human language and history.[2]

Revelation, for Hartman, is about a specific community building a relationship with God. It is "not meant to be a source of absolute, eternal, and transcendent truth," but is rather "an expression of God's love."[3] Unlike the universal availability of Divine knowledge presented by the medieval universalists, Hartman moves to a pluralistic position in which humanity consists of separate religions, each creating their own "historic understanding of the Divine revelation." Now, "historic understanding of the divine" becomes a metaphor for the historic narrative of a specific people. For Hartman, creation is a universal language, but human participation in a particular history is revelation. David Hartman considers Judaism's tradition as the particularities of Jewish history, rabbinic texts, and their interpretation.

Hartman's position seems similar to the universalism of Fayumi in that he believes that God speaks to all nations within their own histories. But here, revelation no longer offers a solid universal religion, rather a means toward a new awareness of or encounter with transcendent meaning.

In this later period, truth claims and the otherness of Sinai have been removed from revelation. Pluralism is needed for human dignity as well as for

appreciating the diversity and complexity of life.[4] Hartman put away hopes
for resolution at the end of days; rather he focuses only on the here and now.
"We cannot in some way leap to some eschaton and live in two dimensions; to
be pluralistic now but monistic in our eschatological vision is bad faith."[5]

> Soloveitchik, claims in his article, "Confrontation" that one can only
> find room for religious tolerance only in the unredeemed present, while
> continuing to believe in eschatological monism. He asserts that it is the
> essence of a faith community's commitment to God... The approach
> to religious pluralism that I shall adopt... is... that acknowledging the
> existence of other faiths in their own right need not be a violation of the
> covenantal faith commitment, but rather the very presence of a digni-
> fied other can create within the Judaic spiritual life an enchantment of
> our consciousness.[6]
>
> Because Buddhism, Hinduism, Christianity, Islam, and Judaism are
> distinct paths, they bear witness to the complexity and fullness of the
> Divine reality. The lack of unity within Christianity and Judaism testifies
> to the radical diversity within human consciousness and to the rich mosaic
> of views and practices inspired by the quest for God in human history.
>
> Does this mean that all humankind must embrace the Jew's history or
> recognize its superiority? No. The knowledge of God that will fill the
> earth on "that day" will be the knowledge derived from "creation" over
> and above "revelation"... The distinction between creation and history
> enables biblical faith to admit the possibility of religious pluralism without
> neutralizing its passionate commitment to the Biblical Lord of History.[7]

Hartman's thought contains a dual ethic—not gentiles and Jews, but a universal experience of the reality of creation that includes Jews and gentile and
the particulars of a given faith commitment. He retains an emphasis on the
historical particularism of Judaism, but his concern with the historical events
of Judaism does not place itself in opposition to other stories. Not only does
it refrain from negative stories about others, it completely avoids all oppositional elements.

Hartman is not sure about any truth claim or the certainty of any path. The
only reason for the Jewish position is because it is rooted in the Jewish story.

> When revelation is understood as the concretization of the universal,
> then "*whose* truth is *the* truth?" becomes the paramount religious ques-
> tions, and pluralism becomes a vacuous religious ideal. If, however,
> revelation can be separated from the claim of universality, and if a com-
> munity of faith can regain an appreciation of the particularity of the

divine-human encounter, then pluralism can become a meaningful part of Biblical faith experiences... "The Jew, the Christian, and the Muslim are all one, insofar as they are creatures of God."[8]

He speaks in the specific covenant language of Soloveitchik, but imparts the universal meaning of the mid-twentieth-century liberal theology that all religions seek ultimate concern. According to Hartman's approach, all humans are under God and encounter God as children of Adam. The Mosaic dimensions are only the particular historical story of the Jewish people.

Hartman's formulation of his ideas was influenced by Paul Van Buren (d. 1998), the Episcopalian radical theologian who considered all religious statements as metaphors for the human experience. Van Buren developed his own theology of Jewish-Christian reconciliation as a fellow of the Shalom Hartman Institute.

Another motivation for this new pluralism is the current religious extremism of those preaching an absolute truth in the Middle East. Hartman, in an important interview with the *New York Times* correspondent Thomas Friedman, connects pluralism with the avoidance of totalitarianism. "The opposite of religious totalitarianism is an ideology of pluralism—an ideology that embraces religious diversity and the idea that my faith can be nurtured without claiming exclusive truth."[9] Offering an ecumenical theism, Hartman offers the quotable aphorism that "God speaks Arabic on Fridays, Hebrew on Saturdays, and Latin on Sundays."

Jospe: An Ethical Pluralism

Raphael Jospe, a Haifa University professor, developed an ethical pluralism consisting of a universal ethic independent from revelation combined with a pluralism based on the multiplicity of human subjectivity. Jospe's importance is the ability to be similar to many of the non-Jewish liberal theologians in combining a universal ethic with pluralism, while remaining with a traditional textual approach.

Jospe, inspired by the 1970s writings of Catholic theologian Hans Kung, asserts that there must be a universal ethic since anything else is triumphalistic and involves making moral judgments upon others. Jospe's paradigm, Hans Kung wrote: "It is a very hopeful sign for us to discover that despite the profound differences we have in these religions, the ethical standards are basically the same."

Jospe accepts the medieval universalism of Sa'adiah and Nathaniel ibn Fayumi, and Mendelssohn's universal tolerance; in turn, Jospe binds his universalism together with the philosophic pluralism of no single truth. He relies

on the contemporary Bar Ilan professor Avi Sagi who wrote that the pluralism of Torah is inherently based on human culture and therefore an inexact
knowledge; religion never consists of fixed doctrines or truth claims. Jospe
accepts from Sagi a "strong pluralism," which "does not affirm only a temporary value of opposing views leading to ultimate truth, but regards different
views as having inherent value of their own."

Jospe also formulates a Judaism that is pluralistic in nature with an internal
pluralism of multiple interpretations within Judaism and an external pluralism
of the availability of Torah outside Judaism in seventy different languages.

> The opponents of pluralism fail to take into account the subjective
> nature of faith and religious experience. The difference between faith
> and knowledge lies unproven and unprovable, it is inherently subjective,
> not objective, and culturally relative.
>
> As for Jewish precedents, there is ample evidence for both internal
> and external pluralism in the sources. For example, we find both inter-
> nal...pluralism supported by rabbinic interpretation of Jeremiah 23:29,
> "Is not my word like fire, says the Lord, and like a hammer smashing a
> rock?" In his commentary to Genesis 33:20 and Exodus 6:9, Rashi cites
> this verse to justify diverse, internal pluralistic interpretations, like the
> sparks set off by the hammer smashing the rock into pieces...
>
> The Talmud (Shabbat 88b) also records Rabbi Yishma'el interpret-
> ing our verse in support of external pluralism, that "as this hammer is
> divided into sparks, so was every single commandment that God spoke
> divided into seventy languages."
>
> Such pluralism...does not imply a strong relativistic conception of
> multiple truths, but of multiple perspectives on the truth, or what the
> rabbis called the "seventy facets of the Torah" (*shiv`im panim la-torah*). I
> think it is not coincidental that the "seventy facets" of the Torah's inter-
> nal pluralism are identical in number to the "seventy languages" of its
> external pluralism.[10]

Mystical Pluralism: Zalman Schachter-Shalomi

Rabbi Zalman Schachter-Shalomi (b. 1924, generally called Reb Zalman),
one of the founders and continuing inspiration of the Jewish renewal movement, offers a unique approach to the mystical pluralist position that cap-
tures many elements of a specific Jewish narrative. With an energetic 1960s
counterculture sensibility he speaks of cybernetics and transpersonal psychol-
ogy and fostered the creation of do-it-yourself multicolored ritual objects.

Many mystical pluralists, including Reb Zalman, started their journey with an encounter with the East or confronting the evolutionary spirit from thinkers such as Teilhard de Chardin (1881–1955, Catholic mystic and paleontologist). Reb Zalman starts with his personal autobiographic perception of a closed and scared post-Holocaust Jewry that needs a renewal to be open and embracing of the wider world through a mystical Judaism. The contemporary age requires a paradigm shift from Judaism to holistic organic thinking, which includes responsibility for the earth, egalitarianism, intuition over intellect, and embracing other religions. His discovery of the spirituality of Trappist monks and Hindu saints led him to want to recreate a Jewish return to Qumran or a new monastery order.

Reb Zalman seeks a theology that flows from actual practice. Famous for his long journey in which he imbibed and experienced many of the world's religious traditions, he advocates learning experiences and practices from other religions.

There are few conversations in this universe as deeply satisfying to the heart as the dialogue of the devout. Unfortunately, such dialogue took place mostly among the people of each religion separately. If this profound sharing were to take place between *tzaddi*k, saint, and dervish, monk, murid, and *hasid*, we would have a model of what one of the highest forms of conversation could be. One of the prime topics of that discourse would be counsel that would help the spirit gain the service of the flesh for the sake of the divine. This dialogue is a sharing of how best to surrender and conform to the divine will, how to receive divine wisdom for our guidance, how to read scripture for the sake of the spirit, how to emulate—imitate—divine attributes. The counsel gained in such dialogue helps the worshiper to worship, the meditator to meditate, the adorer to adore, and the virtuous one who wished to become a devotee to become a virtuoso of devoutness, a saint.[11]

to learn something

Saints to talk to one another

Reb Zalman admires the quest for the philosophia perennis sought by Huston Smith, Frithjof Schuon , and René Guénon, yet feels that in our contemporary world esoteric knowledge from books has become well known and cliché. It is not important to just read about the oneness of reality. Reb Zalman thinks that the direct relationship to God is what counts. He wants to know the spiritual masters who directly experience religion, not the institutional leaders to speak for what is true.

In our new age, Reb Zalman advocates a paradigm shift, in which we accept the truth of all religions as part of the organic whole of the diversity of the world, the same way we accept diversity in the natural realm. "Most religions have claimed triumphalism, that when the final end will come, we'll show we were right and they were wrong. We are in a post-triumphalist situation as we speak of Gaia and of all religions being vital organs of the planet." Using the Halevi metaphor of the heart of the body in a new way, each religion has something else to contribute to the holism of the earth. "I think that there are some issues on which we all need to declare our debt to each other." Reb Zalman applied the Hasidic concept of seeing everything that occurs to a person as an act of Divine providence to embrace the diversity of the world's religions.

> If there is such a thing as divine providence and you believe in it, you have to ask, "what was happening when Jesus was born?" Was God saying, 'Oops, I forgot to look!' Did Jesus and the Buddha somehow happen outside of God's providence?... You have to believe that all we find n the religious world... [was] God making certain that every nation has access to the Divine in the forms that fit the ethnic and environmental ways of that people.[12]

All religions should learn from the other religions. He is ready to teach Torah and *davening* to the world. At this point, traditionalists of all faiths would find his thought bordering on syncretism.

Reb Zalman considers all religious truth as lost and fallen after being driven out from the Garden of Eden. We all seek to get back to the original religious unity, for a brief glimpse in a peak experience that yields only fleeting illuminations, hardly a fixed doctrine. These glimmering from the Garden of Eden and the mystics of the traditions sustain religions. The dogmatists and lawyers of religions, however, turn ecstatic experiential statements into lapidary statements. Faith and experience are the way to cut through the institution doctrine and creeds.

> What this calls for is a willingness to admit that all our formulations about God are nothing but tentative stammerings of blind and exiled children of Eve responding to the light deeply hidden in the recesses of their nostalgic longing for the untainted origin in which one needed not to look through the glass darkly but could see. This can even make us proud of our traditions and heritage as the storehouse of those stammering of the souls that were filled by God with the grace of that holy moment that defied definition and that was forced by ecclesiastical lawyers to be encapsulated in a stateable wording. The mistake that was made was to take the ecstatic exclamations of the overwhelmed souls and to make them numbered articles of creeds instead of acts of faith made in fear and trembling.

It is indeed difficult to say that...that the Torah and all its commentaries—are *deo gratias* what we do have and treasure, but only as the human snapshots of moments of God's nearness; that, although we cannot improve on the divine that flows into our vessels, we can and must take responsibility for keeping these vessels clean and transparent and not at all as essential as the light they contain. Perhaps we are as dogmatists small souls of small faith who do not dare trust that God will be with us as God was with our forebears and that God will not abandon us nor forsake us.

It then behooves the poor of the spirit of all creeds and denominations to support each other in the desperate acts of faith that we make in the face of the exile and the holocausts and enter into a dialogue among fellow servants and children of one Creator.[13]

Rabbi Yitz Greenberg

Rabbi Irving (Yitz) Greenberg (b. 1933) was a congregational rabbi and professor of Jewish studies, then founder and president of CLAL (the National Jewish Center for Learning and Leadership), and finally president of the Jewish Life Network. Greenberg was instrumental in many aspects of Holocaust education and Jewish-Christian dialogue over the last half century. A full presentation of Greenberg's theories of modernity and autonomy are beyond the scope of this book. I will limit my remarks to those that pertain to his covenantal theory of Jewish-Christian dialogue.

Greenberg started his intellectual journey with post-Holocaust anger at Christianity and concludes with respect toward the great post-Holocaust contrition he saw in Christians and Christianity. For Greenberg, the Holocaust was a fall of the humanism of Western civilization and Christianity—therefore, we need for religion to respond to this fall by restoring the image of God, in which each religion seeks to fulfill the biblical covenant of making the world a better place through human action. After the Holocaust, religion must be autonomous and affirming of human dignity, a voluntary existential covenant.

One of Greenberg's starts for his formulation of a voluntary existential covenant was Soloveitchik's in his *Lonely Man of Faith*. Soloveitchik, in line with other thinkers of the 1950s such as Niebuhr, describes the faith community of God as moving beyond universal dignity to accept greater majesty and glory. Soloveitchik wrote: "The element of togetherness of God and man is indispensable for the covenantal community...the paradoxical experience of freedom, reciprocity, and 'equality' in one's personal confrontation with God is basic for the understanding of the covenantal faith community."[14] Rabbi Yitz

Greenberg developed this passage by stressing the aforementioned elements of freedom, reciprocity, and autonomy, and calls the individual goal we are striving to achieve "perfection," with halakhah being the path that will lead us to that goal and covenant being the force that binds us to the path. We are to take personal responsibility, rather than assuming God or some other person will perform the great human task and responsibility that lies ahead of us. We struggle to existentially define our ever-changing relationship with God.

Greenberg generally follows Soloveitchik's *Lonely Man of Faith* where Soloveitchik defines religion as an existential commitment, over the latter's essay *Confrontation* But Greenberg, who interprets the concept of covenant as a personal existentialist decision (following Paul Ramsey and James Gustafson), views covenant as personal in which no one can possess absolute truth. Therefore, we must acknowledge the truth claims of other religions and their very human attempts to seek truth. Greenberg writes:

> Now the presentation of the worlds/faith/truth beyond makes one aware of the limits of one's own position. One comes to recognize that one's own faith occupies an important point or sector along a continuum, but it does note extend over the whole length of the continuum. On a continuum from zero to 100, perhaps my truth extends from 40 to 75; however, before and after it, there are points on the continuum of the very same idea that are left for others to occupy.[15]

Different people each possess some of the truth on a continuum, each with a partial truth but not an erroneous truth. Therefore, we should embrace a living pluralism in which "Each faith must wrestle with humanity to draw closer to God and each other, to recognize the image of God in the other and respond lovingly on a greater scale than ever before."[16]

Greenberg distinguishes among pluralism, absolutism, and relativism. Absolutism is the belief that you possess the truth, the whole truth, and nothing but—an attitude that leads, he says, to degrading and scorning others; in the end, as Jews know well, it leads to murder. Relativism, its opposite, surrenders all claims to truth, assigning equal weight to opposing views. Pluralism, the synthesis that reconciles the two, is an acknowledgment that other religious paths and viewpoints are valid and worthy of respect even while one maintains a firm commitment to one's own path.[17]

In addition to this pluralistic approach, Greenberg makes use of many of the inclusivist themes of R. Yaakov Emden and R. Israel Lipschutz of seeing the moral activities of the gentiles as fulfilling the Jewish moral responsibility. For Greenberg, "Judaism and its offspring brought a powerful message to humanity about God's concern and our responsibility. Blessed are all those who come in the name of Israel even Christians. God's love is not limited to a single group but extends to all humans." Following earlier traditional Jewish thinkers, Greenberg considers the Trinity, from a Jewish perspective, as a departure from pure monotheism. Yet, following Emden, he considers that Christianity is still a monotheistic religion.

Highly noteworthy is Greenberg's innovative development of Yaakov Emden's acceptance of Jesus as a moral teacher (see chapter four). For Greenberg, we can see the teachings of Jesus as similar to the moral teachings of the rabbis. Jesus' messianism was part and parcel of late Second Temple Jewish messianic doctrines. Jesus could therefore be considered a "failed messiah" of Jewish beliefs rather than a false messiah, foreign to Jewish beliefs. "Jesus taught the right values; Jesus tried to bring the righteous kingdom. That's a much more respectful title than 'false messiah.'" Rather than emphasize the Jewish rejection of Christianity and use words like "false," Jesus' own Jewish contemporaries would have recognized his teaching and could have seen him as "failed messiah." He explains incarnation as an ethical teaching that humans can't do alone; they need a leader, a mediator, a role model.

The core of Greenberg's vision is a formulation of the Jewish covenantal message as consisting of three aspects or stories as he calls them, and they are shared by Christianity. The first aspect is that the world has Divine purpose, which is creation; the second is that there is a Divine human partnership, which is covenant; and the third is that human perfection will eventually be achieved, which is redemption.[18] The first two aspects are universalist and the third is an inclusivist perspective. "The covenant is nothing less than God's promise that the goal is worthy and will be realized." The Jewish teaching of covenant guarantees that man is given responsibility for making the world a better place and that it will not be done by divine fiat.

To accomplish equating ethical universalism, redemptive inclusivism, and his aforementioned theological pluralism, as shared by Jews and Christians, he allegorizes Christian doctrine such as the incarnation into a theory of Jewish social activity (*tikkun olam*), part of the universal drive for creation, partnership, and redemption. Greenberg does not entertain a high Christology, an actual divinity to Jesus; he treats him solely as a moral teacher. For example:

> We can say firmly and respectfully, that the logic behind incarnation and God becoming flesh is the shared value system: Both religions believe that life will win out over death—resurrection is the climax of that process—because it's God's will that the world will be made perfect, and that this will be accomplished by a partnership, a covenant between God and humanity, which expresses itself in many religions and many covenants, including Judaism and Christianity.

Dividing points such as the divinity of Jesus, incarnation, and resurrection are treated as "signals" that Jews should not rule out automatically as the form that God communicates to gentiles. He considers Christianity as its own independent set of symbols not broadcast to Jews. This broad definition allows him at many points to proclaim a positive divine mission for Christians as based on Jewish ethics, while a noble appreciation of the other, the reduction of Christianity to a symbol or "signal" of covenant and redemption, lacks the textual strength to allow the real discussion of theology to begin.

Greenberg rejects that the messiah came already by morally arguing that we do not live in a redeemed world. "When people are living on a dollar a day, when women are still being raped in war or sold for sexual use, it's not a redeemed world." For Greenberg, the ground of religion itself is a messianic drive toward the perfection of social relationships and human relations. Theistic and non-theistic traditions alike are motivated by the same longing and commitment. Greenberg writes, "I believe that world religions such as Islam and noncovenantal faiths such as Buddhism and forms of Hinduism should be recognized as movements legitimately striving to fulfill the universal divine covenant with humanity.[19]

In many complementary ways, he asks his listeners to give up triumphalism and to stop using negative images of the other. Hatred needs to be removed and replaced with love toward the world. Like other pluralists, he is terrified about absolutes. "[T]he deepest truth is that unless we hold on to our absolutes in pluralist fashion they turn pathological and tend to destroy others." For some, Greenberg's approach has already relinquished too much of Judaism's truth claims.[20]

Elliott Dorff: Epistemological Pluralism

Rabbi Eliott N. Dorff is rector of the American Jewish University in Los Angeles, and a long-time member of Conservative Judaism's Committee on Jewish Law and Standards. His position proudly presents an epistemological pluralism in which religion is based on the diversity of human experience.

Dorff's conception of Judaism plays a major role in his pluralistic approach to other religions, in that, he stresses that a contemporary conception of religion, especially Judaism, is its personal nature. Dorff writes that Yehudah "Halevi's trust in God's revelation and His actions in history is difficult for contemporary Jews to accept." Yet Dorff seeks to continue the spirit of Halevi, who rejected a philosophical Judaism for a personal and historical one. So too, today we need to take account of the personal and historical aspects of Judaism.[21] According to Dorff, liberal Jews today identity with Judaism for non-theological reasons; they find revelation difficult due to historical criticism, and faith difficult after the Holocaust. Jews today find God through human experience, specifically through action, study, and prayer.[22]

Based on this commitment to personal experience, Dorff is firmly committed to pluralism in all varieties; he accepts an epistemological pluralism due to limits on individual knowledge, an intellectual pluralism since all is based on personal experience, and a moral pluralism based on one's perspective. Dorff asks, "How do Jews understand the truth-status of other religions?" He answers that there are historical, philosophical, and theological grounds for pluralism. Historical grounds for pluralism exist because "religions have changed and continue to change. Today's certainties, even within the boundaries of one's own faith, are not necessarily tomorrow's convictions."[23] The philosophical basis for pluralism rests on the premise that all people have limitations on knowledge and therefore truth claims only lead to "vacuous and inconclusive debates." In reality, our "truths" are based on our personal faith, family, and people. Theologically, Dorff develops an ethical pluralism of individuality from rabbinic texts, which point out that "no human being looks exactly like another" and that all human faces and thoughts are distinct, from which he concludes:

> God...wants pluralism not only to demonstrate his grandeur in creating humanity with diversity, but also to force human beings to realize their epistemological creatureliness, the limits of human knowledge in comparison to that of God. From the standpoint of piety, pluralism emerges not from relativism, but from a deeply held and aptly humble monotheism.

Dorff acknowledges that "traditional sources assign non-Jewish views to a clearly secondary status," and rabbinic tradition does not offer "a validation of other's views" than their own. His remedy is to extend the Jewish sources that discuss pluralism within Judaism to apply to other religions, thereby creating a rabbinic pluralistic attitude toward religions other than Judaism.

Michael S. Kogan

The pluralist position of many academic Christians is to start with our universal quest for transcendence or the universal phenomena of religion, not the doctrine or experience of a given religion. Then, and only then, after accepting a pluralism of positions do they state that since we have so much in common, then every religion, one's own religion, is just one of the many plural paths to God.

Michael S. Kogan, a contemporary Jewish academic, gives his Jewish readers a Jewish version of the classic pluralist approach. Kogan's vision has two parts: (1) that Judaism and Christianity are similar, and related, in their teachings; (2) that pluralism is the approach Jews should take to all religions. Kogan is exceptionally clear in stating his position, so it is easiest to use many of his own words to present his pluralism. He examines the texts of Judaism and finds the verse "In you shall all the peoples of the world be blessed" (Gen., 12:3) as grounds for reaching beyond Judaism into the larger world. Thus God's initial commission to Abram calls for Jewish self-transcendence. Judaism cannot be itself without this moving beyond itself to be a blessing to the world. Where Judaism transcends itself, there is Christianity.

The stories of Judaism and Christianity, for Kogan, "are so closely related that they represent two ways of expressing parallel redemptive concerns." The two faiths share commonality in Bible, liturgy, ethics, and rhythms of daily life. Christianity as a continuity of the biblical message is but "one form of Jewish outreach into the world." Through Jesus' "outreach, the gentiles come to share in the covenant, and in the messianic, redemptive life of the people of God." Christianity is also the fruit of new divine initiate and revelation to open the covenant to the world. Jews need therefore to accept Christianity as part of the Jewish tradition and that Christians share in the promises of the Hebrew Bible.[24]

If one realizes that the two faith are so closely related, Kogan asks the logical question:

How far can Jews and Christians go in affirming the faith of the other?...What we must be willing to do is to reevaluate our negative convictions. In altering our views of the other we recognize that both Judaism and Christianity have crucial roles to play in sacred history...Several church statements have affirmed that while Christianity needs Judaism for its self-understanding, Judaism can fully define itself without reference to Christianity. Not true! Since Christianity has been a conveyer of the word of Israel's God to the nations, it is impossible for Jews to understand their role as inheritors of the commission to Abraham while blinding themselves to the work among the nations of the Church that shares that commission and that inheritance.[25]

Kogan boldly thinks that Judaism cannot be fully understood without taking Christianity into account. In this advocacy of mutual understanding, he is bolder than both Jewish and Christian thinkers such as Yitz Greenberg who affirm a double covenant of separate paths, elucidating and maintaining the differences between the faiths. Kogan, in contrast, uses the Lutheran historical theologian Sigmund Mowinkel (1894–1965) to show a strong continuity between the message of the Hebrew Bible and that of Jesus—in that both messages center on "the Kingdom of God" as a central proclamation. Torah and Christ are just two different readings of the Bible and we should study together and have "mutual learning."[26]

Kogan correctly notes how far he has come by stating that: "for Jews, a new understanding of Christians and Christianity will take them entirely beyond the parameters of their rabbinic faith and biblical sources out of which it grew. Jews never encounter the term 'Christianity' in their biblical or rabbinic studies," and these texts cannot be used to understand the present. But they can help if we are willing to interpret classic texts anew in the light of the contemporary situation. Modern Jews have to develop a living and dynamic approach to interfaith theology and start by asking questions afresh. Kogan credits the great strides made in the past by Menachem Meiri, Moses Mendelssohn, Eliyahu Benamozegh, Martin Buber, Franz Rosenzweig, and the work of Vatican II, and with bequeathing to us the continuing mandate to make great strides in the future toward dialogue and acceptance.[27]

Kogan's second point is that the human reality is greater than either of our religions or interpretations; therefore "we cannot assume that we posses all truth." He rejects the approach that all religion is just human symbols, without a calling by God. Rather he follows Paul Knitter, the pluralistic theologian, who thinks that "religions are not human paths to God, but divine revelations to human beings...God sends different revelations to different people at different points in history." Kogan seeks to follow the fragile religion of the poet Lord Alfred Tennyson, and therefore Kogan declares that "Revelation is the breaking of the infinite into the finite." Hence, we need to grasp the echo of the infinite voice within our finite religions, the divine initiative not systems or dogma.[28]

Kogan concludes from his study of religious pluralism that it requires not just mutual respect but ongoing mutual influence. A pluralistic theory of multiple revelations means we need to learn from one another and share our limited insights to gain a fuller understanding of the infinite God. "If we Jews, with at most 15 million people, insist that we are the only bearers of truth, not only are we narrow and egocentric, we are indulging in a kind of theological madness." Therefore, Kogan advocates "a plurality of pluralities" from within one's own Jewish tradition. "Each group's theology must recognize and make room for the theologies of others."[29] In order to make this mutual influence work, Kogan thinks that there must be a universal ethic to judge the good from the bad within religion and to avoid religion's ability to unleash the demonic.

Kogan praises the document *Dabru Emet*, the 2001 attempt at a Jewish statement of Christianity, for being the first Jewish statement to acknowledge that Christianity is the result of a genuine revelation of God. Most illuminating, however, to Kogan's fundamental commitment to pluralism is that he faults the document for only stating that Jews and Christians have a common God, a common Bible, and a common ethos rather than stating that the two faiths are mutually intertwined and related. They should have stated that Jews need Christianity for a full self-understanding. He also faults the documents for not accepting the pluralistic turn in which there is a plurality of revelations, each religion a divine path to God.[30]

Rabbi Jonathan Sacks

Rabbi Sir Jonathan Sacks (b. 1948), chief rabbi of the United Kingdom, is recognized for his wide role as a spokesman and ambassador for the global Jewish community. According to Sacks, religious communities "have emerged in the twenty-first century as key forces in a global age." Therefore, for Sacks, "if religion is not part of the solution, it will certainly be part of the problem." Religion in his view currently exacerbates violent clashes; therefore, religions need to address the economic, social, and political issues of the times and give moral direction. He has personally expressed moral anguish over the situation in Israel, in which extremism prevails on both sides.

Extremists belong to the very monotheistic tradition that Jews, Christians, and Muslims—who have spent so much of their history in mutual hostility—share. Therefore, "each of us who belongs to a faith must wrestle with the sources of extremism within our own faith." For him, the task of interfaith work is to help stem moral absolutes on all sides, including Judaism and yet, to still maintain a strong moral community based on the diversity of religions.

Sacks' fundamental axiom is that God offers a core of human dignity in human difference, since we are all formed in His image. Sacks takes it for granted that the pious of all nations are under the one universal God, exemplar are the biblical figures Melchizedek and Jethro, whom the Bible acknowledges as worshiping the true God.

Accepting that God is over all humanity means that God has a relationship with all people, without creating a moral absolute of our own religion.[31]

Judaism is a particularist monotheism. It believes in one God but not in one religion, one culture, one truth. The God of Abraham is the God of all mankind, but the faith of Abraham is not the faith of all mankind.

There is a difference between God and religion. God is universal, religions are particular.

Because we know what it is to be a parent, loving our children, not children in general, we understand what it is for someone else, somewhere else, to be a parent, loving his or her children, not ours.[32]

God is over mankind as a whole not as an undifferentiated universalism, rather in the particularism of given religions. Similar to the particularism of the family, in which I know that my love for my family does not negate the love that others have for their families. My love for Judaism does not negate the love others have for their religions.

Sacks portrays Plato (and his medieval followers) as the source of absolute ideas and intolerance for differences between opinions. For Sacks, the opposite of absolute is not relative but the acceptance of difference and the honoring of particularity. If we cherish our own faith, Sacks concludes, "then we will understand the value of others... True tolerance comes not from an absence of faith but from its living presence. In a globalized world exclusive truth is dysfunctional." Like Hartman, the danger of fanaticism drives him to reject any form of absolute truth. "Truth on earth is not, nor can it aspire to be, the whole truth. It is limited, not comprehensive; particular, not universal."[33] Religious moderation flows, according to Sacks, "directly from the proposition that it was not we who created God in our image but God who made us in His."

To provide a theory of the limited nature of truth and the need for pluralism in an age of globalization, Sacks turns to the story of the fall of the tower of Babel. After the fall when every nation has its own language, there are now languages in the plural, without any absolute truth. Sacks leaps forward and concludes that after the fall of Babel absolute revelations and universal truths cannot be expressed anymore. The message of the Babel story was to convey postmodern limits on knowledge and to reject universals. It is worth noting that the widely read pluralist Raimon Panikkar relies on the same metaphor of the tower of Babel to advocate a similar pluralistic rejection of any one religion.[34]

Pluralism, for Sacks, is not a secular doctrine, rather "the celebration of diversity at the very heart of the monotheistic imagination." He offers a theocentric pluralism in which each religion has its own dignity and approach to God without needing to connect to Judaism or the Jewish people.[35] This celebration of diversity, in which each religion helps make the world a better place, creates a sophisticated form of ethical pluralism. In addition, Sacks also offers an ethical pluralism based on the economics of globalization. He cites Thomas Freidman's McDonald's theory of peace—that no two countries having McDonalds ever fought with each other; a unity of Western global capitalism as creating peace.

Nathaniel ibn Fayumi wrote that "God sends a prophet to every people according to their own language." Sacks became embroiled in controversy for, what appeared to his readers as, stating a similar sentiment in the first edition of his work *The Dignity of Difference* (2002). He writes, "In the course of history, God has spoken to mankind in many languages: through Judaism to

Jews, Christianity to Christians, Islam to Muslims." He was forced to clarify the statement in order to temper its potential to allow a pluralistic offering of God's revelation to all people, making a distinction between special and general revelation, or, in his words, between a single divine covenant and natural religion. "As Jews we believe that God has made a covenant with a singular people, but that does not exclude the possibility of other peoples, cultures, and faiths finding their own relationship with God within the shared frame of Noahite law."[36] In the reformulated version, it is clear that it does not mean their own revelation and that the values are those of the Noahite laws.

In addition, another change between the editions is that in the first edition of his book, Sacks states, "The truth at the beating heart of monotheism is that God is greater than religion; he is only partially comprehended by any faith. He is my God, but also your God." Later, Sacks changed the statement to "The truth at the beating heart of monotheism is that God transcends the particularities of culture and the limits of human understanding. He is my God but also the God of all mankind."[37] It was safer, for Sacks, to state that God transcends any culture and human understanding than to have God transcend any religion, which would limit the truth of any one religion. These changes may, or may not, reflect his original intention; nevertheless, they change the meaning of the book.

Sacks' original version of pluralism was quite similar to Hartman's pluralism. Rt. Rev. Richard Harries, the bishop of Oxford, commented on the changes made to the second edition of Sacks' book by noting that: "now if there is not a multiplicity of revelations, then people find their way to God and peaceful co-existence solely through ethics and not the teachings of their religions." If so, then Harris concludes that Sacks revisions no longer give religions any role in the world, since there is a difference between recognizing individual gentile morality and recognizing other religions.[38]

Living in fear to keep his book acceptable to the Kedassia Orthodoxy of England, it was to Sacks' advantage that his right wing critics only understood the religious quotes in the book, and therefore only objected to his religious pluralism and that they did not grasp his epistemological pluralism of denying any absolute or universal. At some points Sacks seems to echo the writings of Hartman, Heschel, and Emmanuel Levinas. An example of the latter's direct influence is Sacks' citation of Levinas' homily "We went into slavery to learn from the inside the need to respond to the stranger." We needed to learn to find God in the face of the stranger.[39] On questions of a halakhic nature, Sacks notably accentuates the ethical approaches to Jewish law, as formulated by Rabbis Kook, and Ben-Zion Uziel, as well as the universal approach of the Lubavitcher Rebbe.

In addition, Sacks has inclusivist themes. He relies on a Maimonidean vision that Islam and Christianity brought the word of God to the world combined with Emden's positive appreciation of Christianity as bringing the Jewish message to the world.

> My views on Christianity are shaped by another great rabbi, Yaakov Emden, who said some very profound things about Christianity. In his view, Christianity was exactly what we would have wished it to be—a way of taking what we call the Noahide Laws to the wider world. It's a very remarkable statement and not very widely known.
>
> Judaism accepts Christianity and Islam as, in a sense, the spiritual children of Abraham. We all worship the God of Abraham, although the way they do in some ways is quite different from us. That I think is what the sages meant when they understood the covenant with Noah to be a universal way of reaching God, whereas ours is a very particular way.[40]
>
> The high priest said on the Day of Atonement: Forgive them father, for they know not what they do. If Jesus said those words on the cross, then Jesus was at his most Jewish. At that moment Jesus was delivering a Jewish message. The Christ delivering the message to the world. We did not take it to the world. We are few. You are many. You took it to the world.[41]

Similar to S R Hirsch, the concept of Noahite laws are recognition that other religions in their own ways have morality and serve God. Yet, Sacks moves the Noahite laws from a universal ethic to an appreciation that the diversity of religions each contribute to Noahite moral order. Further, Sacks moves the Noahite laws from the morality of individual gentiles to the need to follow the Noahite laws through the diversity of other religions.

God created a world that appreciates the differences and unique contributions of each religion in building a moral society.

> Christians, Jews, Sikhs, Muslims, Hindus, Buddhists, Jains, Zoroastrians and Baha'i. Because though we do not share a faith, we surely share a fate. Whatever our faith or lack of faith, hunger still hurts, disease still strikes, poverty still disfigures, and hate still kills. Few put it better than that great Christian poet, John Donne: "Every man's death diminishes me, for I am involved in mankind."[42]

Sacks' pluralism is an appreciation of the fact that the maintenance of the society of men is best performed by the diversity of religions. Specifically, moderate nontotalitarian versions of the religions make for a moral society. Sacks does not create commonalities between religions, or a Judeo-Christian covenant, but an appreciation for traditional religious commitments.

In contrast, Sacks finds multiculturalism as too diffuse and does not offer a moral center the way an established religion can. In 2002, Sacks was the lone non-Anglican voice arguing against the disestablishment of the Church of England, because without an established Church the diversity of minority religions would not thrive and society would degenerate to religious indifference and irrelevance. In 2008, Sacks pleaded with the Anglican Communion to appreciate their "wonderful Church" and their "unique contribution to the world." As an outsider, he observes that the "The Anglican Communion has held together quite different strands of Christian theology and practice more graciously and successfully than any other religion I know."

Religion, for Sacks, once shorn of its absolutes still offers a way to respect the diversity of humanity, an ethical concern for the oppressed in an era of globalization, and more importantly a way to speak of forgiveness.[43] Beyond dignity, one should realize the potential for goodness and working to mend the world can be understood by all, in any faith. Even though "the religious expressions of humankind are incomemmsurable, but goodness—bringing blessing to lives other than one's own—is as near as we get to a universal language."[44]

Conclusions

Attempts at universal ideas of God, even those of medieval universalists, scares pluralists with a specter of exclusivism. They create a false dichotomy between sectarian withdrawal from society and engagement through pluralism. Yet, except for Reb Zalman, none of these thinkers mention a word on whether Christian doctrine might be enriching to them. And except for Sacks, the pluralists make religion an individual matter. In the end, pluralist approaches say we all have our own paths. This generous appreciation for diversity creates several problems for a theology that seeks to encounter the other. (1) It leaves the other religion as a personal decision, another path, an unknown and unknowable; (2) it does not define theologically what I see when I see the other; and (3) it does not delineate specific Jewish ideas from general religious ideas.

Jewish pluralists write that God has chosen Jews to walk the way of the Torah, Christians to follow Christ, the Hindus to be guided by the Vedas, and Muslims to follow the way shown by the Qur'an. Does this statement express a universal truth, obligatory to all, which should be accepted by non-Jews as well? If so, then Jewish pluralism is a camouflaged universalism: it takes for granted that there is a God who chooses people to follow a path. This is a belief that makes sense only on the grounds of biblical religions. Buddhists and Hindus would not recognize themselves in the statement. Maybe, as

S.M. Heim claims (see chapter two), there are many different ultimate goals to which different religions guide people? The other religions may not be answering the same questions as Judaism.[45]

There is a Jain parable used in modernist forms of Hinduism that was adopted and retold by many modern Western pluralists.

> Six blind men were asked to determine what an elephant looked like by feeling different parts of the elephant's body.
>
> The blind man who feels a leg says the elephant is like a pillar; the one who feels the tail says the elephant is like a rope; the one who feels the trunk says the elephant is like a tree branch; the one who feels the ear says the elephant is like a hand fan; the one who feels the belly says the elephant is like a wall; and the one who feels the tusk says the elephant is like a solid pipe.
>
> A wise man explains to them.
>
> All of you are right. The reason every one of you is telling it differently is because each one of you touched the different part of the elephant. So, actually the elephant has all the features you mentioned.

Pluralists are willing to say we are like blind men, but most traditional theology start with certainties, however minimal. The usefulness of acknowledging that other religions have truth is readily apparent in interreligious encounters, but the resonance of pluralistic claims with both actual knowledge of the details of other religions and with a broader theological vision needs to be further discussed.

CHAPTER 7

The Exclusivist Tradition

Jewish exclusivism assumes that the sole domain of truth is the Torah, and Judaism is the sole revealed religion, which differs in meaning from traditional Christian use of the word exclusivism, in that it does not usually deny salvation to gentiles. Instead, Jewish exclusivists limit discussion to acknowledging the merit of individual righteous gentiles, but do not acknowledge the collective virtues in other religious groups.

For Jewish exclusivists, Judaism is the sole path to God; those who are not Jews follow a mistaken path and are at best bystanders in the divine scheme, at worst antagonists. Exclusivist positions tend to be less philosophic than those of the inclusivists and are therefore automatically less universal. The texts recount various typological, and sometimes apocalyptic, struggles between Judaism and Rome. They rely on midrashic texts forged in historical experience, yet raise the ideas expressed therein to metaphysical abstraction.

Some Jewish texts of late antiquity include the debate about *Verus Israel* (*The True Israel*) and contain mockeries of Christianity, such as Kalir and Rashi. Others, such as Maharal and many Hasidic texts, continue the rabbinic approach of viewing the gentile as the opposite of the Jew. Some, such as Bar Hiyya and Zemach Duran, continue the apocalyptic eschatological visions found in the book of Ezekiel and suggest that the gentile will be eradicated at the end of days. Some, like Netziv, focus on the chosenness of the Jewish people minimizing the righteous from among the nations. And finally there are contemporary thinkers who reject gentiles in order to maintain political and social isolationism. In addition, this chapter deals in part with the demonization of gentiles that arises from Lurianic Kabbalah.

Exclusivism

- Historic, Chosen—where there is an oppositional mission of Judaism to other historic religions
- Historic—other religions are one of the evil and transitory kingdoms of the book of Ezekiel or Daniel
- Metaphysical—the other religions are idolatry
- Anti-humanism—where the humanism of others is downplayed or denied
- Revelation—where the other nations are blamed for lacking Torah
- Demonizing—where others are treated as essentially lacking souls, meaning, or value
- Halakhah-centric, institution centered, ecclesiocentrism—in the case of Judaism, the discussion is entirely based on the juridical appraisal by the halakhah (see chapter eight for further discussion)

The True Chosen Religion

Toldot Yeshu

Toldot Yeshu (Life of Jesus) is a derogatory version of the life of Jesus. This non-historical narrative grows out of rabbinic and pagan statements, such as "Jesus the Nazarene practiced magic and deceived and led Israel astray" (Sanhedrin 107b and elsewhere), that denigrate Jesus. The tradition in which *Toldot Yeshu* figures is commonly dated to approximately the sixth century CE, with the principal circulating version dated to the fourteenth century. It signifies a response by the Jewish community to its harsh treatment by Christianity and testifies to its need to define itself through a rejection of Christian history.

A short excerpt from the *Toldot Yeshu* exemplifies its portrayal of Jesus as an impious, marginal man of immoral descent who questioned biblical teachings; this questioning provided an important basis for denying his legitimacy.

One day Yeshu (Jesus) walked in front of the Sages with his head uncovered, showing shameful disrespect. At this, the discussion arose as to whether this behavior did not truly indicate that Yeshu was an illegitimate child and the son of a niddah. Moreover, the story tells that while the rabbis were discussing the *Tractate Nezikin*, he gave his own impudent interpretation of the law and in an ensuing debate he held that Moses could not be the greatest of the prophets if he had to receive counsel from Jethro. This led to further inquiry as to the antecedents of Yeshu, and it was discovered through Rabban Shimeon ben Shetah that he was the illegitimate son of Joseph Pandera. Miriam admitted it. After this became known, it was necessary for Yeshu to flee to Upper Galilee.[1]

The full version of *Toldot Yeshu* contains many other derogatory statements about Jesus and rejects his claims; the story culminates in the Jews killing Jesus to fulfill their duty not to let a sorcerer live.

Contemporary Jews, due to a modern humanistic sensibility, deny any sympathy with this text and do not consider it to be normative. Besides the modern universalism, this rejection is also aided by a modern historical sensibility that supports the removal of the text from the rabbinic corpus due to its lack of historical authority. Today, we can claim that since these texts do not reflect the real Jesus they should not be read. For medieval Jews, however, this text was accepted as part of their historic memory. If they wanted to know the story of Jesus, their Jewish text was the *Toldot Yeshu*. Even today some exclusivist thinkers, such as Rabbi Zvei Yehudah Kook discussed later in this chapter, treat this work as the definitive Jewish teaching on Jesus.

Kalir

Eliezer Kalir (*ca.* Sixth–seventh century, Israel) was the preeminent liturgical poet of his era and set the style for much future Jewish liturgical poetry. Kalir's writings offer a pronounced example from late antiquity of exclusivism based on the falseness of opposing doctrine. He considers the Christian iconography of Byzantium as a continuation of biblical idolatry and urges,

> Do not make idols of the wretched
> They are blind and deaf and without speech;
> They are carried, borne on shoulders;
> Helpless [themselves], they can do nothing for you.[2]

This passage is from the Shavuot liturgy in the *kedushta* in which Kalir compares the truth of the Torah given on Shavuot to the falsehood of the Christian idols. Few synagogues still recite these poems, which are nonobligatory parts of the liturgy, are considered difficult to understand, and are even deemed interruptions to the liturgy by some. Though these verses were written in language that obscured their content for most, contemporary Jews should be aware that such negative statements about Christianity once formed a part of the Jewish liturgical tradition, and there are similar verses about Christianity in the still recited penitential (*selikhot*) supplications.[3]

Early Ashkenazi

Israel Yuval has recently written an important work delineating the role in Ashkenazi Jewry's self-understanding of the dualistic struggle of *Verus Israel*: who is the true Israel, Jews or Christians? Yuval collected a rich sample of texts from late antiquity through the Middle Ages, showing how many Byzantine and Ashkenazi Jews looked forward to an apocalyptic revenge on the gentiles that resulted either in their complete destruction or a wrathful and bloody divine retribution. Even if Yuval has overstated his case about Ashkenazi hatred of Christianity, and is not correct about every text, his basic approach offers a window into Ashkenazi culture.

Ashkenazi Jewry sought divine revenge against the gentiles, drawing on the prior sources promising a downfall of Edom and Rome. For Yuval "the Ashkenazim not only rescued a muted voice from oblivion but also endowed it with new content...vengeance is transformed from a legal event to a universal occurrence, at the very heart of the messianic process."[4] Liturgical poetry for Passover contains lines such as the following from a poem by Shimon ben Isaac: "Let him wreak his vengeance in Edom before our eyes" (based on Ezekiel 25:14, "I will lay my vengeance upon Edom by the hand of my people Israel"). The Jewish practice of searching and burning the leaven before Passover was connected with vengeance in books of the era—"By virtue of burning leaven, Esau will burn."[5]

The Alenu prayer (presented in chapter three), which contains inclusive and universal strains, becomes one of the focal points for the exclusivist Ashkenazi demonization of Christianity. Into the prayer, curses to "send to them angels of malediction, rebuke, and confusion" were inserted, as were outright rejections of Christianity: " 'Pray to a god who cannot save'—man, ash, blood, bile, stinking flesh, maggot, defiled men and women, adulterers and adulteresses, dying in their iniquity and rotting in their wickedness, worn out dust, rot of maggot, and pray to a god who cannot save."[6] This tendency to envision a theological battle between two religions in which there would be only one winner was shared by much of the early Ashkenazi Jewry. These theological tendencies were further exacerbated by Christian persecution of Jews, Christianity's exclusivist claims, and the general experience of living in the medieval culture of violence. I will not delineate these variants, nor will I relate all the negative images of Christianity left in the writings of medieval Ashkenazi Jewry. These texts are part of the larger polemic literature between the two faiths.

The memory of the 1096 massacres of the Jewish communities in the Rhineland by the peasant armies participating in the First Crusade further exacerbated a bitter legacy. This particular elegy is anonymous, but it is one of four preserved in the Ashkenazi rite that preserves the memory of the 1096.

> And each one strengthened the other, helping
> him to cleave [to God] with pure reverence

So as not to bow down to an idol, so as not to have
   mercy on a man or woman,
   or on children, a diadem of glory.

The elegist describes the realization of parents that the situation required them
to imitate Abraham's sacrifice of Isaac by sacrificing their children and each
other rather than becoming idolaters. Here we have strong popular image of
Christianity as idolatry from Jewish liturgy.

Rashi

Rabbi Shlomo ben Yitzhak (1040–1105, Troyes, France), known throughout the Jewish world by his acronym Rashi, was a great eleventh-century
commentator on the Bible and Talmud who wrote the standard basic biblical commentary in the Jewish curriculum. It is difficult to overstate Rashi's
influence on contemporary discourse; both scholars and ordinary Jews see him
as the indispensable commentator. In traditional settings, students approach
the Pentateuch and Talmud first, and often exclusively, through the lens of
Rashi's commentary.

Rashi preserves many of the polemical statements forged in the crucible
of Judaism's late antiquity struggle with Rome and later with Christianity.
He chooses to cite many of the negative rabbinic statements about gentiles
and their typological equivalents in the figures of Laban, Esau, and Bilaam.
Rashi adds to these midrashic stereotypes by adding his own feudal period
glosses. For example, even his very first comment on the Bible contains his
own medieval gloss on the Midrash, depicting a world of armed confiscation
of land. The Barbarian and Feudal marauders are Rashi's exemplar for understanding the world of medieval Christendom.[7]

Many rabbinic texts present Esau as a morally evil figure who does not
achieve any reconciliation with his brother Jacob. A recent comment from
the Bar Ilan University notes the consistency of Rashi's use of this typology
of moral dualism.

Prevailing Jewish interpretation reads the Yaakov-Esav relations as shaping
the relations of the Jewish nation with "the other"—the goy—in general,
and with the Christian nations in particular. The painful history of these
relations fashioned the dominant Jewish commentary in mythic form. It
is stamped with the seal of our essence, and it sketches the Yaakov-Esav
relation exclusively from Yaakov's perspective. Rashi, drawing upon the
Midrashim of our Sages, is the foremost representative of this bias. Yaakov
is forever the righteous victim; Esav is the wicked embodiment of absolute
evil. Esav's red hair testifies to his violent and murderous nature [Rashi on
Bereishit 25:25, 28]. Yaakov is deserving of the birthright, either because

Esav relinquished it so easily, totally trivializing it (Ibid. 32), or because Yaakov was the first to be conceived in the womb (Ibid. 26). Esav is corrupt and a deceiver (Ibid. 28). Yitzchak is the immaculate Torah student.[8]

This moral dualism of biblical figures, in which ancestors of contemporary Jews are regarded as saints while conversely all biblical antagonists are portrayed as wicked precursors of contemporary gentiles, is basic in his commentary.

Avraham Grossman, the leading historian of early Ashkenaz, in his recent scholarly biography of Rashi notes the latter's "deep hatred toward the gentiles" in which they are portrayed as enemies of Israel ready to tear it apart in cruelty and wickedness. Grossman asks: Where did animosity come from? Is it an inheritance of the animosity of the late antiquity and Ashkenaz traditions or was it a personal reaction to the tragic events of the First Crusade? He grants the influence of both of these cause but concludes that the biggest factor was probably Rashi's acute sense of the physical and spiritual dangers of Jewish life under Christendom.[9]

According to Grossman, Rashi considered that "the nations of the world in his time are the inheritors of the great enemies of Israel in the Bible and continue their ways." Even when gentiles are praised in the Bible, Rashi minimizes it or shows that they remain inferior to Israel. In the end of days, the best of the gentiles will convert to serve God but will not attain anywhere near the status of Israel. Rashi displays his exclusivism in statements such as, "I ask from you that your *Shekhinah* should not rest anymore on the nations of the world and we will be separate from all other nations" (Commentary to Exod. 33:16). Rashi's particularism is a separatist exclusiveness based on a moral superiority of Israel and considers other claims as false.[10]

In his Talmud commentary, Rashi offers us specific comments on Jesus in a manner similar to the *Toldot Yeshu* tradition. The Talmud holds that Christians ("minim") and others who reject the Talmud will go to hell and be punished there for all generations. Rashi comments that these apostates are described as the students of *Yeshu HaNotzri* (Jesus of Nazareth) who have twisted the words of the Torah (Rosh Hashanah 17a). These statements have been excised from the standard Rashi commentaries on the Talmud more obliquely; in his Bible commentary Rashi writes, "No Messiah that Jews could recognize could suffer such a death"; for "He that is hanged is accursed of God" (Deut. xxi. 23), "an insult to God."

The extent of Rashi's exegetical concern with Christianity is debated; however, the exegetical school that considered him their model did explicitly deal with Christianity. His intellectual disciples Rabbi Samuel ben Meir (*ca.* 1085–1158, Rashbam) and Rabbi Joseph ben Isaac Bekhor Shor (twelfth century) explain biblical references to Edom through details from contemporary Christianity and seek to refute Christian interpretations of the Bible.

Moral and sectarian particularism is echoed in much of Franco-German Jewish culture; specifically, an aversion to anything having to do with Christianity. For example, *Sefer Hasidim* preserves the pious refusal of medieval German Jews to mention the names of non-Jewish deities and saints, even that of Saint Michael who possesses a Jewish name (656, 427).

Ours is not the first generation of Jews having to grapple with Rashi's exclusionist, anti-gentile tone. Because of the importance of Rashi for the Jewish understanding of Bible, there are over 270 super-commentaries, that is, commentaries written on his commentary. The super-commentaries on Rashi are rich with insights on theological material, adaptations to diverse theologies and communities, and offer moral interpretations of Rashi's thought. They should be examined to see how these passages are dealt with. There has been little study of the over two hundred and seventy super-commentaries on Rashi's commentary and the values that they reflect. This research is especially important because of the predominant role of Rashi's comments in the Jewish educational system.[11] It is important to stress that because of Rashi's central role in the traditional Jewish reading of the Bible, there will always be charitable readings that seek to understand Rashi's commentary as acceptable to all ages and eras.

Historical exclusivism

Abraham bar Hiyya

Abraham bar Hiyya (1070 Barcelona, Spain, to 1136 Provence, France; also known as Savasorda) was a Catalan Jewish mathematician, astronomer, and philosopher. In his works *Meditation of the Soul* and *Scroll of the Revealer*, he presents an apocalyptic eschatology. Bar Hiyya envisions not messianic vengeance, but the uprooting of those who do not fear God in the end of days.

> Most of the nations of the world will be completely destroyed and cut off, and none will remain in the world save for the righteous who fear the Lord, [whether] from among His people or from those who believe in Torah that shall take shelter beneath the wings of the *shekhinah* (earthy indwelling of God) from the other nations.[12]

Shimon ben Zemah Duran

Shimon ben Zemah Duran (1361–1444), a fifteenth-century Spanish philosopher, offers an exclusivist variant of the Zohar theme (discussed in chapter four), in which the two other Abrahamic religions are reincorporated into Judaism, and combines it with the Maimonidean theme, in which Christianity and Islam serve to bring the idea of God to the world. According to Duran, God has a special relationship with the faiths that descend from the patriarchs, yet still seeks their eventual reintegration into Judaism.

God promised the prophets the nullification of the two sects according to their veering from the truth.

Concerning Christianity...it says: "The House of Jacob shall be fire, the house of Joseph flame, and the House of Esau shall be straw" (Obadiah 1:18) and at the end it says, "For liberators shall march up on Mount Zion to destroy in judgment on Mount Esau; and dominion shall be the Lord's" (1:21).

About Islam [lit. Yishmael]...it says an angel said, "Return under her hand." (Gen. 16:9)

And when these two sects are nullified then the whole world will admit to the Torah of truth and say falsehood you lead our ancestors, vanity that does not help and will establish what is written "then the nations will turn to a pure language." (Zeph. 3:9)[13]

The *Zohar*'s image of the three religions springing from Abraham, Duran explains as the other faiths recognizing their falsehood and the eventual triumph of Judaism. According to Duran, Jews let the other religions evangelize the world for Judaism. This will continue until the end of days when Jews will reveal a greater closeness to God. That is, gentiles must be the witnesses to faith in order for Jews to acknowledge their religion.

Maharal: two forces

Rabbi Yehudah ben Betzalel Loewe (*ca.* 1525–1609; called by his acronym Maharal) was an eclectic Renaissance Jewish thinker who served as rabbi in Posen and Prague. His system, like that of many other Renaissance thinkers, Jew and non-Jew, works by creating binary pairs. In this case, Jews sustain the redeemed world, while the gentiles are the opponents of redemption. Maharal embraces a separation and particularism where only the nation of Israel is called man and only Israel has been created in the image of God. Maharal built his theology more on Midrash, with its apocalyptic and typological themes, than on biblical or philosophical universalism. According to Maharal, the ancient struggles of Israel with the seven wicked nations and Amalek are ever with us as is evident in these metaphor-laden pronouncements.

Israel and Edom are inverse and opposite—when one is in ascent then the other is in descent.

At the beginning, Israel is connected to the nations like a shell around a fruit. At the end, the fruit is separated from the shell completely and Israel is separated from them.

The separation from idolaters makes a nation complete in itself and sustains the essence of Israel.

Idolaters are compared to water and Israel to fire. If the two sub-
stances, fire and water, are mixed together the water puts out the fire.
But if the fire remains distant and separate from the water, then the fire
consumes and dries out the water until nothing is left. In truth, this is
the uniqueness (*segulah*) of Israel.

When one hates religion then all of one's thoughts are to destroy the religion of Israel.[14] Maharal creates an exclusivism based on the historical struggle between two forces in the world. Other religions are not just false or
immoral, but prevent the messianic redemption by their very existence.
Whereas Yehudah Halevi used the metaphor of the fruit to refer to the branch
religions that spring with Judaism, Maharal gives the metaphor the opposite valence: Israel is the fruit whose connection with the other nations—
the shell—only decreases with time. This opposition between Israel and the
world—Edom—is real and absolute, a zero-sum game where cooperation is
inconceivable.

Yet, Maharal does have an inclusivist side to his thought. In some places
his distinction between the philosophical first cause, available to all people,
and Torah available only to Jews, leads Maharal to write that anyone who
accepts the first cause, implicitly including Aristotle and Christians, is not an
idolater.[15]

Hasidut

Most Hasidic texts continue the particularism of the Eastern European Jewry.
In almost all cases, hasidim are loath to apply their pantheistic finding of God
in all things to anything having to do with gentiles. The other religions are a
false ensnaring pit or a source of demonic powers that suck energy from the
Torah. Rabbi Levi Yitzhak of Berdichev, one of the major figures of early
Hasidism, who led a large following and whose homilies are widely read,
made use of the then recently republished writing of Maharal to create a
similar binary pair of Israel and the nations. "When God bestows goodness
upon the nations it is in order to give them all of their goodness and reward
in this world and to cut them off from the world to come. With Israel it is just
the opposite: it is to increase their reward in the world to come" [see Eruvin
22a].[16] I choose this passage to show the influence of the Maharal as R. Levi's
ideological base, and to avoid the rawer insulting passages found generally
in Hasidic texts. As a principle, one should avoid ascribing any Romantic
notions about the openness of Hasidism to anything having to do with gentiles or other religions.

One hundred and fifty years after the initial outburst of Hasidism, the
onslaught of modernity led to a sectarian and isolationistic reaction. Rabbi

Shmuel Borenstein, leader of the Sochechew Hasidic group, wrote in 1924 that "the nations pollute the atmosphere with their perverse practices" (*Aharei mot*). His writings have deep feelings of exile and the fallen state left by post–World War I destruction of property and traditional ways of life.

Rabbi Zadok HaKohen of Lublin (1823–1900), a late-nineteenth-century Hasidic thinker, offers an exclusivism that mixes the Midrash, that states that Jews were purified from the immoral human condition through the Torah given at Mt. Sinai, with Maharal's dualism and with Isaac Luria's theory of the soul.

> "You are called 'men,' and not the other nations. The Gentiles were deprived of the title 'men' only where Israel were called 'men,' because in comparison to Israel, who are the primary form of man in the Divine Chariot, it is irrelevant to call any gentile men, at most, they are like animals in the form of men. Taken as themselves, however, all the children of Noah are considered men...and when the Messiah comes...they too will recognize and admit that there are none called 'man' except Israel...anyway, in comparison to Israel even now they are in the category of animals..."[17]

Rabbi Zadok elsewhere creates a typology where gentiles value the intellect, while Jews know how to integrate mind and emotions.

Netziv—chosenness

Rabbi Naftali Zevi Berlin (1817–1893; known as the Netziv) was the head of the Volozhin Yeshiva at the end of the nineteenth century and he wrote an influential Bible commentary called *Haamek Davar*. Known for its worldliness and ethical humanism, his thought continues to play a vital role in many Orthodox circles.

When discussing the religion of people other than his own, Rabbi Berlin chose the particularist path while affirming a universal ethic. He continued the particularism of Rashi, but gave it a new supersessionist twist.

> The nations of the world and their pious had the power of worship from the creation of the world...but from the time that Israel was chosen at Sinai...this ability was limited to Israel. Similarly, the other nations had the quality of loving-kindness...but Israel was chosen to have this power.[18]
>
> Even though every nation has saints [religious men of distinction] who illumine their nation like stars, but they are quantitatively few in number compared to the masses.[19]

Since Netziv accepted a starting point of moral universalism, he had to suppose that the gentiles had lost their original status as conveyers of universalism.

Thus, Israel would be the heir to human ethics, virtue, prayer, and compassion. The original universalism for the world is now Israel's mission. Rabbi Berlin's humanism demands that he acknowledge gentile saints, yet he minimizes its importance; he is equally unimpressed when confronted with examples of gentile ethics. In several texts, he writes that Judaism sustains the world, and that Jews need to be a light unto the gentiles to help foster their precarious relationship with the good.

Rav Kook

Contradictory views have a role to play within an individual's theology. Accordingly, we can find exclusivist views in the theology of Rav Kook notwithstanding his general inclusivist approach. Such exclusivist views surface in the following excerpt, which refers to the Anglican Church's missionizing efforts in Palestine during British rule. Faced with an increased Christian presence in Jerusalem following World War I, Rav Kook counsels absolute separation from the Christian presence.

> From [the church's] wickedness and opinions do not take any aid or support, even from the good aspects. One needs to be careful to avoid the ideas that appear or agree with the good and holy that are found in its treasures... only by separation and loathing, and by absolute resolution not to benefit or to accept any good from their disgusting treasure. Specifically, in this one should fortify the will, clarify the mind, strengthen the good, thereby all that was stolen from the self will return to its place, and Israel will be strong.[20]

Rav Kook's clear anti-gentile comments are not, as published, qualified by any reference to the immediate historic context. Thus, these uncharacteristically exclusivist statements paved the way for some of his students to advocate strongly particularistic sentiments under Rav Kook's banner.[21]

Zevi Yehudah Kook

Rabbi Zevi Yehudah Kook (1891–1982), the son of Rabbi Abraham Issac Kook, was blessed with a long life, many students, and a highly influential messianic theology. Rabbi Zvi Yehudah claimed that the current era was a fulfillment of the biblical messianic prophecies of the return of the Jews to the land of Israel. His theology served as part of a religious ideology for a greater Israel, as in the time of the biblical King David, attained through battle. He was the ideological father of the settler movement and therefore influential in late-twentieth-century Israeli political life.

The ideology itself is noteworthy for a staunch anti-Christianity that culls two millennia of sources without acknowledging any of the countervailing traditions. For Rabbi Zevi Yehudah Kook, his father's attack on Christianity is motivated not by the immediate presence of missionaries, but by a conflict with the entire Western culture, which both threatens the Jewish purity of Israel from within and opposes his messianic settlement drive from without. Zevi Yehudah Kook resurrects many of the classic anti-Christian polemics with a vigor not seen for a millennium. Among these polemics are the ideas that Christianity should be dismissed as an internal Jewish heresy, and that the Jewish God is alive whereas the Christian God is dead. He claims that all references to sectarian heretics (*min, minim*) in rabbinic literature of the later halakhah all refer to Christianity. According to Zevi Yehudah Kook, Christianity is the refuse of Israel, an image in line with the ancient Talmudic portrayals of Jesus punished through boiling in excrement.[22] The stories of *Toldot Yeshu* are considered to be a valid part of the Jewish tradition. Zvei Yehudah originally formulated these ideas in a 1952 essay, immediately after the founding of the state of Israel, that attacked any Jewish attempts to reclaim Jesus, such as those by Joseph Klausner, but he singles out for special venom the works of the Yiddish author Sholem Asch (1880–1957) who in 1939 wrote a popular novel about Jesus, *The Nazarene.*

Rabbi Zevi Yehudah Kook's position serves as the foundation for the Gush Emunim political movement in Israel, which sees a messianic role to new settlements in Israel. But one should not read these statements as merely a polemical work, rather they serve as his actual messianic theology. For Zevi Yehudah, the battle of the second–fourth centuries for the true Israel (*Verus Israel*) is continued in the theological battle for the establishment of the state of Israel, presented as a battle against Western Christendom. Christian theology is considered "the war against the eternality of Israel,"[23] as well as a battle against the very foundation of the oral law as the correct interpretation of the Bible.[24] Jewish exclusivism, for Zevi Yehudah, manifests itself in the meaning of contemporary Israel. Since Zevi Yehudah considers the fulfillment of the biblical prophecy of the messianic age in the current modern state, he deems all deviations from his political vision as the very opposite of his Judaism and of redemption.[25]

Zvei Yehudah's student Rabbi Shlomo Aviner (b. 1943, Rabbi in Beth-El and head of *Ateret Kohanim,* a yeshiva in the Muslim quarter of Jerusalem) carries forth this message by presenting the central message of Christianity as based on the Crusader cry "Jerusalem is lost." Hence, the rebuilding of a Jewish state negates the very essence of Christianity. Even in the year 2000, the year of John Paul II's visit to Israel, Shlomo Aviner writes that the Vatican considers the state of Israel as "a sin for the entire Christian world," and that the Church thinks that it needs to "prevent [the State of Israel] in any possible way." He shows no knowledge of the Fundamental Accord or any current positions of the Church regarding the state of Israel. Aviner responds to his hypothetical Church with the following theological retort about proofs for the true Israel.

> The state of Israel was established by Divine decree, this negates the fundamental principle of Catholic theology, founded on the eternal punishment of Israel. Wandering in exile provides the truth of Christianity...The [State of Israel] proves that the Jewish people...are the true Israel.
>
> Christianity is the number one enemy of the state of Israel. With the Arabs we have a non-essential neighbors quarrel...But with Christianity it is cosmological in essence, whether we are the Jewish people or not.[26]

If one were to ask whether, despite the falsity of Christian truth claims, the religion still constitutes a path to God, Zevi Yehudah would answer by denying any truth to Christianity and all philosophical universals as untrue to Jewish thought. Like the practitioners of Wahabi Fundamentalism within Islam, Zevi Yehudah denies the continuous relevance of the cosmopolitan ages of synthesis, choosing instead to return to the polemical Midrash.

Why was Zvei Yehudah Kook's exclusionist position formulated at the end of the twentieth century? His theology shows the change that comes about from living in a non-Diaspora context, which enables this rejection of Western culture. The state of Israel can lead some to a secure acceptance of the other, especially other religions, or it can allow for a complete xenophobic rejection. Even though the overwhelming majority does not personally entertain these ideas, they are many times passively tolerated.

Exclusive—demonic dualism

Besides the earlier mentioned forms of exclusivism, there is also an undercurrent of demonic dualism in the Kabbalah. What I am labeling the "dualistic" variety of the exclusivist position is really the counterpart to the "metaphysical" variant of inclusivism described in chapter four of this volume. Here too, the real realm of action is not this world, with individual people and nations, but the metaphysical realm of primal and cosmic forces. In this schema, Israel represents cosmic good; the nations represent the primal evil.

The *Zohar* corpus contains two different approaches to gentiles, the inclusivist approach discussed in the inclusivist chapter that places the nations within the divine order of the seventy nations serving God and an exclusivist strand, where the other religion is demonized as part of an evil side.

Rabbi Abba said: soul of the living being, namely, Israel, for they are scions of the Blessed Holy One and their holy souls derive from Him. The souls of the other nations, from whence do they come? Rabbi Elazar said, from those impure aspects of the left, defiling them and anyone approaching them.[27]

In this exclusivist strand, the other nations are Christianity and Islam. *Midrash Ruth* of the Zohar corpus explicitly states that the verse "Do not have other Gods before Me" refers to Ishmael and Esau."[28]

Many fifteenth- and sixteenth-century kabbalists reread the texts of the thirteenth-century kabbalists as exclusivist and dualistic. They took anything negative about Amalek, Edom, the evil side, or idolatry and applied it to Christianity. The fifteenth-century kabbalist Shem Tov ben Shem Tov recasts Islam and Christianity not as right and left branches, as presented by Shimon Duran earlier, but as the right and left shells of the evil side. "The elders of the holy Kabbalah and the sages of the world agree that the holy patriarchs are Abraham and Isaac, corresponding to the attributes of mercy and judgment. Similarly, Yishmael and Edom are rooted in the two roots that are the secret of the shells on the right and left."[29] This exclusivist kabbalistic trend tends to also reject the universalism of philosophy and worldly culture.

An exile from Spain, Judah Hayyat (*ca.* 1450–1510) bitterly went out of his way to reread an explicitly universal rabbinic text as exclusive.

When they said that "the righteous gentiles have a share in the world to come," they meant that they are in the highest level of Gehinnom, and enjoy the pleasure of the Garden of Eden which is next to it, for there is only a hairbreadth between them. But God forbid that they should be in the Garden of Eden.[30]

Another example is the *Sefer Meshiv,* a magical apocalyptic text created from automatic writings dictated by an angel and influential in the circle of Luria, portraying the other religions as demonic. While these dualistic thinkers are widespread in the fifteenth century, they should not be considered to characterize all Kabbalistic works causing one to ignore of the inclusivism of Gikitilla and Cordovero.

Luria

Kabbalist Rabbi Isaac Luria (d. 1572) developed an elaborate theory about souls and reincarnation, which was recorded by his disciple Hayim Vital (1543–1620). This theory, as the basis for later Kabbalah, has devoted adherents even today. In this cosmology, the divine light is obscured in this world by the shells (*klipah, kelipot*) of the demonic side. Gentiles comes from that dark side, while ordinary materiality comes from intermediary shells that can be redeemed (*klipot nogah*). The gentiles are not merely the other, or the anti-Israel, as they appear in the less metaphysical approaches of Rashi; they are of the same stuff as the evil and rupture at the beginning of creation. The internal logic of this myth leads to radical notions.

Developing the *Zohar* passage denigrating gentile souls cited earlier, Luria fills in details based on his system, with particular emphasis on the exclusion of gentiles from mystical knowledge (*daat*).

> Israel possesses the three levels of soul, *nefesh, ruah, neshamah*—from holiness...The gentiles possess only the level of *nefesh* from the feminine side of the shells...for the souls of the nations, come from the *klipot*, are called evil and not good' since they are created without knowledge (*daat*).[31] The animal soul of man is the good and evil inclination. The soul of the gentiles comes from the three *shells*: wind, cloud, and fire, all of them evil. So is the case with impure animals, beasts, and birds. However, the animal soul of Israel and the animal soul of pure animals, beasts, and birds all come from [*klipat*] *noga*.[32]

In Luria's system, the sin of Adam, which destroyed the original cosmic harmony, entails that male Jews are to restore the original sinlessness through the performance of mizvot as the means of rectifying the soul. This scheme leaves gentiles out of cosmic restoration except as bit players who need the sparks that were scattered in them to be raised. "When the Holy One Blessed be He created Adam, all the souls included within him were only the souls of Israel, and if he had not sinned the other nations would have not come to the world. After he sinned the sparks of the souls of the nations were mixed in."[33] According to Luria, Israel is locked into a cosmic battle between kabbalistic redemption through mizvot and earthly gentile impurity. Continuous sins cause Jews to descend into the shells of the gentiles rather than ascend to redemption.

Gershom Scholem credited the expulsion from Spain with influencing the pessimistic worldview of Luria, but current trends ascribe it to his personal selection of thirteenth-century dualistic and demonic approaches to Kabbalah. However, these dualistic statements of Luria became popular in cities such as Damascus, Meknes, Smyrna, and Livorno among the select pietists that devoted their life to the complexity of the system. The kabbalist's perspective turned entirely away from natural encounters with the external world and toward his role in this great cosmic drama—a role that took all of one's intellectual, emotional, and volitional resources. While the influence of Luria on subsequent Jewish history has been overstated, his notion that non-Jews lack significant souls was an important cultural idea that found reception.

The writings of Elijah ben Solomom ha-Kohen, Dayyan of Smyrna (died 1729), who produced over thirty works as a preacher, draws out the implications of the Lurianic ethos. His "Midrash Talpiyyot" contains glosses and comments in 926 (the numerical value of the word "Talpiyyot") alphabetically ordered paragraphs. One of his statements often cited by anti-Jewish racist groups, but heavily embellished with fabricated statements, is his statement that gentiles are compared to animals. In addition, based on the kabbalistic idea that the number thirty-two represents wisdom, he categorically states that gentiles must have 33 teeth; empiricism is far from his mode of thought.[34]

A further example of this approach lies in the writings of the eighteenth-century Moroccan kabbalist Rabbi Hayyim Ibn Attar (1696–1743), known as the *Or HaHayyim* after his biblical commentary of that title. His commentaries are replete with statements that draw out the frightening implications of Luria's writings. These Lurianic exegetical texts are relevant because they, in turn, are cited in Hasidic and other homiletic texts, which contemporary rabbis can and do cite. For example, commenting on "I will separate you from the nations," Attar writes that the separation of Israel from the nations is like the separation from an unclean animal (Comments on Lev. 20:26). Even worse, he uses this logic to consider that killing a Gentile raises sparks: "In the eyes of Israel, killing a Gentile is like drinking their blood." Through this act the holy part of the gentiles cleaves to Israel in the secret of "drink the blood of the slain" (Num. 23:24).[35] While there was indeed persecution in Ibn Attar's Morocco, it should not be seen as the sole cause for the diffusion of these ideas. Even in countries without persecution of the Jews, there are those attracted to these ideas, due to the mystique of the Lurianic system in the eighteenth century.

I have tried to avoid any overt editorializing in the remaining texts mentioned in this volume, but in this case I am compelled to give my own opinion. These passages demonizing the other must be condemned as racist calls to violence. They cannot simply be ignored. This horrific approach moved the exclusivity of the past to a new and potentially dangerous realm. While the influence of Lurianic cosmology has certainly waned with modernity, and these homiletic works have certainly lost their cultural resonance, they nevertheless occasionally and surprisingly appear in the rhetoric of contemporary Jewish separatists and are cited by anti-Semites eager to prove the racism of Judaism. Rather than avoiding them, we must acknowledge their existence and then distance ourselves from them. To repudiate a racist text is not necessarily to relinquish the valuable within exclusivist texts or the concept of a chosen nation.

Luzzatto

Moshe Chaim Luzzatto, an Italian rabbi known for his poetry, Kabbalah, and ethical works, offers a systematic presentation of Lurianic Kabbalah in which the two strands, the inclusivist and the exclusivist, are combined in an exclusivist framework. He accepts that gentiles are at a lower level than Jews, but that they are part of the Divine order of the seventy nations. At the end of time, gentile souls exist as subservient to Jewish souls. His clear presentation of early modern Lurianic Kabbalah speaks for itself.

One of the deepest concepts of God's providence involves Israel and the other nations. With regards to their basic human characteristics, the two appear exactly alike. From the Torah's viewpoint, however, the two are completely different, and are treated as ones belonging to completely different class...

Before Adam sinned, he was on a level much higher than present-day man...However, when Adam sinned, he fell from his original high level, and brought upon himself a great degree of darkness and insensitivity...Mankind in general also fell from its original height, and remained on a degraded level...

The world was then divided into seventy nations, each on its own particular level in the general scheme. All of them, however, remained on the level of man in his fallen state, while only Israel became men in the elevated state.

These nations still have the human aspect, blemished though it may be, so God desired that they should at least have a part of what was actually appropriate for the true mankind. He therefore granted them a divine soul somewhat like that of the Jew, even though it is not on the same level as Jewish souls are, but on a much lower level. They were likewise given commandments through which they could attain both material and spiritual advantages appropriate to their nature—the Seven Commandments given to the children of Noah.

In the World to Come, however, there will be no nation other than Israel. The souls of righteous Gentiles will be allowed to exist in the Future World, but only as an addition and attachment to Israel. They will therefore be secondary to the Jews, just as a garment is secondary to the one who wears it.[36]

Scholarly exclusivism

This dualism found cultured defenders in twentieth-century Central European Jews who fled before the rise of racial anti-Semitism. In this era of emigration, Jewish scholars took conceptual positions of either accepting passively their status as perpetual pariahs or willfully developing a stance as sectarian outsiders. They claimed to share with Rashi and Lurianic Kabbalah a sense of exile and racial alienation from the gentiles, but, because they wrote as historians, they were able to conveniently discuss exclusivism from a distance as a part of the past.

Gershom Scholem, the great Hebrew University scholar of Jewish Mysticism, was the most famous of these émigrés. He rejected the universal vision of the German-Jewish Synthesis—of Moses Mendelssohn, S.R. Hirsch, Herman Cohen, and Martin Buber—by projecting his own alienation from European universalism onto the Kabbalah. Scholem's account of the development of Lurianic Kabbalah as a response to the Spanish expulsion is well rehearsed in the academic literature. Less well-known are the personal comments made in his diaries. For example, during World War I he wrote, "We [Jews] have had a relationship with Europe only to the degree that Europe has acted upon us as a destructive stimulation." And years later, comfortably settled in Jerusalem, Scholem wrote, "I am a 'sectarian' and have never been ashamed of expressing in print my conviction that sectarianism can offer us something decisive and positive..."

Jacob Katz (1904–1998) shared many of these same views, which he projected onto traditional Ashkenazi society. Katz used a racial approach toward these texts and stressed that gentiles were not specifically seen as idolatrous anymore but were symbolically different as a separate order.[37] For Katz, this becomes an unbroken chain of exclusivism from Yehudah Halevi and Kabbalah to Ashkenaz and Poland that encompasses all premodern Jewry.

> The authors of the Midrash and the philosophers like R. Judah Ha-Levi had to distinguish between the natures of Jew and gentile as a basis for the distinction as stemming from a biological-racial factor. Alternately, they might see it as deriving from some differing reaction to a historical-metaphysical event... The difference in creed thus lost its fundamental importance. Difference in belief were now seen only as the product of the deeper division in the biological-metaphysical realm or historical-metaphysical natures of the two camps. This approach which stressed the "underlying nature" of the two groups, became quite popular in our period, especially because of the influence of the Kabbala, and in particular of the *Zohar*. The *Zohar* very much follows this line of argument in distinguishing Israel from the nations, and sees the uniqueness of Israel as a function of the nation's link to the sacred spheres in the divine system, while gentiles were linked by their essence to the impure spheres.

In general, he cites Maharal as the mainstream Ashkenazi Jewish opinion and states that "the distinction between Judaism and Christianity now shifted from the contents of faith to the realm of metaphysics."

Katz personally accepted a universal tolerance based on Mendelssohn; his work highlights his own view by accentuating the alternative. Following Max Weber who described the dual ethics of Judaism, Katz states categorically that in traditional texts there is a dual ethic. "There was one law and ethic for the Jew and another for the gentile...The notion that a single system of justice could control relations between human beings without regard to ethnic and religious origins never occurred to anyone.[38] The sectarianism of the Jerusalem school of Jewish history has had tremendous influence in the late twentieth century. Yet it is worth bearing in mind that they have their counterpoint in the historical schools that presented a world of synthesis and integration.

Dualism: room for rereading

My own personal opinion is that a theology of other religions or an encounter with others requires a sense of at-homeness, either in the Diaspora or in the state of Israel; a full reading of the tradition on these topics can only be achieved when one can feel secure about one's position in the world. During a stable and peaceful era, dwelling alone does not, and will not, serve the best interests of Judaism.

Dualism needs to be reread from our vantage point. We are part of a living tradition of accepting classic texts and applying them to the current generation. As the Lutheran Church has acted to undo the harmfulness of Luther's statements, or as the Catholic Church has worked, through Vatican II, to address the teachings of contempt, Judaism needs to address these texts. It is not enough to cite the Meiri concerning halakhic issues (see chapter eight in this volume) or to write only for moderns who work only with the Enlightenment concerns of tolerance. We cannot ignore problematic texts or flaccidly respond that mid-twentieth-century rabbinic authorities did not teach them. We have to admit that these texts exist, roll up our sleeves, and deal with them. There are traditional means for working with these problematic texts about other religions.

Chajes

An early example of a modern rabbi who dealt with these texts is Rabbi Zvi Hirsch Chajes (1805–1855), an Austrio-Hungarian rabbi who, during the first half of the nineteenth century, was among the first of his colleagues to feel the thrust of modernity in Eastern Europe. To answer the new spirit of the times, he produced a series of apologetic tracts with conservative answers that are still read and accepted among Orthodox apologists today.

Rabbi Chajes dealt with the exclusivist texts in rabbinic literature—the Talmud, Midrashim, and Rashi—by claiming that rabbinic texts were written in a binary black and white, good and evil style for didactic purposes.[39] If one side is praised, then rabbinic rhetoric requires that the other side be condemned as a polar opposite. The goal of the rabbinic text was to encourage the reader to follow the moral exemplar, whose own virtue was amplified by exaggerating the vices of the opposite dystopian exemplar. According to Chajes, rather than simply drawing a demonic caricature of the other, the rabbinic texts offer a continuous reminder that we must praise the good and frown on the bad.

This is a fine approach for dealing with rabbinic texts in traditional "in-house" educational settings, where one has no recourse but to accept this mode of reinterpretation, and it should be developed further. Yet, for interfaith encounters, the apologetic is not sufficient; the demonic dualism and the dehumanization texts need to be addressed directly.

Tanya and Chabad

Another example of the possibilities for rereading appears in the two-hundred-year history of Chabad Chassidic literature. Rabbi Schneur Zalman of Liadi (1745–1812; Alter Rebbe), the founder of the Chabad Hasidic dynasty, wrote the widely read *Likkute Amarim (Tanya)* in 1797. At the beginning, he clearly states a doctrine of metaphysical dualism, as presented in Lurianic writings: Gentiles do not have souls.[40] In bold and daring contrast, the seventh Chabad Rebbe, Rabbi Menachem Mendel Schneersohn (1902–1994), completely rewrote this metaphysical dualism into an embracing inclusivism.

The *Likkute Amarim* of 1797 states that other nations have the same souls as unclean animals and only Jews have souls, while gentiles are considered dead. We read there,

> The souls of the nations of the world, however, emanate from the other, unclean "kelipot" (evil forces), which contain no good whatever. (1:5)
>
> However, the "kelipot" (evil forces) are subdivided into two grades, one lower than the other. The lower grade consists of the three "kelipot," which are altogether unclean and evil, containing no good whatever. From them flow and derive the souls of all the nations of the world, and the existence of their bodies, and also the souls of all living creatures that are unclean and unfit for consumption. (6:25)
>
> To elucidate still further, it is necessary to clarify the meaning of the verse, "The candle of God is the soul of man." What it means is that the souls of Jews, who are called "man," are, by way of illustration, like the flame of the candle, whose nature it is always to scintillate upwards... Now this is a general principle in the whole realm of holiness... This stands in direct contrast to the so-called "*kelipah*" (evil

forces) and *"sitra ahra"* (the other, evil side), where from are derived
the souls of the Gentiles...Therefore they (the Gentiles) are called
"dead"...(19:77,79)

These eighteenth-century ideas were reiterated even as late as 1943 when
the sixth Lubavitch Rebbe, Rabbi Yosef Yitzchak Schneersohn (1880–1950),
advocated spitting at the mention of other religions, and even then to wait
before continuing to pray or study so as not to use the same saliva used in the
mentioning of other religions.[41]

Rabbi Menachem Mendel Schneersohn (1902–1994; Lubavitcher Rebbe),
the seventh leader of Chabad Hasidism, armed with a messianic understanding
of the current era, wanted to bring Hasidism even to the gentiles of America.
He did not need to rewrite the offensive text because, for him, changing times
had made the older text irrelevant. All gentiles were now capable of appreciating the divine light of the Torah.

In this positive approach to gentiles, the Seventh Rebbe could rely on the
writings of Menachem Mendel Schneersohn (1789–1866), the third rebbe of
the Chabad dynasty, who presented the Hasidic vision of unity as based on the
inclusivist philosophic works of Maimonides, Gersonides, Albo, and Arama.
For the latter, the Hasidic approach of finding God in all things is equated
with the unity of God described by the philosophers. The earlier Schneersohn
felt that all Jews need to have knowledge of this unity, while gentiles do
not have to affirm unity. Along the way he states that Christians do indeed
believe in one God but not in unity.[42]

Rabbi Schneersohn was in favor of prayer in public schools and acknowledged the Christian and civil religion of America as a necessary moral force
based on our common belief in one God. In some of his homilies, he even
invokes "In God We Trust," the phrase printed on U.S. currency, as evidence
that we share one God. He explains that gentiles have a God-given destiny to
serve God, and it was only due to prior hostility that Jews did not teach this
basic doctrine of Judaism. He says,

The "spreading of the wellsprings" of Chassidic teachings should not
be limited to Jews alone, but should be extended outward to non-
Jews as well. As [Maimonides] states, the purpose of giving the Torah
was to bring peace to the world (*Mishneh Torah*, Laws of Chanukah
4:14). Similarly, he writes that every Jew is obliged to try and influence those who are not Jewish to fulfill the Seven Laws of Noah.
Maimonides also states that one of the achievements of the Messiah
will be to spiritually refine and elevate the nations of the world until

they, too, become aware of God to the point where Godliness will be revealed to every flesh, non-Jews.

Since the rewards of Torah come "measure for measure" it follows that among the efforts to bring the messianic age must be the effort to spread the Seven Laws of Noah, as well as the wellsprings of Chassidic teachings associated with them, outward to non-Jews. Indeed, the Prophets tell us, "Nations shall walk in your light." Although the Torah was given to the people of Israel, it will also serve as a light to the nations. [43]

Our efforts must be geared to the "final days" in purifying and clarifying ourselves and in influencing the Noachides to accept their God-given destiny which will cause the nations of the world to come before God and give honor to His Name, with the true and complete redemption through our righteous Moshiach, speedily and truly in our days... [T]here was a time when we did not reach out to the Gentiles to encourage them to observe the Seven Noachide Laws... In our generation things are different. There is no danger involved in this activity, and to the contrary, such activity will increase the respect that the nations show us, for they will realize that Jews care not only about their own welfare but also about the good of all humanity and the whole world... This phenomenon adds much momentum to the efforts of convincing the citizens of the world to observe the Seven Noachide Laws. When the President proclaims its importance it is easier to encourage average people to accept it and so the opportunity must not be lost. It also provides us with a clear sign from Above that there is no time to lose in teaching the Gentiles of the world about God.[44]

The Rebbe exhorted several American presidents to work to foster a religious climate in the United States.

The Rebbe even extends the Torah of gentiles to Torah study, prayer, religious holiday celebrations, and respect for the civil government.

Torah Learning: The *Mishnah* states that "Any person who says a [Torah] idea in the name of its author [including a non-Jew] brings Redemption to the world." This is because non-Jews are also enjoined in the mitzvah of Torah study (in the areas in which they are obligated).[45]

Sukkot Rejoicing: This also implies involving others, even Gentiles, in the celebration. Not only must they witness the rejoicing, but they must also take part in the celebrations and attain the unique level of joy appropriate for the present evening. [46]

During the 1991 riots in Crown Heights, Mayor David Dinkins visited the Rebbe and asked for a blessing for peace between the two peoples, Jews and blacks. The Rebbe told him: "Don't say two peoples. One people, under one government and under one God."

A unity that permits no diversity is a limited concept; there is but a single hue. Unity thus becomes only surface-deep. By contrast, a unity that recognizes diversity can thrive. This "unity in diversity" implies a shared acceptance of an inner truth. Common principles and ideals have the power to bring together people with different abilities. So, interdependence is a desirable facet of American life. More can be accomplished when people with varied gifts pull together.

The bold statements of the Lubavitcher Rebbe could only work through the great charismatic force of his leadership. In many respects, he accepted the concept of American civil religion and even certain elements of American Evangelical pre-millenarian dispensational thought, in which current political events are part of the messianic path. His millenarian scenario of the late twentieth century was strong enough to undercut inherited dualism because of his followers' sense of an immanent end-time. The Rebbe resolved the dissonance between the Chabad texts and the accepted tolerance of contemporary life through an all-embracing vision of Judaism. Many Lubavitchers, especially those still living in Chasidic enclaves, rely on the older exclusivism, but those outward looking followers who engage with the world cite the newer readings, In order to interpret the many exclusivist texts from non-Chabad sources in a similar manner would require an equally great acceptance both of the goodness of common American ideals and of a greater universal role for Judaism.

Another recent approach is that of the contemporary kabbalist Yitzhak Nahmani who rejects the theory that gentile souls come from the evil side and by using sources from Midrash, Nahmani argues that all human souls originate in Adam; even Esau and Ishmael have divine lights.[47] Although many modern Jews do not have an interest in kabbalistic or Hasidic doctrine, nevertheless these new understandings show that seemingly rigid texts can be reread, even by conservative thinkers.

Conclusions on Exclusivism

Positions that emphasize Jewish chosenness and uniqueness serve to articulate a foundation of rabbinic thought and possess the positive value of teaching about the special relationship of Jews and God. They create an oppositional identity useful for stability in a world of infinite choices and for creating a strong dedicated community with a sense of mission and uniqueness. Theologically, evaluating these passages needs to be part of a bigger project examining Jewish chosenness and formulating a contemporary theology of the chosen status of Israel. However, some forms of Jewish exclusivism are not merely chosenness, but rather a categorical rejection of other religions combined with a dualistic sense of separatism. Choseness and the special status of Israel itself is not the problem.

Today, these texts are usually only cited by those with special need for isolation, such as those within the settlers' movement or those seeking the isolationism of a life of Torah study in purity. On the other extreme, they are cited by anti-Semites and by anti-religious writers (who are themselves sometimes ex-religious) wanting to show the narrowness of traditional Jewish texts. Most responsible Jews today use these texts in conjunction with the inclusivist and universal texts to create a viable normative position. When teaching, most of the texts are just politely skipped, or explained historically. Usually the way to deal with the difficult texts is to contexualize them historically.

I remember the first time I read Bonaventure's *Collations on Hexameron* and found anti-Judaism to be a serious part of his doctrine of creation. Bonaventure presented Jews as outside the natural realm. My polite instructors, and the visiting lecturers to the campus who were experts on Bonaventure and excited about the theological potential of Bonaventure's doctrines in a non-scholastic post–Vatican II world, ignored these elements entirely, as did the current secondary literature. But history shows the power of such texts on later centuries.

As this chapter makes the reader acutely aware, there is much demonization of other people and faiths in Jewish texts; there is even more small-minded myopia and narcissism wherein the world revolves around Judaism. Much work needs to be done to evaluate the social implications of these ideas and to discuss which can be rewritten and which ought to be outright rejected. All religions have terrible texts that are not usually brought up. The question is of how they are used today and to limit their influence when they do resurface. We need to differentiate between those that can be tempered with inclusive ideas and used in a positive way for pride and self-definition from those texts that are solely polemical, remaining outside the mainstream Jewish textual tradition as vestiges of an age of persecution.

CHAPTER 8

Gentiles

This chapter will give an overview of some of the texts from the Jewish legal literature, the halakhah, in the context of the material presented in the prior chapters. The Jewish legal perspective starts with the assumption that there are texts of the halakhah that favor Jews and considers gentiles as outside the normative system. In this status as outsiders, gentiles occupy a similar legal position as heretics and nonobservant Jews.

Approaching these questions from the perspective of Jewish law is similar to those Christians who approach other religions through ecclesiology. The assumption is that everything is known through the church. In the Jewish case, gentiles are outside the system not because of their religion but simply because they are outside of the ecclesiological structure. The only questions are: How do the members of other religions relate to the Jewish categories and institutions? Can they be tolerated despite not having a formal connection to the system? This legal approach generally considers itself tolerant when it inevitably finds grounds to refrain from condemning those outside the system. However, this ad hoc approach leaves many undeveloped questions about Jewish social theory and the role of religious liberty in Judaism (especially since Orthodox Jewish law lacks the formal statements of the Catholic Church granting religious freedom or vision of the modern world such as those from the 1965 session of Vatican II *Dignitatis Humanae* and *Gaudium et Spes*).

Gentiles

- Idolatry
- Gentiles today and idolatry
- State of Israel

- Gentiles and ethics of the law
- Contemporary issues

I will limit my presentation in this chapter to the following two questions: Is Christianity (and Islam) idolatry? Do those in the halakhic system have to act ethically toward those of other religions? The discussions about the status of contemporary religion as idolatry is explicit in the texts of Maimonides and Ritva, created a range of ad hoc latitude in the terse comments of Tosafot, and are seemingly effaced in the writings of Meiri. Later, many Jewish legal texts from the sixteenth to the nineteenth century attempt to exclude "our gentiles" from the halakhic discourse. The restrictions remain on the legal books; however "our gentiles" are excluded from the restrictions. But, with the recreation of the state of Israel, these exclusions and ambiguities needed to be explicitly stated by Chief Rabbi Herzog. In the nineteenth and twentieth centuries several rabbis sought to present an ethical system, while at the end of the twentieth century the counter valence not concerned with ethics has begun to resurface.

What about the Laws of Idolatry?

In discussing the theological question of how Judaism views other religions, I deliberately set aside a number of other issues that frequently arise in the context of Jewish–Christian discussions, for example, the question of icons and representations. Even if I consider that other religions have the same God, they can still violate Jewish conceptions of monotheism, which in Judaism refers to the means of worshipping God. When Jeroboam set up Golden Calves in the sanctuaries in Bethel and Dan, it was in service to the true God—but it was idolatry. Certainly, even the most pluralistic Jewish legal positions that affirm a common belief in God between Jews and Christians regard the creation of icons as idolatry. The colloquial term referred to as idolatry includes three separate categories: (1) using a statue to worship the biblical God; (2) associating a constellation or saint with the biblical God; or (3) worshiping another deity. However, the first categories are clearly biblical monotheists whose problem is the use of representation, not a foreign god.

Most of the other legal discussions surrounding the Talmudic tractate *Avodah Zarah* deal with creating sectarian restrictions on relating with gentiles for the purpose of creating an isolated community, not theological issues. The Talmud, however, in uncensored versions, states: in the contexts of avoiding the feast days of other religions, "Christians are always forbidden [to conduct business with them on Sundays]" (AZ 9:4).

The two starting points for a discussion of the halakhic issues are Maimonides (d. 1204) and the contemporaneous Talmudic glosses of the Tosafot school (twelfth century). The approach, by the great jurist Maimonides is explicit in considering that "Christians are idolaters" for all legal purposes because of the Trinity.[1] Based on statements elsewhere in his legal code and his theory of idolatry presented in the *Guide of the Perplexed*, Christians would be idolatrous of the second category, correct biblical God, wrong conception.

> Know that this Christian nation, who advocates the messianic claim in all their various sects, all of them are [considered] idolaters. On all their various festivals it is forbidden for us to deal with them. All Torah restrictions pertaining to idolaters pertain to them. Sunday is included among their festivals. Therefore, it is forbidden to deal at all on Sunday with the believers in the messiah. We treat Sunday as an idolatrous festival...We deal with them as we would deal with any idolaters on their festival.[2]

This is the starting position for most Jewish legal deciders concerning the halakhic status of Christians. Yet, it was censored out from the printed editions; hence, few had direct access to this explicit and unambiguous statement. As a note, there is limited validity to the claim that he only wrote this because he did not have familiarity with Christians; Fatimid Egypt, especially Cairo, had a significant Christian population.[3]

This prohibition formulated in the twelfth-century Islamic world was practically tempered in later centuries by citations from the contemporaneous Tosafot, who since they lived in Christian countries could not avoid business dealing with Christians. Tosafot are the twelfth- and thirteenth-century commentaries on the Talmud from medieval France and Germany that sought to harmonize discordant passages and to harmonize the Talmudic text with contemporary medieval reality. These tosafist commentators created limited leniencies for business purposes, which became a backhanded theological aside that allows Christians to have a Trinity because gentiles do not need a pure monotheism. Jewish discussions in this legal tradition of whether trinitarianism can be considered monotheism relate solely to answering a legal question about permitting dealing with gentiles on their holidays, or allowing gentile oaths. Despite its seemingly theological nature, it is a secular question—can Jews do business with Christians on their holidays?[4]

The prime example of this approach of ad hoc thinking is their explanation of the Talmudic passage that states that a Jew should not form a partnership with an idolater or take them to court so as not to cause them to swear by a false god (Sanhedrin 63b). These medieval commentators, the Tosafot, who understood the unfeasibility of applying this in Christian lands excluded

Christians from the category of idolatry. They defined the prohibition of taking an idolater to court does not apply to Christians by acknowledging that Christians and Jews share the same God but that the Christians associate God with other elements.

> It is permissible to [cause a gentile's oath through litigation with one's non-Jewish partner because] today all swear in the name of the saints to whom no divinity is ascribed. They also mention and have in mind God's name, in any event no idolatrous name is actually said. They have the Creator of the world in mind. Even though they associate (*shituf*) God's name with "something else," we do not find that it is forbidden to cause others to associate (*shituf*), and there is no issue of placing a stumbling block before the blind [by entering into litigation with the non-Jewish business partner, thereby causing him to take an oath] because the Sons of Noah were not restricted about it. (*Tosafot Babylonian Talmud Sanhedrin* 63b)

This text, and the other similar ones, which states that there is no prohibition of associations (*shituf*) for gentiles, was created for the purpose of "accepting an oath of a gentile." It permitted Jews to engage in business practices with Christians, even though this could result in the Christian partner taking an oath in the name of Jesus or Christian saints, by saying that the Christian concept of God as including Jesus is not considered to be idolatry but only an association with another entity. There is no direct discussion of the Trinity in the passage or discussion of Christianity, other than use of the vague term "something else." However, there are some manuscripts, unavailable to most legal commentators, that did replace the something else with "Jesus."[5] The Jewish historian Jacob Katz considered these passages as ad hoc legal decisions that did not violate the medieval exclusivism toward Christians. Even if there is a theology in this passage, at best, this is a low theology of assuming that gentiles understood as followers of the laws of Noah (see chapter three) have lower standards of monotheism required of them by God.

This position of allowing Christians to have a monotheism associated with Jesus as a Trinity was in turn codified by R. Moses Isserles (1520–1572), the main legal decider for European Jewry. The version that most legally trained Jews would have known is as follows.

> Today, it is permitted [to form a partnership with Christians], because when they swear on their holy scriptures called the Evangelion, they do not hold it to be divine. Even though when they mention God they mean Jesus, they do not mention idolatry since they really mean the creator of heaven and earth.

Even though they mention jointly God's name and another name, there is no prohibition to cause someone to jointly mention [or associate] God with another...since this association is not forbidden to gentiles...[6]

For Isserles, Christians do not mention another deity when they speak of the Trinity or Jesus since they mean the biblical God of creation, but they retain the problem of a false understanding of it. This argument, probably pragmatically driven, serves as the current default position for most Ashkenazi halakhic deciders.

Rabbi Yosef Karo, the sixteenth-century author of the definitive code of Jewish law, the *Shulkhan Arukh*, codifies Maimonides, but R. Moses Isserles, the Ashkenazi commentator on Karo's legal code, in numerous short glosses, accepts Tosafot. Yet, most of Isserles' comments are limited to "today, the practice of our gentiles is acceptable."[7] In the context of this book, I cannot stress enough that this approach is non-theological and solely ad hoc pragmatic. Especially, since in other places, Moses Isserles still considers Christian worship as idolatry.[8] No Jewish source allows the worship through any form of association; rather, all worship must be directed to the one and only Creator.

The ruling of the Tosafist remains ambiguous enough to allow dispute on whether he deemed Christianity not to fall under the category of idolatry (for Gentiles) or merely permitted Christians to take an oath in the name of the Trinity. Generally, this dictum has been interpreted as stating that Christianity is monotheistic enough for gentiles. Jacob Katz points out that this expansive reading is from the influence of medieval Jewish philosophic literature produced in Arabic countries that used the term association (*shituf*) for those who are polytheist or for Tri-theism. This broad conception allowed interpreters in later centuries to read the legal statement of Tosafot as having wide-ranging implications. It is important to note that none of these Jewish positions discusses any actual Christian understandings of the Trinity, and they blur the lines between actual Trinitarian theology, and non-Trinitarian or Arian theologies.

The later Jewish legalists who see a broad permission created here include Rabbi Shabbtai Hakohen (1621–1662; Shakh), who exerted an influence on later interpretations. (In the earlier chapters we saw Yaakov Emden, who used this statement for a broad inclusivism; Moses Mendelssohn used it for a broad universalism; and as we shall see later, Rabbi Herzog used this to permit the monotheism of Christianity.)

In contrast, Rabbi Ephraim ha-Kohen (1616–1678) rejected the line of reasoning of Rabbi Shabbtai Hakohen. "I have seen many who are mistaken in their explanation that non-Jews are not bound by [the prohibition of] association (shituf), exempting those who worship the Trinity... Why should there be a difference between Jews and non-Jews in this issue?"[9]

Rabbi Yakov Emden follows the lenient position on association as permitted for gentiles and offers an underutilized explanation that association (*shituf*) only applies when one associates God with another deity as two deities of equal power. However, it would not apply to divine intermediaries without independent power, when God remains supreme over a lower divine force, as well as hypostases or representations. According to Emden, "Most idolaters that ever lived believed God to be a God of gods. They believed in an original cause that is the source of all. He is the God of the other gods who were worshiped as intermediaries." In the background to this approach, one senses some of the biblical and rabbinic notions of natural religion and God of gods, yet Emden does not spell them out.[10]

Ritva

Rabbi Yom Tov Asevilli (1250–1330, Seville; Ritva), a major rabbinic figure in his time, was educated in the rabbinic traditions of Catalonia and was an author of an important Talmudic commentary. For Ritva, his Christian and Muslim contemporaries are all outside of God's religion and not ethical or approved by God. He creates a restrictive position negating any natural morality or natural religion to gentiles. "The righteous of the nations judged for an eternal life and who have a share in the world to come are those that keep the seven Noahite laws. But Christians and Muslims are included with the heretics [that do not get eternal life] as Rashi taught 'the students of Jesus are heretics.'"[11] Besides being heretics, Ritva guards against anything used in Christian worship as idolatrous. For him, crosses are considered pagan idols. But impressions of crosses and cross designs on coins and cups are not a problem, since the Talmud had already permitted Greco-Roman forms in public non-sacred usage.

> They worship the image of the cross, but when they regularly place the form of crosses on their silver vessels, we know that they certainly do not worship the vessels. Furthermore, they only worship the images of the crosses when polluted [dysphemism for blessed] by their monks. That is why all permit currency [with crosses] because it is certain that they do not worship it.[12]
>
> Even when the image on the vessel is of Jesus the Nazarene, it is known that that they do not worship it.[13]

On the latter point of functional use of crosses, Ritva's opinion is continued by Rabbi Moshe Isserles, who continues this leniency to consider ornamental crosses as permitted since Christians do not worship them.[14] Some authorities, however, differ in attitude and would not permit crosses even on Swedish flags, window frames, or on the top of kings of chess sets. Some Jews were so averse to using any sign resembling a cross that in arithmetic books they avoided the plus sign.[15]

As a halakhic text, Asevilli is not interested in discussing his apprehension of Christian ritual. There are, however, important antecedents for treating Christianity as full paganism that are part of his cultural heritage of Andalusia. There is a medieval text, *Sefer Ha-Azamim* attributed to R. Abraham Ibn Ezra, that lays out a neo-Platonic theory of idolatry based on pagan sources such as *Book of the Nabatean Agriculture*. The work describes the process by which a cosmic deity is thought to be drawn to inhabit a statue or a human medium.[16] The *Sefer Ha-Azamim* uses this theory to explain the power of the Christian cross without overt mention of any other point about Christianity. In later centuries, there is a general, lingering perception that the sacrament of the Eucharist and the use of crosses have something idolatrous about them and should be avoided, even if Jews are unclear as to what that is, or how to articulate it.[17]

An older contemporary of Ritva, the Rashba (1235–1310; Abraham Aderet), the leading Rabbinic authority of his age, was more dependent on Maimonides, and proffered by ruling that Muslims should not be deemed idolaters, yet remarked that "all the other Gentiles are idol worshippers."[18]

Sometimes honest description about the prohibitions and attitudes in the texts goes further in interreligious encounter than liberal niceties. Medieval authorities who consider Christianity in the legal category of idolatry are in the overwhelming majority. I chose to present the Ritva and Rashba because they lived at approximately the same time as Meiri, in similar geographic regions—the former two in Catalonia, the latter in Provençe. In developing any theology of other religions, placing the complete data on the table before one starts the discussion remains essential.

Meiri

In modern times, the fundamental and widely accepted text for discussions of the laws of idolatry is that of Rabbi Menachem Meiri, the thirteenth-century Provençal Talmudic commentator who explicitly separated rabbinic categories of idolatry from the practices of his contemporary gentiles. In his comments on the Talmud, he broadly reformulates the restrictions of the Talmud, in which idolatry no longer exists in the world.

> It has already been stated that these things were said concerning periods when there existed nations of idolaters, and they were contaminated in their deeds and tainted in their dispositions...but other nations, which are

restrained by the ways of religion and which are free from such blemishes of character—on the contrary, they even punish such deeds- are, without doubt, exempt from this prohibition. (*Beit ha-Bechirah* on *Avodah Zarah* 53)

But anyone who belongs to nations restricted by ways of religion and worshipping the Godhead in any way, even if their belief is very different from ours, are not included in these rules, but are completely like Jews in such matters, including [the obligation of] returning lost items and [the ban on] taking advantage of their mistakes, and all other things, without any difference. (*Beit ha-Bechirah* on *Bava Kama* 113a–b)

In many other places, Meiri writes that gentiles, meaning Christians, have knowledge of the ways of religion (Ketubot 3; Gittin 59) and that therefore the laws of idolatry do not apply to them. He even includes contemporary Christian as brothers, "in the ways of religion" and included with Jews under the prohibition of interest (*Beit ha-Bechirah* on Bava Metziah, 219, 267). The full texts of Meiri's commentary were not available until recently. Until the mid-twentieth century, most rabbinic scholars only had the citations of his opinions available in other works.

The full version of his reasoning opens with an empirical observation that Jews are not avoiding Christian holidays. In order to explain why some of the rabbinic restrictions on gentiles are not fully observed, Meiri explains that the laws of foreign worship only apply to ancient idolatry and do not have to be followed, but the rabbinic dietary and wine restrictions still apply to contemporary religions and are still in effect.

I have seen many people puzzled by the fact that nowadays nobody is careful to observe these laws. But I have already explained which Gentile nations are meant in this tractate; and the names of their holidays will also testify to it: for, as I mentioned above, they all are feasts of ancient nations, not restricted by the ways of religions, but practicing fervently and persistently worship of idols, stars and talismans, which—and all things like them—are essentials of idolatry, as has been already explained. But in any event, with regard to [avoiding] the possibility of violation of the prohibitions concerning Sabbath and the prohibitions concerning food and drinks [of non-Jews]—e. g. [the ban] on wine of libation, and on their wine per se, and all those type of bans, whether it is only consuming something [of theirs] in food which was banned, or getting any advantage of it, or if the bans were made in order to prevent intermarriages—all the [non-Jewish] nations come under these prohibitions... From now on, let these things be settled on your mind, so that it will not be necessary to clarify them specifically on each and every occasion, but you should be able to analyze on your own whether in any particular case the ancient nations are meant or the non-Jews in general; examine things, and you will know them. (*Beit ha-Bechirah* on *Avodah Zarah* 26a)

Gerald Blidstein has shown that Meiri offers a wide philosophic perspective extending the leniency far beyond practical or apologetic concerns. Blidstein points out that when the Talmud seemingly explicitly mentions Christianity, Meiri bends over backward to reinterpret the reference by offering a creative explanation to remove any possible Talmudic reference to Christianity. Meiri writes: "When the Talmud states that "a Christian [*notzri*] is always forbidden" I interpret it to mean watchers [*notzrim*] who come from a far country (Jeremiah 4:16), where it refers to the nation as *notzrim* from [their King] Nebuchad nezzar." Besides the far-reaching removal of Christianity from restrictive laws, he goes further and includes other religions as part of the religious world of Judaism for legal matters. When the Talmud writes, "Israel is not subject to astrology" (Shabbat 156a), Meiri comments, "the name Israel applies to those restricted by the ways of religion." He even makes the surprising corollary that rejects applying the term heretic to a Jewish convert to Christianity since: "One who has completely left the category [of Israel] and becomes a member of another religion is considered by us to be the same as any other member of the religion he has joined" (*Horayyot*, 11a 275, cf. *Teshuva* 597–8). However, the laws of idolatry still apply to iconography and using images even when one follows the ways of religion. Christian worship remains forbidden. And though it is widely cited, ultimately this text remains a practical tool for dealing with gentiles, not a theological treatise about God.

Moshe Halbertal, professor at Hebrew University, presents Meiri's position as a broad universal statement reflecting some of the influence of the Hebrew translations of Al-Ghazzali on Provençal Jewry (see chapter five, especially the sections on Ibn Kaspi and Albalag). For others, the Meiri's position continues the traditional thinking about the category of the resident alien (*ger toshav*) and is less of an innovation.[19]

Rabbi Abraham Isaac Kook in one his letters affirmed that "the fundamental view is the Meiri's, that nations restricted by decent customs between a man and his fellow should be considered resident strangers in regard to all human obligations." In this short quote, Kook offers two important statements about Meiri's position. First that the position is indeed an extension of the laws of resident alien and second that the "ways of religion" are the creation of a moral society. Second, whereas Meiri considered the "ways of religion" as based on correct understanding of religion, Rabbi Kook similar to other early twentieth-century Jewish authors, adapts Meiri to write that gentiles are to be judged by morality not religion.[20]

Meiri's position may also reflect an acceptance of the heretical Cathar, and proto-Unitarian leanings of the surrounding Provençal Christian environment, or at least of the intellectual class.[21] The historian Emmanuel Le Roy Ladurie, for example, in his work *Montaillou*, brilliantly shows how the accounts from the Cathar trials reflect the lived religion of the people in Provençe. Ladurie presents the peasants as far from official Catholicism; they were more concerned with fate, magic, and salvation than the finer points of Christian theology, and the local priests did little to remedy this lack. Ladurie contrasts the "free and easy way of the masses" with "the great God of 'Real Christianity.'" Yet, many, if not most, Jewish historians ignore Ladurie's position for a variety of reasons: as not reflecting the Jewish conception of the historic times or because if it was empirically true then other halakhic figures would have made the same statements, or because they feel that Meiri is fundamentally different from others due to philosophic reasoning, not sociology. To the extent that Jews knew about their neighbors solely through observation of the common man's religion and marketplace interactions, these historical observations should play a greater role in our understanding of their positions.

Max Weber described the double ethic of an ethnic economy, where there is a dual system of law, for example seventeenth-century Protestant Germany that had separate civil laws for Jews, heretics, and Catholics. Does the logic of Sinai commit Jews to a dual ethic? Max Weber answered: "Yes, Judaism affirms a dual ethic." As a double ethic, Jewish law needs to differentiate Jews from Jewish heretics and non-Jews. Meiri's position is useful for moving beyond discriminatory laws and a dual ethic.

Nevertheless, I do not think that a panacea for the negative statements about gentiles is to conceptualize the statements of the Meiri as modern tolerance. Despite the apologetic readings, traditional Jewish texts such as the Meiri are not advocating religious liberties as found in the post-enlightenment world. Furthermore, an avoidance of insult and discrimination is not sufficient to respond to religious encounters. One needs theological formulations, theories of religious liberty, and an acknowledgment of the religious quest of other people of faith rather than solely the social category of gentiles who are moral. More than that, one needs to admit and then deal with the difficult texts in one's tradition, especially since many others in the community still quote them. Tolerance does not lead to a common vision of responsibility, what Chief Rabbi Jonathan Sacks calls "a dignity of difference."

Eliezer Ashkenazi

It is certainly interesting to note that the Polish rabbis who developed this trend of considering Christians as non-idolatrous in the early modern period all lived in Unitarian regions. Rabbi Eliezer Ashkenazi mentions this point explicitly in his writings.[22] More importantly, as a Renaissance figure, he was influenced by current universal trends in Italy, and by his own study of the Maimonidean universalists.

Rabbi Ashkenazi (1513–1585), rabbi in Egypt, Italy, and Poland, was a rational thinker and major influence in his era. He wrote an important biblical commentary and defended the traditional medieval rationalism against Maharal. Ashkenazi, as a universalist and specifically a reader of the medieval Maimonidean universalists, considers that there is no intrinsic special status to Jews. People are different only in cultivated opinion; everyone can use their free will to choose correct opinions. Hence, Christians and Muslims, along with Jews, are all on the path to fulfilling the correct purpose of humanity known through revelation since the Torah was given to everyone in the world. In the end of days, all will be God's children and Israel the first born.[23]

The following passage from his Haggadah commentary played a role in subsequent early modern legal discussions, but seems to have been forgotten in twentieth-century discourse.

"Pour out thy wrath upon the nations"

Some of the Gentiles among whom we are exiled under their protection have thought that God forbid we are cursing them.

It only applies to the nations that do not know Him, that deny the Exodus from Egypt because they don't accept the miracles and wonders. It is quite clear that the Gentiles among whom we are exiled all know about the Exodus and believe in it, and know its details... We only curse the idol worshipers who don't believe in creation and who destroyed the Temple, not the nations who became Edom and Ishmael (Christianity and Islam) because they were still not created... But now our Gentiles and the Ishmaelites know God, and acknowledge the Exodus, forefend for us to curse them from our religion.

And when we do curse those who afflict us and unjustly persecute us, that curse is not from our religion, forefend, but as a person who curses one who afflicts another...

Our holy Torah announces this in the name of the head of the faithful [Abraham] that God does not desire this, as it is written, "Will you destroy the righteous with the wicked?" And the master of the prophets [Genesis 18:23] said, "One person will sin and the whole community should be cut off?" And from the writings it is clarified that we are not allowed from our religion to curse nations that acknowledge the Exodus from Egypt and know God even if they have not received the Torah...

That is why it was not permitted for Israel to conquer the land of
Canaan until after the Exodus, that even after they know about God
they did not believe or accept...[24]

Rabbi Ashkenazi acknowledges that gentiles accept God, creation, and even the
providential Exodus story. Following Nahmanides (cited in chapter four), this passage makes the case that gentiles accept the miraculous providential hand of God,
a crucial element in considering them part of biblical religion. Ashkenazi draws a
distinction between the negative attitude toward gentiles in the Talmud and the
attitude toward contemporary Christians by stating that gentiles at the time of
the Temple were idolaters without a belief in God. He further distances himself
from prior teachings of contempt by stating that the curses that the Midrash heaps
upon Rome have no connection to the later nations of Edom. Ashkenazi further
displays his unique universal exegesis in his interpretation of the four sons of the
Haggadah. The four sons represent the shared Abraham faith. Isaac is the wise
son, Esau, as Christianity, is the wicked son, Jacob is the simple son and Yishmael,
as Islam, is the son that does not know how to ask (*Maaseh Hashem* 122).

Ashkenazi consistently reads the Bible and Rashi as ethical and fought against
the dualistic thinking of Maharal. He invokes the Jewish sense of justice that has
continued since the time of Abraham; he proclaims that Jews do not curse others.
Even when Christians persecute Jews, the persecution stems not from their religion
but from unfortunate occurrences between people. Rabbi Ashkenazi's thinking
is remarkably forward looking, in that he thinks that one cannot hold a people
accountable for the injustice of some of them, and certainly one cannot hold their
religion responsible for the injustice committed by certain members of it.

Yom-Tov Lipman Heller

Rabbi Yom-Tov Heller (1579–1654) was a well-known rabbi in Prague and
Vienna and the author of a famous commentary on the Mishnah, *Tosfot Yom-
Tov*. I include his text here, rather than earlier with his older contemporary
inclusivist R. Avigdor Kara, to contextualize the aforementioned Rabbis Kara
and Ashkenazi and the upcoming Rabbi Rivkes in a single Polish approach.
Rather than apologetics that fly in the face of Ashkenazi exclusivism, these
rabbis clearly reflect the thought of the rabbinic elite in Poland. In the early
modern period, there was a flourishing of positive statements accepting gentiles. These statements are so widespread that they must reflect a common
historical experience and should not be relegated to mere apologetics.

Like R. Eliezer Ashkenazi, Rabbi Heller criticized Maharal, accepted contemporary gentiles, and lived in a Unitarian climate. Heller's academic biogra-
pher Joseph Davis points out that R. Heller absolved the princes and Christianity

for persecutions and placed the blame on the peasants. Jews respected the princes because even though princes were fickle, life would be worse without them. On the anti-Catholic milieu, Davis also notes, "It is possible that Heller was influenced by the rebellious, iconoclastic, and anti-Catholic mood of Prague in 1619. When radical Protestants were denouncing the Eucharist as 'idolatry,' could Heller remain far behind?" Jospeh Davis contends that

> in parallel to the well-known Christian ambition to bring the Gospel to the Jews, certain Jews in Prague, such as Heller, wished to draw the Gentiles by words towards the will of their Creator, that is, towards the perception of their universal moral duty. Heller placed himself in a tradition of Maimonidean universalism, which implied, in principle if not in practice, a duty to enlighten the non-Jewish world.

Rabbi Heller rejected the exclusivism of Maharal, claiming that Maharal's "interpretation is far-fetched." Rabbi Heller affirms, like S.D. Luzzatto after him, that "Love your neighbor" applies to gentiles. And that "when Rabbi Akiva said 'man,' he means all human beings, who are all beloved, all created in the Image" (*Avot* 3:14).[25]

> Rabbi Akiva...used to say: Beloved is man, for he was created in the Image...as it is written. "For in the image of God made He man" (Gen. 9:12). Beloved are Israel, for they are called the children of the All-present...as it written, "you are the children of the LORD your God" (Deut. 14:1). Beloved are Israel, for to them was given the precious vessel [the Torah]...as it is written, "For I give you good doctrine, forsake not my Law" (Prov. 4:2).
>
> Rabbi Akiva came to instruct all the inhabitants of the world, as we have been commanded by Moses our Teacher, as Maimonides explains. For if we are commanded to impose [the laws of the sons of Noah] by the sword...how much more so [are we commanded] to draw them by words towards the will of their Creator and the desire of their Rock. [Therefore Rabbi Akiva] spoke well of them, [saying] that they are beloved, having been created in the image...For it is the law of mankind [*torat ha'adam*] to perform God's laws and statutes out of a sense of commandment, as Maimonides has said...and as Rashi [also] explained. (Avot 3:14)

Moshe Rivkes

One of the strongest statements for the acceptance of contemporary Christianity by a Polish rabbi from this group comes from the pen of R. Moshe Rivkes, an eighteenth-century rabbinic scholar who accepts Rabbi Eliezer Ashkenazi's view. [26]

> The rabbis of the Talmud meant by the term "idolaters" the pagans who lived in their time, who worshipped the stars and the constellations and did not believe in the Exodus from Egypt and in the creation of the world out of nothing. But the nations under whose benevolent shadow we, the Jewish nation, are exiled and are dispersed among them, they do believe in the creation of the world out of nothing and the Exodus from Egypt and in the essentials of faith, and their whole intention is toward the Maker of heaven and earth, as other authorities have written...
>
> So rather than a prohibition not to save them [if they were idolaters], on the contrary, we are required to pray for their welfare as Rabbi Eliezer Ashkenazi wrote at length on the passage from the Passover haggadah "Pour out thy Wrath." King David prayed to God to pour out his wrath on the idolater who did not believe in creation from nothing or the signs and wonders that God performed for us in Egypt and at the giving of the Torah. The nations in whose shadow we live and under whose wings we are protected do believe in all of this. Therefore, we are always required to pray for the welfare and success of the kingdom and the ministers, in all their provinces. Indeed, Maimonides ruled according to Rabbi Joshua, that the pious of the nations have a portion in the world to come. (*Be'er haGolah* to *Hoshen Mishpat* 425:5) [27]

In his formulation, Rivkes uses the ambiguous distinction between "those who lived in their time" and the nations today. Rivkes, following the universalism of Eliezer Ashkenazi, does acknowledge that the Christian conception of God based on Creation, Exodus, and the essentials of faith, presumably providence and afterlife, places Christianity closer to the Jewish biblical conception of religion than to the ancient idolatrous conceptions.

Other eighteenth-century rabbis

Bachrach, Eybeschutz, and Falk

Azriel Shohat, the Hebrew University scholar, pointed out that charitable understandings of Christianity were the norm in the eighteenth century as integration in general society increased. Shohat discussed Emden and Rivkes, and noted that these were not isolated opinions; others shared the approach, including the cleanly stated opinion by R. Yair Haim Bachrach (1638–1702), author of *Havot Yair*, that "Gentiles of our day are not idol worshippers with regard to every issue, since they believe in the Creator of heaven and earth..."[28]

Rabbi Yonathan Eybeschutz, the rabbi of Hamburg (with Altoona and Wansbeck), in a clear statement of solidarity writes:

> The Christian nations among whom we live generally observe the principles of justice and righteousness, believe in the creation of the world and the existence and providence of God, and in the Law of Moses and the prophets, and oppose the Sadducean view that denies the resurrection of the dead and the immortality of the soul. Therefore it is fitting to be thankful to them, to praise and extol them, and to bring upon them blessings and not, God forbid, curses. [29]

It would seem that R. Eybeschutz considered even his Evangelical-Lutheran and Roman Catholic contemporaries to be believers in God.

Another important figure is Rabbi Yaakov Yehoshua Falk (1680–1756), author of the Penai Yehoshua, who offers a similar statement to his contemporaries. [30]

> "It is known in all the earth and in all books and works like the Talmud and poskim...whenever it says *akum* and similar statements. in all of them the specific intention was those nations that worshiped stars and constellations. But those nations among whom we live in their shadow are not included in this. It is not enough that we steal or cheat, or have false weights...but...but we are obligated to continuously pray for the peace of the dominion and the officers.

Rabbi Yehezkael Landau

Rabbi Yehezkael Landau (1713–1793) was chief rabbi in Prague and head of its Yeshiva in 1755. He is best known to us today through his monumental work of *she'alot uteshuvot* entitled *Noda Biyehudah*.

In this famous introductory piece from the 1776 edition of his work, we find a clear acknowledgment of a problem combined with a forceful answer.

> One has to be careful for the honor of the nations of our time. We are protected in their lands and governments. We are obligated to pray for the peace of the monarchs, their ministers, and their armies and to pray for the peace of the nation and its inhabitants. Forefend for us to deny the good which they have bestowed upon us, giving us a life and refuge in the land.
>
> Furthermore, I continuously warn about theft and robbery and make known that there is no difference at all in the prohibition of theft and robbery between the money of a Jew or the money of a gentile...

The nations of our time among whom we dwell believe in the principles of religion, they believe in the creation of the world, in the prophecy of the prophets and in all the miracles and wonders written in the Torah and the books of the prophets. Therefore it is simple and obvious that that we are required and obligated to honor and praise [them]. Therefore I announce and make known that not just in this work but in every place in any work that one finds a derogatory statement about *akum* or *goyim* or *kutim* and similar languages, one should not make the mistake of applying it to the nations of our time. One who explains them thus is mistaken and explains them against the decree of the Torah. Rather the intention was on the ancient peoples who believed in stars and constellations like the Sabian sect mentioned by Maimonides in the *Guide*. Those nations are heretics and sectarians because they do not confess the creation of the world and they deny all the wonders and prophecy. Therefore I warn everyone on these matters. Place them on you heart to remember.

Jacob Katz treated it as apologetic in a negative sense as only for external consumption keeping a separate ethic internally. Meaning that for Katz, either one accepts a single universal ethic for all people like Mendelssohn, or one must adopt the exclusivist position of Jewish law. Yet, even he acknowledged that:

On the one hand, these generalized declarations may be seen as merely attempts to evade the censors... On the other hand we should not conclude that the title page declarations were conspicuously dishonest. The distinction between Christians and pagans were applied in full when it came to practical questions of business ethics. (35)

An inclusivist position such as that presented in Landau's introduction does indeed affect the community, even if written for apologetic reasons. He shows respect for the other, and like most rabbinic elite who trusted the absolute monarchs, credits the government for providing peace. He acknowledges that contemporary Christians are Bible believers and deserve all the respect that entails.

However, it is worth noting that Landau's own son Rabbi Samuel Landau abandoned this early modern line of thinking about Christianity and also he considered the Ashkenaz leniencies as solely pragmatic in nature, to allow an oath in court but not to state any broader position that Christianity is not idolatry.

Even though it is common among many great sages that non-Jews are permitted in association (*shituf*)...nevertheless I have sought and not found this in either the Babylonian or Jerusalem Talmuds, or in the writings of the medieval commentaries... It appears to me that it is based on a printing error in the tosafists...which lead R. Moses Isserles to codify it and thereby mislead many great sages.[31]

Later legalists continue this approach of treating these statements to their original limited pragmatic application.

This chapter does not seek to render legal decisions to the myriad of practical cases that pertain to the obedience to these texts; my goal was solely to organize the material as it relates to the status of other religions. [32]

Herzog: Founding of the State of Israel

Rabbi Isaac Herzog (1889–1959) was chief rabbi of Ireland and then the first chief rabbi for the state of Israel. Due to his political role his positions are especially important.

Rabbi Herzog was responsible for having to set up the Ministry of Religion for the new country, among whose duties it would be to maintain and support Protestant, Catholic, Muslim, and Druze houses of worship in the state of Israel. The state of Israel at its founding gave its citizens of other religions equal rights, based on the continuance of Article 83 of the Palestine Order in Council of 1922, but the houses of worship were placed under the chief rabbinate that had to rely on halakhah to create a tolerant position. In order to offer context for Herzog's goals of supporting the religious liberties mandated as civil law in Israel's Declaration of Independence, I offer a few comparisons. In England, the attempted Jewish Naturalization Act 1753 was repealed after a single year and it took until the middle of the nineteenth century for British Jewry to gain full rights. In the United States, the freedoms of the *Bill of Rights* took until the *1826 Jew Bill* of Maryland to finish the legal incorporation of Jews. Herzog limited his discussion to rabbinic categories, yet he knew about the legal discussions of minority rights, tolerance, and modern democracies.

Chief Rabbi Herzog had considered Islam as monotheistic and therefore had no legal problems with Islam but also no thought over the role of Islam in the new democratic state. He only had the technical question (a debate between Maimonides and Nahmanides) of whether Muslims fit into a rabbinic second-class status as resident-aliens. He preferred to follow the Raavad that they are resident aliens, or the Maimonidean commentators who allow gentiles to live in the land even if they are not resident aliens. "Islam is not in any way idolatry...the question is whether they are resident-aliens (*ger toshav*)"

Christianity was a more troubled discussion. Envisioning the birth of a country, where the new state had to be involved in the upkeep and support of churches, he had to include them as monotheists. He concluded that Christians are monotheists who have an incorrect formation of that monotheism.

> On the question of the small minority of Christians from all denomina-
> tions and sects there will certainly be immense concern by the United
> Nations and the small Christian countries regarding their rights...How
> would it be possible to endanger our chances and existence already at the
> start by restrictions against the Christians?
>   Christians are not in the category of idolatry and the Christians them-
> selves consider themselves monotheists, but our intellects do not grasp
> how they combine faith in God's unity with the trinity. However, there is
> no denying that they have the concept of the creator of the world and His
> providence but unrefined. In the final analysis, their status is dependent
> on whether Noahites are commanded on association (*shituf*). In my hum-
> ble opinion, we accept the view of Rabbi Zev Wolf Boskowitz concluded
> that Noahites were not commanded on association.[33] The rabbinical pro-
> hibition of idolatry on the other hand did not mention warnings about
> association, that is, if one worshiped the One God, without beginnings
> or end, the creator of heaven and earth, who has nothing joined to Him
> together with a celestial power or one of the natural phenomena or elevat-
> ing a man [missing words] to divinity. In the matter, the first is primary
> [one God] and latter secondary [association], even if this is culpable idola-
> try for a Jew, not so for a gentile, for whom it was not forbidden at all.
>   Nevertheless, the Rabbis said that gentiles outside the land of Israel
> are not literally idolatrous but they are following the faith of their
> forefathers (Hullin 13b) so too are the Christians in our age. Even the
> Catholics turn their hearts to heaven, even though they themselves do
> not grasp in their intellect the falseness of the contradiction of mono-
> theism and Trinity.

He sees Christianity as making no sense; he does not have, or attempt, an understanding of the Trinity. Rather, he relies on Rabbi Boskovitz's (1740–1818) broad understanding of Tosafot, which allows association for gentiles.

Rabbi Herzog grants Unitarians special status and all Protestants are considered honorary Unitarians. In the end, he permits all Christian houses of
worship through a string of rabbinic leniencies to argue for his point, rather
than a reformulation of a new religious argument.

> *Concerning maintaining their worship.*
>   For Protestants, [it is permitted to maintain their Churches] since
> even in the worse case their faith is not anything but association. They

do not use statues in their worship only the cross and it is clear that it is only a symbol for remembrance alone and not for worship. But also Catholics know that they are not worshiping the statue as a god but to proclaim the power of those people that the image depicts. Therefore it is certain that we are commanded to avoid entrance to their places of prayer just as it is forbidden for us to have association (*shituf*), to use their religious objects, and to maintain distance for the very purpose of the distance.

But here the question is if we are required to prevent this worship with power of the Jewish state? According to this I say: We are not sinning against our holy Torah if we tolerate their existence because it is unclear if it is mandated from the Torah...and in time of great need even doubts about Torah law are judged leniently...And it is permitted to prevent hatred...and this is passive not active.

Now we should look at the situation as it actually is and to decide the halakhah from a realistic perspective. We have not conquered nor are we able to conquer the land against the will of the nations, even some of them. The Jewish state was accepted by the United Nations by their agreement and there is no doubt that until the messiah comes we will need them for our protection...There is no doubt that they did not give us the state except to be established except by the law and statutes of minority rights for tolerance...

His final conclusion is that even if they are idolatry, we have no choice but to accept modern democracy. For Rabbi Herzog, a modern nation is a partnership of its members Jewish and non-Jewish, in which there cannot be different laws for different religions. The law needs to be the same for all on questions like acquiring land. Therefore, the system of Jewish law must accept the modern democratic nation state of law, civil rights, religious tolerance, and freedom of religion. For Herzog, it is beyond legal questions, there is a need of the hour after the Holocaust to establish a state.

Herzog rejects the opinion, expressed by several Haredi legal authorities, that it is better not to have a sovereign state than violate the imperative not to aid idolatrous practices in any way. In addition, he limits the prohibition of not tolerating idolatry in Israel to the impure, magical, and licentiousness of the idolatry of antiquity. In contrast, Rabbi Yoel Teitelbaum (1887–1979), the Grand rabbi of Satmar and a fierce anti-Zionist, presented an old school argument that it is forbidden to have a ministry of religion because the law requires the destruction of all churches as idolatry.

Within the Religious Zionist approach, Rabbi Ovadiah Yosef, former chief rabbi and a widely respected legal decider, combines the theoretical prohibition of the haredi position with practical leniencies proposed by Rabbi Herzog, "The Israeli government is obligated by international law to guard the Christian churches in the land of Israel, even though those churches are definitely places of idolatry and cult practice." For Rabbi Yosef, we act democratically since Israel is currently too weak politically to demolish churches and the messianic time of redemption had not yet arrived. A similar position was formulated by the religious Zionist authority rabbi Shaul Israeli.[34]

But after the Six- Day war, there was an acute sense among the younger Religious Zionist rabbis that the era of redemption had arrived. Ariel Picard, a scholar of Israeli law, states that there was a real change from a religious to a political approach and a change away from Rabbi Herzog's making the halakhah fit the needs of the state to a militant critique of the state as not following Jewish law. Rabbi Elisha Aviner stated that gentiles should have no equal rights and are to be subjugated. He explicitly rejected the approach of Rabbi Herzog. Rabbi Israel Rozen rejected any rights for gentiles including movement and suggested a need for restriction of movement.[35]

The Problem of Goyim

Claiming that other religions are not idolatrous is not to downplay the holiness of Israel because idolatry and the chosenness of Israel are not necessarily linked. One can still affirm a special relationship with God without having to label the other nations as having no relationship or lacking all connection.

Nevertheless, another more pervasive non-theological issue is that of the relationship of Jews to Gentiles. Regardless of how pure a monotheism a non-Jew is practicing, he is still a gentile. Unlike the topic of other faiths and religions, the subject of gentiles provokes much commentary from the rabbinic tradition— much of it rather derogatory. Raising the theological question of non-Jewish religions should not displace our Jewish, ethical need to address and accept responsibility for the anti-gentile statements in the rabbinic corpus. While Christian efforts in this past generation to deal with the anti-Jewish statements in their tradition may, or may not, serve as models, Judaism must find a way to approach the problem—to deny the significance of the problem is dishonest.

Before we turn to nineteenth- and twentieth-century opinions, we should consider that the historian Jay Berkovits notes that the rabbis in eighteenth-century France from the pre-revolutionary era until the Bourbon restoration assumed that gentiles universally accepted the Jewish monotheistic ethic. In the 1780s, the Assembly of Jewish Notables, with a conservative rabbinic composition, declared that gentiles have moral decent behavior, that there cannot be inequality between faiths, and that Christians are definitely not idolatrous.

In fact Rabbi David Sinzheim said, "we have to love those who observe the seven laws of Noah as our brothers." Especially indicative of this acceptance of gentiles, the rabbi of the traditional community of Alsace–Lorraine, Rabbi Aaron of Worms of Metz, author of the *Me'orei Or* and a student of Rabbi Aryeh Loeb Ginzberg (the *Shaagat Aryeh*), instructed his congregants not to invoke the blessing "thou has not made me a Gentile,"[36] since it made them feel uncomfortable in its lack of congruence with reality.

Chajes

In the first half of the nineteenth century, Rabbi Zvi Hirsch Chajes (1805–1855), an Austro-Hungarian rabbi, discussed attitudes toward Gentiles and wrote inclusivist statements similar to those of R. Yaakov Emden in Germany. In reaction to the Damascus affair of 1840, where the Jews of Damascus were accused of blood libel and European Jewry came to the aid of their co-religionists, Chajes wrote a tract showing that Judaism considers contemporary Christians and Muslims as resident aliens and the righteous of the nations.

> Now, when we see the uprightness of the morals of the Christians who believe in religion and Torah from heaven, and the existence of God and reward in the world to come and the other principles and foundations of religion, it is without a doubt that we judge them as a resident-alien, and those who listen to the seven Noahite commandments because of God's command are the pious Gentiles who have a share in the world to come…The Christians keep the seven commandments and believe in the Torah given from God to Moshe, and believe in the existence of God, but they associate (*shituf*) another thing in their worship…Even not eating a living thing is alluded to in the *Epistles of Paul* [Acts 15 cf. Romans 14]. (489–90)

Chajes provides a précis of his sources in the inclusivist writings of Yehudah Halevi, Maimonides, Meiri, and R. Yaakov Emden. Empathetic reaction to tragic events can push authors to create generous statements; hence, he continues by extending his discussion to Muslims and by quoting Joseph Salvador, an important French Jewish modernist.

> Similar, Muslims are not idolaters and keep the seven commandments…Salvador the Frenchman wrote a special book in our days to show the truth in the matter that these nations are only a forerunner to prepare the world for God's kingdom to make them fit to accept the pure religion of the creator's unity. It was hidden to him that Maimonides, and Kuzari, already foreshadowed this hidden principle.

In contrast, in his commentary on Maimonides' *Mishneh Torah*, Chajes does not exercise the same apologetic power; rather, he enters into a restrained discussion of whether, in fact, gentiles accept the moral commandments as from God or not. He concludes, in contradistinction to his other work, that his contemporary gentiles are not following God. According to Chajes, Christians and Muslims cannot follow their own religion and still tacitly do God's will. Rather, they need to renounce their own religions and acknowledge their Noahite position in the faith of Judaism.

> Since most nations of the world do not keep the commandments because they accepted them upon themselves [as commandments], they do not receive reward as commanded and performing, rather as not commanded and performing. Muslims even though they believe in the unity of the creator, yet accepting their faith is a denial of Moses' Torah because it is better to be a Gentile [who keeps the commandments] than a Christian or Muslim. (1036) [37]

Chajes leaves us with a position common in the halakhic tradition that the nations of the world are devoid of religion because they are not acting from a belief in Moses' revelation. This requirement for the nations to act on knowledge of the unique Jewish faith without any form of general revelation is similar to the hardline Christian position where knowledge of a specific and unique historic event is needed.

Chaim Hirschensohn

Rabbi Chaim Hirschensohn (1857–1935) received his rabbinic ordination in Russia and Jerusalem and served in the rabbinate in Israel, Turkey, and Hoboken, New Jersey. A religious Zionist leader, he wrote dozens of articles and books, several of which are still in manuscript form. They include works on Jewish Law, Talmud, philosophy, the Bible, and education. His writing provides an early-twentieth-century foundation for the principles of human dignity and respect for all.

Whereas most Talmudic commentators restrict Talmudic laws as applying only to Jews, applying them to gentiles only in the interest of "ways of peace" or "to prevent hatred," Hirschensohn finds ways to include gentiles in the Jewish law itself. For Hirschensohn, all people share a common humanity as part of Noahites; for him even Judaism is subsumed under the Noahite laws as a common civil morality. This categorization allows Hirschensohn to create a humanistic, democratic equality between Jews and gentiles. Hirschensohn even rejects the common rabbinic practice to say "to separate (lehavdil)" whenever he compares Judaism and Christianity in the same sentence.

> It is a great error to say "a gentile, to separate (lehavdil)" Gentiles are not separate [from Jews].
>
> There is no separation of holy and profane between Gentiles and Jews because all those in his likeness have the image of God.
>
> All our Gentiles keep the seven Noahite laws since they come from universal reason. They are our brothers in all matters including charity, kindness, and even [not charging] interest.
>
> The state [of America] does not make a separate law for residents and non-residents; nevertheless, we find even in the laws of America, which has one law for residents and non-residents, there are special leniencies and strictures for the non-resident...Similarly Jews have one law for residents and true non-residents who are treated like true citizens...yet, Jews through the Torah are bound in a special constitution how to keep both our obligations to humanity in general and to his nation and God in particular.[38]

Rabbi David Zvi Hoffmann

Rabbi David Zvi Hoffmann (1843–1921), head of the Berlin Rabbinical seminary for Orthodox Judaism, was a leading halakhic authority in his time and wrote an important volume in German defending the *Shulhan Arukh* from charges of anti-gentile bias. Despite its importance, the book has not been translated except for excerpts.

One of the many topics that he discusses is the rabbinic maxim of "ways of peace" in which the law mandates that Jews act with charity toward non-Jews by visiting their sick, burying their dead, and aiding their poor. Rabbi David Zvi Hoffmann states that the rabbinic concept of the "ways of peace" is an ideal universal ethic not just to reduce animosity.

> It cannot be the purpose of these rabbinical rules to obtain peace relations, but rather to offer and promote peace. The rules have been established, not for the sake of our peace, but for the peace and welfare of all men, inhabitants of God's creation.
>
> The religious Christian serving the same God and observing the laws of his religion, must be treated like a resident alien (*ger toshav*) and as such, according to the strict Jewish law, can demand our moral and financial support. The heathen, hostile to God, is not covered by the law; mercy alone motivates our relationship to him.

He includes contemporary Christians with ease under the laws of resident aliens and even includes kindness to the pagan as a required act of mercy, which is how most other legal authorities categorize relationships with Christians.

While giving full discussion about how Jews have to follow the laws of the host countries (*dina demalkhuta dina*) and how to avoid any desecration of God's name, he also attempts to address texts that seem to be unethical. His approach was to say that in the time of the original formulation of the law in Talmudic times all of these laws were ethical and it is only with the changing of economic reality over the centuries that they appear as unethical. Yet, he himself wants to avoid all apologetics about contemporary laws by clearly acknowledging that the current version of the law is unethical and one should not find modern ethics in the law. Rather, today one should rely on the mediating principles of the ways of peace and presenting a desecration of God's name.

> A number of Talmudic laws applying to foreigners have been incorporated in the *Shulkhan Arukh* that a modern observer might consider an encroachment upon the human rights of the alien. Yet, at close inspection, many of these laws are actually revealed as being advantageous for the non-Jew.
>
> In cases where the practice of Talmudic law was likely to result in misinterpretations and possible clashes with the government they called upon their people to consider the demands of "ways of peace," "law of the land," and the danger of desecrating God's name. They could do no more than that. How could we respect Rabbinical leaders who would stoop so low as to falsify the Torah or the old laws of the Talmud as an act of appeasement towards the non-Jews, and who proclaim in the name of the Torah what they have actually derived from modern concepts of ethics?

Many have found his approach of presenting Jewish law as ethical as apologetic. Yet, his approach still flows from the universalism of German Orthodox thinkers. This universalism was an important legacy of those trained in the seminary.[39] Mendel Hirsch, son of the S.R. Hirsch, presents similar universal trends in his essays (see chapter five).

Ethical Texts

An alternate approach to Rabbi Hoffmann's ethical reading of the law itself is to stress the need for ethics to temper the law. Almost all liberal thinkers, following Abraham Geiger, Hermann Cohen, and Leo Baeck, naturally follow the ethics of Judaism over the law. But, ethics were used to temper the law in a variety of modern Orthodox thinkers, including, but not limited to, Rabbis Yehudah Amital, Moshe Avigdor Amiel, Haim David Halevi, Nachum L. Rabinovitch, Ahron Soloveichik, Yehudah Unterman, and Walter Wurzberger. It already has antecedents in the approaches of Emden and Hirsch. A full discussion of their differences in formulation of ethical theories and practical application is beyond the scope of this book. The important common point for all of them is that they all are willing to explicitly invoke ethics to present a moral halakhah; they differ in whether they formulate the ethics as meta-halakhah, part of the law itself, natural morals, or virtue. A strict constructionist, however, could, and would, reject their formulations as not legal and binding.

Rather than cite their writings, the crucial point for our purposes is to cite the two most important sources for this line of thinking. The first is a universal morality based on Ben Azai's statement that we have to care ethically about all of mankind, and Maimonides' statement that we are to show mercy and kindness to gentiles because of the "ways of peace," and "imataio dei." This approach does not create a theology of other religious, but it does avoid the negative statements about gentiles.[40]

> "Rabbi Akiva said: The verse, 'Love your neighbor as yourself' (Leviticus 19:18) is a great principle of the Torah. Ben Azai said: The verse, 'This is the book of the history of mankind' (Genesis 5:1) is a greater principle still." (*Bereishit Rabbah*, Theodor-Albeck edition, Jerusalem 1965, p. 237) "Even [regarding] Gentiles, the Rabbis commanded us to visit their sick and to bury their dead along with the dead of the Jews, and to support their poor along with all the Jewish paupers, because of 'ways of peace.' Behold it was said: 'God is good to all and His mercies are on all His creations' (Psalms 145:9), and it was said: 'Its [the Torah's] ways are ways of pleasantness and all its paths are peace' (Proverbs 3:17)." (Maimonides, *Hilkhot Melakhim* 10:12)
>
> And thus regarding the attributes of God, [through which]...He commanded us to resemble Him...He says: "and His mercies are on all His creations." (*Hilkhot Avadim* 9:8)

Another broad ethical command, not specifically linked to gentiles, is always to sanctify God's name (*kiddush hashem*) and not to do any action that would cause shame or dishonor to Judaism (Lev. 22:32). The Talmud exhorts, "The greater the person, the more he must guard against causing dishonor to God's name" (*Yoma* 84a, 86a; Pes. 49a). "All sins may be atoned for by repentance, by

means of the Day of Atonement, or through the chastening power of afflic-
tion, but acts which cause the desecration of the name of God will not be
forgiven" (*Mek.*, Yitro, 7; *Yoma* 86a).

There are also several kabbalistic texts about loving all people that are
regularly used to not only temper the severity of statements about gentiles,
discussed in the chapter on exclusivism, but also to create an ethic of love.
Hayyim Vital wrote, "One should not get angry even in one's household.
One should love all creations—gentiles included" (*Shaarei Kedushah* 1:5) or
"One should greet in peace every person even a gentile in order that Israel
would be beloved among the gentiles" (*Sefer Hapeliah*).

Meshekh Hokhmah: Natural law or universal morality

Rabbi Meir Simhah Ha-Kohen of Dvinsk (1843–1926), author of two highly
esteemed and widely studied works on Jewish law, *Or Sameah* and *Meshekh
Hokhmah*, offers a sophisticated Eastern European halakhah, which remains
the outer boundary of acceptable humanism for many Orthodox rabbis.

Rabbi Meir Simhah presents the seven Noahite laws as universal and
equally incumbent on all humanity. His innovation, reminiscent of the classics of Enlightenment liberalism, is to understand that these laws are defined
by human convention, and therefore accessible to all. From his short statement one cannot tell if he is more of a proponent of natural law or there is a
rational law available to all.

> The seven Noahite commandments commanded to Adam are the ideas
> for political ordering and natural guidance. (Noah 7)
>   Noahites are warned to keep laws, which are the conventions set by
> men. (Mishpatim 83)
>   A person's soul is the book to know the seven Noahite laws. (Netzavim
> 318–19)
>   "Let us make man in our image": The image of God is our free
> will...we are free to choose good or evil...against our character and
> nature and against the right in the eyes of God. (Gen. 3)[41]

According to R. Meir Simhah, Jews can recognize gentiles as law-abiding
citizens, who in their civil society are fulfilling their biblical mandates. His
thought reverses the classic Christian approach in which Jews uphold an ethic
of law and Christians a higher ethic of love. For R. Meir Simhah, an ethic of
love only applies between Jews, between Jews and gentiles a more utilitarian
ethic applies. But in the end of days, even gentiles will accept a higher ethic.

Jews have a more sublime soul—therefore love only applies to their souls. (Kedoshim 162)

God does not want that [Israel] should mix with Gentiles and the nations should not come to them lest they cause Israel to sin...But in the future, Gentiles will recognize that the Earth and its fullness is the Lord's and then everyone will go up [to Jerusalem] to celebrate together. (Pinhas 245)

Rabbi Meir Simhah offers a still useful respect for secular government as intrinsically fulfilling God's will. For many Orthodox rabbis in the twentieth century, this position meant that one did not have to ask technical questions about whether a given secular government falls within the seven Noahite laws or any specific questions about their formal acceptance of these laws since all governments are now committed to them.

Yehiel Weinberg

Rabbi Yehiel Weinberg (1884–1966) was an instructor in Talmud at the Berlin Orthodox Seminary between the two World Wars and one of the leading legal authorities of his age. His aside comments in his legal writings display a critical sociological edge, accentuated even more by his recently published letters.

In my opinion, it is fitting to put an end to the hatred of the religions for each other. More than Christianity hates Judaism, Judaism hates Christianity. There is a dispute if stealing from Gentiles is forbidden from the Torah, everyone holds that deceiving a Gentile and canceling his debt is permitted, one is not to return a lost object to a Gentile, according to R. Tam intercourse with a Gentile does not render a woman forbidden to her husband, their issue is like the issue [of horses]...We must solemnly and formally declare that in our day this does not apply. Meiri wrote as such, but the teachers and rabbis whisper in the ears of the students that all this was written because of the censor.[42]

The frustration and pain in this text speaks for itself. Rabbi Weinberg acutely senses the strong anti-gentile strand in rabbinical writings. He wants to use the Meiri to create a broad reinterpretation of the tradition, yet he painfully knows that the other legal authorities are actually seeking to avoid any humanistic rapprochement with other religions. The difficulty of creating a lasting ethical approach to gentiles within the Jewish legal tradition remains to this day.

Contemporary Halakhah

In the late eighteenth and nineteenth centuries, Western European Jews seeking to acclimate into their newfound integration into Western society and their new status as citizens naturally rejected the negative statements in the rabbinical corpus about gentiles. Later, nineteenth- and early-twentieth-century rabbis struggled to systematically address these issues. At the end of the twentieth century, many Orthodox Talmudists accept that we live in an age of kind and benevolent governments, so we should not apply the restrictive laws of the Talmud. This means that the sectarian mentality of the Talmud remains the starting point, but the jurist decides how to apply the law in a charitable way for pragmatic reasons. They tended to push thorny texts under the rug rather than acknowledging difficult texts or they only refer to the minority of ethical opinions.[43] However, surprisingly, late-twentieth-century rabbis have returned to the exclusivism and contempt of the early Middle Ages and of Eastern Europe, thereby rejecting their own modern antecedents.

The laws about gentiles in contemporary legal works divide into three categories. The three ascending categories of rabbinic gentiles are (1) idolatrous, (2) pious of the nations or Noahite, and (3) resident alien (*ger toshav*), who accept the Jewish monotheistic ethic and are a part of the Jewish community. We will use these three categories in our further discussions.[44]

Some authorities, including the nineteenth-century Rabbi S.R. Hirsch, Rabbi Chajes (in his Janus-faced writings), the mid-twentieth-century Chief Rabbi Herzog, the contemporary Rabbi Nachum Rabinovitch, and most recently Rabbi Yosef Henkin, consider all modern gentiles within the lenient and expansive category of resident aliens without the need for any formal declaration on their part.

In contrast to these aforementioned tolerant positions of the first half of the twentieth century, the position of many in the latter half of the twentieth century has returned to legally treating gentiles as idolatrous or immoral. The worry of Rabbi Yehiel Weinberg about legal authorities rejecting the Meiri has come to fruition. The nineteenth-century opinion of R. Moshe Sofer (Hatam Sofer), which rejected the Meiri as a forgery, or only written under duress, and exhorted readers to accept that it is a "mitzvah to erase it for it did not emerge from his holy mouth," has become often repeated in late-twentieth-century responsa. Rabbi Moses Sofer's position is that

> It is impossible to say...that the Gentiles of our times are not idolaters, for this may be said only in regard to the issues of going [to court] or situations where he may make thanksgiving [to his god]...because

nowadays they are not so skilled in their religion. Rather, it is clear that their worship is complete idolatry, as stated by Maimonides.[45]

In the twentieth century, R. Moshe Feinstein (1895–1986) wrote that these resident alien categories only apply if gentiles do not adopt a religion of their own, but if they have their own religion, then the gentiles exclude themselves from the inclusive categories. Going further, Yaakov Yisrael Kanievsky (1899–1985; The Steipler) effectively eliminated these categories by writing that the gentile would need to appear before a rabbinic court to accept God, not just to have the status of a resident alien but even not to be considered idolatrous.

Rabbi Moshe Sternbach, a leading contemporary legal authority, head of the Edah Haredit Rabbinic Court in Jerusalem, writes that Christians are idolaters and are therefore liable to the death penalty. From this premise, he draws the ghastly conclusion that Jews can engage in euthanasia, mercy killing, and abortions for gentiles because not only is it permitted to kill gentiles under these circumstances, in fact they present rare opportunities to do so. In a similar vein, he writes that it is forbidden to influence gentiles to observe the Noahite laws. Jews should let them be violent and immoral, and thereby earn their eternal doom and everlasting punishment, which will end the exile.[46]

Not as explicitly dangerous, but with a greater rhetoric of contempt, Rabbi Menashe Klein, a major halakhic authority in the Brooklyn Hasidic community, states categorically that all gentiles are immoral and have violated the Noahite code.[47] Yet, more striking to contemporary sensibilities is his desire to return to the popular folk hatred of gentiles that goes way beyond the statements of the rabbinic elite. Now the rabbinic elite shares the values of the folk teaching of contempt.

> We must laud the customs of our holy ancestors throughout the cities of Europe. May their merit protect us, and may God revenge their blood. When they used to speak about Gentiles or idolaters, they would use euphemistic language in order to accentuate the difference between Jews and Gentiles...When a Gentile treated a Jew kindly, they would describe him as a "dishonest uncircumcised"...when referring to a non-Jewish cemetery, they would use the expression "an impure place...Woe for those who are lost and no longer with us."[48]

Gavin I. Langmuir, in his *History, Religion, and Anti-Semitism,* describes how the popular teachings of hatred for Jews became part of the thinking pattern of the ruling class, superseding the Church's official doctrine of witness. Rabbi Klein offers us an example of the rabbis of the later half of the twentieth century appropriating the folk hatred of gentiles. As a reader of this passage with an acute awareness of the xenophobia of the community, one can only account for such attitudes as based on the experience of the Holocaust linked to the collective memory of the persecution of Jews by Christians. Elements of anti-rationalism and traditional exclusivism also contribute to this attitude.

Rabbinic figures serve the following rhetoric regularly, In 2005, Rabbi Aharon Leib Steinman (b. 1912), former head of the *kollel* at the Ponavitch Yeshiva and major contemporary *haredi* leader, said "Most of the world is evil, especially the gentiles, most of whom are robbers, murderers, thieves and all the bad things. They have no justice or integrity."[49] The Centrist Orthodoxy of Yeshiva University offers a position that does not think of the world as evil, yet retains the same religious isolationism from gentiles. Jews and non-Jews "have different genes, DNA and instincts." "There mere comparison of the Jewish religion with any other religion already constitutes an affront to the Jewish God, as if to imply that there is something substantial shared in common between the two."[50]

A novel twist emerged recently from a work written by a rabbi at the Beit Medrash Gevohah in Lakewood, New Jersey, in which he considers all gentiles as evil in essence. Whereas the rabbinic tradition emphasized the special separate qualities of Israel, an essential goodness, this new work reiterated the negative statements contained in the exclusivist chapter and in this chapter, yet creatively explained them as due to the essential iniquity of gentiles (*pintele goy*), that no matter how good a gentile appears, his core remains impure and corrupt. Unlike past lands and centuries, when a Jew could find comfort in a sense of superiority to gentile peasants, in America, where gentile life is attractive and productive, the rhetoric had to shift from moral superiority to a metaphysical rejection of American gentiles.[51]

Unlike the period from the late eighteenth to the early twentieth centuries, when Jews in Western Europe had to integrate into their host countries and therefore sought universalism, contemporary America does not make any more integration demands on its Jews. Hence, American civility functions as invisible tolerance, not requiring any active program of integration into the host culture. This free gift of civil rights allows those antimodern sectarians to feel at home and to make public demands of civil society, despite their ideology of homelessness and contempt for the civil society. In contrast, in Israel, the haredi isolation from interaction with anyone but Jews allows hardline positions to reemerge. But, explanation does not absolve us of the need to deal with these halakhic texts.

The ecclesiastic approach of looking to Tosafot and Meiri to allow legal dispensations will always lead back to the hardline formulations, since they remain live legal options and are cited in any literature review. Some jurists, therefore, on grounds of legal logic will simply pick the restrictive positions based on seeking original intent of the text, without drawing any moral implications. Moderates seek to sanitize Judaism by stating that they personally do not share these views and that we should be satisfied with their temperate and sensible reading. But moderates do not usually accept responsibility for troubling texts, or their continuous, even though seemingly hushed, role in Jewish society and education. Furthermore, the ecclesiastical moderate never looks to see or understand another religion in its own terms, or give other religions theological meaning. They generally just seek to defend the system and its institutions from charges of racial or religious discrimination.

Conclusions

In 1970, Daniel Sperber (b. 1940), a Jerusalem rabbi and professor at Bar Ilan University, rationally explained the rabbinic approach to gentiles as "motivated by their idolatry, moral laxity, and persecution" of Jews during the Roman era. For him, the other laws are all either "objective reasoning" based on considering gentiles as outside the "Jewish social contract," or serving to discourage social contact.[52]

In the same year, however, Gerald Blidstein, rabbi and subsequently professor of Jewish thought at Ben Gurion University, noted that there is a "wide variety of opinions still found in Tannaitic thought" in which "the Talmudic experience ranges from a gentile society convicted of violence and even bestiality, to those individuals who abide by the law of morality and religion."[53] In a later article, he comments on confronting the difficult passages in which pragmatically over time, restrictive rulings were prudently overruled.

> The ruling that the Sabbath is not to be violated in order to save a [resident alien's] ger toshav's life. Over time, a tradition has developed allowing (or demanding) the violation because such refusal of medical treatment, say, on "religious grounds," would imperil the Jewish community itself. Yet when I once asked Rav Soloveitchik whether he was morally (not halakhically!) satisfied with this prudential permission, he answered flatly "no."[54]

Blidstein stated that traditional Jewish apologetics are "barren and misleading." For Blidstein, in the current age it is no longer sufficient "to cite the

Meiri for his broadmindedness, or to scurry about in the self-satisfaction of saving a gentile's life on the Sabbath." Blidstein urged an examination of the way traditional Jews teach in school or speak in synagogues about Christianity, which he considered still defensive and hostile, "the pieties about Bnai Noah notwithstanding." Chapter 10 will discuss the need to move beyond defensive fear.

CHAPTER 9

The Phenomena of Religion

In our era of globalization, an author such as Rabbi Adin Steinsaltz, without hesitancy, can write:

> A man who offers his prayers must direct his eyes below [to earth] and his heart above [to heaven] (Yevamot 105b). Without going into subtle distinctions, most of the world's religions—including Islam, Buddhism, and Hinduism—suggest that both one's heart and one's eyes should be turned toward Heaven.[1]

Steinsaltz can casually include all the worlds' religions as turning toward heaven, implying a recognition that all faiths are turning, in ways similar to Jewish prayers, to God. If all turn to heaven, then what does Judaism reject?

The important point is that Jews do not formulate this question based on having a monopoly on religious expression; rather medieval texts proceed from a hierarchical sense of superiority. We just ask: Do they turn to heaven? Judaism tacitly accepts a natural ability to turn toward God and to pray. Judaism assumes a natural element to religion and that there are natural experiences of the divine. It also assumes that people are good and God recognizes that goodness. This chapter will offer theoretical accounts for other religions within Jewish teachings.

Explanation for Other Religions

If we can see that all turn to heaven, then why are there pagans? Or at least why did there used to be pagans? What is opposite of heaven?

Those who have empirical observations on other religions are mainly the inclusivists. Part of the reason for this is that since their positions are hierarchical they are comfortable in both observing other faiths and explaining what they consider incorrect beliefs. Universalists look beyond religious communities to the ultimate goal and exclusivists are not usually especially inquisitive about the other or see enough starting commonalities.

Halevi, Maimonides, Nahmanides, Zohar, and Abulafia each offer reasons why they think Judaism is superior empirically. For Yehudah Halevi, other religions are a social creation in order to turn toward heaven. For Maimonides, false ideas and magical thinking delude people into forgetting heaven. For Nahmanides and Zohar, there are lower beings that have power and one can turn to them instead of to God. For Abulafia and Franck, there is a tradition of esoteric knowledge available only to those who have a true tradition. Abulafia and Albo observing other religions focus on diffusion of the one truth to the many nations based on the needs of diversity. In the modern era, Franck and Zeitlin sense a continuity between the phenomena of religion and Judaism, there is an accepted empirical universalism, whereas for others, like Hirsch, the observed commonality is still seen as in discontinuity with Torah.

- Prophecy as greater than naturalism—Halevi
- Truth compared to magic—Maimonides
- Henotheism—Nahmanides, Gersonides
- Mistaking the image for the source—*Zohar*
- Inability to prove truth—Abulafia
- Cultural diffusion—Albo
- Particularist harmonization—Valle
- Perennialism—Franck
- Religion compared to culture—Hirsch
- Natural experiences—Zeitlin
- Mystery—Ehrenpreis

Yehudah Halevi

Yehudah Halevi, the twelfth-century thinker, whose thought is one of the basics of Jewish theology and has been presented in several other contexts in this book, offers a distinctive Jewish theory of religion.

> The first element of religion appeared, no doubt, among single individuals, who supported one another in upholding the faith which it pleased God should be promulgated. Their number increases continually, they grow more powerful, or a king arises and assists them, also compels his subjects to adopt the same creed. In this way only rational religions, of human origin, can arise.[2]

The people believed that Moses held direct communication with God, that his words were not creations of his own mind.[3]

People have an innate faith and receive natural insights and dreams about God's will. This sincere following of God is, however, in turn, assisted and manipulated by political rulers to establish religious communities based on practices of human construction. In contrast, Mosaic religion was a direct prophetic communication from God by means of divine influx.

The Golden Calf offers Halevi an opportunity to discuss how people seeking the Divine influx become diverted into magical thinking both as means of worship and as source of authority. For Halevi the only true source is Divine command.

> The Rabbi: God had forbidden images, and in spite of this they made one. They should have waited and not have assumed power.
>
> This had been done by the advice of the astrologers and magicians among them... The whole affair is repulsive to us, because in this age the majority of nations have abandoned the worship of images.
>
> Al Khazari: The theory I had formed, and the opinion of what I saw in my dream thou now confirmest, viz. that man can only merit divine influence by acting according to God's commands And even were it not so, most men strive to obtain it, even astrologers, magicians, fire and sun worshippers, dualists, etc.
>
> The Rabbi: Thou art right.[4]

Two fruitful theological ideas, not developed yet pregnant with meaning, are in this short piece. The first is the acknowledgment that the majority of nations have already given up images, implying that images are only forbidden when they seek to magically bring a divine influence and not when they are used only as a symbol or remembrance. The second is that the difference between a permitted image and a prohibited golden calf is based on whether God decreed it or not. The question is about whether the need for representation is from heaven or a form of magical thinking?

Maimonides

Maimonides presents a theory of religion in his *Guide of the Perplexed* that has had a significant influence on later thinkers. Since anything in the *Guide* is subject to multiple interpretations, here is one possible explanation of Maimonides' position.

Maimonides discusses religion in general by presenting the religion of the Sabians, an ancient idolatrous religion, based on his reading of Ibn Wahshiyya (tenth-century Nabataean Arab writer) and his *Nabatean Agriculture*. Ibn Ezra, Yehudah Halevi, Maimonides, and others all used this corpus of Sabian documents. They are a rich resource for understanding how Jewish thinkers thought about the world of geography and anthropology. The volumes of the *Nabatean Agriculture* contained discussion of the pre-Adamites, ethnography of the ancient world, a glorification of the tradition of Babylonian-Aramean culture, knowledge of India and Brahmins, the first decipherment of Egyptian hieroglyphics, and details about ancient magical practices. Reading this work formed what many medievals considered as a perfect backdrop to attain a contextual understanding of the Bible against the world of late antiquity Mesopotamian culture and religion.

The Sabians described by Maimonides are, technically, a Mandean Gnostic religion found in Harran, in Northern Iraq, and it is still practiced in the twenty-first century by several indigenous Kurdish faiths. Maimonides is, however, not concerned with the ethnological specifics of who the Sabians were because his intent was to develop the category of "Sabian" as a type that can be used to explain the relationship of monotheism to its pagan environment.

Maimonides broadens his description of this small contemporary sect into an entire theory of religion. First, Harran, the home of the Sabians, was Abraham's birthplace in Genesis, so Maimonides can use the current religion of Harran to explain the religion of Abraham's Chaldean upbringing, and by extension, the idolatry of Baal and Ashera in the Bible and all biblical idolatry. Second, there was a different gnostic group of late antiquity called the Sabians who were one of the protected religious groups (along with Christians and Jews) in the *Koran* (II 6–2, V 69, XXII 17); therefore, the current Sabians can be used to explain the pre-Islamic pagan religion during the age of ignorance (*Jahiliyah*). Third, Maimonides' insistence on calling them Nabateans links them to a forgotten Greco-Roman religion from the trans-Jordan in Petra. The overall effect is a pagan religion of the biblical Akkadean Harran that continued into Greco-Roman times, which was the religion before the Islamic conquests, and which still continues at the margins of thirteenth-century society as various sects. In this sense, we can understand why Maimonides thought that Islam and Christianity brought knowledge of God to the world. The world was originally practicing forms of the Sabian religion until the Abrahamic faiths changed society.[5]

Maimonides explains that before monotheism people prayed to the stars using statues, leading to false prophesies and delusional beliefs.

> The Sabians set up statues for the planets, golden statues for the sun and silver ones for the moon, and distributed the minerals and the climes between the planets, saying that one particular planet was the deity of

one particular clime. And they built temples, set up statues in them and thought that the forces of the planets overflowed toward these statues and that consequently these statues talked, had understanding, gave prophetic revelation to people.[6]

Once they already believed in this level of representation, they descended even further to believe in "the actions of talismans, practices with a view to causing spirits to descend, demons, and ghouls living in deserts."

How did paganism begin according to Maimonides? Originally, Adam had monotheistic faith and knew the account of creation. But his descendents "took the account of the Creation and only listened to the external elements." They mistook the parables for false images of the imagination and mistook causality for magical physics. They did not understanding that the story of Adam was a parable about anthropology, which depicts the human descent from intellect to imagination. The Sabians took the story literally. "Adam was in their belief a human being born from male and female, like the rest of mankind: he was only distinguished from his fellow men by being a prophet sent by the moon; he accordingly called men to worship of the moon." And since in medieval thought Divine wisdom was associated with the sphere of the moon , they mistook the act of cognition of the agent and thought that they needed to ritually worship the moon.

The monotheism of the Abrahamic faiths is, therefore, needed to teach people not to worship the stars and their purified ritual serves to wean people away from paganism. Starting with Abraham and culminating in the twelfth-century rationalism in the time of Maimonides, mankind has to fight the tendency toward idolatry. According to Maimonides, Abraham was the first to use his intellect and understand that religion was about using the intellect.

> You know that in those times the teachings of the Sabians were generally accepted and that all except a few men were idolaters. I mean by this that they believed in spirits, that they believed that those spirits can be made to descend among men, and that they made talismans. At those times everyone who claimed to be listened to, either claimed, like Abraham, that speculation and reason had come to him indicating to him that the world as a whole had a deity, or else he claimed that the spirit of a star or an angel or something similar had descended upon him. Yet that an individual should make a claim to prophecy on the ground that God had spoken to him and had sent him on a mission was a thing never heard of prior to Moses our Master.[7]

Originally, Sabians relied on divination, meaning that knowledge was seen as a spirit descending. Abraham was the first to lead humanity back to an intellectual approach, to know God and nature as a universal, rationalistic understanding of the world, as the creation of a single Creator. Later, Moses was the first who transcended ordinary intellect to reach a prophetic meta-rational state. In his legal code, Maimonides presents the same theory but emphasizes the narrative aspect, of how humanity in the era of Enosh fell into mistaken celestial worship and was only preserved by isolated individuals. Knowledge of religion was restored to the world because of the extraordinary qualities of Abraham. "But the Creator, was not recognized by a single person, except for specific individuals, such as Hanokh, Methuselah, Noah, Shem and Eber. Things continued in this manner until Abraham the Patriarch, supporter of the world, was born." (*Mishneh Torah, Hilkhot Avodah Zarah* 1:2)

Maimonides' story of the origin of idolatry works on a historical level by explaining the descent from Adam to the current irrationality, on an anthropological level explaining the descent from guidance by the human intellect to living though relying on imagination and then returning back again to intellect, and on a religious level in that religion is always fighting those who treat religion as magically efficacious.

Mircea Eliade, the historian of religion, cites Maimonides' *Guide* as an important step in the study of the history of religions. According to Eliade, when Maimonides was published in the sixteenth through eighteenth centuries, his theory of the Sabians was used to explain the ancient Chaldeans, and was also used to explain the religion of Indians of the New World in terms of biblical religious practice. In the eighteenth century, when biblical religion itself was considered as primitive, the Bible was embedded in its Chaldean context. The Sabian thesis leads to the idea of the religion of the Semites where Abraham is the Eastern Sheik, in sharp contrast to the religion of the Aryans, the forerunners of the Indian religions and the Greco-Roman religions. Finally, in the nineteenth century the Semites are portrayed as having an imageless God, and the Aryans have representation. To connect these modern theories of biblical Semitic religion back to the medieval Jewish positions can serve to open new theological possibilities of application.[8]

Nahmanides and Gersonides

Henotheism is a term coined by the German scholar of religion Max Mueller (1823–1900) meaning belief in, and possible worship of, multiple gods, one of which is supreme. It is also called **inclusive monotheism or monolatrism**. According to Mueller, henotheism is "monotheism in principle and polytheism in fact." For traditional Christians of the nineteenth century, this concept allowed them to accept Greco-Roman polytheism as subservient to the philosophic concept of one God and to accept Hinduism as respecting Brahma as the absolute Supreme Being.

Within Jewish literature, the henotheism position has a long pedigree in the writings of most medieval thinkers, including Maimonides, Nahmanides, Kimhi, Gersonides, and Arama. Mueller imagined that the position is part of an evolutionary trend from polytheism to monotheism. In contrast, the medieval Jewish thinkers assumed devolution from primordial monotheism to henotheism.

An example of henotheism, which takes account of a wide range of supernal powers, is that of Nahmanides (1194–*ca.* 1270; Rabbi Moses Ben Nahman, abbreviated to Ramban), a Catalonian Talmudist, biblical exegete, and kabbalist. He rejected Maimonides' dismissal of the power of angels and spirits as mere superstition caused by devolution into irrationality. Instead, he saw pagan religions as a gradual devolution into the service of specific supernal powers, followed by representation and forgetfulness of the original omnipotent divine power, causing idolatry and king worship, followed by worship of earthly spirits.

> There are three categories of foreign worship. The first group began to worship the angels, the separate intelligences, because they knew that they have partial influence on the nations...these are called in the Torah "foreign gods" and "gods of the nations." Even though they worshiped them they admitted that the great power and omnipotence was to the supernal God.
>
> The second group worshiped the visible heavenly hosts, the sun, moon, or constellations...These people started to fashion many forms, statues, images, groves, and astrological images...giving each a power, appointed time, and ability. To these groups the false prophets told the future through magic and augury because the constellations have appointed princes in our atmosphere—like the angels above. There were some terrestrial humans who considered that when they accepted upon themselves the worship of the constellations...and cleaved in thought they increased success in their own souls...This was the approach of Pharaoh and Sennacherib...
>
> The third group worships demons and spirits, earthly creatures that can destroy enemies as known through necromancy. They are also appointed over the nations...but they are not gods at all.[9]

Nahmanides' theory of devolution into representation and then into serving lower non-divine powers seems to be reserved for biblical paganism. Nahmanides does not offer an application to contemporary religions, but he does still accepts the demon and spirit worship as part of his contemporary reality.

In the late fourteenth and early fifteenth centuries, the Nahmanidean idea that the other religions were to draw down the influence of the stars took a turn. At this juncture, various commentaries, such as that of Solomon Al-Constantine considered these processes as factually real. "Know that the Canaanites worshiped to Asherah, Astoret, to pillars...There is no doubt that these activities were to draw down the powers of the stars and the constellations." They also applied the approach to contemporary Indian religions. These thinkers accepted Maimonides' Sabian theory as actually working, but forbidden nevertheless.[10]

Gersonides (1288–1344; Levi ben Gershon), Jewish philosopher, astronomer, and mathematician who lived his entire life in Languedoc, offers an alternative henotheistic model closer to Maimonides' rationalism. For Gersonides, the representations of paganism are patently false; they work through the chicanery of priests found in ancient paganism.

> In order to explain the thought of those who [accepted] Baal, they must have thought that when they made a form the supernal ruling force that rules a given nation and climate would descend into it. The priests of Baal...would perform magic to make it appear that the Baal was the cause.[11]

As recently as in the 1970s, the mythology class at Yeshiva University still taught henotheism as the Jewish position on the Greek and Roman gods. We were to use data from the mythology textbook to prove the henotheism thesis on the final exam.

Zohar

The *Zohar* offers a variety of approaches about the worship of others weaving together many diverse strands of the Jewish tradition. The novel part of the Zohar's presentation is a dramatic narrative depiction of those who worship the sun as henotheism, explaining those who mistake manifestations of God, such as the celestial hierarchy, for the infinite God.

This passage depicts the idolatrous allure of the Golden Calf as similar to the attraction to worship the sun, vividly invoking of the attraction of the sun and showing appreciation of its worship. In using the Sun as the example of idolatry, there seem to be a blurring of the ancient Sabian religion as presented by Maimonides, Egyptian and Greek religion, and the Arabic pagan religion of pre-Islam Arabia. The Talmud already refers to the sun as a name for God, thereby domesticating homage to *Sol Invictus*, the variety of late antiquity veneration of the sun (*Sotah* 10a). This passage also has an explicit Arabic influence in that the text actually uses the Arabic epithet *allah* for God. It seems to echo the *sura* in the Koran, where Abraham tells Nimrod that "Allah brings the sun up from the east "(Sura 2:258). The text also reflects "God is the light of heaven and earth (Sura 24:35), which has antecedents in a variety of extra-biblical texts including *Sefer Hayashar.*

The text effortlessly switches, in the second paragraph, to discuss the archangel Raphael as possessing the gate keys of the sky, similar to Apollo and other late antiquity sun deities. The *Zohar* teaches its readers that the sun and Raphael are not gods but only lower messengers of the higher God.

> R. Yosi and R. Hiyya were walking on the road; as they walked, night fell and they sat down. While they were sitting, morning began to shine, and they arose and walked. R. Hiyya said: "Look at the face of the east, how it shines!" Now all those children of the East of the shining mountains prostrate before this light which shines on behalf of the sun until it comes out. And they worship it. Now when the sun itself comes out, there are many of them who worship the sun, but there are those who worship the light only, and who call this light the God of the shining jewel. And their oath is, "By Allah of the shining jewel!"

> Now you might say: This worship is in vain!
> But since ancient, primordial days
> They have discovered wisdom through it
> When the sun begins to shine, before coming forth
> The deputy in charge of the sun comes forth
> With holy letters of the high holy Name engraved on his forehead
> With the power of those letters, he opens all the windows of heaven
> Knocking home open, then moving on.
> That deputy enters the shining splendor surrounding the sun
> and there he stays until the sun comes forth and spreads
>   over the world.
> That deputy is in charge of gold and rubies and
>   they worship his image there.

The *Zohar* transforms the mythic world of paganism into a monotheistic version, envisioning Divinely appointed celestial deputies with holy names performing the drama of the sunrise. The power of the sacred time of dawn is real and palpable. The reference to the East has added cache for modern readers as an imagined reference to Eastern religions, and not the intended Arabia or Mesopotamia.

In its entirety, this full passage of *Zohar* also presents the positions of Halevi, Maimonides, and a polemical anti-Christian position, finishing the narrative with a snippet of demonizing other faiths. Inclusivism, exclusivism, and empiricism coexist in the same passage. In addition, the *Zohar*'s discussion offers a reformulation of the Talmudic discussion on why God tolerates the idolatrous worship of the celestial powers. The answer is that he will not destroy the sun, moon, and firmaments for fools, who out of their stupidity and lack of awareness call these celestial bodies God. "The Blessed Holy One does not want to destroy His own creations."

The homily continues with a polemic section, not relevant to the themes of this chapter, in which the rabbi meets a *hegemon* (Roman governor), a euphemism for a bishop, who asks: "Why do you consider your Torah true since our kingdom lasted longer?" The answer consists of an ode to how God still cares for Jews as a father for his children, providing providence, personal relationship, and prophesy.

The passage concludes with a completely different approach to the one presented earlier, in which the Golden Calf worship reflects a demonological dualism, and not just a mistaken identity of the manifestation of divine providence, for God Himself. In this approach, a very personified Satan as instigator emerges from the evil side and takes on the image of the Golden Calf.

> Below with the dregs of wine, the evil dregs,
> There emerges an agitator, an accuser, the primordial demon...
> He is disguised in the image of a man when he approaches the holy place...
> He must cloth himself in a garment to victimize the world.
> The first garment that he seizes is the image of the bull.[13]

Abulafia

Abraham Abulafia (1240, Saragosa to *ca.* 1290, Maltese Archipelago), kabbalist and messianic aspirant, has a variety of comments about other religions.

Abulafia presents a version of the ancient parable of three rings, or three pearls, to account for the variety of religions. In the parable the three religions each claim to be true and to having the true ring, or pearl, to prove it and consider the other two false. In some of the prior versions of the parable each of the three monotheistic faiths are like one of the three rings, one original and two copies. But without knowing the truth of the original, all three have to be taken as true, or alternately one is true and two are false. In Abulafia's version, the parable is about a single precious pearl that was hidden away.

Since the pearl was hidden each claimed that they are true because the true religion cannot prove itself.

> It is well known, for some time, among the nations that our people were the first to receive the Torah from God. No nation denies this...If so, what originates in its source is superior to its counterparts. It's language superior to all languages...However we also will acknowledge the truth. Today, the Hebrew scripture lacks these virtues...
>
> It resembles a man who had a beautiful pearl to give as an inheritance to his son. While he was instructing him in the matters of wealth...he hid the pearl in a pit. During this time the servants taunted the son boasting that the master had given him the pearl...eventually the father took the pearl out of the pit and gave it to him.

To complete the analogy, Abulafia thinks that, indeed, we have sinned and God has hidden the pearl. We cannot prove ourselves true anymore. In the version presented by Abulafia, there is only one true pearl, only one son, and the pretenders do not have anything.

The notable point of Abulafia's version is that even Judaism does not have the pearl in hand; it is hidden away so even Judaism does not possess the entirety of religious truth.

> For this reason, the disputation continues about who is beloved of God and who has the truth, we or our opponents. This will persist until the judge will come and take the pearl out of the pit and give it to His chosen, to us or to them. Then the absolute truth will become perfectly clear, and the precious treasure will be radiant. Jealousy and strife, polemics and hatred will cease and mere imagination will be removed from man...all shall know the name from the greatest to the smallest, for the earth will be filled with knowledge of God as the waters that cover the ocean.[14]

Abulafia claims, from his superior knowledge of the Divine name, that he knows Judaism is the true revelation.

There are more universal versions of this story in Immanuel of Rome, Boccaccio, Dante, and others.[15] The most famous version of the tale is the Enlightenment version of Gotthold Lessing's *Nathan the Wise*, in which the judge said that each of the rings was valuable and there should not be a tyranny of one ring.

Abulafia acknowledges that the three faiths of Judaism, Christianity, Islam share the unity of God in which every nation can achieve cleaving to

God—each its desired end. Religion, for Abulafia, is about abstract knowledge of the Divine name and in his opinion neither Jesus nor Mohamed did a better job teaching the divine name.

> The differences between the religions are like the differences between the religion of Moses, the religion of Jesus and the religion of Muhammad, though in all three, the Divine name is necessarily unified, for there is no religion which does not teach the truth of [Divine] unity...on the matter of [Divine] unity, there is no argument between us.
>
> If you will say that in what they expounded, Jesus and Muhammad had no other intention than to unify the Divine name. You are correct, but you can not show that their new teachings were an improvement, materially, spiritually and intellectually, on that which existed previously. Both of them emerged from our nation, and their teachings distanced those who were close to God.
>
> Even so, there are those among them who are *perfecti* (*shalem*) and knowers of the truth,...Recognizing the truth makes them as one who wishes to be attached to our nation. And they are called the righteous of the nations and a merit a portion in the world to come.[16]

Abulafia also explains the differences as based on the different qualities of nations. In some places, Abulafia presents polemical exclusivist rejections of the religion of other nations. Here, he acknowledges the diversity of religions similar to languages and countries.

> The reasons for the differences between nations, religions, languages, and script are all intimately connected. It is known that change of place and time is primarily responsible for the difference between nations; hence, it will also be the reason for the different religions. One could also invert this saying that the differences in religious belief are the reasons for there being different nations...[17]

Albo—Conceptual Acceptance of Diversity

Rabbi Joseph Albo (*ca.* 1380–1444) was a Jewish philosopher and theologian of Spain who is noted for his classic work of Jewish dogmatics, *Book of Principles*. In his work, he reiterates much of what we know about inclusivist approaches to other religions from Sa'adiah, Halevi, Maimonides, and Nahmanides. Albo, however, focuses on the role of law, society, and temperament within religion. After presenting the differences between common law, natural law, and Divine law (as influenced by Thomas Aquinas), Albo asks: Must there be one Divine law for all of mankind or can there be more than one? He answers that since God ordains a single order for all people, there can only be one law.

> However, on more careful consideration we shall find that though we may admit that so far as the giver is concerned there shall be only one, the same result does not follow if we consider the receiver. It is clear that the temperaments of men are different... The differences are so great that we find persons whose qualities are the direct opposites of one another.[18]

For Albo, the various religions differ because of the diversity of human experience, and culture receives the eternal divine word, but all religion at the core is one. Elsewhere in his writings, he presents an inclusivist doctrine, but this passage modifies it by showing not supersessionism or metaphysics, but by simply proclaiming that the qualities of religion are due to receivers.

Particularist Harmonization

An approach that no longer resonates in the modern era is that of Moshe David Valle (1696–1777), a rabbi, physician, and student of the kabbalist Rabbi Moshe Hayyim Luzzatto (1707–1747) in Padua. Valle offers a vision of Jewish truth in which everything that he encounters, science, history, religion, becomes transmuted into kabbalistic doctrine, an eighteenth-century theological book of nature.

He is an example that reminds us that even exclusivist thinkers can venture out and explain other religions as given by God to the other nations. His prime understanding of other religions is the need for everyone to fear Heaven for the sake of morality.

> Why are there many religions in the world? Because God gave to all nations according to what is fitting for them... Israel was worthy to the true God and the true Torah, and the pure language...[19]
>
> God wanted there to be religion in the world even if they are false and deceitful in order that all should worship the Divine, because if not for fear [of heaven] a person would swallow up his neighbor...
>
> The reason that the other nations don't have statutes and laws like Israel is because they are the husk and Israel is the fruit.[20]

Valle offers detailed kabbalistic explanations of Christian practices, untranslatable into English without many introductions to Lurianic doctrine. His comments include observations on Christian burial customs, the full range of the Christian liturgical calendar—Carnival, Lent, Easter, and Christmas—and even reasons for the specifics of clerical clothing and church architecture.

Perennialism

Perennialism, or traditionalism, was the approach to religion in which religious ideas are preserved as ancient tradition, originally associated with the French Catholic thinkers of the early nineteenth century. Traditionalism was essentially a philosophy of history that elevated tradition to a position of divine and absolute authority as opposed to the tradition-less rationalism of Enlightenment philosophers. Perennialism seeks the primordial revelation that is not limited to one religion, but is rather a universal and eternal core that transcends any Enlightenment critique. All sacred traditions were to be regarded as manifestations of a perennial philosophy. Sacred traditions could be numbered in the plural, and thus all religions could be regarded as manifestations of a perennial philosophy that is one and eternal. But the Catholic Church excommunicated this approach in 1855 for its rejection of reason and for seeking a universal source of truth. However, many modern Jewish thinkers and essayists have accepted some form of this approach because of its appreciation of tradition.

An early Jewish proponent of perennialism was Adolphe Franck (1809–1893), a French philosopher and writer; he wrote his works when this position was still considered a traditional approach. His chief work was an attempt at a comprehensive, scientific description of the beginnings and contents of the Kabbalah in popular form and his approach used the Kabbalah as a means of connecting Judaism to this perennial philosophy. For Franck, there is a perennial tradition that predates the differentiation of Judaism and Zoroastrianism. For perennialist, there is a core of tradition from the original revelation and then the ever new interpretations and discoveries are ever dependent on the authority of the tradition. He states that the chain of tradition is always evident in the wildest discoveries, and that tradition is the very power of change and revolution.

The Kabbalah has not been borrowed from Christianity, for all the great principles upon which it stands antedate the coming of Christ.

The striking resemblances which we have found between this doctrine and the religious beliefs of the several sects of Persia, its numerous and remarkable points of similarity with the *Zend Avesta*, the traces that the religion of Zoroaster has left in all parts of Judaism, and the external relations between the Hebrews and their old teachers after the Babylonian captivity—all these force us to the conclusion that the material of the Kabbalah derived from the theology of the ancient Persians.

But this borrowing did not destroy the originality of the Kabbalah for the latter substituted the absolute unity of cause and substance for the dualism in God and nature. Instead of explaining the formation of beings as an arbitrary act of inimical forces, it presents them as divine forms, successive and providential manifestations of the Infinite Intelligence. Ideas take the place of realized personifications and mythology is supplanted by metaphysics. This seems to us to be the general law of the human mind. No absolute originality, but also no servile imitation between nations and centuries. Whatever we may do to gain unlimited independence in the domain of moral science, the chain of tradition will always be evident in our boldest discoveries. No matter how immobile we sometimes appear to be under the sway of tradition and authority, our intelligence paves the way, our ideas change with the very power that weighs them down, and a revolution is bound to break loose.[21]

It would be instructive for further discussion of these topics to compare Franck's work to Franz Joseph Molitor's *Philosophie der Geschichte oder über die Tradition* (1834–1853), which served as the basis for Gershom Scholem's thoughts on the Kabbalah, especially Scholem's ideas on tradition and revelation, in which a textual tradition allows for progressive revelation. In our current age, when perennialism has lost its appeal on both the scholarly and popular levels, Franck serves to remind us of the range of possible solutions in an earlier century.

Hirsch—Human Grasping of God without Revelation

Rabbi S.R. Hirsch, the nineteenth-century founder of neo-Orthodoxy, states that Judaism is divine, while all other religions are man-made. In the following passage, he allows for natural religion as a human process of grasping God without revelation. The natural secular realm does not offer the same truths as God-given revelation.

> to emphasize that the Torah and the Jewish religion are unique in that they are not created by man. This objectivity separates Judaism in an un-ambiguous way from all other religions. Therefore, it alone is absolute and is above all human development because the other religions are based on the grasp of God by man during a given epoch; therefore they evolve with mankind and its enlightenment.[22]

As seen previously in the inclusivist chapter, Hirsch considers Christianity as based on the Jewish concept of God, revelation, and ethical action. Nevertheless, following nineteenth-century thought, he credits Christianity with continuous historical and cultural change, while he views Judaism as eternal and outside history. Hirsch does not develop these thoughts into a full theology, yet the liberal thinker Franz Rosenzweig did develop a similar theology of Christianity.

Natural Theology

Hillel Zeitlin (1871–1942), religious thinker and writer, came from a secular background to become an advocate for Hasidic piety. Among his many literary credits, he was responsible for creating the modernist neo-Hasidic reading of Rav Nahman of Bratzlav. His writings on Hasidism freely quote from a wide range of Hasidic texts in addition to Tolstoy, Nietzsche, Emerson, and Confucius.

As an acknowledgment that there are pious and religious people throughout the world, Zeitlin cites Maimonides on the need for people to sense God and then cites examples from Hasidut about sensing God. He refocuses the discussion on the experiential fact that as seekers of God, members of other religions can sense the divine grandeur; there is a commonality of religious experience.[23]

Zeitlin's writings offer an empirical approach that can align Maimonides, kabbalists, and Hasidism with the variety of religious experience from other religions. Religious experiences are available to all seekers after God—not just to prophets, poets, and mystics, but also to all other people. Zeitlin accepts the empiricism of religion from William James, subdividing religious experience into ten ways to come to God, including God in Nature; Symbolism; Internal Repentance; Depression; Inner Voice, Life Experiences; and the Ascent of the Soul.

> There are even more sublime types of revelation, these revelations ascend from below to above, as a height above height: (1) maggidim, heavenly voices; (2) Holy Spirit in all its unique forms (3) prophecy. These later revelations, their nature, source, and signs are richness and occurrences not just to founders of religions and poets of faith, but by their own testimony of thousands of people in many eras.[24]
>
> There are many, many levels of this emotional closeness. One person feels as if another person comes close to them after an inner cry and pure prayer, while another feels it continuously, both awake and asleep,

upon retiring and awakening, during business, and conversations, while another hears a wondrousness come close to him, ever closer.[25]

The human ear hears the "voice of God in strength," "voice of God in splendor" "voice of a great tremble," or "small still voice," all according to the preparation of the person, his constitution, and the exaltedness of his spirit.[26]

As an empirical modern, he accepts all religious experience as having value, without passing judgment. In contrast, Maimonides' position presented earlier sharply distinguishes between approach of magic and imagination from those of reason and self-perfection.

Respecting Mystery

Marcus Ehrenpreis, chief rabbi in Stockholm between 1914 and 1951, offers us an urbane reminder that ultimately the core in all faith, Jewish as well as Christian, is mysterious, and a secret of God, before which both Jews and Christians should feel humble. Similar to his contemporaries in other faiths, Nathan Soderblom and Jacques Maritain, Rabbi Ehrenpreis acknowledges that deep down all religions contain something mysterious. None of us can penetrate religion's innermost nature; no reading of texts exhausts its revelatory capacity.

There is in every religion, beyond what can be explained, a mystery, a last secret, which remains unreachable for outsiders. We, Jews and Christians, can go a long way together and talk to each other, but sooner or later we will arrive at a closed door, to which the Christians have a key, but we do not. When we come to this closed door, we Jews can do nothing but bow our heads in reverence before it and stay silent. We ask and expect—and this is the purpose of our dialogue—that the Christian world shall learn to revere the mystery that is the innermost core of the Jewish religion, that which is difficult for outsiders to grasp and difficult for us to explain.[27]

Conclusions

This chapter mainly dealt with medieval ideas. For all of them, there was a natural sense of God's accessibility to all. They each portray the other religions, collectively, as a lower form of religion than Judaism since the other faiths either use representation in worship, accept magical thinking, or serve other forces than God. For each of these, they paint an ideal and then find wanting those who do not live up to it. From a distance of time, many of these criteria seem like internal debates concerning what they considered imperfections in their own Judaism. Their rejections of superstition, magic, and representation seem to say much about the Jews themselves. It is as if the other religions are on their shadow side.

If we only have the medieval positions, then we are limited to a hierarchal approach to the other. When the sixteenth-century Catholic Spaniards considered the religions of the New Worlds, they relied on the Spanish Bishop Jose Sepulveda. He advised, following medieval thought, that hierarchy, not equality, is the natural state of human society. Everyone has the same ability but some religions are more perfected than others. The medieval Jewish inclusivists discussed the issues in terms that Bishop Sepulveda would have understood, a hierarchy created and evaluated by only one side. Yet, the medieval could indeed see the religious traits of the other religions, provided the other religions turned toward heaven.

In the modern era, the medieval positions were rejected through the adaptation of the either/or choice of universalism or particularist revelation. The former position, associated with William James, accepts universals of religious experience, whereas the latter, associated with Karl Barth, voids medieval hierarchy but states that one should consider one's own revelation as sui generis and not in continuity with the natural phenomena of religion. As typified by Rabbi Soloveitchik, "R. Saadyah Gaon and Maimonides, by stressing the continuity between the two domains—where the rational ends, the revelational begins—ignored the distinctive marks that give them their unique character and different patterns."[28]

Nevertheless, the medieval are still especially useful for reminding us that there are middle positions toward other religions between universal human and divine revelation. Yehudah Halevi, Maimonides, and Nahmanides, as do most philosophers, all have continuity between knowledge of God and Torah.

The position of Marcus Ehrenpreis that the difference between religions is a mystery bears the brunt of rejecting the medieval positions but is unable to move forward.

Those who moved beyond medieval positions will be discussed in the follow-up volume to this work. In the subsequent volume, *Judaism and World Religions*, we will deal with Buber, Rosenzweig, Herberg, Heschel, Soloveitchik, and many others. It will also discuss those Jewish authors who have had first hand observed knowledge of other religions.

CHAPTER 10

At the Dawn of a New Century

My view of a theology of other religions, as presented in prior chapters, is that the discussion cannot go forward without a sound grounding in the past texts and engagement with past theological rubrics.

Analyzing the prior texts allows us to know the contours of potential overlooked useful perspectives, and conversely, to diagnose correctly the problems of inherently problematic texts. Inclusivism teaches us to see the universal call of God in ethics, metaphysics, or revelation, the basis of theological study. Particularism teaches us the need to preserve and take pride in the holiness of Israel, the basis of textual study. But particularism needs to be curtailed of its potentially demonic and harmful side. Universalism opens us to the natural human elements in coming toward God and the brotherhood of man, the basis of religious humanism. Pluralism lends dignity to human difference and diversity.

We need to appreciate what the wide palette of traditional texts says about other religions and stop thinking that we already know. The range of opinions as shown in previous chapters is larger than most people think it is. As I explained in the first chapter, we regularly employ all the positions in different contexts in our lives. The goal is to know which position is needed in a specific context. Now, in an age of globalization, the theological agenda has become even more crucial. This chapter will offer some perspectives on the role of encountering other religions in the age in which we live.

The debate should not deliberate whether we should be encountering the other but how we encounter the other. What are the various methods of relation, commonality, confrontation, and respect that we use? Differences between religions are not arranged in either a clear hierarchy or dissolved in universality or pluralism. In our era, it is not an either/or choice of exclusivist or tolerance, rather a both/and relationship is needed. Any opinion that we formulate is based on knowing that many positions—inclusivist, exclusivist, universalist, pluralist, and empiricist—all exist. The positions are mutually correcting and they presuppose one another, thereby limiting, protecting, and offering reciprocal adjustment to the other opinions. The combination of opinions is greater than the parts. The very concept of religion implies interreligious, but then how can we ward off the triumphalism of acknowledging only our own religion and the indifference of not differentiating between religions. By knowing that it is a both/and choice and to be familiar with the other positions.[1]

In order to learn about other religions and to see ourselves through the eyes of the other, as stated at the beginning of the book, we have to kick the secularism habit. To see the religious other, we have to acknowledge that we encounter religious people outside of Judaism and consider them as people of other religious communities, as religious individuals, and as people that also have secular sides. The goal is not a common narrative or a secular tolerance where we do not give dignity to the other faith, where I ignore the religion of the other or socially tolerate a predetermined incorrect opinion. Tolerance of the other is not sufficient for moral responsibility; rather we need a self-understanding of other religions.

The opposite of intolerance is not necessarily tolerance, but humanity. This is not the humanity of putting our religions aside, or a subjective humanism that does not make demands on us. It is a humanism that demands that we cultivate the religious virtues of mercy, kindness, truth, and peace.

To overcome intolerance, we need hospitality. Hospitality is simultaneously theological and ethical; it teaches us not to make serious misrepresentations of the other and to meet others in a way that makes demands upon us for welcome. The invitation to the other, and the subsequent time spent together, generates actual relationship, familiarity, and a potential for change in ourselves. How do we offer hospitality? Conversation, graciousness, listening, and mutual respect are the keys. By engaging in hospitality we receive the other as a stranger in our life. As if receiving a stranger in one's home, in each other's presence, we learn the patterns of behavior of the other. Tolerance offers no insight into the other faith because there is no actual encounter with the other religion.

The art of listening, however, turns out to be a crucial factor in building healthy encounter. Careful listening deepens into a discernment that goes beyond words. We come to these events truly knowing nothing about the other side, and have to listen to the most basic elements. Interfaith relationships tend to be about friendship, cooperation, and collaboration around shared stories, values, and goals—not a search lowest common religious denominator. Universals and common denominators play a role in the opening encounters to help alleviate the initial apprehension toward those that one meets and inherited fear of the other side. But the real encounter occurs through understanding difference. One grows through experiences that stand out in memory as an encounter outside the normal "safety zone." When one meets a member of the other faith, one seeks to be open to surprise or to be humbled, an experience of healing and hope. One seeks the genuine experience of friendship. Hospitality is a commitment to a character trait and a culture of life, not just civil tolerance. Hospitality needs a genuine openness to the other, which will hopefully lead to self-transformation.[2]

We should not confuse the public policy decision of whether to engage in actual theological dialogue, or meeting in person, with the theoretical question of whether Judaism actually has a theology of other religions. If one respects the Orthodox restrictions on dialogue and at the same time is not seeking to find converts though theological discussion, then what is one's activity? The activity of hospitality offers a twofold answer—to expand our global vision and to seek to diminish hatred and avoid derogatory statements about others.

As stated by Krister Stendahl (1921–2008), former Lutheran bishop of Stockholm and professor of religion at Harvard university, "how to sing my song to Jesus with abandon without telling negative stories about others! Or, if you want to sound more academic: Towards a Christian theology of religions." How do we tell a Jewish story without minimizing parts of our tradition or speaking negatively about others? Basically, by using a Jewish theology of other religions. This requires familiarity with other positions and hospitality.

We can talk about our religions without harmful statements about others. In doing this, we would be coordinating and institutionalizing the de facto reality that confronted by modernity, Jewish and Christian theologians have profited by encountering the other faith.

Emmanuel Levinas mentions the ethical crime of the tyranny of the same, in which I impose my categories on the other. We need to move beyond the smugness of thinking that we know anything about the other. Just as an understanding of the past is necessary for political reconciliation between communities, we need to study and engage the other's community of faith in order to work for the future, where we can confront the issues of the day.

Another way to overcome intolerance is to learn to engage in practical work together, now in a global context. Active encounter creates stories—positive stories of possibilities. Even when faiths clash in encounter or practice, we can still tell the story of where things went wrong and how we navigated the troubled times. Political states regularly engage in diplomatic relationships, cordial encounters, and practical negotiations without sharing a common political ideology.

To move the discussion forward, there are several broad topics that need to be addressed to appreciate my position. The first topic is the need to overcome Jewish xenophobia of other religions. Friendship is needed to overcome hostility and to create trust. Second, we need to overcome fears of the past. Third, we have to address the new fears of the age of globalization and to understand that it is a new religious American landscape. Fourth, we need to come to accept and internalize the changes in the Church. Here, I discuss these issues as they pertain to interreligious encounter.

Fear of the Other

First, and foremost, Jews need to put aside their frightened mentality, and recognize the age in which they live. We have a choice of how to see the world: Is Abraham the start of monotheism, a father of many nations, blessed among people, or is he someone who dwells alone (*"ivri,"* literally other bank of the river) or in opposition?

Historians estimate that at the start of the first millennium at least 7 percent of the Roman Empire of late antiquity was Jewish or God-fearing. Jews were integrated into Roman society with observers in the Senate and significant presence in the urban areas. So what happened to that integration? Jews turned inward, and in many communities dwelled alone after the Hadrianic persecution. But what would have happened if Jews had not done that?

In the Middle Ages we did not always dwell alone; rather we adapted to each age. Jewish history is usually portrayed as one of continuous persecution, what Salo Baron called the lachrymose theory. But prior centuries of Jewish life were not continuous persecution.. In most countries, Jews embraced the opportunities of their culture from 800 until 1800. Some may know of the Golden Age in Spain, when Jews were political leaders, financiers, and poets. But a comparable situation existed in most regions: North Africa, Italy, Provence, the Ottoman Empire, and Greece. And not just in the eleventh and twelfth centuries, but in most places until the 1800s. In 1100, 95 percent of world Jewry lived around the Mediterranean Sea or around the Fertile Crescent in security, while in the era of the crusades, only 5 percent of Jewry lived in Ashkenaz. We spend disproportionate amounts of time envisioning the crusades, and minimal time discussing the periods of social integration, tranquility, and productivity.

The great Hebrew University historian Ben-Zion Dinur portrayed each age of the Diaspora as concerned with politics, economics, and success. He depicted Jewish life as willing to engage the surrounding world, not as scared of building strong communities. This approach was formally portrayed in the Nahum Goldman Museum of the Jewish People in the Diaspora in Tel Aviv (*Beit Hatefusot*). In the displays, Dinur sought to point out how Jews were not passive but part of the systems of the age. He wanted to show how each age produces poetry, philosophy, science, and community leaders. To take some examples, Jews had representation at the fourth Lateran Council of the Church (1215). Those Jewish representatives to the Council certainly did not sit there not understanding the discussions as they pertained to the Jews, nor were they attending to sit cowering in the background. Rabbi Abraham Aderet (Rashba) was a financier, political leader, and a close ally of the King, and handled civil and communal matters in Spain. He did not rise in political power without integration into the legal and economic structures of Aragon. A generation later Rabbanu Nissim (Ran) formulated theories of the importance of secular government in Jewish life.[3]

Cecil Roth, the historian of Western European Jewry, also showed the richness of the period of early Modern Europe (1500–1800) when Jews did not dwell alone. Jonathan Israel, a current Princeton University historian, states that because of this outgoingness and success, "Jews had it better in absolute and relative terms than in modernity." Once again, to give several examples, R. Ovadiah Seforno was a rabbi, rabbinic scholar, exegete, and philosopher in Renaissance Italy, noted for teaching Torah to gentiles, and dedicating his theology work *Light of the Nations* to King Henry of France. Seforno suggests that Christians share with Jews a universal relationship with God, and that all humanity is the chosen people. Rabbi Menashe ben Israel, humanist rabbi in Holland, widely respected as a theologian, served as model for Western European Jewry from the seventeenth until nineteenth centuries. His confident and open manner was modeled on Shimone Luzzato, a rabbi from Italy, who wrote "how profitable are the Jews" for mercantilism. There are many other examples of social integration, a contemporary reader can rely on many of the recent cultural histories of Judaism to provide a corrective narrative of Jewish integration into society.[4]

However, in the modern period, the Czarist policy, pograms, and the Holocaust have made Jews scared. The Jewish history taught in 1860 by Heinrich Greatz (updated throughout the 1950s by Grayzel, Margolis, and Marx, and others) was one of continuous persecutions and the miracle of survival. There are historical countertrends to this history of persecution and passivity, but this lachrymose history where the Christian was always killing Jews became the unofficial ideology of modern Jewry. The aforementioned historian Ben-Zion Dinur did not accept this ideology of persecution and described the period of 1881–1948 as one of catastrophe, and offers the resounding contrast of how the post-1948 era of security, growth, and prosperity produced the state of Israel and the American Jewish community.

Nevertheless, as the loss of the Holocaust was internalized by American Jews, the lachrymose version had renewed resonance. The theologian and essayist Arthur A Cohen, in his book on the impact of the Holocaust, poignantly notes how before 1939, one could read the sad litany of pograms, riots, and massacres presented by Graetz and find it unremarkable and predictable. One could account for the events sociologically, historically, and psychologically and thereby provide context. After the death camps, Cohen argues that the past became illuminated by the present image of the mass killings. Now, it is as if the small medieval riots naturally culminated in the tremendum of the Holocaust. Many are blinded to our own current prosperity and security. We have forgotten both past and present periods of tranquility and instead have internalized a story of a millennium of persecution and a need to fear.[5]

Now we have to choose not to dwell alone and move beyond seeing ourselves as victims. We need to return to engaging the world, as defined by living in an age of globalization, which requires a response. . We have to reexamine the role of collective memory, family ties, and liturgy in our holding on to hatred. More importantly, much of the memory was created by these recent narratives Jewish history, which emphasize the negative at the expense of the positive.

Carlos Ginzburg, the noted Italian Jewish historian, observes that we actually have precious little collective memory. Much of what we know does not actually correspond to the actual contours of either medieval safety or persecution. Much of the polemical narratives, such as the crusade chronicles, are currently not considered reliable accounts. Yet, we still give these accounts deference over other possible narratives of Jewish history. When we teach prior ages, do we tell narratives of harmony, coexistence, and sharing of culture? Why do Jews accept only the negative stories when they teach? If we are going forward to a new future, then the more pressing question becomes of what we teach in the coming years?[6]

To return to our opening question about our dual image of Abraham as either blessed among people or dwelling alone, Rabbi S.R. Hirsch offered a model for openness and not dwelling alone:

And I will make you into a great nation, and I will bless you, and I will make your name great; become a blessing (Gen. 12:2)

"The people of Abraham, in private and in public, follow one calling: to become a blessing. They dedicate themselves to the Divine purpose of bringing happiness to the world by serving as a model for all nations and to restore mankind. God will grant His blessing of the renewal of life and the awakening and enlightenment of the nations, and the name of the People of Abraham shall shine forth."

Rabbi Hirsch's model of Abraham is open to the world rather than set apart from the rest of humanity. Jews need to reclaim the Divine purpose of encountering the world and working for the benefit of humanity. Rabbi Hirsch was not advocating the denial of Abraham's differences from the religiosity in Ur of the Chaldeans; rather he grasped both elements.

Looking back on four decades of Christian-Jewish dialogue and looking ahead to our future encounters, I'm convinced that what has transpired between Judaism and Christianity in this past generation has set the stage for an important milestone for the Jewish people. It is time for Judaism to take its rightful place as part of the global parliament of religions. Theologically, we believe God called us: "through you will the nations of the world be blessed." But historically, the reality led us to shut ourselves off. We became "a nation who dwells alone," not because of our embrace of God or holy purpose, but because of the world's rejection of Jews.

Following the nadir of that isolation in the darkest days of the past century, we have been strengthened and enabled to achieve a new place, both as a nation—through the state of Israel—and as a religion—through the flourishing of Judaism. It is time for us to put aside the role of a nation of victims that we assumed due to circumstance of history, and return to the role played by our ancestors Abraham, Isaac, and Jacob: heroes of Divine history, called by God to greatness and responsibility. The Jewish people, as a people and a community of the faithful, must address the challenges that so many individual Jews have eagerly taken part in. As Jews we must do our part in working for a better global order, one that promotes freedom, justice, peace, and human dignity.

I am not saying that Judaism—or any religion—can solve the economic and political problems our world faces. But we can do our part through supporting programs that can make a difference. This challenge—which I believe we must bravely confront—requires Jewish thinkers to begin articulating visions of a just social and economic order. We must begin to discuss—within our own community and with other communities—the task of applying our theories of local and community building to the global community.

In building communities, we are called upon to take our virtue of *zedek,* righteousness, a virtue similar yet distinct from those of charity and philanthropy, and apply it to creating a world of *zedek,* of righteousness. Maimonides lists righteousness as one of the cardinal Jewish virtues—the others being mercy and judgment. Elsewhere he adds three more virtues to his list, truth, loving-kindness, and peace. We need to ground our pragmatic activities in the sources of our traditions. For us, the defining Talmudic principle commanding us to act in the world is *mipnei darkhei shalom,* "because of the ways of peace."[7]

For Maimonides, this reflected our command to emulate God, whose name is peace, and who by His example showed us the virtues of righteousness and mercy. For this ethic, the God who opens His hand and provides for every living thing is highlighting our responsibility to open our own hands and feed the hungry. This teaches us that our concern as Jews is for righteousness (*tzedek*), justice (*mishpat*), charity (*hesed*), truth (*emet*), loving-kindness (*rahamim*), and peace (*shalom*).

There is another interpretation of this principle of the ways of peace, found in halakhic sources, though, which should not be overlooked. This interpretation explains that Jews are commanded to provide charity to everyone to avoid hatred (*mipnei eivah*). We must be open in discussing how both of these interpretations, the virtuous and the pragmatic, can each play a role to enable, justify, and perhaps command Jewish action in the world arena. Sometime we need to act pragmatically to avoid enmity and sometimes we need to act based on higher values.

As individuals, members of the Jewish people are called by God to fulfill the work of Creation, to serve as stewards of the world, and to enhance the respect of the image of God by helping those who embody it. Rabbi Moses Cordovero, the great sixteenth-century Safed ethicist and kabbalist, wrote, "It is evil in the sight of the Holy One, blessed be He, if any of His creations are despised."[8]

However, even in considering our very notions of a call to action and ethical processes, we see our differences. Halakhah is not the same as the magisterium or an appeal to conscience. In working together, in emphasizing the commonality, we must be careful to ensure that the differences are not erased or elided.[9]

New Fears

The other major change for Judaism is the rise of globalization. The debates between proponents of Huntington's *Clash of Civilizations* and those of Thomas Friedman's *Lexus and the Olive Tree* have replaced the local concerns of the 1950s. Like modernity and nationalism, globalization has potential for both good and bad, creating a new reality that demands confrontation and response. Globalization offers very real and very immediate threats. It is based on a culture of the marketplace, divorced from any constraints, be they ethical, religious, moral, or national. Globalization creates a need to choose greater openness in place of fear and closure, and to choose real politics over academics.

To respond to the current decade, rehearsing old parameters is academic. We should be seeking guidance for the contemporary issues. We need to provide sanctity to the world. Social issues need a religious perspective. In the tension between globalization and preserving tradition, we can be secure at this point and use our tradition to aid in globalization. Not entering the modern world of globalization and dwelling alone is a form of "triumph without battle." In our age there are no victories resulting from isolationism and silence. Creating closed ethnic enclaves does not address global issues or make the world a better place. If we do not engage the world, our seeming religious victories would be hollow.

Recently, a select group of religious Zionist rabbis sought to show that religious Jewry remains relevant in an age of international factories and renewed human trafficking. They stated that "we must expand our field of moral studies" in order to create a broader vision of social and economic concerns beyond the local. One of its leaders discussed the need for greater sensitivity to the new social and economic issues not legislated by halakhah by turning to ethical literature (*mussar*) and nonlegal rabbinic literature (*aggada*). "In avoiding halakhic discussion of these issues, we abstain from the improvement of the world and passively contribute to its destruction." Under these new conditions, "social sensitivities become more significant...If we can only build on this sensitivity, we can create a more just world." Religious encounters are an essential part of the process.

As individuals, members of the Jewish people are called by God to fulfill the work of Creation, to serve as stewards of the world, and to enhance the respect of the image of God by helping those who embody it. That much of this work will take place in conjunction with non-Jews is self-evident. What is not self-evident, however, is the desirability of carrying out this work under a specifically Jewish framework and in conjunction with other religious groups. As my teacher Walter Wurzburger taught when dialogue started in the 1960s, "When Jews and Christians embark on joint social action, they do so not merely qua fellow citizens of a secular society but as members of faith communities seeking the implementation of their socio-religious message." Almost fifty years later we ask again: Why should these acts of humanity be undertaken under a banner of interreligious joint action, rather than as a response to God's call to each individual? The answer, I think, lies in the tenor of the times.

The Midrash tells how the great events in this world are only known to God, and only He understands the outcome of current human actions.

"A nation that dwells alone"..."Who alone performs great wonders" (Tehillim 136:3)—What is the meaning of "alone"? Rabbi Prozdik bar Nachsha explains: He alone knows what He is doing. Rav Avdimi of Haifa said: The things that we have seen are hidden; we ourselves do not know what we have seen. (*Yalkut Shimoni*)

We need to sow seeds of new ventures, of entering a wider arena, of working with others. It is our current perspective, our vision of the world. Levinas notes in this passage that we need to embrace the unknown future and enter the world, even though we can make no claims of knowing the outcome of our actions or even the correct choice. Those are left hidden for God's perspective; nevertheless, we have to be part of the events.

Locally

These encounters between religions occur not just nationally and globally, but even locally. Every Sunday my local community center in my predominately Jewish suburb, also containing a strong Christian and Muslim presence, has a continuous stream of Hindu, Buddhist, Sikhs, and Zoroastrian services using the classrooms. Diana Eck, a professor at Harvard University, points out that it is a new religious America. "We the people of the United States of America are now religiously diverse as never before and some Americans do not like it." She advocates active engagement and real constructive understanding of others, without relativism or abdication of differences.[10]

Whereas in the 1950s people saw America as Protestant, Catholic, and Jewish, now every country has Muslims, Buddhists, Hindus, Sikhs, and others. Numerically many of these groups are quite small, and America remains predominately Protestant. However, the response to their presence is similar to the acceptance of Jews in the 1950s as one of the three faiths of America, despite their small numbers. Mosques, halal shops, Buddhist shrines, and a Bahai Temple are in my seemingly Jewish neighborhood and Hindu and Buddhist altars with food offerings are ever present in my local shopping area. There was a time when we met others only as foreigners—as travelers in strange locations. In America they are now our coworkers, schoolmates, and neighbors.

In an event like the Asian tsunami at the end of 2004, we find ourselves working together locally on global projects. I have a classmate Rabbi Chaim Steinmetz who leads a congregation in Montreal. After the Asian tsunami he held a citywide commemoration for the victims in his synagogue Shabbat morning. His account of the event portrays the type of events occurring in our own synagogues.

> It was not your average synagogue service. On this particular Saturday morning, Jews, Christians, Muslims, Hindus, Sikhs and Buddhists gathered together in my Montreal synagogue for a service on behalf of the victims of the Asian tsunami. Diplomats from India, Indonesia, Israel and

Sri Lanka, as well as the Canadian Minister of Justice, all offered words of sympathy. And indeed, solidarity was in the air. Representatives of the Sinhalese and Tamils both attended, and a representative of the largest Muslim country in the world, Indonesia, thanked the Jewish community for their efforts on behalf of the disaster victims. You could say it was a morning of strange bedfellows; in actuality, it was a true moment of grace.

In the aftermath of this tsunami, we remember again that all human beings are brothers and sisters. That is why people all around the world are coming forward to help the victims. With this disaster came a world-wide moment of grace.[11]

About the meetings of religions today, I could not have said it any better. For public events we pragmatically work together, yet learning to engage in the encounter opens the participants up to greater self-understanding, or as Rabbi Steinmetz boldly states "a true moment of grace."

Christianity

In the last forty years, Jews have a greater sense of security in the world stemming from their internalizing the existence of the state of Israel. We also have witnessed the great strides of the Catholic Church, moving from persecutor to greatest friend, from offering us eternal damnation to recognition of the state of Israel. I have many times met educated Jews who have studied aspects of medieval history and who are convinced that contemporary Christians still follow early medieval Church theology and attitudes. They do not realize that just as Jews are not living twelfth-century lives at present, neither are Christians still accepting medieval views and they are not to be judged on millennium-old opinions. Many Jews have little cognizance of *Nostra Aetate* or the changes to the very structure of Christian thought in modern times.

When *Nostra Aetate* was written in 1965, it irrevocably ended the culture of contempt. But it was John Paul II who publically recognized the state of Israel, condemned the Holocaust, and accepted Judaism as an ongoing living faith that permanently changed the relationship. He had a personal understanding and empathy for Judaism. When he was the authority in charge of Catholic-Jewish relations, Walter Cardinal Kasper stated that there is "no mission to the Jews. There is dialogue...and dialogue respects the difference of the other and brings mutual enhancement." Many, both locally and globally, think the same. There have been several important statements in later decades that Jews have not internalized the change such as the *Fundamental*

Accord between the Holy See and Israel (1993). Finally, Pope Benedict XVI has shown sincere respect for Jewish ritual, vision of kingship, and acknowledged that the "Jewish messianic hope is not in vain." He has repeatedly worked to condemn Holocaust denial and remove anti-Jewish interpretations of Christian texts.[12]

In recent years there have been other changes. The Presbyterian Church has the following position in its "1987 paper on Judaism": "We are willing to ponder with Jews the mystery of God's election of both Jews and Christians to be a light to the nations...As Christians we acknowledge that Jews are in covenant relationship with God." Far from thinking that Jews need to be perfected, they state that "We believe and testify that this theory of supersessionism or replacement is harmful." The United Methodist Church states: "God is steadfastly faithful to the biblical covenant with the Jewish people. The covenant God established with the Jewish people...continues because it is an eternal covenant." Thoughtful Christians will usually take these statements a step further and state that even Christians themselves need to be perfected in faith, hope, and charity. The meeting of Jews and Christians as religious individuals is no longer a rare occurrence. According to one study, 77 percent of American Christians have been to at least one synagogue service, and many have been to several.

Many Evangelical churches have attained an understanding of the importance of Israel for Jews. Currently, a strong plurality of America is Evangelical; we should stop referring to America as a secular country. God and religion, for better or worse, are part of the national vocabulary. There have been more references to God by politicians from 1976 to 1996 than there were in the first two hundred years of this country, and now we have stopped counting. Evangelicals understand the role of nationalism and peoplehood within our religion, and have thereby attained a rapid sense of political mutuality with the Jewish community despite the lack of theological rapprochement, and even despite their theological agenda. They support and fund Jews from American suburbs to move to Israel, yet Christian Zionists are waiting for a war of Armageddon in Israel and the eventual conversion of all the Jews who make Aliyah. Paradoxes abound.

Many Jews still say that Christianity, especially the Catholic Church, was responsible for horrible crimes in the past, so how can we trust them? Many have similar feelings about Islam.

Jews need to work to overcome their fear and distrust of the Church. The current climate requires Jews to overcome their sense of minority status and find a new social model for their interactions. We need to move beyond bitterness, both in our relationship with the Church and in our own self-understanding of our place in the world community. And we will need to consider how we have relied on this culture of victimhood even when the other who surrounds us does not wish to destroy us. Since the Jewish theological tradition offers us models ranging from exclusivism to pluralism, we should learn to cultivate a self-understanding appropriate for our current confrontations.

So how are we to go forward in interfaith encounter, given the broad and deep memory of the Jews living in fear of the Church? I do think that there are traditional theological models for reconciliation, but I am not sure of their ability to be accepted in the current climate.

For example, theologically, reconciliation is not forgiveness. As Jews, we are in no position to offer atonement to the Church. From our standpoint, atonement from God through repentance cannot be offered in cases of sins performed against one's fellow man, especially murder. In today's world when human memory vanquishes theology, the model of South Africa may be useful for us. There, "truth commissions have been set up under the assumption that getting people to understand the past will somehow contribute to reconciliation between those who were enemies under the ancient regime."

The philosopher Jonathan Lear points out that people want to hold onto humiliation because they enjoy destructive hatred, and the humiliation justifies their continuous hatred. The memory the Jewish people now hold of the past millennia is one that evokes hostility. We should begin the task of overcoming hatred by thinking of the virtues of peace and reconciliation. In this, we are mindful of the warnings of Bulgarian philosopher Tzvetan Todorov that academic understanding or pragmatic knowledge can be used to defeat or harm another religion, as likely as it will be used to foster good relationships.[13] "Understanding the narratives of other people can be used for reconciliation or it can be used to help undermine the other side." Knowledge of history or even first-hand encounters with others does not automatically lead to reconciliation. In fact, it can just as likely be used to foster hatred toward the other. Todorov points out that even when a dialogue is created, it is impossible to abandon prejudices and hostility. But that is a risk we must all take.

I was once discussing the rabbinic hatred of Rome in an interfaith encounter setting that included James Carroll, the author of *Constantine's Sword*, a book that strongly condemns the church, showing its responsibility and guilt for anti-Semitism. In the discussion of Rome and Judaism as Esau and Jacob, Carroll understood that prior Midrashic languages of hatred in Jewish texts are not our current reality. Contextualizing them historically can remove their negative influence.[14]

In contrast, Judaism's distrust of Catholicism was forged not so much by these theological texts, but by the day-to-day experience, over centuries, of living among members of the Catholic faith who followed their local parishes in prejudiced acts based on cultures of contempt and violence. Our encounter needs to look at the lay people and the events of these centuries, and in particular, the role of the Church in fostering hatred. In this, we join contemporary Catholic historians who think that the Church has to discuss its role in the culture of violence. We understand that learning to see the other side's perspective constitutes a painful process. Accordingly, it cannot be rushed. Appreciating the pain of the process is itself part of the moral understanding we aim to achieve.

I seek now to expand our encounter concerning history precisely to overcome humiliation and repudiate hatred. The Jewish historical consciousness is one that evokes revenge. I pray that the process of joint historical exploration creates a new memory, one based in mutual honesty and respect that can enable reconciliation.

After fifty years in which there have indeed been changes of history, theology, and policy, our real questions are not exegetical nor do they concern who gets to interpret older essays. Rather, how do we have confrontation between religions in the world of the twenty-first century?

Conclusion

Everyone has now encountered other faiths. Globalization has hastened these trends. A Jewish theory of other religions is not about who is saved or if another religion is idolatrous, but understanding and working with diversity. To treat non-Jews as secular is not respectful of other people. I can recognize the pious of the nations and acknowledge that non-Jews have devotion and give witness to their faiths. If we acknowledge that these are not secular acts then we can hear others through mutual testimony, narrative, and questioning. There is a need not just for tolerance, but also to offer, as Rabbi Jonathan Sacks advises, dignity to our differences. He wrote: "The choice is ours—will the generous texts of our tradition serve as interpretive keys to the rest, or will the abrasive passages determine our ideas of what we are and what we are called on to do?"[15]

In conclusion, there is a gap between the original situations of the texts mentioned in this book and today's reality. This book offers an overview of traditions and counter-traditions for future possibilities and new situations. Theology is not a closed activity. We are not outside history, and people in real situations will always adopt the texts for the current situation. Every day people work through and around texts and ideas without leaving the contours of the textual traditions. Real life is complex and social, and does not head in a single direction. Today, there are many complex dialectic relationships of the faiths. Texts do not form complete systems in interfaith settings. As Levinas notes, I am not in control to create an isolated approach since I am confronted by the other. I can remain isolated only if I choose not to be confronted and not hear the other. We need ways for the other to speak or be heard.

To do this we need to show vulnerability and acquire the called-for skills and virtues. We need to embrace the complexity of texts that parallel the complexity of life. All contemporary theologies are only a temporary order. The past, prior texts, and neglected opinions usually return. Texts are capacious and keep returning with ever new meanings and applications.

For us, the non-Jew will perforce remain an other; Jews and Christians, Muslims, Hindus, and Buddhists do not constitute one religion. We are not envisioning an irenic rapprochement. We respect that for any other religion to return under the emblem of Israel would require a renunciation of its deepest, most cherished beliefs—something we neither seek nor encourage. We need to ensure that our work under shared banners of common beliefs does not obscure what differences may exist. In the Jewish tradition, expressions such as "the image of God" and "the dignity of the created" have a range of meaning that is different from that of other faiths. We should be sensitive to the theological differences.

Moving forward will require a move beyond provincialism towards understanding Judaism as a faith among faiths. Does God ignore or destroy the beautiful in world cultures and religions? If one has a restricted view of the world limited to the ethnography of rabbinic texts, then de facto God is not concerned with the cultures of the world. If one is willing to view the world in broader terms then one can, and must, see that God likes many flowers in His bouquet. God does not reject the overwhelming majority of the world humanity. He does not ignore 99.75 percent of the world. Jews forget that they are less than .22 percent of the world's religious population. Yes, they were the Abrahamic basis for the faith of 55 percent of the world, the four billion Christians and Muslims, but the number of actual Jews in the world is miniscule. Is religious diversity simply an accidental fact of history or something willed positively by God? Do other religions have elements of truth, worship, and moral teachings as a positive meaning in God's single overall plan.

Abraham was the model for openness and hospitality. He ran to receive his guests as the presence of God (*shekhinah*). On this verse, the great Biblical exegete Rashi comments that this was despite the fact that the guests worshiped the dust of their feet as an idolatrous practice. According to the commentators on Rashi, Abraham knew that there was no problem in bringing idolaters into one's home for hospitality; the only problem is not to bring the object of idolatrous worship into one's home. Abraham had to differentiate between the practices that posed difficulties and those that did not.

Can we host everyone in our home? Or reciprocate and feel comfortable as guests wherever we go? There are still limits—we cannot approach another religion with our own projections of sameness. Jews cannot worship Christ or Vishnu as an avatar of the Holy One Blessed be He. We cannot ignore the differences of the other religions. But to encounter the other in hospitality is not, and should not be, the problem. Rather, it is a sign that God has concern for the world.

Jonah, in the biblical account, was called to go on a voyage to Nineveh. He was resistant and uncooperative in his response to the critical situation his world, as represented by the boat he sailed on, was in. Even if he and the others might die, Jonah sits stubbornly in the bottom of the boat, caught up in his preconceptions. They could pray without him. Later when he arrives in Nineveh, and despite himself and his attitude to the world he helps the world, he is chagrined, even angry. How dare God care about the world! If his Jewish people are not at center stage, he had no need to include them in his domain of concern. The years of political fear of Assyria, Egypt, and other empires of the Fertile Crescent set the framework to Jonah's attitude to the world. Those years and their pains led to Jonah's fear and anger. Jonah teaches a powerful and fertile message to our times.

Just as Jonah on his voyage confronted each religion calling out to its own god, so too do we need to have an understanding of our daily encounters with people of other faiths in an age of globalization. And as Jonah needed to learn that he could not dwell alone, or ignore that each man sincerely called "in the name of his god," and he certainly had to be taught that he could not refrain from traveling to speak the word of God to the gentiles of Ninveh, we need to learn that we have to encounter the broader world, and cannot refrain from engaging other religions in an age of globalization. Hence, in our age, we need our own theology of other religions.

NOTES

1 Beginning the Conversation

1. Jacob Katz, *Exclusiveness and Tolerance: Jewish-Gentile Relations in Medieval and Modern Times* (New York: Schocken, 1969).
2. John Micklethwait, "In God's Name: A Special Report on Religion and Public Life," The Economist, London November 3–9, 2007.
3. Mark Lila, "Earthly Powers," *NYT*, April 2, 2006.
4. When we mention the clash of civilizations, we think of either the Spengler battle, or a more benign interplay between cultures in individual lives. For the Spengler battle, see Samuel P. Huntington, *The Clash of Civilizations and the Remaking of World Order* (New York: Simon & Schuster, 1996). For a more benign interplay in individual lives, see Thomas L. Friedman, *The Lexus and the Olive Tree* (New York: Farrar, Straus, Giroux, 1999).
5. Micklethwait, "In God's Name."
6. Robert Wuthnow, *America and the Challenges of Religious Diversity* (Princeton, NJ: Princeton University Press, 2005). "Interview with Robert Wuthnow" *Religion and Ethics Newsweekly* April 26, 2002. Episode no. 534 http://www.pbs.org/wnet/religionandethics/week534/ rwuthnow.html
7. Wuthnow, *America and the Challenges of Religious Diversity,* 291.
8. Eric Sharpe, "Dialogue," in Mircea Eliade and Charles J. Adams, *The Encyclopedia of Religion*, first edition, volume 4 (New York: Macmillan, 1987), 345–8.
9. Archbishop Michael L. Fitzgerald and John Borelli, *Interfaith Dialogue: A Catholic View* (London: SPCK, 2006).
10. Lily Edelman, *Face to Face: A Primer in Dialogue* (Washington, DC: B'nai B'rith, Adult Jewish Education, 1967).
11. Ben Zion Bokser, *Judaism and the Christian Predicament* (New York: Knopf, 1967), 5, 11.
12. Ibid., 375.
13. Robert Gordis, *The Root and the Branch* (Chicago: University of Chicago Press, 1962), 49.
14. Ibid., 55–6, 63.
15. Leon Klenicki, *Toward a Theological Encounter: Jewish Understanding of Christianity* (New York: Paulist Press, 1991), 1; Eugene Fisher, *Visions of the Other: Jewish and Christian Theologians Assess the Dialogue* (New York: Paulist Press, 1994).
16. Avery Dulles, "Christ Among the Religions," *America* 186, 3 (2002): 8.
17. See Lenn Evan Goodman, *Monotheism: A Philosophic Inquiry into the Foundations of Theology And Ethics* (Totowa, NJ: Rowman & Littlefield, 1982).

2 Theological Categories

1. Alan Race, *Christians and Religious Pluralism: Patterns in the Christian Theology of Religions* (Maryknoll, NY: Orbis Books, 1983); John Hick, *God Has Many Names* (London: Macmillian, 1980). Current readable summaries are provided by Paul F. Knitter, *Introducing Theologies of Religions* (Maryknoll, NY: Orbis Books, 2002); Veli-Matti Kärkkäinen, *An Introduction to the Theology of Religion: Biblical, Historical, and Contemporary Perspectives* (Downers Grove, IL: InterVarity Press, 2004).
2. John Hick and Paul F. Knitter, *The Myth of Christian Uniqueness: Toward a Pluralistic Theology of Religions* (Maryknoll, NY: Orbis Books, 1987); Langdon Gilkey, "Plurality and Its Theological Implications," in *The Myth of Christian Uniqueness.*
3. Terry Muck, "Instrumentality, Complexity, and Reason: A Christian Approach to Religions," *Buddhist-Christian Studies* 22, 1 (2002): 115–21.
4. George Lindbeck, *The Church in a Postliberal Age* (Grand Rapids, MI: William B. Eerdmans Pub., 2003); Holmes Rolston, *Religious Inquiry—Participation and Detachment* (New York: Philosophical Library, 1985), 244.
5. Francis X. Clooney, *Hindu God, Christian God* (New York: Oxford University Press, 2001); *Divine Mother, Blessed Mother: Hindu Goddesses and the Virgin Mary* (New York: Oxford University Press, 2005).
6. S. Mark Heim, *The Depth of the Riches: A Trinitarian Theology of Religious Ends.* (Grand Rapids: Eerdmans, 2001).
7. Kathryn Tanner, "Respect for Other Religions: A Christian Antidote to Colonialist Discourse," *Modern Theology* 9 (1993): 1–18.
8. Henry Siegman, "Ten Years of Catholic-Jewish Relations: A Reassessment," *Encounter Today* 11, 2–3 (1976): 87–8.
9. Jerome Gellman, "Mysticism," *Stanford Encyclopedia of Philosophy* (January 10, 2005), http://www.science.uva.nl/~seop/entries/mysticism/;Ewert H. Cousins, *Global Spirituality toward the Meeting of Mystical Paths*, Madras University Philosophical Series, 42 (Madras, India: Radhakrishnan Institute for Advanced Study in Philosophy, University of Madras, 1985); Steven T. Katz, *Mysticism and Philosophical Analysis* (New York: Oxford University Press, 1978); Paul J. Griffiths, "Modalizing The Theology of Religions," *Journal of Religion* 73 (1993): 382–9.
10. Paul Griffiths, *Problems of Religious Diversity* (Oxford: Blackwell, 2001), 54; Jerome Gellman, "In Defense of Contented Religious Exclusivism," *Religious Studies* 36:4 (December 2000): 401–17; Gavin D'Costa, *The Meeting of Religions and the Trinity* (Maryknoll, NY: Orbis Books, 2000).
11. Schubert Miles Ogden, *Is There Only One True Religion Or Are There Many?* (Dallas: Southern Methodist University Press, 1992); David Lochhead, *The Dialogical Imperative: A Christian Reflection on Interfaith Encounter* (Maryknoll, NY: Orbis Books, 1988).

3 Biblical and Talmudic Texts

1. Yehezkel Kaufmann, "The Bible and Mythological Polytheism," *JBL* 70 (1951): 179–97; idem., *The Religion of Israel, from Its Beginnings to the Babylonian Exile* (Chicago: University of Chicago Press Chicago, 1960).
2. Naomi Janowitz, "Good Jews Don't: Historical and Philosophical Constructions of Idolatry," *History of Religions* 4, 2 (2007): 239–52.
3. Morton Smith, *Palestinian Parties and Politics that Shaped the Old Testament* (New York: Columbia University Press, 1971); Mark S. Smith, *The Early History of God: Yahweh and the*

Other Deities in Ancient Israel (San Francisco: Harper, 1990); Ziony Zevit, *The Religions of Ancient Israel: A Synthesis of Parallactic Approaches* (London: Continuum, 2001).

4. Robert Goldenberg, *The Nations that Know Thee Not* (New York: New York University Press, 1998); Gerald R. McDermott, *God's Rivals: Why Has God Allowed Different Religions?* (Downer's Grove, IL: IVP Academic, 2007), 62.

5. C.J. Labuschagne, *The Incomparability of Yahweh in the Old Testament* (Leiden: E.J. Brill, 1966).

6. Smith, *The Early History of God*, 36, 47.

7. David Goodblatt, *Elements of Ancient Jewish Nationalism* (Cambridge: Cambridge University Press, 2006), 13–15.

8. Ruth 1; Zephaniah 3:9; Zechariah 14:9.

9. BT *Avodah Zarah* 46a; BT *Megillah* 25b; Sif. Deuteronomy 61.

10. BT *Sanhedrin* 10:2; Maimonides, *Mishneh Torah*, Teshuvah 3:13; Kings 8:11.

11. *Genesis Rabbah* 38:13.

12. Judith 5:6–7; Jubilees 11:16–17; 12:1–3, 6–7; *Genesis Rabbah* 38:13.

13. Emmanuel Friedheim, "Who Are the Deities Concealed Behind the Rabbinic Expression a Nursing Female Image?" *Harvard Theological Review* 96 (2003): 239–50; *Rabbinisme et paganisme en Palestine romaine: étude historique des Realia talmudiques (Ier-IVème siècles)* Religions in the Graeco-Roman world, v. 157 (Leiden: Brill, 2006). Emmanuel Friedheim; idem., *Tarbiz* 69 (2000): 167–75; idem., *Tarbiz* 70 (2001): 403–15.

14. Noam Zohar, "Idolatry, Idols, and Their Annulment" (Hebrew), *Sidra* 17 (2001–2002): 64–77.

15. Moshe Halbertal and Avishai Margalit, *Idolaty* (Cambridge, MA: Harvard University Press, 1998).

16. Azzan Yadin, "Rabban Gamliel, Aphrodite's Bath, and the Question of Pagan Monotheism," *Jewish Quarterly Review* 96 (2006): 149–79.

17. Plotinus, *Enneads* 3:9:3. Celsus, *On the True Doctrine* and Julian the Apostate, *Against the Galileans*—both books are translated in *Celsus and Others: Early Attacks on Christianity* (London: T. Rodd, 1830).

18. "God created two evil inclinations in the world, that toward idolatry and the other toward incest; the former has already been uprooted; the latter still holds sway" (*Song Rabbah* 7:8; cf. *Yoma* 69b).

19. Moshe Halbertal, "Coexisting with the Enemy: Jews and Pagans in the Mishnah," in *Tolerance and Intolerance in Early Judaism and Christianity*, ed. Graham N. Stanton, Guy G. Stroumsa (Cambridge: Cambridge University Press, 1998), 159–72. And see the recent articles Yair Furstenberg, "Nullification of Idolatry" *Reshit* 1 (2009): 117–144. In the same volume Noam Zohar sees this passage as already pointing to the approach reached by Meiri, see "Partitions Around a Shared Cultural Space" *Reshit* 1 (2009) 145–164.

20. Josephus reported that there existed groups, such as the Hasmonean family in the first century BCE, who produced human representations. Some rabbinic passages make reference to the widespread existence of Jewish figurative art (JT, *Avodah Zarah* 3:2; 3:3) but opposing views existed (e.g., *Mekhilta de Simeon bar Yochai, Ki Tisei* 31).

21. On the rabbis approaching the Greco-Roman cult as civil religion, see E.E. Urbach, "The Rabbinical Laws of Idolatry in the 2nd and 3rd Centuries in the Light of Archaeological and Historical Facts," *IEJ* 9 (1959): 145–69. Gerald Blidstein, "R. Yohanan, "Idolatry, and Public Privilege," *Journal for the Study of Judaism* 5, 2 (1974): 154–61.

22. TB *Megillah* 13a, but this statement was not developed in the legal discussions of halakhah.

23. Menachem Hirschman, *Kol ba'ei Olam: [All Humanity: a Universalist Stream in Tannaitic Literature and its Attitude toward Gentile Wisdom]* (Tel-Aviv: Ha-Kibbutz Ha-Meuhad, 1999); Marc Hirshman, "Rabbinic Universalism in the Second and Third Centuries," *Harvard Theological Review* 9, 2 (2000): 101–15.

24. Paula Fredrickson, *From Jesus to Christ: The Origins of the New Testament Images of Christ* (New Haven, CT: Yale University Press, 1988), 150; E.P. Sanders, *Jesus and Judaism* (Philadelphia:

Fortress Press, 1985). Some of the relevant statements include R. Abahu's interpretation of Hosea 14:8, "Those who sit in his shade shall be revived," as the gentiles who take refuge in the shade of the Holy One, Blessed be He. (*Leviticus Rabbah* 1:2) and Targum Pseudo-Jonathan on Deut. 23:16 who sees a prohibition against returning back to idolatry a gentile who desires to be under the shade of the shekhinah.

25. Cf. Paul Eph 6:19: Pray also for me, so that, when I begin to speak, the right words will come to me. Then I will boldly make known the secret of the gospel.

26. Sasha Stern, *Jewish Identity in Early Rabbinic Writings* (Leiden: E.J. Brill, 1994), 33. Yehezqel Kohen, *Ha-yahas el ha-nokhri ba-halakhah u-ve-metsi'ut bitequfat ha-tanna'im* doctoral dissertation, Hebrew University, Shevat 5735, 1975.

27. Stern, *Jewish Identity in Early Rabbinic Writings*, 156; and "The Death of Idolatry?" *Le'ela* (April 1993): 26–8; Gary Porton, *Goyim: Gentiles and Israelites in Mishnah-Tosefta* (Atlanta: Scholars Press, 1988), 196, 199 ff., 215–17, 241–3.

28. There are some of the little read texts from the early Ashkenaz period (ninth–twelfth centuries) that offer visions of heaven and hell, where these ideas play a role. See Adolf Jellinek, *Beit ha-Midrash*, 6 vols (1853–78, 1938), II, 48–51.

29. Aaron Lichtenstein, *The Seven Laws of Noah* (New York: The Rabbi Jacob Joseph School Press, 1981; Z. Berman Books, 2d ed. 1986); David Novak, *The Image of the Non-Jew in Judaism: An Historical and Constructive Study of the Noahide Laws* (New York: E. Mellen Press, 1983).

30. Book of Jubilees 7:20–28.

31. Nahum Rakover, *Law and the Noahides: Law as a Universal Value* (Jerusalem, Israel: Library of Jewish Law, 1998).

32. Stern, *Jewish Identity in Early Rabbinic Writings*, 204.

33. Naomi Janowitz, "Rabbis and their Opponents: The Construction of the 'Min' in Rabbinic Anecdotes," *Journal of Early Christian Studies* 6 (1998): 449–62.

34. Daniel Boyarin, "Rethinking Jewish Christianity: An Argument for Dismantling a Dubious Category (to which is Appended a Correction of my Border Lines)," *Jewish Quarterly Review* 99, 1 (Winter 2009): 7–36; Richard Kalmin, "Christians and Heretics in Rabbinic Literature of Late Antiquity," *HTR* 87 (1994): 155–69, citation on p. 157; Marcel Simon, *Verus Israel: A Study of the Relations Between Christians and Jews in the Roman Empire (Ad 135–425)* (Oxford: Oxford University Press, 1986).

35. Christina Hayes, *Gentile Impurities and Jewish Identities: Intermarriage and Conversion from the Bible to the Talmud* (Oxford: Oxford University Press, 2002); Aharon Shemesh, "The Origins of the Laws of Separatism: Qumran Literature and Rabbinic Halacha," *Revue de Qumran* 18, 2 (1997): 223–41.

36. On the complex dynamic deity of Judaism, see Moshe Idel, *Ben: Sonship and Jewish Mysticism* (London; New York: Continuum, 2007).

37. R. Travers Herford, *Christianity in Talmud & Midrash* (Jersey City: Ktav, 2006).

38. Stern, *Jewish Identity in Early Rabbinic Writings*, 28.

39. Daniel Boyarin, *Dying for God: Martyrdom and the Making of Christianity and Judaism* (Stanford: Stanford University Press, 1999).

40. Richard Kalmin, "Jesus in Sasanian Babylonia," *Jewish Quarterly Review* 99, 1 (Winter 2009): 107–12; Joshua Kulp. *"Jesus* in the Talmud (review)." *Shofar: An Interdisciplinary Journal of Jewish Studies* 27.2 (2009): 132–134.

41. TB *Gitten* 57a; *Vikkuah Yehiel of Paris*, ed. Margulies, 15ff.

42. For more details, see the article on *Encyclopedia Judaica*, vol. 2, "Aleinu"; Naphtali Wieder, "Regarding an Anti-Christian and Anti-Muslim Gematria (in the *'Alenu le-shabeah'*) prayer)," *Sinai* 76 (1998): 1–14: Michael D. Shwartz, "Alley le-Shabbeah: A Liturgical Prayer in Ma'aseh Merkabah," *JQR* 77(1986–87): 179–90.

43. E.E. Urbach translates Micah with an *and* rather than a *but* in the last sentence: *and* we will walk..., "Self-Isolation or Self-Affirmation in Judaism in the First Three Centuries,"

in E.P. Sanders, Albert I. Baumgarten, and Alan Mendelson, *Jewish and Christian Self-Definition. Vol. 2, Aspects of Judaism in the Graeco-Roman Period* (London: SCM Press, 1981), 298.

44. Goldenberg, *The Nations that Know Thee Not*, 108.

4   The Inclusivist Tradition

1. Yehudah Halevi, *Kuzari* II: 36. Translated by Hartwig Hirschfeld (1905).

2. Halevi, *Kuzari* IV: 23.

3. On the ability of gentiles receiving revelation provided a distinction is made between prophets and ordinary revelation, see Robert Eisen, "The Problem of the King's Dream And Non-Jewish Prophecy in Judah Halevi's 'Kuzari,'" *JJTP* 3, 2 (1994): 231–47. See also Charles Manekin, "Hierarchy and Race in the Thought of Judah Ha-Levy," in *Proceedings of the Ninth International Congress of Medieval Philosophy, 1992* (Louvian: Peters, 1996).

4. Halevi, *Kuzari* I: 103.

5. There is a large literature on Maimonides' attitude toward other religions including: David Novak, *Maimonides on Judaism and Other Religions* (Cincinnati: Hebrew Union College Press, 1997). Gerald Blidstein, "The Status of Islam in Maimonidean Halakhah," in *Studies in Halakhic and Aggadic Thought* (Beer Sheva: Ben Gurion University Press, 2004), 237–47; Stephen D. Benin, "The Search for Truth in Sacred Scripture; Jews, Christians, and the Authority to Interpret," in Jane Dammen McAuliffe et al., eds, *With Reverence for the Word: Medieval Scriptural Exegesis in Judaism, Christianity, and Islam* (Oxford: Oxford University Press, 2003), 13–32; Yosef Kapah, "Islam and the Relation to Muslims in Maimonides' Teachings" [Hebrew], *Mahanayim* 1 (1992): 16–23; A. Hacohen, "Islam and Its Believers" [Hebrew], *Mahanayim* 1 (1992): 41–5; A. Sloshberg, "The Relationship of Maimonides to Islam," *Paamim* 42 (1990): 42–5; George F. Hourani, "Maimonides and Islam Studies," in William M. Brinner and Stephen David Ricks, eds, *Studies in Islamic and Judaic Traditions* (Atlanta: Scholars Press, 1986), 153–66; Howard Kreisel, "Maimonides on Christianity and Islam," *Jewish Civilization* III (1985): 153–62.

6. Moses Maimonides, *Guide of the Perplexed*, III: 29.

7. Moses Maimonides, *Teshuvot ha-RaMBaM*, ed. Joshua Blau (Jerusalem: Mekitse Nirdamim, 1960), 284f.

8. Nahmanides, *Writings & Discourses*, ed. Charles Chavel (New York: Shilo Pub. House, 1978).

9. *Abraham Maimonides' Commentary on Genesis & Exodus*, ed. E. Weissenberg (S.D. Sassoon: Letchworth, 1958).

10. Isaac Abarbanel, *Sefer Yeshuot Meshiho* (Jerusalem, 1967), 74b; David Kimchi, *Commentary of David Kimchi on Isaiah* (New York: AMS Press, 1995) 159: 7.

11. Isaac Abarbanel, *Sefer Yeshu'ot Meshiho*, 473a; Kimchi, *Commentary of Isaiah*, 160.

12. Sid Z. Leiman, "Abarbanel and the Censor," *Journal of Jewish Studies* 19 (1968): 49–61. On the censorship of Abarbanel, see Amnon Raz-Krakotzkin, "Censorship, Editing, And The Reshaping of Jewish Identity: The Catholic Church and Hebrew Literature in the Sixteenth Century," in Allison Coudert and Jeffrey S. Shoulson, eds, *Hebraica Veritas?: Christian Hebraists and the Study of Judaism in Early Modern Europe* (Philadelphia: University of Pennsylvania Press, 2004), 125–155.

13. Moses Maimonides, *The Eight Chapters of Maimonides on Ethics (Shemonah Perakim)*, trans. Joseph Isaac Gorfinkle (New York: Columbia University Press, 1912).

14. Yaakov Emden, *Seder Olam Rabbah veZuta*, cited in Chapter 1 of Harvey Falk, *Jesus The Pharisee: A New Look at the Jewishness of Jesus* (New York: Paulist Press, 1985). On the full text of Emden's approach to Christianity with the eighteenth-century discussions retained, see

the superb new critical edition of the Hebrew text by Lior Gottlieb, "*The Breaking of Those who Lead Astray* by Rabbi Yaakov Emden, First and Second Editions, with Introduction, Textual Comparisons, and Explanatory Notes," in Binyamin Ish Shalom and Amihai Berholts, eds., *Be-darkhe Shalom: iyunim be-hagut Yehudit, Mugashim* le-Shalom *Rosenberg* (Jerusalem: Beit Morahsa, 2007), 295–321. For those who cannot read the Hebrew edition, see Moshe Miller, "Rabbi Jacob Emden's Attitude Toward Christianity," in Michael A. Shmidman ed. *Turim: Studies in Jewish History and Literature: Presented to Dr. Bernard Lander* (New York: Touro College Press—KTAV Pub., 2007), 105–36.

15. Cited in Eugene J. Fisher, A. James Rudin, and Marc H. Tanenbaum, *Twenty Years of Jewish-Catholic Relations* (New York: Paulist Press, 1986), 69, 101.

16. Abraham Joshua Heschel, *No Religion is an Island: Abraham Joshua Heschel and Interreligious Dialogue*, ed. Harold Kasimow and Byron L. Sherwin (Maryknoll, NY: Orbis Books, 1991), 3–22; J.B. Levinsohn, *Éfés Dammím: A Series of Conversations at Jerusalem Between a Patriarch of the Greek Church and a Chief Rabbi of the Jews* (London: Longman, Brown, Green and Longmans, 1841). I have analyzed this document in a paper delivered in Thessaloniki at "The Fifth Academic Meeting between Judaism and Orthodox Christianity," May 27–29, 2003.

17. Samson Raphael Hirsch, *The Pentateuch*, trans. Isaac Levy (Gateshead: Judaica Press, 1989), commentary on Numbers 29:13.

18. The verses that Hirsch used, which are based on the comments of Radak and Rabbi David Kimchi, include: Isaiah 2:2–4, 11:6–9, 42:5–7, 55:3–5, 60:3; Psalm 67; Zechariah 9:1, 14:9.

19. Samson Raphael Hirsch, "Talmudic Judaism and Society," in *Principles of Education* (New York: Feldheim Publishers, 1991), VII, 226.

20. Ibid., 225–7.

21. Judah Aryeh Leib Alter, *Sefer Sefat emet: al ha-Torah* (Jerusalem: 1990).

22. Abraham Isaac Kook, *Igrot Harayah* (Jerusalem: Mossad Harav Kook, 1985), 112.

23. Abraham Isaac Kook, *Arpelei Tohar* (Jerusalem: Mosad Harav Kook, 1993), 33.

24. Abraham Azulai, *Hesed leAvaram* (Jerusalem: 1996), 50b.

25. Adin Steinsaltz, "Peace without Conciliation: The Irrelevance of 'Toleration' in Judaism," *Common Knowledge* 11, 1 (2005): 41–7.

26. Joseph Gikitilla, *Gates of Light,* trans. Avi Weinstein (San Francisco: HarperCollins, 1994). My presentation follows Weinstein's translation that considers the divine forces as actually divine and not just as celestial.

27. Ibid., all quotes are from gate 5.

28. *The Zohar III*: 161b; II: 84a; on the concept of seventy nations, see *Targum Yonathan, Deuteronomy* 32:8, *Pirkei deRebbi Eliezer,* 24.

29. *Zohar* I: 13a.

30. *Zohar* III: 215a.

31. Ibid.; cf. Joseph Gikitilla, *Shaarei Orah*, gate 2, 39ff.

32. Shlomo Alkebetz, *Berit Levi* (Brooklyn, 2003), 19a.

33. Yaakov Yosef Polnoye, *Toldot Yakov Yosef* (Jerusalem, 2001), introduction.

34. Jacob Joseph of Ostrog, Rav Yevi…(Kiryat Yoel, 1994), *yaveshev.*

35. Solomon ben Abraham Aderet, *Teshuvot ha-Rashba*, ed. Haim Z Dimitrovsky (Jerusalem: Mosad Harav Kook, 1990), 162–4; on the topic, see Harvey J. Hames, *The Art of Conversion: Christianity and Kabbalah in the Thirteenth Century* (Leiden: Brill, 2000).

36. Trude Weiss-Rosmarin, *Judaism and Christianity: The Differences* (New York: 1943).

37. Aderet, *Teshuvot ha-Rashba,* 212.

38. John Hood, *Aquinas and the Jews* (Philadelphia: University of Pennsylvania Press, 1995).

39. Isaac Arama, *Akadat Yitzhak* (Tel Aviv, 1960), gate 70.

40. Ibid., cf. 73.

41. Ibid., gate 60.

42. Ibid., 60: 36; see also his comments on Deuteronomy 4:35, 26:1, and Exodus 12:1, where it might imply that Israel means any zaddik whether of Jewish or gentile origin. The French

report is found in "Christianity in Jewish Theology," *Revue des Études Juives* 160 (2001): 495–7; Leopold Zunz, *Das gedachtniss der Gerechten in gesschichte und Literatur* (Berlin, 1919), 371–89, citation from page 384.

43. Eliyahu Soloweyczyk, *Kol kore o' Hatalmud ve haberit Hahadashah* (1867).

44. Ovadiah ben Jacob Seforno, *Commentary on the Bible* (Jerusalem: Mosad ha-Rav Kook, 1980), Exodus 19:5–6; Deuteronomy 33:3.

45. Jospeh Shapira, *Hagut, halakhah ve-Tsiyonut: al olamo ha-ruhani shel ha-Rav Yitshak Yaakov Raines* (Tel-Aviv: ha-Kibuts ha-Meuhad, 2002).

46. Frank Talmage, "Angels, Anthems, and Anathemas" in Barry Walfish, ed., *The Frank Talmage Memorial Volume* (Haifa: Haifa University Press, 1993), 17–18.

47. Yehezkel Kaufman, *Christianity and Judaism: Two Covenants* (Jerusalem: Magnes Press, Hebrew University, 1988), 48.

48. Ibid., 163.

5   The Universalist Tradition

1. Sa'adiah Gaon, *The Book of Beliefs and Opinions*, trans. Samuel Rosenblatt (New Haven, CT: Yale University Press, 1948), x.

2. Raphael Jospe, "Ha-Hagadah Ha-Ne'emenet Shel Rabbi Sa'adiah Gaon: Mi Hem Qehal Ha-Meya hadim?" *Da'at* 41 (Summer 1998): 5–17; and "Additional Note" in *Da'at* 42 (Winter 1999): IX. He rejects Pines who interprets "the community of monotheists" exclusively as the Jews; S. Pines, "A Study of the Impact of Indian, Mainly Buddhist, Thought on Some Aspects of Kalam Doctrines," *Jerusalem Studies in Arabic and Islam* 17 (1994): 182–203; This section is indebted to Raphael Jospe, "Pluralism out of the Sources of Judaism: Religious Pluralism Without Relativism" *Studies in Christian-Jewish Relations* volume 2 issue 2 (2007) 92–113.

3. Sa'adiah Gaon, *The Book of Beliefs and Opinions*, 16.

4. Raymond P. Scheindlin, *The Gazelle: Medieval Hebrew Poems on God, Israel, and the Soul* (Philadelphia: Jewish Publication Society, 1991), 45.

5. Aaron Hughes, *The Texture of the Divine: Imagination in Medieval Islamic and Jewish Thought* (Bloomington, IN: Indiana University Press, 2004), 111, 206.

6. Maimonides, *Guide* I: 36, Pines edition, 83–4.

7. Joseph Ibn Kaspi, *Amudei Kesef u-Maskiyot Kesef*, ed. S.A. Werbloner (Frankfurt: a/M, 1848), 51, 67.

8. Jacob Anatoli, *Malmad Hatalmidim* (Lyck, 1866), *Noah* 12a.

9. *Shut Harashba* 1: 415.

10. Gitit Holtzman, "Rabbi Moshe Narboni on the Relationship Between Judaism and Islam," *Tarbiz* 65, 2 (1996): 277–99; "Universalism and Nationality in Judaism, and the Relationship between Jews and Non-Jews the Thought of Rabbi Eliyahu Benamozegh," *Pe'amim* 74 (1998): 104–30.

11. Yair Shiffman, *Shem Tov ben Joseph Ibn Falaquera, Moreh ha-Moreh* (2001): 141.

12. Isaac Albalag, *Sefer Tikkun Hadaot*, edition Georges Vajda (Jerusalem, 1973), 69.

13. Menachem Kellner, "Respectful Disagreement—A Reply to Professor Jospe," in Alon Goshen-Gottstein and Eugene Korn, eds., *Jewish Theology of the Other* (Oxford; Portland, OR: Littman Library of Jewish Civilization, forthcoming).

14. Immanuel Ben Solomon, *Tophet and Eden: <Hell and Paradise>. In imitation of Dante's Inferno and Paradiso*, trans. Hermann Gollancz (London: University of London Press, 1921), 64–65.

15. Fabian Alfie, "Immanuel of Rome, alias Manoello Giudeo: The Poetics of Jewish Identity in Fourteenth-Century *Italy*," *Italica* 75, 3 (Fall 1998), 307–29.

16. Aaron W. Hughes, "Transforming the Maimonidean Imagination: Aesthetics in the Renaissance Thought of Judah Abravanel," *Harvard Theological Review* 97, 4 (2004): 461–84; Judah Abarbanel, *The Philosophy of Love* (Dialoghi d'Amore) (London: Soncino Press, 1937).

17. Shoshanna Gershenzon, "Myth and Scripture: The *Dialoghi d'Amore* of Leone Ebreo," *A Crown for a King* (2000): 125–45.

18. Norman Roth, "The 'Theft of Philosophy' by the Greeks from the Jews," *Classical Folio* 32 (1978): 52–67; Abarbanel, *The Philosophy of Love*, 345.

19. Abarbanel, *The Philosophy of Love*, 349, 416–17.

20. Ibid., 277–328.

21. Steve M. Wasserstrom, *Between Muslim and Jew: The Problem of Symbiosis under Early Islam* (Princeton, NJ: Princeton University Press, 1995); Shelomo Dov Goiten, *Jews and Arabs, their Contacts through the Ages* (New York: Schocken Books, 1955).

22. Goiton, *Jews and Arabs*, 59.

23. Ibid., 130.

24. Ibid., 167.

25. Cecil Roth, *The Jews in the Renaissance* (Philadelphia: Jewish Publication Society of America, 1964).

26. A similar universalism is shown *Tanna Debei Eliyahu* to including gentiles under brethren with regards to theft. See *Tanna Debei Eliyahu* 16: "Your fellow is like your brother and your brother is like your fellow. This teaches that it is forbidden to steal from a Gentile because it is theft, since it need not be said that theft from your brother is forbidden."

27. D. Levene, *The Garden of Wisdom* (Columbia University Press, 1907), chapter 6.

28. Ibid.

29. Moses Mendelssohn, *Selections from his Writings*, trans. Eva Jospe (New York: Viking Press, 1975), 116–17.

30. Moses Mendelssohn, *Jerusalem and Other Jewish Writings*. Translated and edited by *Alfred Jospe* (New York: Schocken, 1969), 134.

31. Zvi Jonathan Kaplan, "Mendelsohn's Religious Perspective of Non-Jews," *Journal of Ecumenical Studies* 41, 3 (2004): 355.

32. Israel Lipschutz, *Tiferet Yisrael*, Avot 3:17.

33. Ibid., Avot 3:14.

34. Ibid., Avot 3:17.

35. Marc Gopin, "An Orthodox Embrace of Gentiles? Interfaith Tolerance in the Thought of S. D. Luzzatto and E. Benamozegh," *Modern Judaism* 18, 2 (May 1998): 176. Noah H. Rosenbloom, *Luzzatto's Ethico-Psychological Interpretation of Judaism; a Study in the Religious Philosophy of Samuel David Luzzatto* (New York: Yeshiva University, 1965), 181.

36. Rosenbloom, *Luzzatto's Ethico-Psychological Interpretation*, 151–3.

37. Gopin, "An Orthodox Embrace of Gentiles?" 176.

38. Rabbi Yaakov Tzvi Meklenburg, *HaKtav VeHaKabbalah* (Leipzig, 1839); *Commentary on Lev* 19:18. Ernst Simon, "The Neighbor (re'a) Whom We Shall Love," in M. Fox, ed., *Modern Jewish Ethics* (Columbus, OH: Ohio State University Press, 1975), 29–56.

39. Harold Fisch, "A Response to Ernst Simon," in Marvin Fox, ed., *Modern Jewish Ethics: Theory and Practice* (Columbus: Ohio State UP, 1975), 57–61.

40. Rosenbloom, *Luzzatto's Ethico-Psychological Interpretation*, 180.

41. Samson Raphael Hirsch, *The Nineteen Letters*, trans. Bernard Drachman (New York: Bloch Publishing, 1942), letter 15.

42. Mendel Hirsch, *Judaism and Humanism* (London: Beddoe Press, Staines, 1928), reprinted in Jacob Breuer, *Fundamentals of Judaism: Selections from the Works of Rabbi Samson Raphael Hirsch and Outstanding Torah-True Thinkers* (New York: Published for the Rabbi Samson Raphael Hirsch Society by P. Feldheim, 1949).

43. Hirsch, *Judaism and Humanism*.

44. Menashe ben Israel, *The Conciliator* (London, 1842), 192–3.

45. Ibid.

46. Ibid., 194.

47. Ibid., 195–6.

48. Ibid., 209.

49. Aime Palliere, *The Unknown Sanctuary* (New York: Bloch Publishing, 1928), 157.

50. Elijah Benamozegh, *Israel and Humanity*, trans. Maxwell Luria (Mahwah, NJ: Paulist Press, 1995), 53.

51. Ibid., 68.

52. Ibid., 50.

53. Ibid., 77

54. Ibid., 75.

55. Ibid., 55.

56. Ibid., 51.

57. Ibid., 54–5.

58. Ibid., 194.

59. Ibid., 54.

60. Ibid., 51.

61. Henry Pereira-Mendes, "Orthodox or Historical Judaism," in *The Dawn of Religious Pluralism: Voices from the World's Parliament of Religions, 1893*, edited with introductions by Richard Hughes Seager (La Salle, IL, Open Court, 1993), 328–30; reprinted from Walter R. Houghton, ed., *Neely's History of the Parliament of Religions* (Chicago, 1894), 217–18. One should also note H. Pereira-Mendes, *The Jewish Religion Ethically Presented* (New York, 1905), where he presents twenty-one objections to the current practice of Christianity followed by a statement wishing that Christians would return to the religion of Jesus himself. He was also against the ecumenical trends in Reform Judaism that blurred their distinction from Unitarians.

62. J.H. Hertz, *Pentateuch and Haftorahs* (London: Soncino, 1963), 103, 759.

63. *Orot haKodesh* (Jerusalem: Mosad Harav Kook, 1969), 3:15.

64. *Iggrot HaRiyah* (Jerusalem: Mosad Harav Kook, 1962), 1:112

65. Joshua Hoffman, "Rav Kook's Mission to America," *OROT* 1, 5751 (1991): 78–99.

6   Pluralism

1. David Hartman, "On the Possibility of Religious Pluralism from a Jewish Viewpoint," *Immanuel* 16 (1983): 101–13.

2. David Hartman, *Conflicting Visions: Spiritual Possibilities of Modern Israel* (New York: Schocken Books, 1990).

3. Ibid., 248.

4. David Hartman, *A Heart of Many Rooms* (Woodstock, Vt.: Jewish Lights, 1999).

5. David Hartman, "Jewish and Christian in a World of Tomorrow," *Immanuel* 6 (1976): 79.

6. David Hartman, "Judaism Encounters Christianity Anew," in Eugene Fisher, ed., *Visions of the Other: Jewish and Christian Theologians Assess the Dialogue* (Stimulus Books, 1994), 69.

7. David Hartman, *Heart of Many Rooms*, 160, 164.

8. Ibid., 165.

9. Thomas Friedman, "The Real War," *New York Times*, November 27, 2001, Foreign Affairs. It is interesting to note that the Muslim thinker Ibn Sabin (1216–1270) ascribes a similar statement, that God listens to a different group on different days to Maimonides's *Guide*, cited in Jacques *Waardenburg*, editor. *Muslim Perceptions of Other Religions: A Historical Survey* (New York: Oxford University Press, 1999), 191.

10. Raphael Jospe, "Pluralism Out of the Sources of Judaism: Religious Pluralism Without Relativism," *Studies in Christian-Jewish Relations* 2, 2 (2007): 92–113.

11. Rabbi Zalman Schachter-Shalomi, "Bases and Boundaries of Jewish, Christian, and Moslem Dialogue," http://www.havurahshirhadash.org/rebzalmanarticle7.html (January 20, 2009).

12. Zalman Schachter-Shalomi and Netanel Miles-Yepez, *A Heart Afire: Stories and Teachings of the Early Hasidic Masters* (Philadelphia: Jewish Publication Society, 2009), 32.

13. Rabbi Zalman Schachter-Shalomi, "Jesus in Jewish-Christian-Moslem Dialogue," http://www.havurahshirhadash.org/rebzalmanarticle8.html (January 20, 2009).

14. Joseph Dov Soloveitchik, *The Lonely Man of Faith* (New York: Doubleday, 1992), 29–30.

15. Irving Greenberg, *For The Sake of Heaven and Earth: The New Encounter Between Judaism and Christianity* (Philadelphia: Jewish Publication Society, 2004), 204.

16. Ibid., 101.

17. Irving Greenberg, "Theology after the Shoah: The Transformation of the Core Paradigm," *Modern Judaism* 26, 3 (2006): 213–39.

18. Greenberg, *For The Sake of Heaven and Earth,* 185.

19. Irving Greenberg, "Judaism and Christianity, Covenants of Redemption," in Tikva Frymer-Kensky, David Novak, Peter Ochs, David Fox Sandmel, and Michael A. Signer eds. *Christianity in Jewish Terms* (Boulder, CO and Oxford, England: Westview Press, 2000), 158

20. Greenberg, *For The Sake of Heaven and Earth,* 204.

21. Elliot N. Dorff, "This Is My God: One Jew's Faith," in John Hick, ed., *Three Faiths One God: A Jewish, Christian, Muslim Encounter* (Albany: State University of New York Press, 1989), 10–11.

22. Elliot N. Dorff, *To Do the Right and the Good: A Jewish Approach to Modern Social Ethics* (Philadelphia: Jewish Publication Society, 2002), chapter 2.

23. Ibid., 271.

24. Michael Kogan, *Opening the Covenant: A Jewish Theology of Christianity* (New York: Oxford University Press, 2008), 68.

25. Ibid., 118.

26. Ibid., 132; Sigmund Mowinckel, *He That Cometh:The Messiah Concept in the Old Testament and Later Judaism* (Grand Rapids, Mich: William B. Eerdmans Pub. Co., 2005).

27. Kogan, *Opening the Covenant,* 168.

28. Ibid., 176.

29. Ibid., 183.

30. Ibid., 170–1, 175–6.

31. Jonathan Sacks, *The Dignity of Difference: How to Avoid the Clash of Civilizations* (London: Continuum, 2002), 4, 9, 19.

32. Ibid., 53, 58.

33. Ibid., 64, 209. See Paul Lakeland, "Not So Heterodox," *Commonweal* 134, 2 (January 26, 2007): 19–23.

34. Raimon Panikkar, "The Myth of Pluralism: The Tower of Babel—A Meditation on Non-Violence," *Cross Currents* 29 (1979): 197–230.

35. Sacks, *The Dignity of Difference,* xi.

36. World Wide Religious News, February 15, 2003: *http://www.wwrn.org/article.php?idd=14438&sec=35&con=55*; http://www.wwrn.org/article.php?idd=14435&sec=35&con=55.

37. Richard Allen Greene, "Britain's Chief Rabbi Tries to Fend off Orthodox Fury," *The Jewish Weekly of Northern California,* Friday, March 28, 2003: http://www.jewishsf.com/content/2–0–/module/displaystory/story_id/20022/edition_id/408/format/html/display-story.html (January 20, 2009). A full list of changes between the two editions is available at M.A. Sherif, "Will Courage Prevail? An Essay on Jonathan Sacks," *http://www.salaam.co.uk/books/show_comm_review.php?commreview_id=21*; for a good discussion of the

controversy and the issues involved, see Marc B. Shapiro, "Of Books and Bans," *Edah Journal* 3, 2 (2003): 2–16.

38. Richard Harries, *"Jonathan Sacks's* The Dignity of Difference: How to Avoid the Clash of Civilizations," *Scottish Journal of Theology* 57, 1 (2004): 109–15.

39. Sacks, *The Dignity of Difference,* 59. I subsequently found that Avi Ravitzky already noted the similarity of Sacks to Heschel, Hartman, and others in his article "Judaism Views Other Religions," in J.D. Gort, Henry Jansen, and H.M. Vroom, eds, *Religions View Religions: Explorations in Pursuit of Understanding* (Amsterdam and New York: Rodopi, 2006), 75–107.

40. Dan Goldberg, "Interview with Chief Rabbi Sir Jonathan Sacks," October 24, 2006: http://www.ajn.com.au/news/news.asp?pgID=1868 (January 7, 2009).

41. Johnathan Sacks, "Exposition of the Hebrew Scriptures: The Relationship Between the People and God—the Covenant": http://www.bc.edu/research/cjl/meta-elements/texts/cjrelations/news/Sacks%27_Lambeth_Address.htm.

42. Ibid.

43. Sacks, *The Dignity of Difference,* 177.

44. Jonathan Sacks, *To Heal a Fractured the World* (New York: Schocken, 2005), 10.

45. Piotr Sikora, "Judaism Open to the Religions of the Nations A Polish Catholic Theologian Reads an American Jewish Pluralist": http://www.jcrelations.net/en/?item=2804.

7 The Exclusivist Tradition

1. Morris Goldstein, *Jesus in the Jewish Tradition* (New York: Macmillian, 1950), 148–54.

2. Leon J. Weinberger, *Jewish Hymnography: A Literary History* (Portland, OR: Littman, 1998), 38.

3. See the translated selections in Gustaf Dalman, *Jesus Christ in the Talmud, Midrash, Zohar, and the Liturgy of the Synagogue* (Cambridge, 1893; reprinted New York: Arno Press, 1973).

4. Israel J. Yuval, *Two Nations in Your Womb: Perceptions of Jews and Christians in Late Antiquity and The Middle Ages* (Berkeley: University of California Press, 2006), 99.

5. *Sefer Rokeah* (Jerusalem, 1967), sec 271, 230–1.

6. Yuval, *Two Nations in Your Womb,* 119.

7. S.J.D. Cohen, "Does Rashi's Torah Commentary Respond to Christianity? A Comparison of Rashi with Rashbam and Bekhor Shor, " in H. Najman and J.H. Newman, eds, *The Idea of Biblical Interpretation: Essays in Honor of James L. Kugel* (Boston: Brill, 2004), 449–72.;Elazar.Touitou, "Rashi's Commentary on Genesis 16 in the Context of Judeo-Christian Controversy," *Hebrew Union College Annual* 61 (1990): 159–83; idem, "Rashi and His School: The Exegesis on the Halachic Part of the Pentateuch in the Context of the Judeao-Christian Controversy," in Shimon Schwarzfuchs, Yvonne Friedman, and Bat-Sheva Albert, eds, *Bar Ilan Studies in History IV. Medieval Studies in Honor of Avrom Saltman* (Ramat Gan: Bar-Ilan University Press, 1995), 231–51.

8. Menachem Klein, "Rethinking Jew-Gentile Relations": http://www.netivot-shalom.org.il/parshaeng/toledot5763.php (January 4, 2009).

9. Avraham Grossman, *Rashi* (Jerusalem: Merkaz Zalman Shazar, 2006), 194–9.

10. Ibid., 195, 198, 210.

11. Shabbatai Bass, *Sifthei Hakhamim,* a sixteenth-century commentary on Rashi consistently reworks Rashi to impose a more ethical reading.

12. Abraham bar Hiyya Savasorda, *The Meditation of the Sad Soul,* ed. Geoffrey Widoger (New York: Schocken Books, 1968), 111, 128–9.

13. Shimon ben Ẓemaḥ Duran, *Keshet U-Magen: A Critical Edition,* trans. Prosper Murciano, PhD thesis (New York University, 1975), 25b.

14. The quotes are from Maharal, *Commentary on Sanhedrin* 21b; *Gevurat Hashem*, chapter 23; *Nezah Yisrael*, chapter 25; *Be'er ha-Golah*, chapter 7.

15. Maharal's Be'er ha-Golah, chapter 7 (pp. 144–6 in Ch. Y. L. Hanig's edition, Jerusalem, 1971); "anyone who accepts upon himself to worship the First Cause [alone] becomes thereby a resident stranger and is not subject to the discriminative laws like that in Bava Kama 4:3." Compare his commentary on *Tur Yoreh De'ah*, which states unequivocally that only a Gentile "who accepted upon himself the Seven [Noahide] Commandments" is a resident stranger.

16. Kedushat Levi *vayehi*, cited in Or Rose, "The Non-Jew in Hasidism: The Case of Levi Yitzhak of Berditchev,"(Unpublished manuscript)

17. Zadok Hakohen, *Sefer Maḥshevot ḥaruts; Poḳed Aḳarim*, 19; on Rabbi Zadok, see Alan Brill, *Thinking God* (Ktav: New York, 2002).

18. Naftali Zvei Berlin, *Haamek Davar* (Deut. 33:2 and 8:3).

19. Naftali Zvei Berlin, *Haamek Davar*, commentary on Genesis 15:5.

20. Abraham Isaac Kook, *Shemonah Kevazim* 5:57. Compare the passage in Zvei Yehudah Kook edited *Orot*, where Rabbi Kook writes: "Christianity abandoned the laws of the Torah, and established itself on a false mercy and kindness that uproots and destroys the foundation of the world. By denying the Divine source of justice, it becomes overwhelmed by the basest evil. The pollution penetrates the private life of the individual and spreads massively to the soul of nations. This becomes the foundation for the hate between nations and for the unfathomable evil of bloodshed" [*Orot* (Northvale, NJ: Jason Aronson, 1993), 21].

21. In the volume of his writings edited by his son Yehuda Zvei *Orot* (5:10) we do find the following passage that reflect his son's views: "The difference the Jewish soul—its essence, inner light, vitality, construction, and status—from the souls of all the gentiles despite their achievements [or perfections] is greater and deeper than between the human soul and the soul of an animal. The later distinction is only quantitative, but the former there is an essential qualitatitive difference." The widely cited passage is discussed in Zvei Judah Kook and Shelomoh Ḥayim Aviner, *S'iḥot ha-Rav Tsevi Yehudah ha-kohen Ḳuḳ al Sefer orot* (Jerusalem: Aṭeret Kohanim, 2004), 156.

22. Zvei Yehudah Kook, *Judaism and Christianity* [Hebrew] (Sifriyat Chava: Beit El, 2001). One of Zvei Yehudah Kook's students, with Kahanist leanings, considers Islam as idolatry based on its alleged pagan folk customs such as the Kaaba. Ariel understands, against their grain, the inclusivists as agreeing with him, even those who explicitly state Islam is monotheistic,; see Israel Ariel, "Israel One Nation in the Land," *Zefiah* 3 (1989): 115–222.

23. Zevi Yehudah Kook, *Li-netivot Yiśrael: ḳevutsat maamarim* (Jerusalem: Menorah, 1966), 23.

24. Ibid., 36, 58, 62.

25. Ibid., 62–3.

26. Kook, *Judaism and Christianity*, 77–9. He also notes that Muslims are monotheists and share the laws of circumcision and the dietary laws of meat. "But belief in their prophet nullifies all prior beliefs,... Islam calls that the prophet Mohamed the seal of the prophets,... while cannot leave the Torah of Moses" (39).

27. Daniel Chanan Matt, *The Zohar 1* (Stanford: Stanford University Press, 2006), 47a, 252.

28. Reuven Margaliot, ed., *Zohar Hadash* (Jerusalem: Mossad Ha-Rav Kook, 1978), 78d.

29. Shem Tov ben Shem Tov, *Sefer haEmunot* 5:4 53b–54a;

30. Judah Hayyat (*ca.* 1450–1510), cited in Joseph Davis, *Yom-Tov Lipmann Heller* (Oxford: Littman Library, 2004), 93.

31. Isaac Luria, *Etz Chaim*, Heichal Abi'a, Sha'ar HaKlipot, chapter 2.

32. Isaac Luria, *Etz Chaim*, Sha'ar Klipat Noga, chapter 3.

33. *Shaar Hagilgulim*, 31ff.

34. *Midrash Talpiyyot* (Amsterdam, 1698).

35. For full explanation, see Hayyim Ibn Attar, commentary on Numbers 19:2. A similar statement from Islam, a century before, is brought by Andrew G. Bostom, *The Legacy of Islamic*

Antisemitism: From Sacred Texts to Solemn History (Amherst, NY: Prometheus Books, 2008). "Whenever a Jew is killed, it is for the benefit of Islam."

36. Moses Hayyim Luzzatto, *Derech Hashem* (New York: Feldheim, 1997), part 2, section 4.

37. Jacob Katz, *Tradition and Crisis* (New York: NYU Press, 1993), 23. Katz footnotes to Isaac Heinemann, "The Dispute over Nationality in the Aggada and in Philosophy during the Middle Ages," in Yitzhak Baer et al., eds, *Sefer Dinaberg* (Jerusalem: Kiryat Sefer, 1949), 132–50; On the *Zohar* see Y.F. Lachower and Isaiah Tishby, *The Wisdom of Zohar* (Jerusalem: Mossad Bialik, 1957), I: 290 ff.

38. Katz, *Tradition and Crisis*, 32.

39. Z.H. Chajes, *The Student's Guide through the Talmud* (New York: Feldheim, 1960).

40. *Tanya,* chapter 1; Shnuer Zalman of Liadi, *Iggeret haKodesh*, 25.

41. Joseph Isaac Schneersohn and Menahem Mendel Schneersohn, *ha-Yom Yom—: luah Or Zarua le-Haside Habad* (Bruklin, NY: Kehot, 1988), Thursday Tevet 9 5703. Our custom in Aleinu (*Siddur Tehilat Hashem*, 84) is to say "for they bow to vanity and nothingness," and markedly not to say "and pray." They write "The expectorating is after these words; the reason is that speech stimulates saliva, and we do not wish to benefit from this saliva."

42. *Derekh Mizvotekha* (Brooklyn: Kehot Publication Society, 1998).

43. Menahem Mendel Schneersohn, *Likute Siihot.* hekhal 9, shaar 3 (Brooklyn, NY: Kehot, 2000). *Likkute Sikhot* 19 kislev 5743–1982.

44. Menachem Mendel Schneersohn, *Sichos in English*, vol. 35 (Brooklyn, NY: 1978), *Parshat Tzav,* 5747, 75–6.

45. Menahem Mendel Schneersohn, *Hisvaduyos* 5748, 4:39, cited in *HaMaaseh hu ha-Ikar* (n.p. n.d), 388.

46. Menachem Mendel Schneersohn, *Sichos in English*, 6th night of Sukkos (Brooklyn, NY: 1978), 5747, 139.

47. Yitzhak Nahmani, *Sefer Torat ha-gilgul, nefesh, ruah u-neshamah* (Netanyah: 1995).

8   Gentiles

1. Maimonides, *Mishneh Torah, Laws of forbidden foods* 11:4 [11:7 in some editions], uncensored editions.

2. *Commentary On The Mishnah: Avodah Zarah*, 1.3, 1:4 ed. Y. Kafih (Jerusalem, 1965), 2:225; *Mishneh Torah: Avodah Zarah*, 9.4 (uncensored text of Mishneh Torah cited in Kafih's ed., *Commentary on the Mishnah*, 2:225, n. 10).

3. Yaacov Lev, *Saladin in Egypt* (Leiden: Brill, 1999), 185–93.

4. On the historical background of allowing association (*shituf*) for gentiles, see Jacob Katz, *Exclusiveness and Tolerance: Jewish-Gentile Relations in Medieval and Modern Times* (New York: Schocken, 1969), 35–6. Katz also discusses the ad hoc decision of Rabbenu Gershom (eleventh century), to permit trade with Christians on their holy days based on a statement of Rabbi Yohanan, namely that "Gentiles outside the Land of Israel are not idolatrous, but they are merely following the customs of their ancestors" (B. Hullin 13b).

5. There are a variety of versions of this text, some more explicit than others; see Rabbenu Yerucham, *Sefer Adam ve havvah* 17:5 and the discussion in Katz, *Exclusiveness and Tolerance*, 35.

6. Moses ben Israel Isserles, *Darkhe Mosheh mi-Tur Yoreh Deah*, 15.

7. Ibid., 151; Rama, *Yoreh Deah* 129:4, 20 and 132:1.

8. Isserles, *Darkhe Mosheh,* 141, 150.

9. See Shakh on Yoreh Deah siman 151: 7 in the name of Isserles; for a full discussion, see Ephraim Hakohen, *Shaarei Ephraim* (Sulzbach, 1668), # 24, 38; Yehezkel Landau, *Nodeh Beyehudah* Yoreh Deah, 148, Yaakov Tzvi Hirsch ben Yaakov Eisenstadt, *Pitkhei Teshuvah*

Yoreh Deah 147 siman 2; *Samuel Kolin Mahasit Hashekel* Orekh Hayim 146:2 ; Samuel ben
Yosef, *Olat Tamid Orekh Hayim* 156. Avraham Isaiah Karlitz, *Hazon Ish* 62:19.

10. *Shilat Yaavetz* (Altona, 1738), 1:41; 2: 133; *Mor u-Ketziah* 224. On these passages, see Moshe
    Miller, "Rabbi Jacob Emden's Attitude Toward Christianity," *Turim: Studies in Jewish
    History and Literature: Presented to Dr. Bernard Lander* (New York: Touro College Press-
    KTAV Pub., 2007), 105–36.
11. *Commentary on Rosh Hashanah* 17 and Rashi ad loc.
12. *Commentary Avodah Zara* 40b.
13. Ibid., 43b.
14. Moshe Isserles, on Yoreh Deah siman 141:1.
15. Kaufman Koehler, "Cross," *Jewish Encyclopedia* IV (1901): 369.
16. Abraham Ibn Ezra, Sefer Ha-Az'amim, *Kitvei R. Avraham Ibn Ezra*, vol. 2 (Jerusalem, 2001),
    15–21; London 1901, 17–19.
17. R. Ishmael ben Abraham Isaac ha-Kohen (1723–1811), in *Zer'a Emet*, vol. 2 (Leghorn, 5556),
    fol. 34b., held that the Eucharist is an idolatrous service with a magical element; cited by
    J. Faur, "The Legal Thinking of the Tosafot," *Dine Yisrael*, 6 (1975): 67 n. 50.
18. Shelomo ben Aderet, *Torat ha-Bayit,* book 5, chapter 4.
19. Moshe Halbertal, "Ones Possessed of Religion: Religious Tolerance in the Teachings of
    the Me'iri," *Edah Journal* 1,1 (2001): 1–25; cf. Aryeh Klapper, "The Meiri's Halakhah about
    Christians and Christianity: A Response to Halbertal," unpublished AJS paper, who thinks
    Meiri is just continuing the *ger toshav* tradition and not creating a new category. Also see Yehudah
    Henkin, *Shut Benai Banim* III (1997): 121, who also limits the range of application of Meiri.
20. *Igrot ha-Raayah,* I: 89 (Jerusalem: Mossad ha-Rav Kook, 1962).
21. J. David Bleich, "Divine Unity in Maimonides, the Tosafists and Meiri," in Lenn Goodman, ed.,
    Neoplatonism and Jewish Thought (Albany: State University of New York Press, 1992), 237–54.
22. Eliezer Ashkenazi, *Maaseh Hashem* on the haggdah ad loc.
23. Neta Ecker, "Universlaism in the Thought of Rabbi Eliezer Ashkenazi" (Unpublished
    Dissertation presented to Haifa University, 2010).
24. Ashkenazi, *Maaseh Hashem,* 36–7.
25. Joseph M Davis, *Yom-Tov Lipmann Heller: Portrait of a Seventeenth-Century Rabbi* (Oxford:
    Littman Library of Jewish Civilization, 2004), 93–7.
26. *Jacob Katz, "The Vicissitude of Three Apologetic Passages," Zion* 23–24 (1957–58): 175–93
27. Moses Rivkes, *Be'er Hagolah*, Hoshen Mishpat 425:5.
28. Frankfurt edition, 5:2; Azriel Shohat, "The German Jews's Integration Within Their Non-
    Jewish Environment in the First Half of the Eighteenth Century," [Hebrew] *Zion* 21 (1956):
    230–1.
29. Jonathan Eybeschutz, *Kreti uPleti* (1776 edition) introduction- not reproduced in most of
    the later editions; cf. Abraham Zevi Eisenstadt, *Pitkhei Teshuvah* Yoreh Deah 147 and 152,
    footnote 2; Katz, *Exclusiveness and Tolerance*, 35–6.
30. Yaakov Yehoshua Falk, *Penai Yehoshua* on *Bava Metzia* (first edition, 1756).
31. Yehezkel Landau, *Nodah be Yehudah* II Yoreh Deah 148.
32. For example, on the topic of entering churches, the following contemporary legal authori-
    ties provide an summary of relevant sources: Ovadiah Yosef, *Yabia Omer* II Yoreh Deah 11:4;
    idem., *Yehaveh Daat* 4:45; Eliezer Walenberg, *Teitz Eliezer* 14:91; David Hayim Halevi, *Ashe
    Lekhah Rav* vol. 1 (2009): 59; 4:53. The first two legal authorities ban entering a church,
    the latter writes that one can visit a church that is no longer active. On entering Mosques,
    Obadiah Yosef allow one to enter, even to pray, in a mosque, and Eliezer Walenberg bans
    it. Rabbi Eliezer Berkovis permits entrance into a church for aesthetic and tourist reasons:
    see "Responsa on Entering a Church," *Millin Havivin* (2009).
33. Isaac Herzog, *Tehumim* 2 (1981): 169–79. Herzog's preferred interpreter of tosafot was
    [Binjamin] Zev Wolf Boskowitz, *Seder Mishneh: beurim al Yad ha-hazakah le-rabenu* ha-
    Rambam (*i*Prague: 1820).

34. Yoel Teitelbaum, *Va-Yoel Moshe*, Maamar Gimmel shevuos 90–8; *Yated Ne'eman* (September 1989).

35. Ariel Picard, "The Status of the Gentile in the State of Israel in the Legal Decisions of Religious Zionist Rabbis" *Reshit* 1 (2009): 187–208.

36. Jay R. Berkowitz, *Rites and Passages: The Beginnings of Modern Jewish Culture in France, 1650–1860* (Philadelphia: University of Pennsylvania Press, 2004), 130; idem., "Authority and Innovation at the Threshold of Modernity: The *Me'orei Or* of Rabbi Aaron Worms," in Ezra Fleischer, et al., eds, *Me'ah She'arim: Studies in Medieval Jewish Spiritual Life in Memory of Isadore Twersky* (Jerusalem 2001), 275–77.

37. R. Zvi Hirsch Chajes, *Hilkhot Melakhim* 10:9 *Kol Sifrei Maharatz Chajes* (Jerusalem, 1958): vol. 1, 483–91; vol. 2, 1036.

38. David Zohar, "Jewish Commitment in a Modern World" [Hebrew] (Tel-Aviv, 2003), 227, 233.

39. David Zvei Hoffmann, "Problems of the Diaspora in the Shulkah Arukh," in Jacob Breuer, ed., *Fundamentals of Judaism* (New York: Feldhiem, 1969), 181–91.

40. See the correspondence between R. Haim David HaLevy and Prof. Aviezer Ravitzky that was published in Zvi Zohar and Avi Sagi, eds, *Yahadut shel Hayyim: Iyyunim BeYetzirato ha'Hagutit-Hilkhatit shel HaRav Hayyim David HaLevi* (Jerusalem: Hartman Institute, 2007), 255–85.

41. Meir Simkhah of Dvinsk, *Meshekh Hokhmah* (Jerusalem, 1974); Yonah Ben-Sasson, *Mishnato Ha 'Iyunit shel Baal Meshekh Chokhmah* (Jerusalem, 1984).

42. In a letter of November 15, 1965, to Prof. Samuel Atlas; quoted in Marc Shapiro, "Scholars and Friends," *Torah U-Madda Journal* 7 (1997): 118.

43. On "gezel hagoy," see *Baba Kama* 113a; 38a. On the permissibility of the error of a gentile [i.e., property of which he deprived himself due to an error], similar to the case of his lost item, see *Baba Kama* 113b: Rashi permits deceiving him, Tosfot does not allow deception. Tosfot does, however, allow one not to point out his error if the gentile does discover it and it does not cause a desecration of God's name. See Maimonides, *Mishneh Torah* The Laws of Robbery and Lost Items, 11: 4; *Tur Hoshen Mishpat*, 348: 3 and SMA and other ad loc for pragmatic limitations. Maharasha, *Yam shel Shlomo* (Baba Kama chap. 11, para 20) and the Vilna Gaon also reject deception. Since, many of these laws apply equally to heretical Jews, the main problem is the fundamental use of a double ethic as described by Max Weber in his description of an ethnic economy. The problem is the dual system of law not unlike the seventeenth-century laws in Protestant Germany that had separate civil laws for Jews, heretics, and Catholics; on "heretic" Jews as outside the economy, see *Hoshen Mishpat* 425:5 and *Hazon Ish Yoreh Deah* 2:16.

44. There are three main categories of gentiles: see R. Yom Tov ben Avraham Alshevili, *Hiddushei ha-Ritva—Masekhet Makkot* (Jerusalem: Mossad ha-Rav Kook, 1984), Makkot 9a, 113–14.

45. Moshe Sofer, *Hatam Sofer*, 90. R. David Zvi Hilman considers the Meiri's position as an insincere smokescreen against gentile authorities, similar to the notes in the Czarist era editions of the Talmud that state "All these laws applied only in the ancient era, but now everything should be managed according to the laws of His Majesty the Czar." R. David Zvi Hilman, "Leshonot ha-Meiri she-nichtevu le-tshuvat ha-minim," *Zefunot* 1, 1 (September–October 1988): 65–72.

46. Moshe Sternbach, *Teshuvos VeHanhagos* (1997), #365. For the Sternbach and Klein responsa, I am indebted to Chaim Rapoport, "Attitudes Towards Gentiles in Post Holocaust Rabbinic Literature," unpublished dissertation (Institute of Jewish Studies at University College London, 2001).

47. Menashe Klein, *Mishnah Halachot*, volume 5, #141.

48. Ibid., introduction.

49. Shahar Ilan, "What does Aryeh Deri Regret?" *Haaretz*, October 20, 2005.

50. Rabbi Hershel Schachter, Temple and the *Mikdash Me'at*," available at Torahweb http://www.torahweb.org/torah/special/2004/rsch_mikdash.html; http://www.thejewishweek.com/viewArticle/c361_a4821/News/Breaking_News.html.

51. S. Grama, *Ḳuntres Romemut Yissrael* (Lakewood: 2002).

52. Daniel Sperber, "Gentile," *Encyclopedia Judaica*, first edition 7, 410–14.

53. Gerald Blidstein, "Jews and the Ecumenical Dialogue," *Tradition* 11 (1970): 103–10.

54. Gerald Blidstein, "The Non-Jew in Jewish Ethics," *Sh'ma* 7, 125 (1977).

9   The Phenomena of Religion

1. *The Jewish Week* (September 17, 2004), 28.

2. Judah ha-Levi, *Kuzari: The Book of Proof and Argument*, trans. Yiẓhak Heinemann (Oxford: East and West Library, 1947), 80, 81.

3. Ibid., 87.

4. Ibid., 97–9.

5. Tamara M. Green, *The City of the Moon God: Religious Traditions of Harran* (Leiden: E.J. Brill, 1992).

6. Moses Maimonides, *The Guide of The Perplexed* (Chicago: University of Chicago Press, 1963), III: 29.

7. Ibid., I: 63.

8. Mircea Eliade, *The Sacred and the Profane* (New York: Harcourt, Brace, 1959), 226.

9. Naḥmanides, *Commentary on the Torah* (New York: Shilo Pub. House, 1971).

10. Rabbi Solomon Al-Constantine, *Megaleh Amukot*, cited in Dov Schwartz, *Studies on Astral Magic in Medieval Jewish Thought* (Leiden: Brill, 2004), 167–8.

11. Gersonides, Commentary on Kings 18:21.

12. *Koran, Surah Al Baqara* (the calf) ayah 258.

13. Daniel Matt, *The Zohar: The Book of Enlightenment. Classics of Western Spirituality* (Mahwah: Paulist Press, 1983), 259 based on II: 188a.

14. Harvey J. Hames, *Like Angels on Jacob's Ladder: Abraham Abulafia, the Franciscans, and Joachimism* (Albany: State University of New York Press, 2007), 69–70.

15. *The Three Rings—Textual Studies in the Historical Trialogue of Judaism, Christianity and Islam*, eds. Barbara Roggema, Marcel Poorthuis, and Pim Valkenberg (Utrecht: Peeters Leuven, 2005).

16. Hames, *Like Angels on Jacob's Ladder*, 60, 64.

17. Ibid., 57–8.

18. Joseph Albo, *Sefer ha-'Ikkarim*, trans. and ed. I. Husik (Philadelphia: The Jewish Publication Society of America, 1929), 196.

19. Moses ben Samuel Valle, *Sefer ha-Liḳuttim* (Jerusalem: 1997), 42.

20. Ibid., 80

21. Adolphe Franck, *The Kabbalah. or, The Religious Philosophy of the Hebrews*, trans. I. Sossnitz (New York: 1926), 224.

22. S.R. Hirsch, *The Pentateuch. Vol.2. Exodus*. 2nd ed. (London: 1960); Exodus 21:6.

23. Moses Maimonides, *Mishneh Torah* Yesodei Hatorah 2:1–2.

24. Hillel Zeitlin, *Sifran Shel Yeḥidim: Ketavim Meḳubatsim* (Jerusalem: Mosad ha-Rav Ḳook, 1979), 44.

25. Ibid., 43.

26. Ibid., 39.

27. *Judisk Tidskrift* 6 (1933): 229.cited in "The Ways of God: Judaism and Christianity. A Document for Discussion within the Church of Sweden" (June 1, 2003): http://www.jcrelations.net/en/?item=1965 (December 12, 2008).

28. Joseph Dov Soloveitchik, *And from There You Shall Seek* (Jersey City, NJ: Ktav, 2008), 162.

10   At the Dawn of a New Century

1. Ulrich Beck, *Cosmopolitan Vision* (Cambridge: Polity Press, 2006), 430–1.
2. Alon Goshen-Gottstein, "Jewish-Christian Relations: From Historical Past to Theological Future": http://www.jcrelations.net/en/?item=1754 (January 20, 2009).
3. Ben Zion Dinur, *Israel and the Diaspora* (Philadelphia: Jewish Publication Society of America, 1969).
4. Cecil Roth, *A Short History of the Jewish People* (London: East and the West Library, 1969).
5. Arthur A. Cohen, *The Tremendum: A Theological Interpretation of the Holocaust* (New York: Crossroad, 1981).
6. Carlo Ginzburg, Martin H. Ryle, and Kate Soper, *Wooden Eyes: Nine Reflections On Distance, European perspectives* (New York: Columbia University Press, 2001).
7. Maimonides, *Guide of the Perplexed* III: 52–4. Cf, Mishneh Torah, *Laws of the Sabbath*, 2:3.
8. Moses ben Jacob Cordovero, *The Palm Tree of Deborah* (New York: Hermon Press, 1974), *gate of hokhmah*; see also Nahman of Bratzlav, *Sihot Haran*, 89.
9. J.M. Ta-Shema, "Yemei Eideihem" ["Their Festival Days"], *Tarbits* 47 (1977/78): 197–210.
10. Diana L. Eck, *A New Religious America* (San Francisco: Harper, 2002).
11. "Chaim Steinmetz—Happiness Warrior" (Monday, January 10, 2005): http://chaimsteinmetz.blogspot.com/2005/01/last-saturday-morning-we-held-service.html (January 20, 2009).
12. Eugene J. Fisher, "The New Agenda of Catholic-Jewish Relations: A Response to Edward Kessler": http://www.bc.edu/research/cjl/meta-elements/texts/cjrelations/resources/articles/Fisher_New_Agenda.htm (January 20, 2009).
13. Jonathan Lear, *Freud* (New York: Routledge, 2005); Tsvetan Todorov, *The Morals of History* (Minneapolis: University of Minnesota Press, 1995).
14. James Carroll, *Constantine's Sword: The Church and the Jews: A History.* (Boston: Houghton Mifflin, 2001).
15. Jonathan Sacks, The Dignity of Difference: How to Avoid the Clash of Civilizations (London: Continuum, 2002), 207.

SELECTED BIBLIOGRAPHY

Abarbanel, Judah. *The Philosophy of Love (Dialoghi d'Amore)*. Trans. F. Friedeberg-Seeley and Jean H. Barnes. London: Soncino Press, 1937.

Abraham bar Hiyya. *The Meditation of the Sad Soul*. Trans. Geoffrey Widoger. New York: Schocken Books, 1968.

Abraham Maimonides' Commentary on Genesis & Exodus. Eds. Ernest J Wiesenberg and Solomon David Sassoon. Letchworth, 1958.

Abravanel, Isaac. *Sefer Yeshuot Meshiḥo*. Jerusalem: 1967.

Adret, Solomon ben Abraham. *Teshuvot ha-Rashba*. Ed. Haim Z Dimitrovsky. Jerusalem: Mosad Harav Kook, 1990.

Albo, Joseph. *Sefer ha-Ikkarim; Book of Principles*. Trans. Isaac Husik. Philadelphia: The Jewish Publication Society of America, 1929.

Anatoli, Jacob. *Malmad Hatalmidim*. Lyck: 1866.

Beck, Ulrich. *Cosmopolitan Vision*. Cambridge: Polity Press, 2006.

Benamozegh, Elijah. *Israel and Humanity*. Trans. Maxwell Luria. Mahwah, NJ: Paulist Press, 1995.

Berkowitz, Jay R. "Authority and Innovation at the Threshold of Modernity: The *Me'orei Or* of Rabbi Aaron Worms." In *Me'ah She'arim: Studies in Medieval Jewish Spiritual Life in Memory of Isadore Twersky*, edited by Ezra Fleischer et al., 275–77. Jerusalem: Hebrew University Magnes Press 2001.

———. *Rites and Passages: The Beginnings of Modern Jewish Culture in France, 1650–1860*. Philadelphia: University of Pennsylvania Press, 2004.

Bleich, J. David. "Divine Unity in Maimonides, the Tosafists and Meiri." In *Neoplatonism and Jewish Thought*, edited by Lenn Goodman, 237–54. Albany: State University of New York Press, 1992.

Blidstein, Gerald. "Jews and the Ecumenical Dialogue." *Tradition* 11 (1970): 103–10.

———. "The Non-Jew in Jewish Ethics." *Sh'ma* 7, 125 (1977). http://www.clal.org/e15.html

———. "R. Yohanan, Idolatry, and Public Privilege." *Journal for the Study of Judaism* 5, 2 (1974): 154–61.

———. "The Status of Islam in Maimonidean Halakhah." In *Studies in Halakhic and Aggadic Thought*, edited by Gerald Blidstein, 237–47. Beer Sheva: Ben Gurion University Press, 2004.

Bokser, Ben Zion. *Judaism and the Christian Predicament*. New York: Knopf, 1967.

Boyarin, Daniel. *Border Lines: The Partition of Judaeo-Christianity*. Philadelphia: University of Pennsylvania Press, 2004.

———. "Rethinking Jewish Christianity: An Argument for Dismantling a Dubious Category (to which is Appended a Correction of my Border Lines)." *Jewish Quarterly Review* 99, 1 (Winter 2009): 7–36.

Brill, Alan. *Thinking God.* New York: Yeshiva University Press, 2002.

———. *Thinking God: The Mysticism of Rabbi Zadok of Lublin* (Jersey City, NJ: Yeshiva University Press *KTAV Publishing*, 2002).

Brumberg-Kraus, Jonathan D. "A Jewish Ideological Perspective on the Study of Christian Scripture." *Jewish Social Studies* 4, 1 (1997): 121–52.

Buber, Martin. *Origins of Hasidism.* New York: Horizon Press, 1960.

Chajes, Z.H. *The Student's Guide through the Talmud.* New York: P. Feldheim, 1960.

Clooney, Francis X. *Divine Mother, Blessed Mother: Hindu Goddesses and the Virgin Mary.* New York: Oxford University Press, 2005.

———. *Hindu God, Christian God.* New York: Oxford University Press, 2001.

Cohen, Arthur A. *The Tremendum: A Theological Interpretation of the Holocaust.* New York: Crossroad, 1981.

Cohen, S.J.D. "Does Rashi's Torah Commentary Respond to Christianity? A Comparison of Rashi with Rashbam and Bekhor Shor." In *The Idea of Biblical Interpretation: Essays in Honor of James L. Kugel,* edited by H. Najman and J.H. Newman, 449–72. Boston: Brill, 2004.

Cousins, Ewert H. *Global Spirituality toward the Meeting of Mystical Paths.* Madras, India: University of Madras, 1985.

Davis, Joseph. *Yom-Tov Lipmann Heller.* Oxford: Littman Library, 2004.

D'Costa, Gavin. *The Meeting of Religions and the Trinity.* Maryknoll, NY: Orbis, 2000.

Dinur, Ben Zion. *Israel and the Diaspora.* Philadelphia: Jewish Publication Society of America, 1969.

Dorff, Elliot N. "This Is *My God*: One Jew's Faith." In *Three Faiths One God: A Jewish, Christian, Muslim Encounter,* edited by John Hick, 7–29. Albany: State University of New York Press, 1989.

———. *To Do the Right and the Good: A Jewish Approach to Modern Social Ethics.* Philadelphia: Jewish Publication Society, 2002.

Dulles, Avery. "Christ among the Religions." *America* 186, 3 (2002): 8–15.

Eck, Diana L. *A New Religious America.* San Francisco: Harper, 2002.

Ecker, Neta "Universlaism in the Thought of Rabbi Eliezer Ashkenazi" (Unpublished Dissertation presented to Haifa University, 2010).

Edelman, Lily. *Face to Face: A Primer in Dialogue.* Washington, DC: B'nai B'rith, Adult Jewish Education, 1967.

Eisen, Robert. "The Problem of the King's Dream and Non-Jewish Prophecy in Judah Halevi's 'Kuzari.'" *JJTP* 3, 2 (1994): 231–47.

Falk, Harvey. *Jesus the Pharisee: A New Look at the Jewishness of Jesus.* New York: Paulist Press, 1985.

Falk, Ze'ev. "Nokhri ve-ger toshav be-mishpat ha-ivri." *Mahalkhim* 2, 5729 (1968–69): 9–15.

Fenton, Paul B. "Jewish Attitudes to Islam: Israel Heeds Ishmael." *Jerusalem Quarterly* 29 (Fall 1983): 84–102.

———. "Judaeo-Arabic Mystical Writings of the XIIIth-XIVth Centuries." In *Judaeo-Arabic Studies,* edited by Norman Golb, 89–100. Amsterdam: Harwood Academic Publishers, 1997.

Fisch, Harold. "A Response to Ernst Simon." In *Modern Jewish Ethics: Theory and Practice,* edited by Marvin Fox, 57–61. Columbus: Ohio State University Press, 1975.

Fisher, Eugene. *Visions of the Other: Jewish and Christian Theologians Assess the Dialogue.* New York: Paulist Press, 1994.

Fisher, Eugene J., A. James Rudin, and Marc H. Tanenbaum. *Twenty Years of Jewish-Catholic Relations.* New York: Paulist Press, 1986.

Fitzgerald, Michael L., and John Borelli. *Interfaith Dialogue: A Catholic View.* London: SPCK, 2006.

Franck, Adolphe. *The Kabbalah; or, the Religious Philosophy of the Hebrews.* Trans. I. Sossnitz. New York: Kabbalah Pub. CO., 1926.

Fredrickson, Paula. *From Jesus to Christ: The Origins of the New Testament Images of Christ.* New Haven: Yale University Press, 1988.

Friedheim, Emmanuel. *Rabbinisme et paganisme en Palestine romaine: étude historique des Realia talmudiques (Ier-IVème siècles).* Leiden: Brill, 2006.

———. "Who are the Deities Concealed behind the Rabbinic Expression a Nursing Female Image?" *Harvard Theological Review* 96 (2003): 239–50.

Friedman, Thomas L. *The Lexus and the Olive Tree.* New York: Farrar, Straus, Giroux, 1999.

———. "The Real War." *New York Times,* November 27, 2001, Foreign Affairs.

Gellman, Jerome. "In Defense of Contented Religious Exclusivism." *Religious Studies* 36, 4 (2000): 401–17.

Gershenzon, Shoshanna. "Myth and Scripture: The *Dialoghi d'Amore* of Leone Ebreo." *A Crown for a King* (2000): 125–45.

Gikkitila, Joseph. *Gate of Lights.* Trans. Avi Weinstein. San Francisco: HarperCollins, 1994.

Gilkey, Langdon. "Plurality and Its Theological Implications." In *The Myth of Christian Uniqueness: Toward A Pluralistic Theology of Religions,* edited by John Hick and Paul F. Knitter, 37–52. Maryknoll, NY: Orbis Books, 1987.

Ginzburg, Carlo, Martin H. Ryle, and Kate Soper. *Wooden Eyes: Nine Reflections On Distance, European Perspectives.* New York: Columbia University Press, 2001.

Goiton, Shlomo Dov. *Jews and Arabs.* New York: Schocken Books, 1955.

Goldenberg, Robert. *The Nations that Know Thee Not. New York: New York University* Press, 1998.

Goldstein, Morris. *Jesus in the Jewish Tradition.* New York: Macmillian, 1950.

Goodblatt, David. *Elements of Ancient Jewish Nationalism.* Cambridge: Cambridge University Press, 2006.

Goodman, Lenn Evan. *God of Abraham.* New York, NY: Oxford University Press, 1996.

Gopin, Marc. "An Orthodox Embrace of Gentiles? Interfaith Tolerance in the Thought of S.D. Luzzatto and E. Benamozegh." *Modern Judaism* 18, 2 (May 1998): 173–96.

Gordis, Robert. *The Root and the Branch.* Chicago: University of Chicago Press, 1962.

Goshen-Gottstein Alon. "Jewish-Christian Relations: From Historical Past to Theological Future." International Council of Christians and Jews. http://www.jcrelations.net/en/?item=1754.

Green, Tamara M. *The City of the Moon God: Religious Traditions of Harran.* Leiden: E.J. Brill, 1992.

Greenberg, Irving. "Judaism and Christianity, Covenants of Redemption." In *Christianity in Jewish Terms,* edited by Tikva Simone Frymer-Kensky et al., 141–74. Boulder, CO: Westview Press, 2000.

———. *For the Sake of Heaven and Earth: The New Encounter Between Judaism and Christianity.* Philadelphia: Jewish Publication Society, 2004.

———. "Theology after the Shoah: The Transformation of the Core Paradigm." *Modern Judaism* (2006): 213–39.

Griffiths, Paul J. "Modalizing the Theology of Religions." *Journal of Religion* 73 (1993): 382–89.

———. *Problems of Religious Diversity.* Oxford: Blackwell, 2001.

Hacohen, A. "Islam and Its Believers" [Hebrew]. *Mahanayim* 1 (1992): 34–51.

Halbertal, Moshe. "Coexisting with the Enemy: Jews and Pagans in the Mishnah." In *Tolerance and Intolerance in Early Judaism and Christianity,* edited by Graham N. Stanton and Guy G. Stroumsa, 159–72. Cambridge, UK: Cambridge University Press, 1998.

Halbertal, Moshe. "One's Possessed of Religion: Religious Tolerance in the Teachings of the Me'iri." *Edah Journal* 1, 1 (2000): 1–24.

Halbertal, Moshe and Avishai Margalit. *Idolaty.* Cambridge, Mass: Harvard University Press, 1998.

Halevi, Yehudah. *Book of Kuzari.* Trans. Hartwig Hirschfeld. New York: 1905.

Hames, Harvey J. *The Art of Conversion: Christianity and Kabbalah in the Thirteenth Century.* Leiden: Brill, 2000.

———. *Like Angels on Jacob's Ladder: Abraham Abulafia, the Franciscans, and Joachimism.* Albany: State University of New York Press, 2007.

Harries, Richard. *"Jonathan Sacks's The Dignity of Difference: How to Avoid the Clash of Civilizations."* Scottish Journal of Theology *57, 1 (2004): 109–15.*

Hartman, David. *Conflicting Visions: Spiritual Possibilities of Modern Israel.* New York: Schocken Books, 1990.

———. *A Heart of Many Rooms.* Woodstock, VT: Jewish Lights, 1999.

———. "Jewish and Christian in a World of Tomorrow." *Immanuel* 6 (1976): 70–81.

———."Judaism Encounters Christianity Anew." In *Visions of the Other: Jewish and Christian Theologians Assess the Dialogue,* edited by *Eugene Fisher,* 67–80. Mahwah NJ: Stimulus Books, 1994.

———. "On the Possibility of Religious Pluralism from a Jewish Viewpoint." *Immanuel* 16 (1983): 101–13.

Heim, S. Mark. *The Depth of the Riches: A Trinitarian Theology of Religious Ends.* Grand Rapids: Eerdmans, 2001.

Herford, R. Travers. *Christianity in Talmud & Midrash.* Jersey City, NJ: Ktav Pub. House, 2006.

Hertz, J.H. *Pentateuch and Haftorahs.* London: Soncino, 1963.

Herzog, Isaac. "Right and Obligation According to Torah." *Tehumin* 2 (1981) [Hebrew].

Heschel, Abraham Joshua. *No Religion is an Island: Abraham Joshua Heschel and Interreligious Dialogue,* edited by Harold Kasimow and Byron L. Sherwin. Maryknoll, NY: Orbis, 1991.

Hick, John. *God Has Many Names.* London: Macmillian, 1980.

Hick, John and Paul F. Knitter. *The Myth of Christian Uniqueness: Toward A Pluralistic Theology of Religions.* Maryknoll, NY: Orbis Books, 1987.

Hirsch, Mendel. *Judaism and Humanism.* London: Beddoe Press, Staines, 1928, reprinted in Jacob Breuer. *Fundamentals of Judaism: Selections from the Works of Rabbi Samson Raphael Hirsch and Outstanding Torah-true Thinkers.* New York: Published for the Rabbi Samson Raphael Hirsch Society by P. Feldheim, 1949.

Hirsch, Samson Raphael. *Nineteen Letters.* Trans. Bernard Drachman. New York: Bloch Publishing, 1942.

———. *The Pentateuch.* Trans. Isaac Levy. London: 1960. n.p.

———. "Talmudic Judaism and Society." In *Principles of Education,* vol. VII. New York: Feldheim Publishers, 1991.

Hirshman, Marc. *Kol ba'ei olam: zerem universali be-sifrut ha-tanna'im ve-yahaso le-hokhmat ha-amim.* Tel-Aviv: Ha-Kibbutz Ha-Meuhad, 1999.

———. "Rabbinic Universalism in the Second and Third Centuries." *Harvard Theological Review* 9, 2 (2000): 101–15.

Hoffmann, David Zvei. "Problems of the Diaspora in the Shulkah Arukh." In *Fundamentals of Judaism,* edited by Jacob Breuer, 181–91. New York: Feldhiem, 1969.

Hoffmann, Joshua. "Rav Kook's Mission to America." *OROT* 1, 5751 (1991): 78–99.

Holtzman, Gitit. "Rabbi Moshe Narboni on the Relationship Between Judaism and Islam." *Tarbiz* 65, 2 (1996): 277–99.

———. "Universalism and Nationality in Judaism, and the Relationship Between Jews and Non-Jews the Thought of Rabbi Eliyahu Benamozegh." *Pe'amim* 74 (1998): 104–30.

Hood, John. *Aquinas and the Jews*. Philadelphia: University of Pennsylvania Press, 1995.

Hourani, George F. "Maimonides and Islam Studies." In *Studies in Islamic and Judaic Traditions*, edited by William M. Brinner and Stephen David Ricks, 153–65. Atlanta, Ga: Scholars Press, 1986.

Hughes, Aaron W. *The Texture of the Divine: Imagination in Medieval Islamic and Jewish thought*. Bloomington, Ind: Indiana University Press, 2004.

———. "Transforming the Maimonidean Imagination: Aesthetics in the Renaissance Thought of Judah Abravanel." *Harvard Theological Review* 97, 4 (2004): 461–84.

Huntington, Samuel P. *The Clash of Civilizations and the Remaking of World Order*. New York: Simon & Schuster, 1996.

Immanuel, Ben Solomon. *Tophet and Eden*: <Hell and Paradise>. Trans. Hermann Gollancz. London: University of London Press, 1921.

Janowitz, Naomi. "Good Jews Don't: Historical and Philosophical Constructions of Idolatry." *History of Religions* 4, 2 (2007): 239–52.

———. "Rabbis and their Opponents: The Construction of the 'Min' in Rabbinic Anecdotes." *Journal of Early Christian Studies* 6 (1998): 449–62.

Jospe, Raphael. "Ha-Hagadah Ha-Ne'emenet Shel Rabbi Sa'adiah Gaon: Mi Hem Qehal Ha-Meya ḥadim?" *Daat* 41 (Summer 1998): 5–17.

———. "Pluralism out of the Sources of Judaism: Religious Pluralism without Relativism." *Studies in Christian-Jewish Relations* 2, 2 (2007): 92–113.

Kalmin, Richard. "Christians and Heretics in Rabbinic Literature of Late Antiquity." *HTR* 87 (1994): 155–69.

———. "Jesus in Sasanian Babylonia." *Jewish Quarterly Review* 99, 1 (Winter 2009): 107–12.

Kapah, Yosef. "Islam and the Relation to Muslims in Maimonides' Teachings" [Hebrew]. *Mahanayim* 1 (1992).

Kaplan, Zvi Jonathan. "Mendelsohn's Religious Perspective of Non-Jews." *Journal of Ecumenical Studies* 41, 3 (2004): 355–66.

Kärkkäinen, Veli-Matti. *An Introduction to the Theology of Religion: Biblical, Historical, and Contemporary Perspectives*. Downers Grove, IL: InterVarity Press, 2004.

Katz, Jacob. *Exclusiveness and Tolerance: Jewish-Gentile Relations in Medieval and Modern Times*. New York: Schocken, 1969.

———.*Tradition and Crisis*. New York: NYU Press, 1993.

Kaufmann, Yehezkel. "The Bible and Mythological Polytheism." *JBL* 70 (1951): 179–97.

———. *Christianity and Judaism: Two Covenants*. Jerusalem: Magnes Press, Hebrew University, 1988.

———. *The Religion of Israel, from its Beginnings to the Babylonian Exile*. Chicago: University of Chicago Press Chicago, 1960.

Kellner, Menachem. "Respectful Disagreement—A Reply to Professor Jospe." In *Jewish Theology of the Other*, edited by Alon Goshen-Gottstein and Eugene Korn (Forthcoming).

Klausner, Joseph and Herbert Danby. *Jesus of Nazareth*. Boston: Beacon Press, 1964.

Klenicki, Leon. *Toward a Theological Encounter: Jewish Understanding of Christianity*. New York: Paulist Press, 1991.

Knitter, Paul F. *Introducing Theologies of Religions*. Maryknoll, NY: Orbis Books, 2002.

Koehler, Kaufman. "Cross." *Jewish Encyclopedia* IV: 369.

Kogan, Michael. *Opening the Covenant: A Jewish Theology of Christianity*. New York: Oxford University Press, 2008.

Kohen, Yehezqel. *Ha-yahas el ha-nokhri ba-halakhah u-ve-metsi'ut bitequfat ha tanna'im*, doctoral dissertation. Hebrew University: Shevat 1975.

Kook, Abraham Isaac. *Arpelei Tohar*. Jerusalem: Mosad Harav Kook, 1993.

Kook, Abraham Isaac. *Igrot Harayah*. Jerusalem: Mossad Harav Kook, 1985.

―――. *Orot*. Jerusalem: Mosad Harav Kook, 1963.

―――. *Orot*. Trans. Betsalel Naor. Northvale, NJ: Jason Aronson, 1993.

―――. *Orot haKodesh*. Jerusalem: Mosad Harav Kook, 1969.

Kook, Zvei Judah. *Judaism and Christianity* [Hebrew]. Beit El: Sifriyat Chava, 2001.

―――. *Li-Netivot Yiśrael*. Jerusalem: Menorah, 1996.

Kook, Zevi Yehudah ben Abraham Isaac and Shelomoh Ḥayim Aviner. *Siḥot ha-Rav Tsevi Yehudah ha-kohen Ḳooḳ al Sefer Orot*. Jerusalem: Aṭeret Kohanim, 2004.

Kreisel, Howard. "Maimonides on Christianity and Islam." *Jewish Civilization* III (1985): 153–62.

Kulp, Joshua. "Jesus in the Talmud (review)." *Shofar: An Interdisciplinary Journal of Jewish Studies* 27.2 (2009): 132–34.

Labuschagne, C.J. *The Incomparability of Yahweh in the Old Testament*. Leiden: E.J. Brill, 1966.

Lear, Jonathan. *Freud*. New York: Routledge, 2005.

Leiman, Sid Z. "*Abarbanel and the Censor.*" *Journal of Jewish Studies* 19 (1968): 49–61.

Lev, Yaacov. *Saladin in Egypt*. Leiden: Brill, 1999.

Levene, D. *The Garden of Wisdom*. New York: Columbia University Press, 1907.

Levin, Israel. *Abraham Ibn Ezra Reader: Annotated texts with Introductions and Commentaries*. New York and Tel Aviv: Israel Matz, 1985.

Lichtenstein, Aaron. *The Seven Laws of Noah*. New York: The Rabbi Jacob Joseph School Press, 1981.

Lila, Mark. "Earthly Powers." *NYT*. April 2, 2006.

Lindbeck, George. *The Church in a Postliberal Age*. Grand Rapids, Mich.: William B. Eerdmans Pub, 2003.

Lochhead, David. *The Dialogical Imperative: A Christian Reflection on Interfaith Encounter*. Maryknoll, NY: Orbis Books, 1988.

Luzzatto, Moses Hayyim. *Derekh Hashem*. New York: Feldheim, 1997.

Maimonides, Moses. *The Eight Chapters of Maimonides On Ethics (Shemonah Perakim)*. Trans. Joseph Isaac Gorfinkle. New York: Columbia University Press, 1912.

―――. *The Guide of the Perplexed*. Trans. Shlomo Pines. Chicago: University of Chicago Press, 1963.

―――. *Teshuvot ha-RaMBaM*. Ed. Joshua Blau. Jerusalem: Mekitse Nirdamim, 1960.

Manekin, Charles. "Hierarchy and Race in the Thought of Judah Ha-Levy." In *Proceedings of The Ninth International Congress of Medieval Philosophy, 1992. Louvian: Peters, 1996*.

Matt, Daniel Chanan. *The Zohar*. Stanford, CA: Stanford Univ. Press, 2006.

―――. *Zohar, The Book of Enlightenment*. The Classics of Western Spirituality. New York: Paulist Press, 1983.

McDermott, Gerald R. *God's Rivals: Why has God Allowed Different Religions?* Downer's Grove, III: IVP Academic, 2007.

Menashe ben Israel. *The Conciliator*. London: 1842.

Mendes, Henry Pereira. "Orthodox or Historical Judaism." In *The Dawn of Religious Pluralism: Voices from the World's Parliament of Religions, 1893*, edited with introductions by Richard Hughes Seager, 328–30. La Salle IL, Open Court, 1993; reprinted from Walter R. Houghton, ed. *Neely's History of the Parliament of Religions*. Chicago: 1894.

Micklethwait, John. "In God's Name: A Special Report on Religion and Public Life." *The Economist*. November 3–9, 2007. London: Economist Newspaper.

Moses Mendelssohn: Selections from his Writings. Trans. Eva Jospe. New York: Viking Press, 1975.

Muck, Terry. "Instrumentality, Complexity, and Reason: A Christian Approach to Religions." *Buddhist-Christian Studies* 22, 1 (2002): 115–21.

Naḥmanides. *Commentary on the Torah*. Ed. Charles Chavel. New York: Shilo Pub. House, 1971.

———. *Writings & Discourses*. Ed. Charles Chavel. New York: Shilo Pub. House, 1978.

Novak, David. *The Image of the Non-Jew in Judaism: An Historical and Constructive Study of the Noahide Laws*. New York: E. Mellen Press, 1983.

———. *Jewish-Christian Dialogue: A Jewish Justification*. Oxford: Oxford University Press, 1989.

———. *Maimonides on Judaism and Other Religions*. Cincinnati: Hebrew Union College Press, 1997.

Ogden, Schubert Miles. *Is There Only One True Religion or are There Many?* Dallas: Southern Methodist University Press, 1992.

Panikkar, Raimon. "The Myth of Pluralism: The Tower of Babel—A Meditation on Non-Violence." *Cross Currents* 29 (1979): 197–230.

Pines, S. "A Study of the Impact of Indian, Mainly Buddhist, Thought on Some Aspects of Kalam Doctrines." *Jerusalem Studies in Arabic and Islam* 17 (1994): 182–203.

Porton, Gary. *Goyim: Gentiles and Israelites in Mishnah-Tosefta*. Atlanta: Scholars Press, 1988.

Race, Alan. *Christians and Religious Pluralism: Patterns in the Christian Theology of Religions*. Maryknoll, NY: Orbis Books, 1983.

Rakover, Naḥum. *Law and the Noahides: Law as a Universal Value*. Jerusalem, Israel: Library of Jewish Law, 1998.

Rapoport, Chaim. "Attitudes Towards Gentiles in Post Holocaust Rabbinic Literature," unpublished MA dissertation (Institute of Jewish Studies at University College London, 2001).

Ravitzky, Aviezer. "Judaism Views Other Religions." In *Religions View Religions: Explorations in Pursuit of Understanding*, edited by J.D. Gort, Henry Jansen, H.M. Vroom, eds, 75–107. Amsterdam and New York: Rodopi, 2006.

Raz-Krakotzkin, Amnon. "Censorship, Editing, and the Reshaping of Jewish Identity: The Catholic Church and Hebrew Literature in the Sixteenth Century." In *Hebraica Veritas?: Christian Hebraists and the Study of Judaism in Early Modern Europe*, edited by Allison Coudert and Jeffrey S. Shoulson, 125–55. Philadelphia: University of Pennsylvania Press, 2004.

Reines, H.Z. "Yaḥas ha-yehudim le-nokhrim." *Sura* 4 Jerusalem and New York, 5724 (1963–64): 192–221.

Roggema, Barbara, Marcel Poorthuis, and Pim Valkenberg. *The Three Rings: Textual Studies in the Historical Trialogue of Judaism, Christianity, and Islam*. Leuven: Peters, 2005.

Rokeah, David. "Le-parashat yaḥasam shel ha-hakhamim la-goyyim ve-la-gerim." *Mahalkhim* 5, 5731 (1970–71): 68–75.

Rolston, Holmes. *Religious Inquiry—Participation and Detachment*. New York, NY: Philosophical Library, 1985.

Rosenbloom, Noah H. *Luzzatto's Ethico-Psychological Interpretation of Judaism; A Study in the Religious Philosophy of Samuel David Luzzatto*. New York: Yeshiva University Press, 1965.

Roth, Cecil. *The Jews in the Renaissance*. Philadelphia: Jewish Publication Society of America, 1964.

———. *A Short History of the Jewish People*. London: East and the West Library, 1969.

Rothschild, Fritz A., ed. *Jewish Perspectives on Christianity*. New York: Crossroad, 1990.

Sa'adiah. *The Book of Beliefs and Opinions*. Trans. Samuel Rosenblatt. New Haven: Yale University Press, 1948.

Sacks, Jonathan. *The Dignity of Difference: How to Avoid the Clash of Civilizations*. London: Continuum, 2002.

———. *To Heal a Fractured the World*. New York: Schocken, 2005.

Sagi, Avi and Zvi Zohar, eds. *Yahadut shel Hayyim: Iyyunim BeYetzirato ha'Hagutit-Hilkhatit shel HaRav Hayyim David HaLevi*. Jerusalem: Hartman Institute, 2007.

Sanders, E.P. *Jesus and Judaism.* Philadelphia: Fortress Press, 1985.

Sandmel, D.F. "Joseph Klausner, Israel, and Jesus." *Currents in Theology and Mission* 31, 6 (2004): 456–64.

Schachter-Shalomi, Zalman. "Bases and Boundaries of Jewish, Christian, and Moslem Dialogue." http://www.havurahshirhadash.org/rebzalmanarticle7.html.

———. "Jesus in Jewish-Christian-Moslem Dialogue." http://www.havurahshirhadash.org/rebzalmanarticle8.html.

Schäfer, Peter. *Jesus in the Talmud.* Princeton, NJ: Princeton University Press, 2007.

Scheindlin, Raymond P. *The Gazelle: Medieval Hebrew Poems on God, Israel, and the Soul.* Philadelphia: Jewish Publication Society, 1991.

Schneersohn, Menahem Mendel. *Sichos in English.* Brooklyn, NY: 1978.

Schwartz, Dov. *Studies on Astral Magic in Medieval Jewish Thought.* Leiden: Brill-Styx, 2004.

Sforno, Obadiah ben Jacob. *Commentary on the Bible.* Jerusalem: Mosad ha-Rav Ḳook, 1980.

Shapira, Jospeh. *Hagut, Halakhah ṿe-Tsiyonut: al Olamo ha-Ruḥani shel ha-Rav Yitsḥaḳ Yaaḳov Reines.* Tel-Aviv: ha-Kibbutz ha-Meuḥad, 2002.

Shapiro, Marc. "Scholars and Friends." *Torah U-Madda Journal* 7 (1997): 105–21.

Sharpe, Eric. "Dialogue." In *The Encyclopedia of Religion,* edited by Mircea Eliade and Charles J. Adams, first edition, volume 4. New York: Macmillan, 1987.

Shemesh, Aharon. "The Origins of the Laws of Separatism: Qumran Literature and Rabbinic Halacha." *Revue de Qumran* 18, 2 (1997): 223–41.

Siegman, Henry. "Ten Years of Catholic-Jewish Relations: A Reassessment." *Encounter Today* 11, 2–3 (1976).

Sikora, Piotr. *"Judaism Open to the Religions of the Nations a Polish Catholic Theologian reads an American Jewish Pluralist." Jewish-Christian Relations.* http://www.jcrelations.net/en/?item=2804.

Simon, Ernst. "The Neighbor (re'a) whom we Shall Love." In *Modern Jewish Ethics,* edited by M. Fox, 29–56. Columbus OH: Ohio State Press, 1975.

Simon, Marcel. *Verus Israel: A Study of the Relations Between Christians and Jews in the Roman Empire (Ad 135–425.)* Oxford [u.a.]: Oxford University Press, 1986.

Schlossberg, Eliezer. "The Relationship of Maimonides to Islam." *Peamim* 42 (1990): 38–60.

Smith, Mark S. *The Early History of God: Yahweh and the other Deities in Ancient Israel.* San Francisco: Harper, 1990.

Smith, Morton. *Palestinian Parties and Politics that Shaped the Old Testament.* New York: Columbia University Press, 1971.

Soloveitchik, Joseph Dov. *And from There You Shall Seek.* Jersey City, NJ: Ktav, 2008.

Soloweyczyk, Eliyhau. *Kol kore o' Hatalmud ve haberit Hahadashah* (1867).

Sperber, Daniel. "Gentile." In *Encyclopedia Judaica,* 7:410–14.

Steinmetz, Chaim. "Monday, January 10, 2005." Chaim Steinmetz—Happiness Warrior. http://chaimsteinmetz.blogspot.com/2005/01/last-saturday-morning-we-held-service.html.

Steinsaltz, Adin. "Peace without Conciliation: The Irrelevance of 'Toleration' in Judaism." *Common Knowledge* 11, 1 (2005): 41–47.

Stern, Sasha. "The Death of Idolatry?" *Le'ela* (April 1993): 26–28.

———. *Jewish Identity in Early Rabbinic Writings.* Leiden: E.J. Brill, 1994.

Talmage, Frank. "Angels, Anthems, and Anathemas." In *The Frank Talmage Memorial Volume,* edited by Barry Walfish, 195–222. Haifa: Haifa University Press, 1993.

Tanner, Kathryn. "Respect for Other Religions: A Christian Antidote to Colonialist Discourse." *Modern Theology* 9 (1993): 1–18.

Ta-Shema, J.M. "Yemei Eideihem" ["Their Festival Days"]. *Tarbits* 47 (1977/78): 197–210.

Todorov, Tsetan. *The Morals of History.* Minneapolis: University of Minnesota Press, 1995.

Touitou, E. "Rashi and His School" The Exegesis on the Halachic Part of the Pentateuch in the Context of the Judeao-Christian Controversy." In *Bar Ilan Studies in History IV. Medieval*

Studies in Honor of Avrom Saltman, edited by Shimon Schwarzfuchs, Yvonne Friedman, and Bat-Sheva Albert, 231–51. Bar-Ilan University Press, 1995.

———. "Rashi's Commentary on Genesis 16 in the Context of Judeo-Christian Controversy." *Hebrew Union College Annual* 61 (1990): 159–83.

Urbach, E.E. "The Rabbinical Laws of Idolatry in the 2nd and 3rd Centuries in the Light of Archaeological and Historical Facts." *IEJ* 9 (1959): 145–69.

———. "Self-Isolation or Self Affirmation in Judaism in the First Three Centuries; Theory and Practice." In *Jewish and Christian Self-definition Vol. 2, Aspects of Judaism in the Graeco-Roman Period*, edited by E.P. Sanders, Albert I. Baumgarten, and Alan Mendelson, 269–98. London: SCM Press, 1981.

Wasserstrom, Steve M. *Between Muslim and Jew: The Problem of Symbiosis under Early Islam.* Princeton, NJ: Princeton University Press, 1995.

Weinberger, Leon J. *Jewish Hymnography: A Literary History.* Portland, OR: Littman, 1998.

Weiss-Rosmarin, Trude. *Judaism and Christianity: The Differences.* New York: The Jewish Book Club, 1943.

Werblowsky, R.J. Zwi. *Joseph Karo, Lawyer and Mystic.* London-Oxford: Oxford University Press, 1962.

Wieder, Naphtali. "Regarding an Anti-Christian and Anti-Muslim Gematria in the *'Alenu le-shabeah*" prayer." *Sinai* 76 (1998): 1–14.

Wuthnow, Robert. *America and the Challenges of Religious Diversity.* Princeton, NJ: Princeton University Press, 2005.

Yadin, Azzan. "Rabban Gamliel, Aphrodite's Bath, and the Question of Pagan Monotheism." *Jewish Quarterly Review* 96 (2006): 149–79.

Yuval, Israel J. *Two Nations in Your Womb: Perceptions of Jews and Christians in Late Antiquity and the Middle Ages.* Berkeley: University of California Press, 2006.

Zeitlin, Hillel. *Sifran shel Yeḥidim.* Jerusalem: Mossad ha-Rav Ḳooḳ, 1979.

Zevit, Ziony. *The Religions of Ancient Israel: A Synthesis of Parallactic Approaches.* London: Continuum, 2001.

Zohar, Noam. "Idolatry, Idols, and their Annulment." (Hebrew) *Sidra* 17 (2001–2): 64–77.

Zunz, Leopold. *Zur Geschichte und Literatur.* Berlin: L. Lamm, 1919.

INDEX

Abarbanel, Isaac   71–3
Abarbanel, Judah   109–10
Abraham   5, 34, 42, 43, 45, 48, 56, 70,
    76, 77, 84, 85, 115, 116, 142, 144,
    147, 155, 158, 164, 185, 186, 210,
    211, 212, 215, 228, 230, 231, 239
Abraham bar Hiyya   151, 157, 215
Abraham Maimuni   38, 70
Abulafia, Abraham   216–18
Acceptance Model   25–6
    Comparative Theology   25–6
    Different Ends   25, 26, 149
    Post Liberal   25
Adam   24, 34, 46, 66, 76, 77, 82, 88,
    92, 93, 94, 99, 109, 116, 118, 120,
    125, 133, 165, 167, 173, 200, 211,
    212
Aderet, Solomon   86– 8, 105, 229
Akiva, Rabbi   40, 187, 199
Albalag, Isaac   106–7, 183
Albo, Joseph   218–19
Al-Constantine, Solomon   214
Alenu   41, 59–62, 154
Allah   89, 214, 215
Amalek   39, 158, 164
Amiel, Moshe Avigdor   199
Amital, Yehudah   199
Ammonite   39
Amos   54, 64, 119
Anatoli, Jacob   104–6
Arama, Isaac   80, 88–90
Arugat Ha-Bosem   60

Asevilli, Yom Tov (Ritva)   176, 180,
    181
Ashkenazi, Eliezer   107, 184–6, 188
Assyrian   39
Aviner, Elisha   194
Aviner, Shlomo   162–3
Avodah Zarah   40, 44, 45, 50, 51, 59,
    176, 181, 182, 183, 212
Avot (tractate)   93, 187
Azariah, Eleazar ben   55
Azriel, Abraham b.   60
Azulai, Abraham   78–9

Baal Shem Tov   85
Baba Kama   48, 49, 202
Baba Metzia   182
Bachrach, Yair Haim   188–9
Baeck, Leo   199
Balaam   58, 76, 90, 112
Baron, Salo   228
Barth, Karl   224
Bayme, Steven   57
Benamozegh, Elijah   99, 121–4, 143
Ben Azzai, Shimon   199
Ben Sira   83
Ben Stada   57
Benedict XVI, Pope   236
Berkovits, Jay   194
Berlin, Naftali Zevi   160–1
Bikkurim   48
Blidstein, Gerald   183, 205–6
Blood libel   195

Boadt, Lawrence   75
Bokser, Ben Zion   6–7
Boyarin, Daniel   56
Buber, Martin   5, 143, 168, 224
Buddhism   26, 30, 36, 79, 81, 132,
    140, 207

Canaanite Religion   33, 214
Carroll, James   237
Catholic Church   5, 169, 175, 220, 235,
    236
Chajes, Zvi Hirsch   169–70, 195–6, 202
Chardin, Teilhard de   135
Christian Zionists   236
Christianity   vii, ix, xi, 6, 7, 8, 18, 20, 24,
    27, 36, 38, 41, 55–6, 58, 59, 60, 61,
    62, 63, 65, 67, 68, 69, 70, 71, 72, 73,
    74, 75, 79, 81, 84, 85, 86, 87, 88, 89,
    90, 91, 92, 94, 95, 96, 97, 98, 100,
    113, 114, 122, 123, 124, 126 ,132,
    137, 139, 140, 142, 143, 144, 146, 147,
    151, 152, 153, 154, 155, 156, 157,
    158, 162, 163, 164, 168, 176, 178,
    179, 181, 183, 184, 185, 186, 187, 188,
    190, 191, 192, 197, 201, 206, 210,
    217, 220, 222, 231, 235–8
  Christians   2, 5, 6, 7, 8, 21, 27, 28,
    31, 40, 45, 52, 53, 55, 56, 59, 60,
    67, 79, 70, 72, 73, 75, 77, 80, 81,
    87, 90, 97, 109, 122, 124, 137, 139,
    140, 141, 142, 143, 144, 146, 147,
    148, 154, 156, 159, 171, 175, 176,
    177, 194, 195, 196, 198, 200, 203,
    204, 210, 212, 223, 229, 233, 234,
    235, 236, 239
  Falsity of   10, 189, 192, 211, 213, 219
  Idolatry   18, 24, 32–4, 35, 36, 44
  Rejection of   56, 139, 152
Clooney, Francis X.   25
Cohen, Arthur A.   230
Cohen, Hermann   117, 168, 199
Cordovero, Moses   232
Covenant   5, 8, 32, 39, 62, 75, 77,
    93–7, 111, 115, 116, 131–3, 137–42,
    146, 147, 236

Crescas, Hasdai   67
Cross   147, 180, 181, 193

Daniel   68, 83
Darkhei Shalom   199, 231
Demonic dualism   163–8, 170, 220–1
Deuteronomy   32, 36, 39, 45–8, 56–8,
    80, 94, 121, 156, 187
Deuteronomy Rabbah   50
dialogue of religions   5
Dina Demalkhuta Dina   198
Dinur, Ben-Zion   228, 229
Dorff, Elliott   130, 140–1
Douglas, Mary   20
Dulles, Avery   10
Duran, Shimon ben Zemah   157–8, 164

Ebionites   59
Ecclesiastes   59, 102
Eck, Diana   21, 234
Egyptian   38, 39, 57, 210, 214
Ehrenpreis, Marcus   208, 223, 224
Eliade, Mircea   212
Eliezer, Rabbi   41, 185, 188
Emden, Yaakov   12, 52, 63, 73–5, 79,
    90, 91, 98, 114, 123, 138, 139, 147,
    179, 180, 188, 195, 199
Empiricism   25, 166, 216, 222
Enlightenment   2, 3, 18, 19, 73, 74, 76,
    78, 105, 108, 112–14, 127, 169, 184,
    200, 217, 220, 221, 230
Epstein, Isadore   52
Esther Rabbah   50
Ethics / Ethical   7, 18, 20, 23, 29, 35,
    36, 50, 63, 64, 74, 75, 78, 96, 97,
    99, 112, 114, 115, 116, 117, 126,
    127, 130, 132, 133, 139, 140, 141,
    142, 143, 145, 146, 147, 148, 160,
    161, 166, 169, 176, 180, 184, 186,
    190, 194, 197, 198–202, 222, 225,
    226, 227, 232, 233
Exclusivism   xii, 2, 4, 5, 9, 10, 16, 19,
    20, 23–4, 26, 29, 40, 41, 49, 71, 94,
    111, 119, 129, 148, 151–74, 178,
    186, 187, 200, 202, 204, 216, 237

Exclusivist   xiii, 4, 6, 9, 11, 15, 17,
    18, 19, 20, 21, 22, 24, 28, 29, 30,
    36, 52, 60, 84, 130, 151–74, 190,
    204, 208, 218, 219, 225, 226
    Historical Exclusivism   157–63
    Scholarly Exclusivism   167–9
Exodus   38, 42, 47, 134, 185, 186, 188
Exodus Rabbah   47, 49, 52
Eybeschutz, Yonathan   188–9
Ezekiel   39, 154

Falk, Yaakov Yehoshua   188–9
Falquera, Shem Tov   106–7
Fayumi, Nathaniel Ibn   99, 111, 112,
    131–3, 145
Feinstein, Moshe   203
Fourth Lateran Council   229
Franck, Adolphe   208, 220, 221
Friedman, Thomas   133, 232

Gamaliel, Rabban   40, 45, 46
Genesis   34, 48–52, 85, 134, 142, 158,
    187, 199–200, 230
Genesis Rabbah   43
Gentiles   20, 21, 24, 31, 32, 34, 40, 41,
    42, 46, 47, 48, 49, 50, 51, 52, 53,
    54, 61, 69, 72, 73, 74, 75, 78, 79,
    81, 83, 85, 90, 93, 104, 105, 107,
    108, 111, 113, 114, 120, 121, 123,
    132, 138, 140, 142, 147, 151, 154,
    155, 156, 158, 159, 160, 163, 164,
    165, 166, 167, 168, 170, 171, 172,
    175–206, 229, 240
Gershon, Levi ben (Gersonides)   80,
    171, 209, 212–14
Gikitilla, Yosef   63, 81–3, 84, 164
Ginzberg, Aryeh Loeb   195
Ginzburg, Carlos   230
Gittin   49, 50, 182
Globalization   2, 11, 13, 66, 79, 129,
    145, 148, 207, 225, 228, 230, 232,
    233, 238, 240
Gnostics   40, 53, 54
Golden Calf   44, 92, 209, 214, 216
Goldenberg, Robert   62

Gordis, Robert   7
Greatz, Heinrich   299
Greenberg, Irving   8, 130, 137–40,
    142
Griffiths, Paul   28, 29
Grossman, Avraham   156
Guénon, René   135

Halakhic   20, 47, 50, 68, 104, 146, 169,
    176, 177, 179, 181, 184, 196, 197,
    202, 203, 204, 232, 233
Halbertal, Moshe   46, 183
Halevi, Haim David   199
Halevi, Yehudah   7, 11, 17, 63, 64–7,
    68, 73, 75, 79, 84, 85, 136, 140,
    159, 168, 195, 208–9, 210, 215,
    218, 224
Hama, Levi b.   50
Harries, Richard   146
Hartman, David   8, 9, 130–3, 145, 146
Hasidism   159, 171, 222
Heller, Yom-Tov   186–7
Henotheism   35, 36, 88, 208, 212, 213,
    214
Herford, R. Travers   55
Hermes   66
Hertz, Joseph Herman   99, 126
Herzog, Isaac   176, 179, 191–4, 202
Heschel, Abraham Joshua   75, 146, 224
Hick, John   9, 15, 18, 19
Hierarchy   24, 63, 66, 72, 80–6, 93,
    122, 214, 224, 225
Hinduism   30, 36, 79, 81, 123, 132,
    140, 149, 207, 212
Hirsch, Mendel   99, 118–19, 198
Hirsch, Samson Raphael   76–9, 94,
    147, 168, 198, 199, 202, 208,
    221–2, 230, 231
Hirschensohn, Chaim   196–7
Hobbes, Thomas   19, 28
Hoffmann, David Zvi   197–8
Holocaust   vii–xi, 6–8, 135–7, 141,
    193, 204, 229–30, 235–6
Hosea-   47
Hullin   54, 192

Huntington   232
Hyrcanus, Eliezer b.   50

Ibn Ezra, Abraham   37, 45, 83, 99, 101,
    102, 105, 181
Ibn Gabirol, Solomon   22, 67, 101
Ibn Kaspi, Joseph   104–6, 183
Icons   33, 44, 45, 47, 92, 94, 153, 176,
    183, 187
Idol   32–4, 40, 42, 43, 44, 45, 46, 47,
    48, 49, 50, 51, 54, 59, 60, 61, 72,
    73, 74, 75, 95, 103, 152, 153, 155,
    180, 182
  Idolatry   18, 24, 32–4, 35, 36, 43,
    44, 45, 46, 47, 50, 51, 54, 59, 70,
    74, 75, 78, 80, 88, 89, 91, 95, 97,
    106, 152, 153, 155, 164, 175,
    176–91, 192, 193, 194, 203, 205,
    210, 211, 212, 213, 214
Immanuel of Rome   99, 107–9, 217
Inclusivism   8, 9, 16, 17, 18, 22, 23, 26,
    47–9, 52, 63–98, 139, 163, 164,
    170, 179, 216, 225
  Inclusivist   9, 15, 17, 18, 19, 21, 22,
    28, 34, 41, 59, 60, 61, 63–98, 99,
    100, 102, 126, 129, 130, 138, 139,
    151, 159, 161, 163, 167, 171, 174, 186,
    195, 207, 218, 219, 222, 224, 226
Isaac   56, 84, 116, 125, 127, 155, 164,
    186, 231
Isaiah   22, 32, 37–8, 60, 63, 69, 72, 80,
    93, 119
Ishmael, Rabbi   40, 58, 68
Islam   vii, x, 2, 12, 18, 24, 37, 61, 63,
    68, 69, 71, 72, 73, 79, 84, 85, 86,
    87, 95, 96, 98, 100, 106, 110, 132,
    140, 146, 147, 157, 158, 163, 164,
    176, 185, 186, 191, 207, 210, 214,
    217, 236
Ismaeli   56, 66, 72, 84, 127, 164, 173,
    185
Israel, Jonathan   229
Israel, Menashe ben   35, 99, 120–1,
    203, 229
Isserles, Moses   178, 179, 180, 191

Jacob   38, 39, 56, 58, 66, 84, 116, 127,
    155, 158, 186, 231, 237
James, William   222, 224
Janowitz, Naomi   53, 55
Jeremiah–   32, 50, 120, 134, 183
Jeremiah, R.   48
Jesus   7, 21, 28, 41, 53, 55, 56–9, 60,
    68, 69, 74, 75, 90, 91, 92, 96, 97,
    116, 124, 136, 139, 140, 142, 143,
    147, 152, 153, 156, 162, 178, 179,
    180, 218, 227
  Historical Context   7, 56–9
  Toldot Yeshu (*Life of Jesus*)   152–3
Jew Bill of Maryland   1826 191
Jewish Law   50, 52, 67, 81, 86, 92, 140,
    146, 175, 179, 184, 190, 193, 194,
    196, 198, 200
Jewish Naturalization Act   1753 191
Job–   49
John Paul II, Pope   162, 235
Jonah   240
Joshua–   39
Joshua, Rabbi   41, 188
Jospe, Raphael   100, 130, 133–4
Jubilees   54

Kabbalah   21, 24, 55, 56, 30, 81, 83,
    84, 88, 97, 124, 151, 163, 164–8,
    173, 200, 219, 220, 221
  Kabbalist   51, 67, 70, 78, 79, 81, 83,
    121, 164, 165, 166, 173, 213, 216,
    219, 222, 232
Kalir, Eliezer   151, 153–5
Kanievsky, Yaakov Yisrael   203
Kara, Avigdor   94–6, 186
Karo, Yosef   179
Kasper, Walter Cardinal   235
Katz, Jacob   2, 168, 169, 178, 179, 190
Kaufman, Yehezkel   33, 34, 37, 96, 97,
    126
Ketubot   182
Kimkhi, David   60, 63, 72, 76
Kings   33, 35, 36, 52, 68
Klausner, Joseph   162
Klein, Menashe   203, 204

Knitter, Paul   9, 19, 143
Kogan, Michael   130, 141–4
Kook, Abraham Isaac   7, 22, 63, 78–9,
    94, 126–7, 146, 161, 183
Kook, Zvei Yehudah   153, 161, 162,
    163
Koran   69, 87, 210, 215
Kung, Hans   9, 133

Ladurie, Emmanuel Le Roy   184
Landau, Yehezkel   189–91
Langmuir, Gavin I.   204
Lear, Jonathan   237
Lessing, Gotthold   2, 9, 217
Levensohn, Isaac Bar   75
Levinas, Emmanuel   90, 146, 227, 234,
    238
Leviticus-   47, 117, 166, 199
Lila, Mark   2
Lindbeck, George   25
Lipschutz, Israel   99, 114–15, 138
Locke, John   2, 165
Loewe, Yehudah ben Betzalel   93,
    158–9, 93, 187, 248
Lull, Raymond   86, 87
Luria, Isaac   160, 164–6
Luzzato, Shimone   229
Luzzatto, Moshe Hayyim   166–7, 219
Luzzatto, Samuel David   99, 115–19,
    187

Maccabee   22
Magic   54, 57, 58, 152, 164, 184, 193,
    208, 209, 210, 211, 212, 213, 214,
    223, 224
Mahzor Vitry   59
Maimonides   xii, 17, 35, 37, 42, 52, 60,
    63, 67–71, 73, 77, 91, 96, 101, 102,
    103, 104, 105, 106, 111, 112, 116,
    171, 176, 177, 179, 181, 187, 188,
    190, 191, 195, 196, 199, 203, 208,
    209–12, 213, 214, 215, 218, 222,
    223, 224, 231, 232
    Guide   101, 209–12
    Mishneh Torah   52, 70, 171, 196, 212

Universalism   102–3
    Ways of peace   196, 197, 198, 199,
        231, 232
Malachi   35, 80, 112, 120, 126
Megillah   50
Meir, Rabbi   47, 117, 156, 200, 201
Meir Simhah Ha-Kohen of
    Dvinsk   200–1
Meiri, Menachem   7, 104, 143, 169,
    176, 181–4, 195, 201, 202,
    205, 206
Menachot-   121
Mendelssohn, Moses   2, 74, 99, 112–14,
    127, 133, 143, 168, 169, 179, 190
Micah-   62
Min   53, 54, 162
Minim   53, 55, 59, 156, 162
Moabite   39
Molitor, Franz Joseph   221
Monolarity   36
Monotheism   vii, 9, 12, 17, 20, 32, 33,
    34, 36, 37, 38, 47, 54, 55, 56, 59,
    62, 63, 64, 69, 75, 81, 87, 94, 95,
    96, 99, 100, 102, 103, 121, 122,
    123, 124, 139, 141, 144, 146, 176,
    177, 178, 179, 192, 194, 210, 211,
    212, 213, 228
Mowinkel, Sigmund   142
Mueller, Max   212, 213
Museum of the Jewish People   229
Mysticism/Mystical   18, 23, 29, 30, 78,
    83, 84, 97, 98, 102, 110, 124, 126,
    127, 130, 134, 135, 136, 168, 222

Nabatean Agriculture   181, 210
Nahman, of Bratzlav   222
Nahmanides   52, 63, 70, 80, 186, 191,
    208, 212–14, 218, 224
Narboni, Moses ben Joshua   104,
    105–6
Natural Theology   222–3
Neo-Hasidic   222
Neo-Orthodoxy   221
New Testament   52, 74–5, 195
Nissim, Rabbbanu (Ran)   229

Noahide Laws   20, 41, 51–2, 77, 85, 98,
     104, 113, 121, 146, 147, 180, 192,
     195–7, 200–3
Nostra Aetate vii,   5, 6, 8, 65, 116, 235
Notzrim   59, 183
Numbers-   43, 76, 166

Obadiah-   158
Ogden, Schubert   29

Pagans   40, 44, 46, 60, 123, 188, 190, 207
Peor   43
Pereira-Mendes, Henry   99, 125
Perennialism   208, 220–1
Philosophy   5, 12, 18, 71, 76, 88, 99,
     100, 101, 103, 104, 106, 109, 110,
     117, 164, 196, 220, 229
Pious of the Nations   42, 105, 188,
     202, 238
Pluarlism   x, 4, 5, 8, 9, 10, 16, 17, 18,
     19, 22, 23, 26, 27, 29, 35, 98,
     129–49, 225, 237
   Absolutism   138
   Epistemological   17, 23, 27, 130,
     140–1, 146
   Ethical   18, 23, 130, 133–4, 141, 145,
     146, 148
   Mystical   18, 23, 29, 126, 130,
     134–7
   Pluralist   xii, xiii, 1, 9, 10, 15, 16, 18,
     19, 21, 22, 23, 26, 27, 28, 29, 86, 111,
     121, 126, 127, 129, 130, 131, 132,
     134, 135, 138, 140, 141, 142, 143,
     144, 145, 146, 148, 149, 176, 226
   Relativism   4, 10, 138, 141, 234
   Theocentric   23, 63, 64, 145
Polemics   2, 12, 53, 69, 80, 88, 126,
     162, 217
Polytheism   32, 33, 37, 44, 81, 100,
     179, 212, 213
Porton, Gary   50
Proverbs   35, 47, 187, 199
Psalms   33, 37, 39, 41, 233

Rabinovitch, Nachum L.   199, 202
Race Alan   15–16

Rav   46, 59, 121
Reincarnation   114, 164
Relativism   4, 10, 138, 141, 234
Resident alien (*ger toshav*)   183, 191,
     195–8, 202–5
Restrictivism   20
Revelation   2, 16, 17, 18, 19, 23, 24,
     28, 29, 40, 48, 51, 63, 64, 65, 66,
     70, 73, 77, 84, 86–92, 93, 95, 96,
     97, 99, 100, 102, 103, 111–12, 114,
     118–19, 121, 122, 123, 127, 131,
     132, 133, 140, 141, 142, 144, 145,
     146, 152, 185, 196, 211, 217, 220,
     221–2, 224, 225
Rivkes, Moshe   186, 187–8
Rosenzweig, Franz   143, 222, 224
Rosh Hashanah   59, 61, 82, 156
Roth, Cecil   111, 229

Sa'adiah (Saadyah)   100–1, 224
Sabians   210, 211, 212
Sacks, Jonathan   75, 130, 144–8, 184,
     238
Sagi, Avi   134
Salvador, Joseph   195
Sanhedrin   41, 43, 45, 51, 52, 57, 177,
     178
Sarna, Nachum   36
Schachter-Shalomi, Zalman   130,
     134–7
Schneersohn, Menachem Mendel   170,
     171
Schneersohn, Yosef Yizchak   171
Scholem, Gershom   165, 168, 221
Schuon, Frithjof   135
Second Temple   40, 42, 54, 55, 59, 83,
     91, 139
Second Vatican Council   5, 65
Sectarian   30, 40, 41, 53–5, 59, 62, 148,
     157, 159, 162, 167, 168, 169, 176,
     190, 202, 204
Seforno, Ovadiah   63, 93–4, 98, 108,
     131, 229
Sepulveda, Jose   224
Shabbat (tractate)   134, 183
Shabbtai Hakohen, (Shakh)   179

Sharpe, Eric 5, 6
Shemesh, Aharon 54
Shetach, Shimon ben 57
Shituf 113, 178, 179, 180, 190, 192, 193, 195
Siegman, Henry 26, 27
Sifre Deuteronomy 45, 47, 51, 56, 111
Sinai Revelation 40, 93, 122
Sinzheim, David 195
Smith, Huston 135
Smith, Mark 33, 36
Smith, Morton 33
Socrates 66
Sofer, Moshe (Hatam Sofer) 202
Sol Invictus 214
Soloveitchik, Joseph B. 94, 131, 132, 133, 137, 138, 205, 224
Soloweyczyk, Eliyahu 75, 90–2
Sotah 214
Soteriology 42
Sperber, Daniel 205
Steinman, Aharon Leib 204
Steinmetz, Chaim 234, 235
Steinsaltz, Adin 81, 207
Stendahl, Krister 62, 227
Stern, Sacha 50, 52, 55
Sternbuch, Moshe 203

Taanit (tractate) 56
Tanner, Kathryn 26
Teitelbaum, Yoel 193
Tennyson, Lord Alfred 143
Todorov, Tzvetan 237
Tosafot 7, 47, 113, 176, 177, 178, 179, 192, 205
Trinity 55, 67, 87, 88, 89, 91, 92, 100, 101, 105, 107, 109, 122, 123, 124, 139, 177, 178, 179, 180, 192
Truth 2, 5, 9, 13, 16, 17, 18, 19, 20, 21, 23, 24, 26, 27, 28, 29, 34, 48, 49, 61, 64, 71, 74, 79, 87, 96, 99, 100, 102, 103, 107, 108, 112, 121–4, 126, 129, 130, 131, 132, 133, 134, 135, 136, 138, 140, 141, 143, 144, 145, 146, 148, 151, 153, 158, 159, 163, 173, 195, 208, 217, 218, 219, 220, 221, 226, 231, 232, 237, 239

Unitarian 92, 95, 184, 185, 186, 192
Universalism 9, 17, 18, 19, 21, 22, 26, 29, 32, 35, 37–8, 40, 47–9, 62, 99–127, 130–3, 139, 145, 148, 153, 158, 160, 161, 164, 168, 179, 187, 188, 198, 204, 208, 224, 225
Universalist 9, 15, 18, 19, 21, 22, 28, 32, 60, 61, 67, 76, 99, 127, 129, 130, 131, 139, 148, 185, 208, 226
Urbach, E.E. 46, 62

Valle, Moshe David 208, 219
Van Buren, Paul 133
Vatican II 5, 6, 7, 8, 17, 143, 169, 174, 175
Vital, Hayyim 164, 200

Wahshiyya, Ibn 210
Weinberg, Yehiel 201–2
Worms of Metz, Aaron 195
Wurzberger, Walter 199
Wuthnow, Robert 4–5, 21
Wyschogrod, Michael 8

Yedidyah HaPenini 105
Yevamot 207
Yitzhak, Shlomo ben (Rashi) 37, 134, 151, 155–7, 160, 165, 167, 169, 180, 186, 187, 239
Yochai, Shimon b. 40, 50
Yosef, Yaakov of Polnoye 85, 194
Yuval, Israel 154

Zakkai, Yohanan b. 40
Zechariah 32, 39, 62, 76, 78, 82, 243, 246
Zedek 231
Zeitlin, Hillel 208, 222–3
Zephaniah 32, 39, 68–9, 74, 93, 94, 158, 243
Zevit, Ziony 33
Zohar 63, 84–5, 157, 158, 163, 164, 165, 168, 208, 214–16
Zoroaster 66, 220